BUSINESS STUDIES

2nd Edition

FOR YOU

David Needham ● **Robert Dransfield**

First published in 1996 by:
Stanley Thornes (Publishers) Ltd

Second edition 2001 published by:
Nelson Thornes Ltd
Delta Place
27 Bath Road
CHELTENHAM
GL53 7TH
United Kingdom

01 02 03 04 05 / 10 9 8 7 6 5 4 3

A catalogue record for this book is available from the British Library

ISBN 0 7487 6393 7

Illustrations by Shaun Williams
Page make-up by Hardlines
Printed and bound in Spain by Graficas

Contents

UNIT 1

THE BUSINESS ENVIRONMENT

UNIT 2

THE OWNERSHIP OF A BUSINESS

UNIT 3

BUSINESS ORGANISATION

Acknowledgements

We would like to thank Sandy Marshall at Nelson Thornes for her detailed work in helping us to produce this new and updated version of *Business Studies for You*.

Our aim has been to develop a usable book with a lively and interesting style and presentation which students from all backgrounds and abilities can enjoy. We have also endeavoured to provide thorough and detailed coverage of all specification areas with the objective of helping students to pass with flying colours.

The authors and publishers would like to thank the following individuals and organisations for their help with the preparation of this book and for permission to reproduce photographs and other material:

Abbey National PLC; Ark Geophysics Ltd; Katherine Beane; British Airways plc; British Gas; British Nuclear Fuels plc; British Telecommunications plc; The Body Shop PLC; Cancer Research Campaign; the Co-operative Union Ltd; Dyson Ltd; easyJet airline company limited; the Ford Motor Company; Greenpeace UK; Jaguar Cars; Eurostar; Franchise Development Service; Jean Hooper; Levi Strauss Co.; Marks and Spencer PLC; the Metro Centre; Nestle UK Ltd; Bryan Oakes; P & O Portsmouth; Raymonds Press Agency; Syndicated International Network; Sainsbury's ; the Samaritans; Shell Education Service; SmithKline Beecham PLC; Societe Bic SA; Sue Woollatt; Tesco; Transport and General Workers Union; Unilever UK; Virgin Group; Voluntary Service Overseas.

Every effort has been made to contact copyright holders and we apologise if any have been overlooked.

David Needham
Robert Dransfield

Photo credits

The Advertising Archive Ltd (p. 148), Associated Press (p. 317), Denis Doran (p. 323), Environmental Picture Library (p. 330), Greenpeace UK (p. 334), PA News (pp. 303, 335), Pictor International (p. 66), PowerStock Photo Library (pp. 19, 72), Raymonds Press Agency (pp. 21, 54), S.I.N. (p. 45)

A message from Frankie and Cleo...

Welcome to Business Studies For You!

We hope that reading and working through this book will give you a firm foundation for your business studies course.

The text provides you with a detailed coverage of everything you will need for a good exam pass, as well as a colourful and interesting insight into all the latest developments in business.

More than that, we hope it encourages you to ask questions and to challenge existing ideas.

Enjoy your time with us!

Best wishes.

Frankie

1 1 Learning About Business

Why learn about business?

Learning about business is both interesting and useful. It is also challenging and requires imagination.

In learning about business you will need to be creative and to have a questioning mind. Business decisions are open-ended. There may be more than one way of going about things. Therefore you will need to ask lots of questions and to weigh up alternative ideas and proposals.

Frankie and Cleo

In this book we would like you to follow the model of Cleo and Frankie. They are keen to set up their own business making shortbread in their town. However, first they want to find out as much as possible about business and business activities. Throughout this book they ask questions in order to find out information that will help them to make better decisions. Having found out information, they try to make sense of it in order to draw balanced conclusions and make sound judgements.

'We are both looking forward to learning about business!'

Ron Rust

In contrast, the model we *don't* want you to follow is that of Ron Rust. Ron is a bit of a 'know-it-all' who has worked for a number of years as a scrap metal dealer. His business hardly ever makes a profit and he is always getting into scrapes. However, he thinks that because he has 'experience' of business everyone should listen to his opinions.

When you come across Ron in the text, examine the things that he says, and try to explain why he is getting it wrong. What is he saying that doesn't quite make sense?

'You win some, you lose some!'

Latest news

Because business is continually changing it is helpful to keep up to date with the very latest developments. We have therefore included a series of sections which bring you right up to date with changes in the modern business environment. These pieces of information are supplied to you by our very own Internet newshound.

LATEST NEWS

Spix

Spix's macaw is the very last of his kind living in freedom. He lives in the Amazon rainforest in South America. Spix helps to remind us of the harm that humans are causing to the environment and the importance of businesses operating in a moral way. Every now and then Spix has something to say about the modern world of business. To what extent do you agree with his comments?

Tasks

Throughout the book there are tasks for you to carry out. The tasks should only take 5 to 10 minutes and should be copied up into your notebook or file. Some will be more difficult than others. The tasks headed with a yellow band will take you longer and require more thought. Tasks with a blue band are easier.

Coursework

Coursework activities are activities for you to carry out in your own private research time. For these, you will need to find out information for yourself. This information will increase the breadth of your knowledge of business.

Case Studies

Case Studies appear in nearly all the chapters. These provide examples of business activities and problems, usually taken from the real world. At the end of each Case Study, there are a number of questions for you to answer in your notebook or folder.

Match It!

At the end of nearly all the chapters you will find 'Match It!' activities. The aim of these is to help you to build up a business dictionary.

Each 'Match It!' consists of a list of business terms, and a list of definitions. Your job is to list the terms in your notebook or folder and write the correct definitions alongside them. As you do so, you build up your own glossary of business terms.

The world of business

All businesses set out to achieve a particular result. Different businesses set out to achieve different results.

◆ For example, the e-business Amazon.com sets out to sell books to customers over the Internet while at the same time making a profit for its owners.

◆ The charity Oxfam sets out to raise funds, and to provide famine relief and other help to people throughout the world.

◆ Newcastle United Football Club sets out to play attractive, winning football that will attract spectators through the turnstiles and into the club shops so as to make a profit and to raise pride in the city of Newcastle.

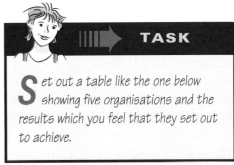

TASK

Set out a table like the one below showing five organisations and the results which you feel that they set out to achieve.

Organisation	Desired result
Newcastle United	Play attractive, winning football, achieve high gate figures, sell club souvenirs, make a profit, raise pride in the City of Newcastle, etc.
Halifax (bank)	?
Greenpeace (pressure group)	?
My school/college	?
Internet company (.com)	?

What do businesses do?

Business involves adding value to **inputs** so as to create more valuable **outputs**. For example, if you buy ingredients worth £1, you may be able to make a cake which you can sell for £3. The value you have added to the ingredients is therefore £2.

Value of cake ingredients	Value added	Value of cake
£1	£2	£3

The difference between the price paid for the inputs needed to create the cake and its selling price is the **value added**. Business activity is concerned with adding value in making things.

◆ Oxfam receives donations from the public and channels them to its projects overseas. This requires a lot of organisation. Oxfam adds value to the donations by making sure that they are used in the best way possible. If Oxfam carried out any of its activities in a disorganised way, it would fail to add value to the donations.

'When does most value get added? In the early stages of production or later on? For example, in the producing of Coca Cola, breakfast cereals, or chocolate bars?'

Being organised

Businesses need to be organised. As we shall see later (Chapters 10–23), there are a number of ways of organising. However, whether you are talking about a large organisation employing tens of thousands of people or a small corner store, you will find that a disorganised business will never be successful for long.

There are a number of characteristics of organisations:

1 Organisations have a **name** – e.g. Iceland.com, Manchester United, etc.

2 Organisations set out to achieve particular **end results** – e.g. to be the biggest company in their field in the country, to make high profits, etc.

3 Organisations have **rules and regulations** which govern the way they operate – e.g. a school's code of discipline, or a business's procedures for dealing with customer complaints, etc.

4 Organisations have **posts and offices** – e.g. managing director, supervisor, etc.

5 Organisations have a **public image**. All organisations will try to create an image which reflects the way the business runs. For example, a hospital will want to create an image of being a caring organisation.

COURSEWORK ACTIVITIES

Choose a particular organisation that you are familiar with. This may be a small business near you, an organisation that you work for on a part-time basis or an organisation to which you belong, e.g. a sports club, school, etc.

Produce a short illustrated report setting out:

- The name of the organisation
- The end results that it is working towards
- The rules and regulations of the organisation
- The posts and offices in the organisation
- The public image of the organisation

Compare the organisation you have chosen with those looked at by other members of your class.

Business ideas

All business organisations start out from an original idea. Many new business ideas have come 'out of the blue' to inventive people. An example of this is the Sony Walkman. Other ideas have resulted from careful work over a period of time. Examples are the development of the ballpoint pen, the photocopier and the dishwasher.

There are many ways of coming up with a bright idea. They include:

◆ Spotting a gap in the market

◆ Improving on an existing product or service

◆ Listening to people and finding out what they want or need

◆ Using a special skill or talent that you have

◆ Developing a hobby

◆ Combining two or more existing products or services

◆ Setting out to solve a particular problem

'Our idea is to produce shortbread. It is something we are already good at, and we know that our product is popular with friends. We also know that the costs of production are low compared with the price we can sell at. We can produce the shortbread in a bakery oven in part of an industrial unit that has been rented out by my uncle Abe. Do you think we have a good "business idea"?'

  TASK

Working in a group with two or three other students, brainstorm 10 ideas for setting up a small business in your area. You need to make sure that your ideas meet the criteria listed below.

1   Think of at least one idea for each of the sources of ideas listed above – i.e. at least one idea that involves solving problems for people, one idea that involves developing a hobby, etc.

2   Each idea must be capable of being developed for less than £1,000.

3   Each idea must be practical given the skills of the group you are working with.

Choose the best idea and decide how you would go about setting up your business and making your idea work. For example, what resources would you need? Who would be involved? How much would it cost to buy the resources you need, and how much could you sell your product or service for?

Present your idea to the rest of your class. Be prepared to answer questions.

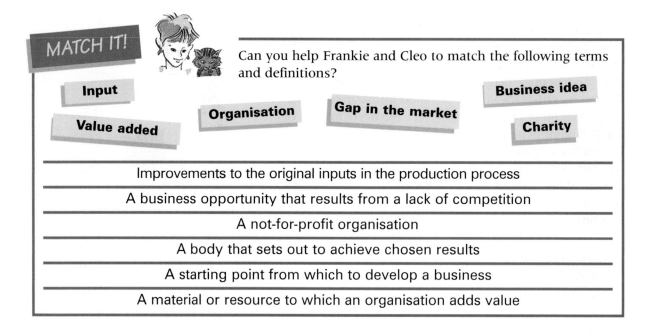

Can you help Frankie and Cleo to match the following terms and definitions?

Input

Value added

Organisation

Gap in the market

Business idea

Charity

Improvements to the original inputs in the production process
A business opportunity that results from a lack of competition
A not-for-profit organisation
A body that sets out to achieve chosen results
A starting point from which to develop a business
A material or resource to which an organisation adds value

2 Making Use of Scarce Resources

Needs and wants

Businesses exist because they meet needs and wants. The person or people who run these organisations have identified a need. This applies equally to:

◆ The ice-cream van selling cones and choc-ices outside a park or a school gate

◆ The large multinational shoe and clothes manufacturer like Nike, selling its brands throughout the world

◆ The public service organisation, such as the meals-on-wheels service

◆ The charity organisation such as Oxfam, working to provide famine relief

What are needs and wants? At a basic level we all **need** a minimum standard of food, liquid, heat, shelter and clothing (although a walk through Central London makes it apparent that not everybody achieves this).

We also have psychological and emotional needs, such as the need to feel loved and to feel that we are valued.

'Like millions of other football supporters I wanted to watch England's football match versus Finland on October 10th, 2000 on television. I wasn't able to watch the match live because it was a pay-per-view match costing £10, which was only available live to households with Sky Digital, cable company ntl, or ONdigital.'

Not many people are content to live with only having their basic needs met. Our **wants** go beyond our basic needs, and it would appear that many of them can't be met. For example, Frankie was not able to watch the Finland–England match live. The tennis enthusiast who buys a tennis racket, balls, trainers, wristband and clothes soon moves on to a better racket, more expensive trainers, and a collection of 'designer' tennis clothes. Most people want better and more up-to-date goods. What sorts of things would you want to buy if you won the lottery? A bigger house? A car? More clothes?

Scarcity, choice and opportunity cost

We can't have everything that we want because there aren't enough resources to produce everything that society wants.

There are two main types of resource:

◆ **Physical or natural resources** such as soil, climate, water, minerals, forests, and fisheries

◆ **Human resources** – people and their various skills

Imagine society had all the land, labour, raw materials and other resources it needed. Then we could produce all the goods we wanted without making sacrifices. In reality resources are **scarce**. When we use resources to produce an item, we are taking away these resources from producing something else. This is a major problem for all societies.

Decision-making over the use of resources involves:

◆ making a **choice** (we can do either this or that)

◆ making a **sacrifice** (if we choose to do this with a resource we can not also do that)

The real cost of using resources for one purpose is the loss of the next-best use to which they could have been put. The **opportunity cost** of any activity is the next-best alternative which is given up.

TASK

Classify the following into needs and wants:

soap	tea
perfume	a bed
fruit	underwear
bread	shoes
milk	a new CD
cake	a newspaper
a DVD player	a textbook
sugar	vegetables
chocolate	eggs
orange juice	a pen

TASK

Cleo's favourite type of cat food is 'Vegichunks', which costs 50p a tin. Her next favourite is 'Superveg', which also costs 50p a tin.

Every week Frankie has £3.50 available for cat food. She buys Cleo seven tins of 'Vegichunks'.

What is the opportunity cost?

  TASK

In some hospitals there are wards where elderly people who don't have long left to live are looked after. From time to time these patients have heart attacks and it has to be decided whether to save their lives. Often patients are given lower priority if they don't have any remaining family and if they have expressed a wish not to be saved. How does saving a patient's life involve an opportunity cost? Can you think of other items of hospital spending where the opportunity cost needs to be considered?

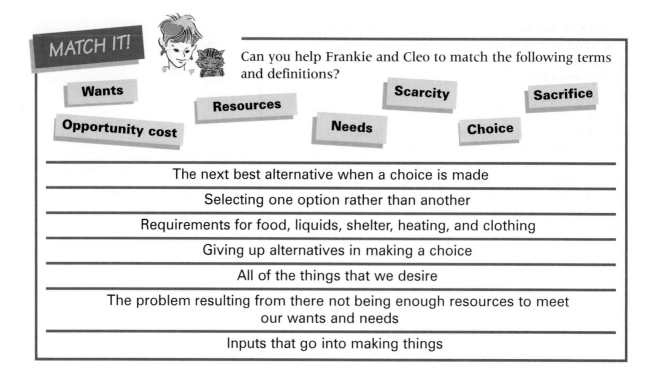

MATCH IT!

Can you help Frankie and Cleo to match the following terms and definitions?

Wants

Resources

Scarcity

Sacrifice

Opportunity cost

Needs

Choice

The next best alternative when a choice is made
Selecting one option rather than another
Requirements for food, liquids, shelter, heating, and clothing
Giving up alternatives in making a choice
All of the things that we desire
The problem resulting from there not being enough resources to meet our wants and needs
Inputs that go into making things

3 How Businesses Add Value and Help to Satisfy the Needs of Customers

What is added value?

To keep a share of the market, businesses need to give their products an edge over their competitors. They can do this by finding out what the customer really wants from a product and then supplying it – by adding value.

James Dyson was doing some housework in 1979. His first job was to vacuum the living room using a Hoover Junior machine. The vacuum cleaner that he was using employed the standard technology of the time – the air being sucked through the nozzle and the dirt and dust trapped in a cloth bag between the intake and the exhaust.

James felt that the system was very inefficient because there was so much dirt and dust that wasn't being sucked up. As a consumer he felt that the existing method did not fully meet his needs. He felt that given time he could add value to the machine to make it better. **Adding value** is the process of making a product more desirable for a consumer.

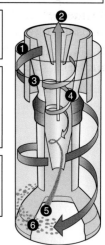

❶ Outer rotating cyclone forces large debris and 90% of the fine dust to edge of outer cylinder where it collects at the bottom of the chamber ❷

❸ Air is sucked through shroud filter into inner cylinder which separates dust and fluff

❹ Inner cyclone exerts centrifugal force on the fine dust particles separating them from the air and forcing them to the edge where they collect at the bottom ❺

❻ Clean air is sucked out through the top of the chamber. The cylinder is detached and the dust is tipped out

The Dyson Dual Cyclone

James was already a well known designer, having invented (among other things) the 'ballbarrow' (a wheelbarrow with a ball rather than a wheel). As chance would have it, his business was installing a powder coating plant for the ballbarrows. To capture dust that wasn't being sprayed onto the barrows they were using an industrial cyclone made of steel and about 6 m tall. Cyclone towers are a well known industrial filtering system, with air being dragged into a tower and whirled round, at very fast speeds, forcing the dust against the outer wall of the cyclone.

James Dyson realised that the cyclone system could be applied to vacuum cleaners to enable them to work more efficiently. He started to work on the task, which took him four years and 5,127 prototypes (i.e. trial models). He realised that for household vacuuming you need a dual cyclone – one to separate out larger items like cigarette ends and dog hairs and the second to catch the smaller particles. Unlike traditional vacuum cleaners, the Dyson Dual Cyclone does not use bags. The product has proved to be a great success story, revolutionising the industry.

The Dyson Dual Cyclone has been a hit because it has been able to add value in a way that previous vacuum cleaners were not able to. It met **customer requirements** for a really efficient vacuum cleaner.

The example of the Dyson Dual Cyclone shows us that in the modern **market place** (where goods and services are bought and sold) the **customer** (the person that buys a good or service) is king.

Businesses need to understand the wants and needs of their customers. Often they will find out this information by carrying out **market research**, which involves asking questions about the wishes of customers.

'This satisfies all my needs – it sucks up all Cleo's hairs!'

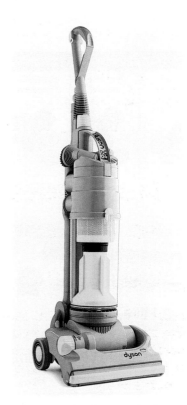

The Dyson bagless method

The business that best understands the wants and needs of its customers is best placed to add value to its products.

Value can then be added at various stages in the production process. For example, a confectionery business may already be producing a range of round chocolate sweets in red, orange, green, yellow, and white. Market research may reveal that customers would also like to buy a blue sweet and that even more value can be added by putting little faces onto the sweets. Further value can be added by putting the sweets in a new exciting bag, and advertising the sweets on television.

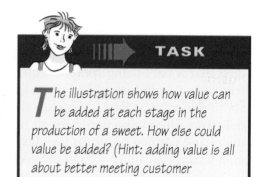

TASK

The illustration shows how value can be added at each stage in the production of a sweet. How else could value be added? (Hint: adding value is all about better meeting customer requirements.)

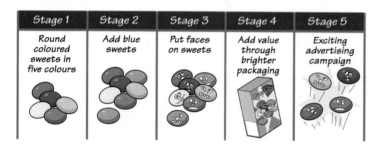

Stage 1	Stage 2	Stage 3	Stage 4	Stage 5
Round coloured sweets in five colours	Add blue sweets	Put faces on sweets	Add value through brighter packaging	Exciting advertising campaign

Adding value in sweet production

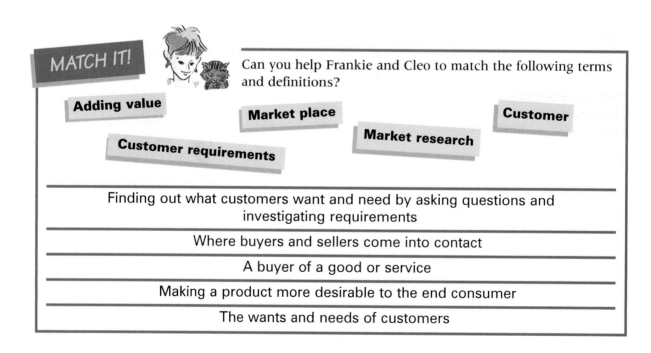

MATCH IT!

Can you help Frankie and Cleo to match the following terms and definitions?

Adding value   **Market place**   **Customer**

Customer requirements   **Market research**

Finding out what customers want and need by asking questions and investigating requirements
Where buyers and sellers come into contact
A buyer of a good or service
Making a product more desirable to the end consumer
The wants and needs of customers

4 Types of Business Activity

The way in which value is added will vary from one type of industry to another and between businesses within the same industry.

Business activity is often broken down into three types:

◆ Extractive (primary industry)

◆ Manufacturing and construction (secondary industry)

◆ Services (tertiary industry)

Extractive industries

These are concerned with using **natural resources.** They include farming, mining and oil drilling. Farmers grow and harvest crops and farm livestock, while miners take out fuel and minerals from the ground.

Farming: a primary industry

Left: Car production – a manufacturing industry

Primary industries sometimes produce raw materials like iron ore (for making steel) and oil (for making petrol, plastics, fibres, etc.). They also produce final products like fish and oranges.

Manufacturing and construction industries

These are concerned with making and assembling products. Manufacturers use raw materials and parts from other industries. A **semi-manufactured good** is one that is only partly made. Most products go through several stages of production. Examples of manufactured products are furniture, cars, chocolate and oil rigs.

Below: Banking – a service industry

Service industries

Service/tertiary industries are particularly important in Britain today. **Services** give something of value to people, but are not physical goods. You can physically touch or see a sandwich, a car, or a television set. You cannot touch or hold life insurance, a haircut, or the protection offered by the police. These are all services. Other examples are banks and public transport.

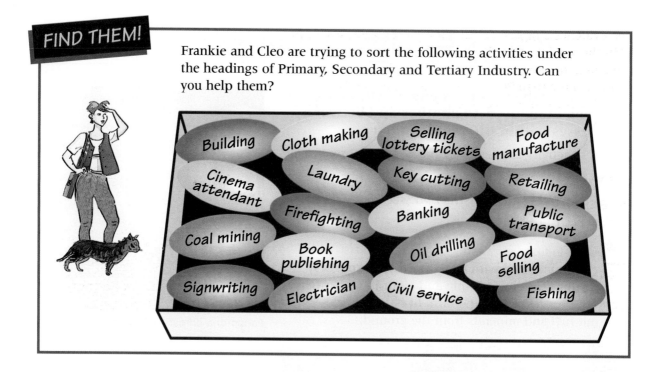

FIND THEM!

Frankie and Cleo are trying to sort the following activities under the headings of Primary, Secondary and Tertiary Industry. Can you help them?

Building · Cloth making · Selling lottery tickets · Food manufacture · Cinema attendant · Laundry · Key cutting · Retailing · Firefighting · Banking · Public transport · Coal mining · Book publishing · Oil drilling · Food selling · Signwriting · Electrician · Civil service · Fishing

Services are sometimes classified as **direct** (to people, e.g. the police, hairdressing) or **commercial** (to businesses, e.g. insurance, banking). However, the difference is not always clear-cut. Some commercial services like banking are used by individuals as well as by other businesses.

The changing face of business activity

Many experts talk about **three waves** of industrial development.

In the first wave, countries are dominated by agriculture and farming. This was the case in Britain until the Industrial Revolution of the late eighteenth and early nineteenth century.

In the second wave, countries are dominated by manufacturing, when industries such as coal, steel, car manufacture and shipbuilding become important.

In the third wave, services become the most important sector of the economy, with many people working in insurance, banking, office administration, leisure and similar industries. This is sometimes called **de-industrialisation**.

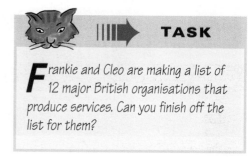

TASK

Frankie and Cleo are making a list of 12 major British organisations that produce services. Can you finish off the list for them?

Marks and Spencer – Retailing
National Westminster Bank – Banking
Central Television – Television Broadcasting

The evidence suggests we are now in the third wave. In 1959 the service sector in the USA produced a greater value of goods than manufacturing. Today, services produce more than 70% of the value of all goods in the USA, Britain and France, and just over 60% in Germany and Japan.

'I buy some of my books from Amazon. They are cheaper and are quickly delivered through my letter box.'

LATEST NEWS

New economy versus old economy

In the 2000s many people make a distinction between the 'old economy' and the 'new economy'.

The old economy is made up of the businesses that have been around for a long time making products and services that we are familiar with – construction companies like Blue Circle Cement, chemical companies like ICI, retailers like Marks and Spencer, oil companies like Shell and BP.

From the late 1990s onwards we saw the development of what was termed the 'new economy', made up of new .com ('dot com') companies like Lastminute.com, which sell a range of last-minute items such as last-minute tickets to pop concerts, or last-minute holidays abroad. Another of the famous new .coms is Amazon, the online bookseller. These new companies are involved in e-commerce (buying and selling things over the Internet).

In 1999 lots of people were trying to buy shares in the .coms, hoping to make a lot of money very quickly. Unfortunately, people soon realised that many of the new businesses were not going to make much profit in the short period (many made losses and went bankrupt).

However, what has happened is that companies in the old economy have moved into Internet trading – e-commerce. Many big companies today buy their supplies over the Internet, and advertise and sell their products through online Internet sales. Most large companies have set up their own websites for e-commerce.

MATCH IT!

Can you help Frankie and Cleo to match the following terms and definitions?

New economy   Primary industries   Semi-manufactured   Old economy   E-commerce

Natural resources   Manufacturing industries   Service industries

Goods that are only partially made or finished
Typical form of industry in third-wave societies
Buying and selling using the Internet
Making things, usually using raw materials
Modern businesses trading through the Internet
Materials that are not manufactured
Industries such as farming, fishing and mining
Established industries such as retailing, textiles, confectionery manufacture, chemicals

5 Factors of Production

Imagine that you are visiting a modern food processing plant. What do you see?

The first and most obvious sight would be large areas of land and building. Inside, you would find machinery, equipment and employees. In order for the machines to work, they need energy, raw materials and semi-finished products. Enter a production area and you will find people blending and mixing food. Other workers will be loading and unloading supplies and finished goods. Others will be tending equipment.

The **factors of production** are the ingredients that make a business work: land, labour, capital and enterprise.

◆ In the case of our food processing plant, the **land** includes the site on which the factory is built.

◆ The **labour** is the factory employees.

◆ The **capital** is the buildings and equipment which are used to make the products.

◆ Finally, **enterprise** is the art of bringing together the other factors of production to make a successful business.

We use the French word **entrepreneur** to describe someone who brings together factors of production in order to achieve business objectives. The entrepreneurs in a food processing plant would include the people who set up the plant in the first place.

Definitions

Over the years the four factors of production have come to mean more than the examples used above.

◆ **Land** is now used to refer to *all* natural resources, e.g. farm land, water, coal, etc.

◆ **Labour** is used to refer to *all* the physical and mental contributions of an employee. So it is more than just the physical effort of digging coal, or making car parts. It also includes the mental effort of an accountant or the services provided by a bank clerk.

◆ **Capital** includes all those items that go into producing other things, e.g. a machine manufactures products, tools contribute to this process, and so on.

Machines, tools and buildings are all examples of physical capital. In order to purchase these items you would need money capital.

◆ **Enterprise** is the factor that brings the other factors together to produce goods in order to make profits.

COURSEWORK ACTIVITIES

Talk to the owner of a small local business. Find out how the business uses its land and capital, the type of labour employed, and the enterprise skills needed to ensure that the venture is successful.

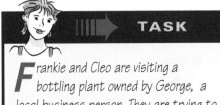

TASK

*F*rankie and Cleo are visiting a bottling plant owned by George, a local business person. They are trying to identify the factors of production employed there. Can you identify:

• 4 items of capital
• 2 items of labour
• 1 entrepreneur
• 1 item of land?

CASE STUDY

Rewards to factors of production

Richard Branson is a good example of an entrepreneur. He is able to make things happen by bringing together factors of production in exciting combinations to produce products as different as airline flights, contraceptives, and cola drinks.

However, in order to run his business successfully, he needs to reward the factors of production that work for his business organisation – Virgin.

Richard Branson rewards:

- **Labour** with **wages**
- **Land** with **rent**
- **Capital** with **interest**
- **Enterprise** with **profits**

Wages

Attractive salaries and wages have to be paid to the employees who work for the organisation.

Rent

Virgin needs to pay rents to any landlords that have rented out land or other natural resources to the company.

Interest

Like most other major businesses, the Virgin organisation will borrow money capital from banks and other lending institutions. Interest must be paid at regular intervals for these loans.

Profits

Finally, profits are the reward for enterprise. The profits of Virgin will be shared among the company's owners. These are the shareholders, and will include Richard Branson himself. Many of his managers and employees may also be shareholders.

LATEST NEWS

The importance of intelligence

Labour is one of the most productive factors today. This is particularly true in the new economy in which intelligent workers like Information and Communications Technology specialists can earn very high wages.

Today we have a shortage of what are called 'knowledge workers' – people who work with their brains and often use computers as a key part of their work. Although machinery is very important in many companies, particularly in manufacturing, it is probably true to say that the intelligent worker is the most important factor of production.

Intelligent workers don't just work in a back room with computers. Very often they also deal with customers – over the phone and in face-to-face relations. Highly skilled workers therefore need to have good communications, presentation, interpersonal and information and communications technology skills.

TASK

1 Why is Richard Branson often described as an entrepreneur?

2 What are the rewards of being an entrepreneur?

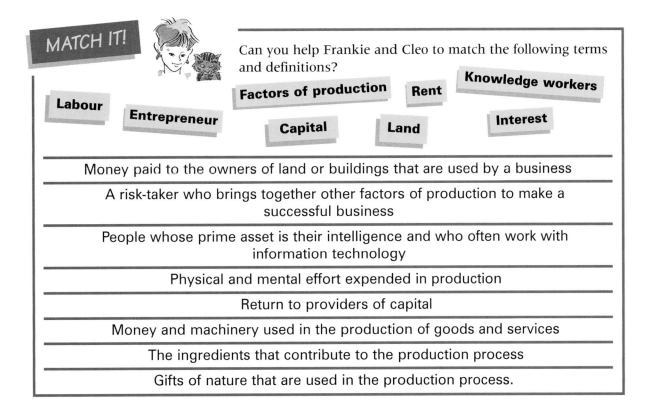

MATCH IT!

Can you help Frankie and Cleo to match the following terms and definitions?

Labour   Entrepreneur   **Factors of production**   Rent   **Knowledge workers**   Capital   Land   Interest

Money paid to the owners of land or buildings that are used by a business
A risk-taker who brings together other factors of production to make a successful business
People whose prime asset is their intelligence and who often work with information technology
Physical and mental effort expended in production
Return to providers of capital
Money and machinery used in the production of goods and services
The ingredients that contribute to the production process
Gifts of nature that are used in the production process.

6 Types of Economic System

In the UK we have an economic system in which there are a number of key decision makers.

These key decision makers are:

1 **Households** made up of people like you and me. As households we make important consumer decisions – for example to buy one good rather than another (*The Guardian* rather than *The Sun*, fresh orange juice rather than Coca-Cola, and so on). We make important decisions as employees – e.g. to work more or fewer hours, to take one job rather than another. We also make important decisions as citizens – e.g. to vote for one political party rather than another.

2 **Businesses** decide what goods and services to make, what factors of production to use in production, how much to pay in wages, how much profit to distribute to shareholders, etc.

3 The government is the other important decision maker – for example, deciding how much to charge people in taxes, which industries to put directly under government control, and so on.

Alternative systems for making economic decisions

Because resources are limited, it is necessary for society to decide how its available resources will be used. Important questions to consider are:

◆ **What** will be produced?

◆ **How** will it be produced?

◆ **For whom** will it be produced?

TASK

Look at the following newspaper headlines and sort them out according to whether they raise a 'what', a 'how' or a 'for whom' issue:

Pensioners to get higher benefits

Wages increase for key workers

Teachers to lose out in a new pay deal

Textiles in decline while leisure centres boom

NEW TECHNOLOGY BOOSTS OUTPUT

Call for revival of craft skills

UK to produce more machine tools

In the distant past, decisions about what to produce, how to produce it, and for whom, were made by custom and tradition. For example, the way that crops were grown and shared out was decided by folk tradition. In most parts of the world, traditional economies have given way to three major systems:

◆ The **centrally planned system**

◆ The **free market** system

◆ The **mixed system**

Central planning

In a centrally planned system, many decisions are made by a central planning organisation. Smaller groups such as factories and other business units submit their plans to a local committee. The local plans are then fed back for approval at the centre. The central organisation may decide what resources to make available to each local area. In turn, resources are allocated to each factory, farm or other productive unit.

Up until the end of the 1980s, most Eastern European countries had centrally planned systems. Today, however, many of them have moved towards a free market system.

A centrally planned economic system

CASE STUDY

The end of the line for the Trabant

In 1990 the new Germany was created. Former East Germany had been a centrally planned economy. West Germany had been a mixed economy in which prices had been free from government interference.

Before reunification, a car known as the Trabant was almost the only model available in East Germany. More than three million Trabants had been sold since production began in the late 1950s. The same model of car was sold from 1964 to 1991. Because people could only buy one make of car there was no competition. The planners saw no need to change the design because they could sell every car that they produced.

The Trabant was functional (i.e. it served the purpose of getting a driver from place A to place B), cheap to run and easy to repair. It was said it could be repaired with a hammer, a ball of string and chewing gum. However, it was an environmental disaster. It was noisy and gave off a lot of exhaust fumes. It was made largely from a cheap fibre-glass material called Duroplast, which is

Trabant cars pouring out of East Germany at the time of reunification

everlasting. The car could only be destroyed by burning, which gave off poisonous fumes.

Before the joining together of East and West Germany there was a long waiting list for the Trabant. After reunification, nobody wanted to buy a Trabant. The Trabant was obsolete in a modern market. It was no longer possible to continue producing a car which cost 11,000 DM (£3,700 in 1991) and could only be sold for 9,000 DM. In May 1991 the company was forced to close down and 9,000 employees lost their jobs.

  TASK

1   Why do you think that so little change was made to the Trabant over the years?

2   What would be the benefits to (a) producers and (b) consumers of sticking to the standard model?

3   Why would free market forces introduce change?

4   How could the Trabant survive in a free market?

5   What problems do you think would have been caused by the disappearance of the Trabant?

6   Explain in detail why you think that the disappearance of the Trabant was a good or a bad thing for (a) people living in former East Germany, and (b) the world economy.

The free market

In a **free market** the decisions about what to produce, how, and for whom, are made by consumers and producers. The government does not intervene.

In a free market, producers are forced to pay attention to the wishes of consumers in order to survive. Of course producers often try to manipulate consumers into buying their goods by aggressive marketing and advertising campaigns. These techniques can be very persuasive.

The mixed economy

The mixed economy combines elements of both the free market and a centrally planned system. Some decisions are made solely by individual businesses and consumers. Other decisions are made by the government.

The UK is an example of a **mixed economy**: Some parts of industry are owned and run by the government, but large sections of the business world remain in private hands.

TASK

1 What factors decide whether consumers have more power to keep prices low, or producers have the power to push prices up?

2 List five advantages that (a) the free market has over central planning; and (b) central planning has over the free market.

TASK

1 In recent years the demand for videos has increased. How have producers responded?

2 In recent years the demand for black and white television sets has fallen. How have producers responded?

3 Every year the fashion industry spends a lot of money on advertising clothes. How do consumers react?

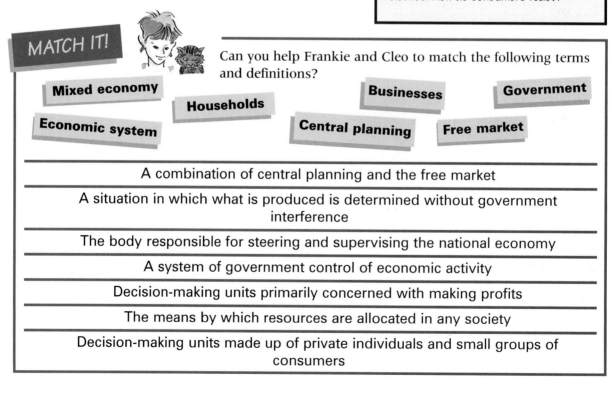

MATCH IT!

Can you help Frankie and Cleo to match the following terms and definitions?

Mixed economy   Households   Businesses   Government
Economic system   Central planning   Free market

A combination of central planning and the free market
A situation in which what is produced is determined without government interference
The body responsible for steering and supervising the national economy
A system of government control of economic activity
Decision-making units primarily concerned with making profits
The means by which resources are allocated in any society
Decision-making units made up of private individuals and small groups of consumers

7 Demand and Supply in the Market Place

The price of football shirts with top players' names is high because there is a great demand for them

Demand for goods and services

The **demand** for a good or service is a want backed up by the money to purchase it. If a good is in 'great demand', there will be a lot of people wanting to buy it at the current price.

Business organisations want to know how much the demand will be for their products at different prices. They will then be able to decide what to make, and how much to make in order to meet demand.

Plotting demand

The demand for a product can be plotted on a table of figures. This shows how many items would be demanded at given prices. It is also useful to plot the demand for a product on a graph. When you look at the graph, it becomes obvious that larger quantities of any good will be bought at lower prices, and lower quantities at higher prices.

For example, the table on the right shows the demand for apples at different prices per kilo. The graph shows the same figures transferred onto a **demand curve**.

The demand curve is constructed by showing prices on the vertical axis and quantities demanded along the horizontal axis. You can see that:

◆ Higher prices lead to lower quantities being bought.

◆ Lower prices lead to higher quantities being bought.

Price per kg	Quantity demanded
45p	1,000 kg
35p	3,000 kg
25p	4,500 kg
15p	6,500 kg

Above: Demand for apples at different prices per kilo

Below: The same data displayed in graph form

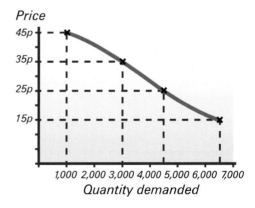

Supply

The **supply** of any good is the quantity that producers and sellers supply at different prices. Suppliers will supply more to a market if the price is higher than if it is lower. In other words:

◆ Higher prices lead to higher quantities being supplied to the market.

◆ Lower prices lead to lower quantities being supplied to the market.

This rule applies both for individual producers – e.g. a single farmer growing tomatoes – and for the whole market, i.e. all the tomato growers in a particular area.

Plotting supply involves plotting the quantities that would be supplied at different prices. For example, if there are three bakers in a town, we add their individual supplies of bread together to arrive at market supply as follows:

'Are there any goods that suppliers would produce more of at lower prices, and fewer at higher prices?'

What do you think?

Price per loaf	Supply			
	Jolly Bakers	Better Bakers	Healthy Bakers	Market supply
15p	100	150	200	450
20p	200	300	400	900
25p	400	600	800	1,800

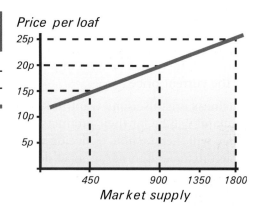

A typical supply curve

A **supply curve** can then be drawn on a graph *(right)* showing the quantities that would be supplied at different prices. A typical supply curve slopes upwards from bottom left to top right.

The market price

All markets are made up of buyers and sellers. We can show the relationship between buyers and sellers by placing the demand curve and supply curve for a product on the same diagram.

The point at which the two curves cut shows the **market price**. This is the only point at which the wishes of buyers and sellers match at a given moment in time.

For example, the graph on the right illustrates the demand and supply for chocolate spread.

You can see that, at a price of 60p for a 250 g jar, 100,000 tonnes of chocolate spread would be bought each week. At this price consumers are happy to buy 100,000 tonnes and sellers are happy to supply this quantity.

This is called the **equilibrium point** because there is nothing forcing a change from it.

We can see why this point is an equilibrium point by considering non-equilibrium ones.

For example, at 80p a jar, consumers would purchase only 75,000 tonnes while suppliers would make 125,000 tonnes available to the market. At this price, sellers would be left with unsold stocks and would quickly reduce supply to the equilibrium point.

If the price were below the equilibrium – at say 40p – demand would be for 150,000 tonnes with producers only willing to supply 50,000 tonnes. In this situation chocolate spread would be snapped up as soon as it was put on the shelves, and stocks would run out. Prices would soon be raised towards the equilibrium point.

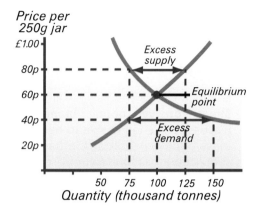

The market for chocolate spread (250 g jars)

TASK

*F*rankie and Cleo have been finding out how much demand there would be for their shortbread at different prices. Can you plot their demand curve on a piece of graph paper?

'Please could you answer our questions? First try a piece of our shortbread. How many pieces would you buy per week if the price was 20p?'

Later:
'At a price of 20p we would be able to sell 1,500 pieces per week…'

'…And at 30p we could sell 850 squares.'

'But at 40p we would only be able to sell 200 squares.'
'Let's plot our figures on a demand curve..'

CASE STUDY

The demand for chocolate biscuits

Midwich village shop sells – amongst other things – one very popular brand of chocolate biscuits. The shop is able to buy stocks of these biscuits in bulk at 15p per packet. The shopkeeper has found out from five local families how many packets they would buy per month at different prices.

Price per packet	Amount bought by families					Total
	Jones	Patel	Cray	O'Rourke	Sylvio	
10p	15	15	20	20	15	85
15p	12	12	20	15	11	70
20p	8	8	15	10	9	50
25p	7	7	12	9	5	40
30p	6	6	9	7	2	30
35p	5	4	6	5	-	20
40p	-	2	3	-	-	5
45p	-	-	-	-	-	-

  TASK

1 What is the relationship between price and quantity demanded in the table?

2 How would you explain this relationship?

3 Why might it be more sensible for the shop to charge a price of 25p for its biscuits, rather than 15p or 40p?

 **COURSEWORK ACTIVITIES**

Choose a product which you use regularly, e.g. a brand of toothpaste, chewing gum, or a particular chocolate bar.

Set out a list of possible prices for the product. Interview five of your friends to find out how much they would buy at each of the prices you have chosen. Construct a demand curve using the information you have researched.

The importance of the market place

The market brings together buyers and sellers. Buyers show what they prefer by 'voting' with their money for certain goods and services.

Every day millions of buying and selling decisions are made. When you go shopping, you may make a decision to buy a particular kind of breakfast cereal. Your decision has a great impact if thousands of other consumers make the same choice as you.

If we all decide to buy a particular type of cereal, then cereal manufacturers will benefit by switching resources (such as labour, machinery and materials) into making that cereal.

The diagram below shows how important the market is in bringing together consumers and producers.

The market place: bringing together producers and consumers

Meeting customer requirements

Not all consumers are customers. For example, a mother may buy the type of cereal her children prefer. The children are the **consumers**, but the mother is the **customer** because she makes the decision to buy that particular product from that particular shop.

Customers are the lifeblood of any company. Without enough customers a business will close. To keep their customers, companies need to be sure that they are producing goods that meet the customers' needs at the right quality, time and price.

The demand curve for a product does not always stay in the same place. Tastes and fashion change, incomes rise and fall, population changes and the prices of other goods change. Suppliers need to be aware of these changes in the market and react to them.

'When I buy cat food for Cleo who is the customer and who is the consumer?'

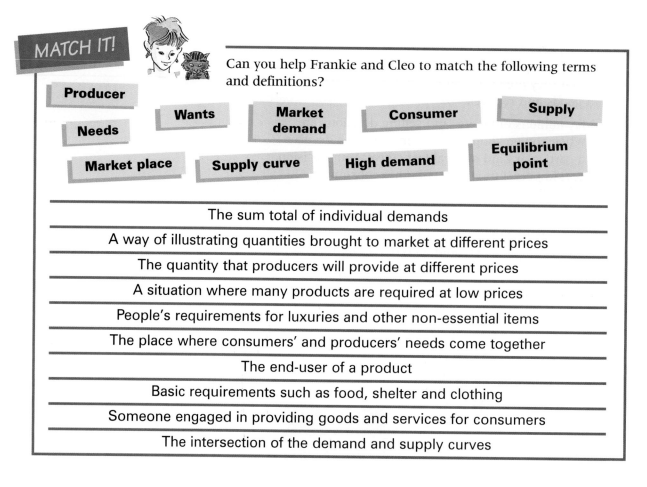

MATCH IT!

Can you help Frankie and Cleo to match the following terms and definitions?

Producer

Wants

Market demand

Consumer

Supply

Needs

Market place

Supply curve

High demand

Equilibrium point

The sum total of individual demands
A way of illustrating quantities brought to market at different prices
The quantity that producers will provide at different prices
A situation where many products are required at low prices
People's requirements for luxuries and other non-essential items
The place where consumers' and producers' needs come together
The end-user of a product
Basic requirements such as food, shelter and clothing
Someone engaged in providing goods and services for consumers
The intersection of the demand and supply curves

8 The Changing Economy

The twentieth century saw the replacement of manufacturing by service industries as the main type of employment in the economy. This change is illustrated in the following table:

	Total employment (thousands)	Manufacturing industries (thousands)	All service industries (thousands)
1988	22,688	4,907	15,806
1989	23,100	4,900	16,216
1990	23,364	4,780	16,601
1991	22,702	4,362	16,478
1992	22,356	4,137	16,500
1993	22,032	3,951	16,479
1994	22,121	3,967	16,603
1995	22,454	4,069	16,912
1996	22,706	4,110	17,192
1997	23,253	4,173	17,615
1998	23,742	4,193	17,973
1999	24,020	4,049	18,379

'Why do you think that between 1991 and 1992 the numbers of people employed in services and manufacturing both fell, and both rose between 1993 and 1994?'

The twentieth century saw the decline of many of the UK's traditional heavy industries leading to job losses in coal, shipbuilding, textiles, motor car manufacture, and many other industries

There was a rise in service and leisure industries

The revolution in service industries has been accelerated by the use of ICT

The development of the 'new economy'

At the same time as there were job losses in manufacturing, there were gains in the service industries such as retailing, hotel and catering work and the leisure industries.

These new service industries involve employees working closely with customers – for example, in face-to-face contacts, over the telephone and through electronic communications such as e-mail.

The revolution in the service industries has been accelerated by the use of information and communications technologies, which have helped to bring people into much closer contact than ever before.

At the end of the twentieth century it became common practice to refer to the 'new economy' as consisting of firms that make frequent use of Internet technology and telecoms. Typical jobs in the new economy are desktop publishers, web designers and software architects.

There can be no doubt that the growth of the new economy helped the economy to grow at the end of the twentieth century and in the early part of the twenty-first century.

A business planning to use the Internet to buy goods and services from other businesses can save huge amounts of money. A business planning to use the Internet to sell goods and services to customers can reach a much bigger market, and reduce its selling costs. **E-commerce** (buying and selling using the Internet) is made up of **business-to-business** (B2B) links and **business-to-consumer** (B2C) links.

B2C links — Consumers buy books from Amazon.com using the Internet

amazon.com

B2B links — Amazon buys from book publishers using Internet ordering systems

B2B and B2C links

The relationship between the 'old' and the 'new' economies

The **old economy** is defined by experts as being made up of more traditional established companies such as Cadbury Schweppes (the confectionery and soft drinks manufacturer), Barclays Bank and Unilever (making a range of products from soap powder to margarine).

Today, however, many traditional companies are being forced to change the way they run in order to keep up with new technology. Failure to do so may result in them being left behind, and, losing business to new e-commerce companies.

The creation of Amazon.com (the UK's largest Internet bookstore) resulted in WH Smith losing so much business in book sales that they had to urgently rethink their whole business strategy. In 1998 they purchased Internet Bookshop, the largest Internet bookshop in Europe and Amazon's main rival in Britain.

The banking industry provides an excellent example of how a traditional old economy industry has embraced the technology available in the new economy and become a thriving part of it.

Many banks now offer:

◆ Automated cash machines

◆ Some voice-activated telephone automatic services

◆ Telephone banking

◆ 24-hour Internet banking, which allows customers to have access to their bank account and be able to do all their own banking transactions

---

CASE STUDY

Hi-tech sector creates thousands of jobs

On 25 July, 2000 two technology-driven firms announced the creation of thousands of new jobs, underlining the shift within the British economy from manufacturing to services.

Pay-TV group ONdigital said it was creating 1,500 jobs, while telecommunications equipment maker Marconi announced a £2 billion deal with BT, which will boost employment at its Coventry plants.

The news came as Asda Wal-Mart opened the first of ten planned supercentres, which are expected to create 3,000 jobs over the next 5 years and help change the face of British retailing.

This good news on the jobs front followed the previous week's reports that Corus, the steelmaker formed by the merger of British Steel and the Dutch group Hoogovens, would be cutting a further 1,600 jobs, bringing the total job losses announced by the group to 4,000 in July. A further 600 jobs were lost at Courtaulds Textiles because of the closure of its knitwear factories near Nottingham.

LATEST NEWS

UK second only to US in online shopping

Research shows that the UK is second only to the US in online shopping. Most customers usually access e-commerce websites by keying in a known site address, indicating the importance of establishing a recognised brand name.
In the UK, France and Italy the most popular items bought online are books, CDs, computers and IT products.

Market research shows that consumers are keen to be able to buy their groceries online because visits to supermarkets take up so much of their leisure time.

Customers say that their primary reason for shopping online is competitive prices. This is followed by range of products, convenience and good delivery speed. The biggest causes for concern are credit card security, lack of choice and guaranteed privacy of personal information submitted while making a transaction.

  TASK

1   Which of the businesses mentioned in the case study are most typical of the 'new economy'?

2   Which of the businesses mentioned in the case study are most typical of the 'old economy'?

3   What does the case study tell you about the changes that are taking place in the economy?

MATCH IT! Can you help Frankie and Cleo to match the following terms?

New economy   Manufacturing   E-commerce   Business-to-business

Service industries   Old economy   Business-to-consumer

Buying and selling using the Internet
Links between an organisation and its end consumers
Traditional companies that are well known in particular product fields
Industries made up of organisations that provide services to people and to business
Modern organisations using the Internet and electronic communications systems
The production of tangible goods
Electronic communications between one business organisation and another

9 The Competitive Business Environment

Organisations must be competitive if they are to survive. They need to have a good understanding of the competition in their environment.

FIND THEM!

Frankie and Cleo are trying to sort the following companies into ones which are competing closely with each other. Can you help them?

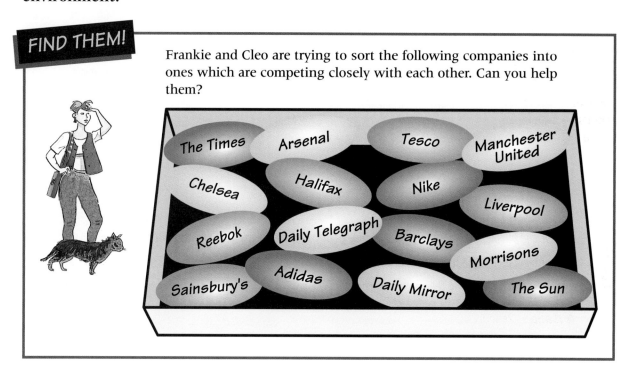

The Times Arsenal Tesco Manchester United

Chelsea Halifax Nike

Liverpool

Reebok Daily Telegraph Barclays

Morrisons

Sainsbury's Adidas Daily Mirror The Sun

Direct and indirect competition

Some products and companies are in **direct competition** with each other in that they produce identical or almost identical products. For example, there are many different mobile phone companies (such as Nokia) producing very similar phone products; one brand of soap powder, such as Persil, is in direct competition with another, like Daz; Reebok trainers are in direct competition with Nike ones.

In addition, most businesses face **indirect competition**. One firm competes with another for you to spend your money with them. A firm producing women's fashion clothes is in indirect competition with a firm producing women's underwear. A firm producing teenage magazines is in indirect competition with a DVD producer. The magazine producer, by providing a really enticing front cover and interesting stories, may persuade the teenager to buy the magazine rather than the DVD they were thinking of buying.

Positional maps

In weighing up the competition it is often useful for a company to create a **positional map** to see where it stands in the market in relation to the competition. The positional map should set out the two most important ingredients that make the business more competitive than its rivals. Two important elements are price and quality. The map below shows why an Italian restaurant – 'Mario's' – in a Midlands city decided to go for the **upmarket** (high-quality/high-price) segment of the market. There were already six other Italian restaurants operating in the mid-market area (medium quality and medium prices), and three operating in the **downmarket** sector (low quality and low prices). There was no existing competition in the upmarket sector.

TASK

1   What would Mario's restaurant need to do to retain its upmarket position?

2   What do you think would be the characteristics of a restaurant like Italian Delights?

3   How would Italian Delights be able to beat off the competition?

Competition in the local market place

There are many ways in which firms are able to be competitive in the local market. For example, in the case of service stations one firm might be able to gain a competitive edge by:

◆ Being in a better location than rivals

◆ Offering lower prices

◆ Offering a wider range of services

◆ Offering additional features such as free air and water

◆ Using lighter hoses

◆ Giving a more friendly service, etc.

COURSEWORK ACTIVITIES

Examine two businesses that are competing in the local market place such as rival newsagents, sweetshops, supermarkets, clothes shops, hairdressers. What are the key areas which the two businesses compete over?

International competition

Internationalisation refers to the way in which companies expand their operations overseas in order to exploit new markets.

Globalisation refers to the way a company sets out to operate in exactly the same way across the globe – using the same packaging, the same products, the same adverts, etc, in every country in which it operates.

'What is the difference between internationalisation and globalisation?'

Today many companies find that their home market is no longer rich in opportunity. Companies are forced to operate on a more international scale because of increased competition at home and because there are often opportunities to grow faster in other regions of the world.

Being competitive

Being competitive involves taking a long hard look at everything an organisation does, as well as at how rival firms operate. Firms not only need to look at what the competition is doing now, but also at what they are likely to do in the near future.

To be competitive an organisation needs to make sure that it:

◆ Provides high-quality products that meet customer requirements

◆ Values its people – the most important resource of any organisation

◆ Uses modern technology, including information technology, to its full potential

◆ Ploughs back funds into new investment, research and product development

◆ Experiments with new ideas and sets out to lead rather than follow the field

◆ Makes sure that it has outstanding customer and community relationships as well as respecting the environment

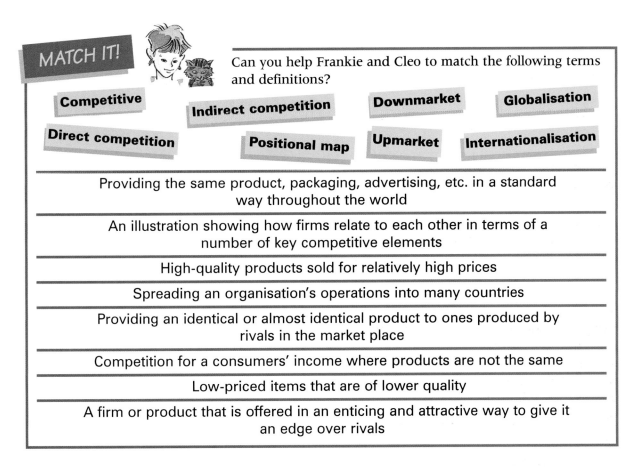

MATCH IT!

Can you help Frankie and Cleo to match the following terms and definitions?

Competitive   **Indirect competition**   **Downmarket**   **Globalisation**

Direct competition   **Positional map**   **Upmarket**   **Internationalisation**

Providing the same product, packaging, advertising, etc. in a standard way throughout the world
An illustration showing how firms relate to each other in terms of a number of key competitive elements
High-quality products sold for relatively high prices
Spreading an organisation's operations into many countries
Providing an identical or almost identical product to ones produced by rivals in the market place
Competition for a consumers' income where products are not the same
Low-priced items that are of lower quality
A firm or product that is offered in an enticing and attractive way to give it an edge over rivals

10 Globalisation

One of the major changes affecting business in recent times has been the spread of globalisation. The term globalisation refers to the way in which businesses such as Shell (the oil company), Nestlé (the food manufacturer) and Ford (the car manufacturer) operate in many parts of the globe, making and selling products. Many of these products are global products – for example, the Ford Ka that you buy in Paris will be very similar (if not identical) to the Ka that you could buy in Brazil, Australia or South Africa.

A company that thinks globally will look at the whole world (or at least large parts of it) as a place where:

◆ It can sell its products

◆ It can make its products

◆ It can employ people to work for it

Take for example, the case of Nestlé, which claims to be 'the world's food company' – making products from Nescafe (coffee) to Quality Street and Smarties (sweets and confectionery). Go into a supermarket in India, Australia, Japan, the United States, Mauritius, France or the United Kingdom and you are almost certain to be able to buy a can or bottle of Coca-Cola. The actual product *may* have been made in a Coca-Cola bottling or canning plant in the United States but it is just as likely to have been made in a Coca-Cola plant near to the end consumer, employing Coca-Cola staff who may be Indians, Australians, Japanese – or any one of scores of other nationalities who live in a country were Coca-Cola is made.

It is not hard to think of global products – for example:

◆ Mars bars

◆ Heinz tomato ketchup

◆ Marlboro cigarettes

◆ Coca-Cola soft drinks

◆ Sony DVD players

◆ Philips televisions

◆ Nike trainers

The importance of multinational and transnational companies

Multinational companies produce many of the goods and services that we consume. A **multinational** is a company with its headquarters in one country but which produces and sells its products in other countries.

Today it has also become popular to use the term **transnational** companies as well as multinational companies. A transnational may have a number of regional Head Offices in different parts of the world and be owned by people from many different countries. It is difficult to identify a transnational with any particular country.

The terms transnational and multinational are often used to refer to the same companies – e.g. Royal Dutch Shell and Unilever – to emphasise the way in which businesses are increasingly global.

SPIX

'One of the problems of globalisation is that when a global company produces products in a country where the government does not protect workers. This can lead to bad pay and conditions, even the employment of child labour.'

What do you think? Do you know of any examples of bad practice?

TASK

Can you make a list of ten products you could buy that would be more or less identical in lots of different countries? Think of examples from holidays abroad.

Unilever

The British–Dutch company Unilever employs about quarter of a million people around the globe. They have 300 local factories and own companies in 88 countries. Annual sales for 1999 were £27 billion (you can find up-to-date information about Unilever on www.Unilever.co.uk).

Today Unilever is concentrating on producing 400 well known brands.

Some of these brands are identical throughout the globe – e.g. Lipton tea or Magnum ice cream. Other brands are produced by Unilever specially for a particular country or area – for example, in teas there are PG Tips in the UK, Home Cup in Africa and Ting Hua in China.

The importance of globalisation to UK business

The spread of globalisation is very important to UK businesses for a number of reasons.

◆ Large UK businesses need to look at the globe as their market place. Although there are only about 60 million people in the UK to sell to there are literally billions in the global market.

◆ Foreign companies are increasingly selling their own products in the UK market. Many of these companies are very big – like the US retailer Wal-Mart, which took over Asda in 2000. If UK businesses lose some of their UK market they have to make up for these losses by selling abroad.

◆ In the world today billions of consumers are for the first time earning enough money to buy modern consumer goods like Mars bars, Johnny Walker whisky, Thorntons confectionery, Lipton tea, etc. UK businesses therefore will benefit from seizing this opportunity to expand sales. We are seeing the rise of **global consumers**, who have similar tastes and lifestyles whatever country they live in.

TASK

Why do you think that Unilever produces some global brands and some brands for local markets?

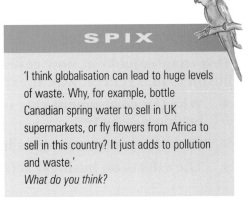

SPIX

'I think globalisation can lead to huge levels of waste. Why, for example, bottle Canadian spring water to sell in UK supermarkets, or fly flowers from Africa to sell in this country? It just adds to pollution and waste.'
What do you think?

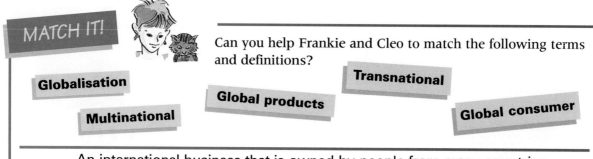

MATCH IT!

Can you help Frankie and Cleo to match the following terms and definitions?

Globalisation

Transnational

Global products

Multinational

Global consumer

An international business that is owned by people from many countries and has a range of regional head offices

People who have similar buying patterns and lifestyles wherever they live

Items that are presented and sold in an identical way across the world

A company with its headquarters in one country but with plant and selling operations in many different countries

The reduction in the size of the planet through modern communication links to create similar lifestyles, buying patterns and production patterns across the world

11 The Importance of Government in the Business Environment

'How and why does the government get involved in business activity in this country?'

This chapter looks at how government affects business in a general way. It explains:

◆ Why the government gets involved in business activity

◆ How the government gets involved

◆ The effects on business activity

Left: The 15 member states of the European Union

Levels of government

Today there are three levels of government which affect us all:

1 European Union government

The UK is one of 15 countries belonging to the **European Union**. The EU is responsible for policy making on economic and social issues, and member states co-operate closely on a wide range of other issues. The European Commission and European Parliament are bodies representing all 15 member states. EU laws override national laws in important areas and the **European Court** makes sure that these laws are enforced. National governments signed over responsibility for making these decisions to European bodies when they joined the Union and when they signed the Maastricht Treaty in November 1993.

2 Central government

Central government runs the country. Citizens choose Members of Parliament. MPs belong to political parties which have leaders. Central government passes new laws in Parliament. Civil servants run the day-to-day activities of the state, such as collecting taxes.

3 Local government

Local government looks after only a small part of the country, e.g. a county like Lincolnshire or a heavily built-up area such as Manchester. Citizens vote for councillors to represent them at local-government level.

Organising refuse collection is a responsibility of local government

The importance of the European Union

Today business people are very interested in new regulations and directives that are produced by the **European Commission**, which is situated in Brussels. Business people know that when the European Commission passes a regulation or directive – for example, directives about controlling pollution, regulations about how many hours people are allowed to work, regulations about keeping the workplace safe and so on – it will have to be enforced in the UK.

Most business people are happy that we are a member of the European Union. With our 14 other trading partners we now have a market of 380 million people (instead of 60 million in the UK). Goods and services can cross borders freely without the importer having to pay any import taxes. People can also move freely within the union to get jobs and can invest money in any of the 14 other countries.

This means that there are plenty of business opportunities for British companies in the European Union. At the same time competition between companies in the 15 member states means that UK consumers can enjoy high-quality products at competitive prices.

'I can vote for my Euro MP, who represents me in the European Parliament at Strasbourg'

'I can vote for my local MP, who represents me in the UK Parliament at Westminster'

'There are three ways I can vote for people to represent me in government'

'I can vote for my local councillor, who represents me at the local council in Nottingham'

CASE STUDY

The importance of the Euro

Most big businesses in the UK would like us to be part of the Euro – a single currency for the European Union. At the moment, however, Britain has not joined the Euro, and is unlikely to do so until at least the middle of this decade.

Businesses would like to join because it would take away the cost of changing pounds into other currencies. Also, because businesses would be paid in Euros they would not have to worry about the exchange rate between the Euro and the Pound varying. For example, suppose I sell £100 worth of goods to France on credit to be paid in 3 months time in Euros and the exchange rate is currently £1 to 3 Euros – I would expect to receive 300 Euros. However, during the payment period the Pound falls against the Euro and becomes worth only 2 Euros. Instead of receiving 300 Euros as I had expected I would now get only 200 – making me worse off and reluctant to trade in the Eurozone.

Why does the government get involved in the economy?

To understand the role of government, take a walk in a group along a road outside your school or college. List ways in which the government influences everyday life. For example, who has paid for the roads, street lighting and maintenance of the pavements and parks? Why are drivers wearing seatbelts, and why are lorries only allowed to use certain roads?

◆ Some goods and services are provided by the government because it is felt that all citizens benefit from them, either directly or indirectly. For example, most people in the UK believe that children should have some form of healthcare and education.

◆ Some goods and services from which everyone benefits can be provided adequately only if they are funded and organised at national level. The armed forces are one example.

◆ Some people believe that the government should try to reduce inequality in society. They believe the government should tax some people at a higher rate than others and give more benefit to those who are worse off. Others see inequality as a useful way of encouraging people to try to better themselves.

◆ The government can also try to make the economic system run more smoothly. For example, it passes laws to protect consumers and takes measures against pollution and other antisocial practices.

A very important role played by the government is to set the rules within which business activity takes place. These rules are constantly changing, so some people lose out and others benefit. It is important to think about the following questions:

1 Who makes the rules? For whom?

2 Why do the rules change?

3 How do they change?

4 Who loses, and who benefits when they change?

TASK

*S*ome British companies have already decided to do most of their buying and selling abroad in Euros rather than Pounds. Why do you think they have done this?

TASK

*U*se the four questions listed on the left to analyse the following recent changes in the law:

a) New powers given to the army and police to ensure that fuel supplies get through if there are fuel blockades in this country

b) European Union directives setting a maximum 48 hour working week

c) Relaxation in the licensing hours to enable pubs to stay open for longer

d) Restrictions on the speed at which trains are allowed to travel while essential repairs are made to the rail track network

How the government becomes involved in the economy

There are many areas of government involvement in the economy, which are looked at later in the book. These include:

◆ Policy for the steady growth of the economy

◆ Employment policy

◆ Inflation policy

◆ Industrial relations policy

◆ Taxation policy

◆ Education and training policy

◆ Regional policy

The effect of government activity

The effects of government legislation vary from one sector of the economy to the next, but inevitably the government has an important influence on how businesses behave. Today, businesses need to be familiar with local, national, and European-wide issues and rules.

SPIX

'Government plays a very important role. It provides many services that would not otherwise be provided and stops activities which can be harmful.'
Can you list three services that the government provides which might not otherwise be provided? Can you list two harmful activities which the government seeks to prevent? Do you agree with Spix about the importance of government?

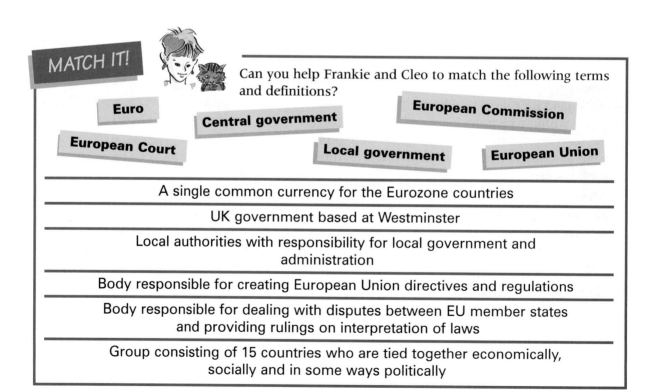

MATCH IT! Can you help Frankie and Cleo to match the following terms and definitions?

Euro · Central government · European Commission · European Court · Local government · European Union

A single common currency for the Eurozone countries
UK government based at Westminster
Local authorities with responsibility for local government and administration
Body responsible for creating European Union directives and regulations
Body responsible for dealing with disputes between EU member states and providing rulings on interpretation of laws
Group consisting of 15 countries who are tied together economically, socially and in some ways politically

12 The Technological Environment

'Today we need to learn to surf the wave of continually changing technologies.'

International companies that have failed to realise the power and influence of the Internet have fallen behind in the competitive race.

Advances in computer technology have changed the economy for ever, reducing distances and costs as never before.

The **Internet** is a world-wide computer network. It was originally planned by military and educational institutions in the United States during the 1960s and has never looked back.

SPIX

'The use of the Internet is creating a bigger gap between the haves and have-nots in the world than ever before. This is a bad rather than a good thing!'
Do you agree with Spix?

LATEST NEWS

Internet access

In May 2001 the Internet content and technology provider Screaming Media announced that it had reached a deal with Boeing, the world's largest commercial aircraft maker, to provide passengers with broadband access services, including Internet and e-mail, while they fly.

Passengers will pay a fee to use this service. For example, when a passenger gets on a plane from Los Angeles to New York he or she will get all the information they want about the weather, where to go, concerts in New York, etc. This is just one more example of the way in which the Internet has turned into a business opportunity by providing customers with what they want and where they want it – in this case in the sky.

Why might business people be prepared to pay for Internet access while they are flying?

CASE STUDY

Ex-students net £10 million web deal

Four Internet entrepreneurs are celebrating after clinching a £10 million business deal just months after leaving University.

The four graduates began their Net adventures while they were still at college. They set up the Student-Net.co.uk site, which provides information about student life in Nottingham. The site proved such a success that it was taken over by an American media giant for £10 million. The deal with Nevada-based firm IMPG saw the website firm become a global company, containing information about virtually every university in the world. The company is based in Nottingham and is employing increasing numbers of people (50 in its first year, 2000).

The four entrepreneurs saw a sudden change in their lifestyle. One minute they were living in student accommodation and trying to scrape by on student loans, next they were directors of an international computer firm.

There can be no doubt that new technology has played a major part in transforming business activity in the UK, and the developed world. Today most large businesses have developed B2B (business-to-business) and B2C (business-to-consumer) links using databases and extensive websites.

To many people in the UK today the Internet, e-mail and mobile phone communications have become a way of life.

The **World Wide Web** is a development of the Internet, and took off in the early 1990s. It uses **special transmission protocols** to deliver text, graphics and audio materials over the Internet. These materials are linked to other materials by 'hypertext links'. The way in which the information is available over the Web through the use of these links is completely in the hands of the computer user. So the World Wide Web is a highly powerful way of exchanging information.

By improving the flow of information between buyers and sellers the Internet and the World Wide Web have caused changes in the business world: a new marketplace, a new form of communication, a new way of getting goods to people, and a new information system. Buying and selling can now be carried out using the Internet and the World Wide Web. Internet-enabled commerce has been called '**e-commerce**', 'electronic commerce', 'Internet commerce', 'e-trade' or 'e-business'. Perhaps the biggest impact has been in cutting costs.

CASE STUDY

easyJet to sell 100% of seats on the Net

easyJet, the low-cost airline, will become the first carrier to take seat bookings completely over the Internet. In Spring 2001 the company was selling all its seats over the Internet.

The Luton-based airline estimated that by cutting out travel agents and teams of telesales agents it can make savings of 30% compared with airlines that sell tickets through traditional outlets.

Today, **Internet companies** can build new brand names very quickly. An example is Amazon.com, the book retailer. Awareness of Amazon was developed very quickly through Internet links.

The success of Amazon is typical of the way in which transactions can now be made between one part of the world and another, very quickly and efficiently. Private and business consumers are quickly able to find out information about the availability of goods in different parts of the world – they can select goods and have them delivered from other countries rather than from close to home.

Large companies like the American retailing giant Wal-Mart are using the Internet to make bulk purchases across continents in order to minimise their buying costs and get the goods to the consumer.

TASK

*W*hy do you think easyJet made this move? How are rival firms likely to respond?

The technology revolution

The **technology revolution** of the late twentieth century was in many ways more dramatic than the revolutions at any previous period of history. Many firms went out of business because they failed to introduce new technology, or because rivals did it quicker. Many new firms came into being because they were able to run large operations very cheaply by using the latest technologies.

And, of course, new technologies are being developed all the time – many of which do not involve computer technology.

Technological breakthroughs simply involve using scientific discoveries to the benefit of humanity. Technological breakthroughs often involve the creation of new products.

For example, in 2000 the British biotechnology firm Protherics was the first company in 50 years to develop an antidote to rattlesnake bites. The antidote was extracted from Australian sheep. When the company was given the licence to sell the new product in America its share price leaped.

In a market worth an estimated $40 million, the only antidote at the time was horse serum, which causes unpleasant side-effects. Up to 40,000 people are bitten by rattlesnakes every year, mainly in the southern United States and Mexico. This technological breakthrough was a tremendous boost to the company.

All businesses need to keep up to date with technological changes that affect their industries, and make sure that wherever possible they lead technological change rather than lag behind.

Up to 40,000 people are bitten by rattlesnakes every year

'Next time I get bitten by a rattlesnake I won't be so upset!'

MATCH IT!

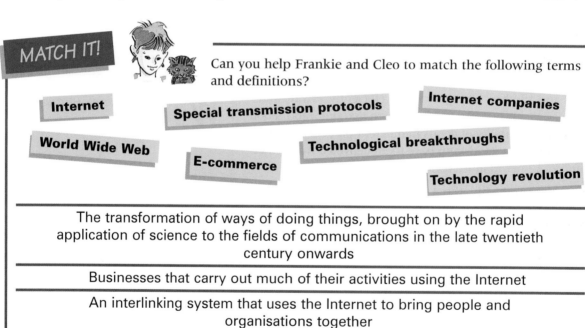

Can you help Frankie and Cleo to match the following terms and definitions?

Internet

Special transmission protocols

Internet companies

World Wide Web

E-commerce

Technological breakthroughs

Technology revolution

The transformation of ways of doing things, brought on by the rapid application of science to the fields of communications in the late twentieth century onwards
Businesses that carry out much of their activities using the Internet
An interlinking system that uses the Internet to bring people and organisations together
A means of delivering text, graphics and audio-visual materials over the Internet
A world-wide computer network originally used by the defence and education industries
Leaps forward in technology, enabling new developments
The buying and selling of goods, services, information, etc. through the medium of the Internet

13 The Social Environment

Affecting fashions and tastes: Britney Spears, Craig David and Eminem

Business takes place in a social environment in which there are all sorts of changes taking place.

Typical changes are in:

◆ fashions and tastes

◆ lifestyles

◆ spending patterns

◆ popular recreational activities

◆ working patterns

◆ the age distribution of the population

Fashions and tastes

Fashions and tastes change regularly – for instance, first we are told that black is the 'in' colour, then that grey is the 'new black' and so on. The Internet replaces newspapers, DVDs replace CDs, alcopops become the rage, and then something else. Today fashions and tastes are changing faster than ever before. For example, the rate at which songs enter the Top Twenty and then exit is the fastest it has ever been.

Businesses need to try to keep up with changes – if a business produces platform shoes when flat shoes are in fashion its sales will be much lower than required. Organisations can find out more about fashions and tastes by carrying out market research, through which they find out about what customers want and need by asking the right questions. They can also use published information such as government surveys into social trends and family expenditure patterns and market research information provided by specialist companies such as MINTEL, who do surveys on all sorts of topics. A more expensive way of gathering information is to pay for market research to be carried out especially for your company.

CASE STUDY

Net to take 20% of video and CD sales

A survey carried out by the retail consultants Verdict in early 2000 revealed that online sales of music and videos and associated software are on course to account for 20% of the total market within 5 years. Although online entertainment sales accounted for only about 1.5% of sales in early 2000, advances in technology mean that the market is on the threshold of an electronic revolution. The development of 'downloadable' CDs and DVDs, where music can be recorded from the Net on to a CD or DVD, will threaten the role of middlemen in the music and video industries, including retailers and record companies.

Lifestyles

Lifestyles are patterns of social behaviour associated with groups of people. For example, teenagers may have a lifestyle that is different from their parents – they might spend more on going to the cinema, buying DVDs, etc., whereas their parents may be more involved with buying washing machines and new cars. Some people enjoy a lifestyle which involves going on holiday to exotic places and regularly eating out in expensive restaurants, while others may just have a few days' holiday each year at a British seaside resort and regularly eat fish and chips.

Businesses need to be aware of the lifestyles of different groups of people, and how these lifestyles are changing. In the UK, as living standards increase people are able to enjoy a lifestyle which involves more travel, the purchase of more expensive clothes, and so on. Many businesses, when they market products, will plan their advertising and other promotional activities to appeal to a potential consumer's total lifestyle.

Spending patterns

As people become better off their **spending patterns** alter. The person who once was happy to travel to work by public transport and to have just a few clothes might feel that travelling by car and having a wardrobe bursting with clothes is necessary for a happy life once their income rises above a certain level.

Generally, as people earn more they have more **disposable income** (money available for spending). As people become richer their spending patterns alter – with an increasing emphasis on luxury and more expensive goods.

Businesses need to have a good picture of the spending patterns of the consumers they are trying to sell to. For example, UK supermarkets such as Sainsbury and Tesco have increasingly looked to selling more upmarket products as their customers' incomes have risen.

Popular recreational activities

In the modern world people are able to enjoy more leisure. This is because as they have become better off they have been able to afford to work fewer hours. In the UK we have seen a boom in leisure and **recreational activities**. For example:

TASK

What sorts of businesses have been able to take advantage of the growth of the leisure and recreational activities listed on the left?

◆ There is more interest in personal fitness and grooming

◆ More people play sport

◆ More people buy equipment for leisure and sporting activities

◆ More people eat out

◆ More people take holidays abroad

Working patterns

In recent years we have seen a decrease in the number of full-time jobs and a lot more people doing part-time jobs. There has been a dramatic increase in the numbers of women at work (although many still do part-time jobs). Increasingly women are going back to work soon after having children. More men are doing part-time work than in the past. These changes in **working patterns** are of importance to business. The growth in part-time work has enabled businesses to cut some of their labour costs because part-timers are paid less.

The change in work patterns has had a major impact on consumption patterns. For example, it has led to a massive increase in the demand for ready-made meals and for fast food, as the traditional family meal has fallen into decline. Increasingly, people who live busy lives are seeking to buy labour-saving gadgets such as tumbledryers and dishwashers. Businesses need to understand these changes and to respond to them.

COURSEWORK ACTIVITIES

How has the development of new working patterns in recent years changed the lifestyle of the household that you are a member of? How has this changed buying patterns? What sorts of businesses have been able to benefit from the changes that you have described?

The age distribution of the population

Another major social change that affects business is population change. A census of population is carried out every ten years to record changes in population – the most recent in 2001.

One of the key findings of the census is that the average age of the population in the UK is increasing, and that there are fewer young people entering the labour force. One effect of this is that some businesses are increasingly seeking to employ and retrain older people who may prove to be more reliable (e.g. in DIY stores).

Another impact of the 'greying of the population' has been to change the demand for goods and services. There is more scope for providing goods for the over-50s – e.g. specialist holidays for 'older' people – and many people have set up retirement homes. Businesses need to have a good understanding of the age structure of the population to know where opportunities lie.

'What other business opportunities are there resulting from the ageing of the population?'

LATEST NEWS

The ageing population

The government is very worried about the ageing population. Today there is more pressure on those in work to support older people than ever before. Those in work pay National Insurance contributions to pay for pensions and other benefits such as sickness and accident benefits. The worry is that older people will be taking more out of the National Insurance kitty than the working population is able to pay into it. There is a real worry that state pensions may have to fall.

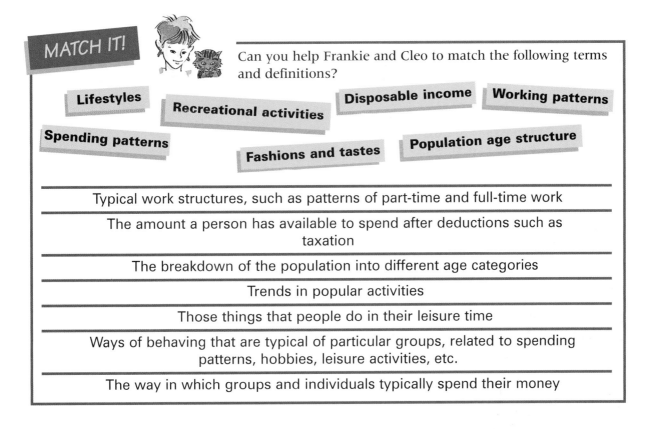

MATCH IT!

Can you help Frankie and Cleo to match the following terms and definitions?

Lifestyles

Recreational activities

Disposable income

Working patterns

Spending patterns

Fashions and tastes

Population age structure

Typical work structures, such as patterns of part-time and full-time work
The amount a person has available to spend after deductions such as taxation
The breakdown of the population into different age categories
Trends in popular activities
Those things that people do in their leisure time
Ways of behaving that are typical of particular groups, related to spending patterns, hobbies, leisure activities, etc.
The way in which groups and individuals typically spend their money

14 The Ethical Environment

What is meant by ethics?

An ethic is a moral principle or set of moral values held by an individual or a group.

Ethical behaviour is behaviour which is considered to be correct and moral.

'Is it sometimes possible for businesses to forget about ethics in the pursuit of profit or some other business goal?'

CASE STUDY

Passenger safety or punctuality?

In a letter to the Cullen inquiry into the Ladbroke Grove rail disaster, written by Gerald Corbett (the chief executive of Railtrack) it was admitted that passengers' safety had taken second place to punctuality.

In the letter Gerald Corbett expressed the view that maintenance standards had suffered in the drive for improved performance.

Business ethics

Ethics are the values and principles which influence how individuals, groups and society behave. Business ethics are therefore the values and principles that operate in the world of business.

In business, it is possible to carry out many practices which are not strictly ethical, and yet stay within the letter of the law. However, many successful companies are based on strict ethical principles, and most people would argue that businesses ought to keep within some form of moral framework.

Anita Roddick set up The Body Shop because she was tired of the way the beauty industry in this country was exploiting both consumers of cosmetics and the producers of ingredients in other countries. Examine The Body Shop's website to find out how they seek to operate in an ethical way.

Ethical decisions

Whether business owners and managers recognise it or not, all business decisions have an ethical dimension.

For example, here are some of the ethical questions that a business might have to face:

◆ Should products which might damage the health of consumers (e.g. cigarettes) be withdrawn from the market?

◆ Should the firm make sure that its business activities do not damage the environment? For example, should a DIY store sell mahogany and other rare woods?

◆ Should money be spent on wheelchair access to workplaces and retail outlets?

◆ Should the firm reject a bribe given to secure an overseas contract?

◆ Should part-time staff be offered the same rights as full-time staff?

◆ Should a workplace crêche be provided for working parents?

A firm that answers 'Yes' to these questions might be described as operating in an **ethical** way.

In contrast, a firm that pays a 17-year-old employee £1.47 an hour for working in a shop, or one that imports cosmetics ingredients from the Amazon region of South America, paying only a pittance to the local people, could be considered to be behaving in an **unethical** way.

TASK

What do you think should be the priority – rail safety or train punctuality? Why might the emphasis have been put on punctuality? In your view is this emphasis correct?

THE BODY SHOP

CASE STUDY

Whale hunting

The illustrations below show the stages in hunting for whales in a modern whaling fleet.

1 The hunt
The quarry is the 10-metre-long whale. The factory ship is about the size of a cross-channel ferry and is accompanied by 'catcher ships' with harpoons.

2 The attack
The harpoon holds a powerful grenade and a large hook. The grenade blasts a hole in the whale's side. The hook is used to pull the animal to the side of the ship.

3 The kill
Electrodes are fired into the body of the whale. A strong electric charge immobilises the whale. Death may take up to 25 minutes.

4 The sale
The factory ship strips the whale in 35 minutes. During a whaling season as many as 330 whales may be caught by a fleet. This produces more than 3 million pounds of meat sold at £130 per pound.

TASK

Do you consider the modern whale-hunting techniques that you see illustrated in these pictures to be ethical? Explain your arguments.

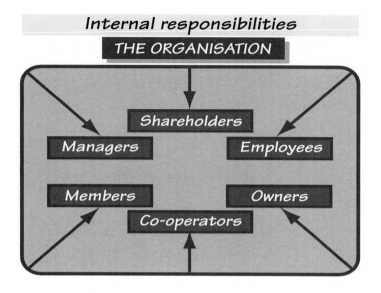

Internal responsibilities

Internal and external responsibilities of a business

External responsibilities

Social responsibility

A firm which behaves ethically towards the local community and society as a whole can be described as being **socially responsible**.

What then makes an ethical business?

Different individuals and groups will have different views about what makes an **ethical business**. The diagram on page 53 illustrates some of the characteristics of a 'good business'.

TASK

Make a list of what you consider to be the twelve most important characteristics of an ethical business.

Think about areas such as its relationship with its employees, the environment, the community, its obligation to pay taxes, etc.

Write each characteristic in the form of a statement, i.e.:

"An ethical business is one which ...."

Characteristics of an ethical business

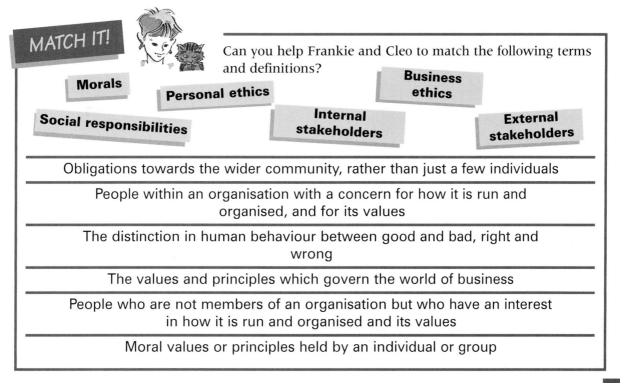

MATCH IT!

Can you help Frankie and Cleo to match the following terms and definitions?

Morals   Personal ethics   Business ethics

Social responsibilities   Internal stakeholders   External stakeholders

Obligations towards the wider community, rather than just a few individuals

People within an organisation with a concern for how it is run and organised, and for its values

The distinction in human behaviour between good and bad, right and wrong

The values and principles which govern the world of business

People who are not members of an organisation but who have an interest in how it is run and organised and its values

Moral values or principles held by an individual or group

15 Locating a Business

Choosing a location

One of the most important decisions affecting the success of a business is its location.

◆ Local businesses need to decide on the best location within a particular town or area.

◆ National businesses need to decide on the best spot in a country.

◆ International companies often search all over the world for the right location.

Costs should be borne in mind when choosing a location but cost is not necessarily the only factor. For example, some shops selling luxury goods will probably want branches in city centres where property costs are at their highest. The best site will be the one where the business gains the most commercial advantage.

Pride Park Stadium – the new Derby County Football ground, which has been relocated to the outskirts of Derby where there is easy access to motor vehicles, and good public transport links. Rates and rents are lower because the location is not in central Derby.

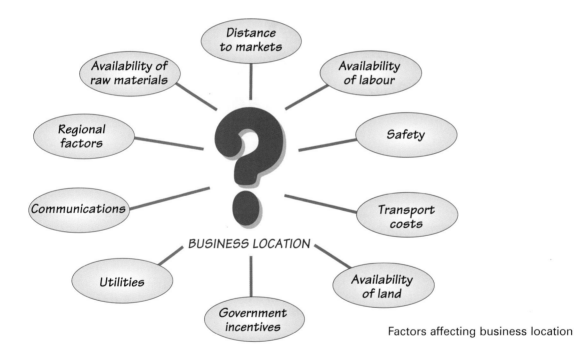

Factors affecting business location

1 Distance to market

Many businesses need to be located close to their market, i.e. their customers. Think of the florist at a railway station, or the local newsagent.

Service industries such as entertainment and banking also have to locate near their markets to be available for their customers. Many manufacturing industries locate close to their markets, particularly if they produce bulky or fragile items which are expensive to transport.

Centres of population tend to attract **bulk-increasing industries**. These are industries where the output is more expensive to transport than the raw materials. They need to be close to their market in order to minimise transport costs. For example, London is ringed by bulk-increasing consumer goods industries.

Bulk-increasing industries are better placed near their market.

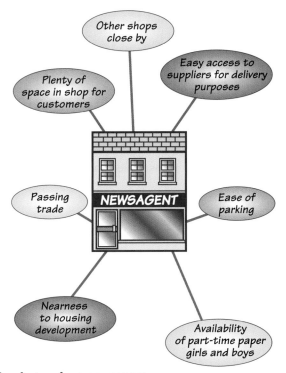

Location factors for a newsagent

TASK

Following the example shown on the left, set out a diagram on a piece of paper with one of the following types of business at the centre:

- *A sports centre*
- *A coffee shop*
- *A fashion clothes shop*
- *A steelworks*
- *An insurance company*

Around the edge of the diagram, list six factors which you think would be important in determining whether the location of the business would be a success or not.

2   Availability of raw materials

Some businesses use a lot of heavy and bulky raw materials in the construction of their products. However, these products may be a lot smaller and lighter than the ingredients which have gone into them. For example, finished steel is a lot lighter than the ore, limestone and other materials which have gone into making it.

If raw materials are bulky and expensive to transport, it makes sense to locate near them. These industries are known as **bulk-decreasing industries**, as their output is much cheaper to transport than their input.

3   Transport costs

Different industries have different **transport** needs. Two major influences are the pull of the market and of raw materials. These depend on whether the industry is bulk-increasing or bulk-decreasing. However, many industries' markets are spread out and raw materials come from several suppliers.

4 Availability of land

Land costs vary a lot from area to area. Some firms dealing with large quantities of goods require a lot of space. Others may need to check that a site has the right geology to support heavy weights, or the right climate for producing certain goods.

5 Availability of labour

The right sorts of labour and skills are easier to find in some areas than others. If a firm moves to an area which does not have the right sort of labour, it will have to pay employees to 'relocate', or train people in the skills it needs. This costs money. In some areas there may be a tradition of work in a particular industry and a large pool of workers with the right skills already available.

Footloose industries are ones which do not have to be located anywhere in particular. These industries will be attracted to areas where labour is cheap.

6 Safety

Some industries have to locate well away from heavily populated areas – for example, nuclear power stations, munitions factories and some chemical plants.

7 Utilities

A business must consider five standard **utilities**:

◆ Gas   ◆ Electricity

◆ Water   ◆ Disposal of waste

◆ Drainage

Aluminium smelting, for example, uses vast quantities of cheap hydro-electric power. Industries such as food preparation and paper production use large quantities of water. Food-processing creates waste, and the cost of disposing of this waste is a key locational factor.

8 Communication

Access to motorways, ports and airports has become an increasingly important locational factor in recent years. These services and other vital communication links make up what is called the **infrastructure** of a region. A good infrastructure can attract businesses to move to an area. Many towns have expanded partly as a result of good communications. For example, the M4 corridor between London and South Wales has been very successful in attracting industry to Wales.

Bulk-decreasing industries are better placed near their source of raw materials.

'What sorts of businesses require a lot of land for their business needs?'

SPIX

'Too many resources are wasted because of distribution costs. Take, for example, the export of meat. In the UK we typically export as much meat as we import. It seems silly to export British beef to France and at the same time import French beef!' *What do you think?*

9 Regional factors

Locating in an area which contains similar businesses, suppliers and markets may be a considerable advantage. The quality of local schools, housing, leisure and recreational facilities can also help to maintain the quality of staff and keep them happy and motivated.

10 Government incentives

Unemployment rates vary considerably between regions. The government tries to reduce these differences by rewarding firms which set up in areas of hardship. However, such incentives can make problems worse in neighbouring areas. In some cases the new industries created have not been very labour-intensive.

The European Union provides funds for poorer regions of Europe, to encourage businesses to set up there.

TASK

1 Set out a table like the one below to identify the key locational factors that you consider to be important in the location of the following types of businesses. Tick the boxes which you think are most important (a worked example is shown for the steel industry, which depends on many of the locational factors listed).

	Confectionery plant	Sewage works	Petrol station	Nuclear plant	Steelworks	Television studios
Distance to market					X	
Availability of raw materials					X	
Transport costs					X	
Availability of land					X	
Availability of labour					X	
Safety					X	
Utilities					X	
Communications					X	
Regional factors					X	
Government incentives					X	

2 For one of the businesses shown in the chart explain in greater detail the locational factors that affect that business.

||||⟫ **TASK**

What do you consider would be the key locational factors in encouraging the following?

1 A Japanese car manufacturer setting up in the UK.

2 Video advertising companies setting up in the Soho area of London.

3 High-quality retailers setting up in the Knightsbridge area of London.

4 High-tech companies setting up in Reading.

5 Web page designers setting up in many of the UK's larger cities.

Can you help Frankie and Cleo to match the following terms and definitions?

Regional advantages	Utilities	Bulk-decreasing industries	Footloose industries
Infrastructure	Bulk-increasing industries	Transport costs	

The network of communications and other services which create a foundation for business activity
The five standard services of gas, electricity, water, waste disposal and drainage
The costs involved in moving products and people around in business activity
Industries which locate near to their market because their output is bigger, bulkier, or heavier than their inputs
Industries which are not influenced by any particular locational factors and set up where labour costs are low
Industries which locate close to their raw materials because their inputs are reduced in size and weight in the process of production
The benefits of setting up in a particular locality

16 The Main Types of Organisation

Organisations are set up to serve a particular purpose. They therefore need to have a clear aim – something they are trying to achieve.

For example, the aim of a Premier League Football Club may be 'to win the Premier League on a regular basis while delighting the spectators with high-quality play'. The aim of a leading supermarket chain may be 'to be the customer's first choice in supermarket shopping and to be the largest single firm in the market'.

'Is the only purpose of an organisation to make a profit?'

Business organisations

Most business organisations seek to make a profit for their owners. Profit is thus a major purpose of a business organisation that is owned by individuals or **shareholders** (people who have bought a share in a company).

Most businesses that are owned by people in this country have a **'for-profit'** element to them – a restaurant owner may enjoy running a business because of the freedom it gives them to make decisions for themselves and to be creative but they would not be able to continue in business if they did not make a profit.

Not-for-profit organisations

In this country there are also many **not-for-profit organisations**, including **charities** such as Oxfam, the British Heart Foundation and the Cancer Research Campaign.

A charity is an organisation set up to raise funds, or a surplus, for use in helping other people or causes. A surplus is a balance from the income of a charity after all costs have been paid. This contrasts with the profit-based purposes of a 'for-profit' organisation. The management of charity work is overseen by a group of trustees. Many of these trustees will have a variety of experience in both charity and business activities. Charities have to register as such and must produce annual accounts that are available for anyone to see.

Charities employ paid managers and workers (unlike **voluntary organisations**, which rely on the good will of their staff). A voluntary organisation is set up, organised, staffed and run by people who are working purely on a voluntary basis, usually for a 'good cause'. Examples of voluntary organisations are the Women's Royal Voluntary Service (WRVS) and Voluntary Service Overseas (VSO).

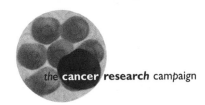

the **cancer research** campaign

CASE STUDY

Problems for Oxfam in 2000

The Oxfam shop is a landmark of the British high street. But fierce competition among retailers has left the shops facing a financial crisis.

Despite subsidised business rates, donated goods and an army of volunteer staff, Britain's most famous charity shop chain's revenues are falling. A radical review of the 850 stores is leading to cost cutting and job losses.

The main reason for plunging profits is higher costs, such as Oxfam's decision to professionalise shop management in 1998 by hiring some 500 paid managers to replace volunteers at the busiest outlets. This occurred just at the time when the retail sector was moving into a slump.

While overall sales of the shops have remained constant at £60 million, surpluses passed on for aid projects have fallen from £16.5 million in 1997–1998 to £7.6 million in 2000. Only about 20p of every £1 donated to Oxfam was available for projects to aid the needy in 2000, the rest was going on running the charity. The decision to use paid managers added £3 million a year to costs.

Government-run organisations

As well as private businesses, charities and voluntary organisations, some organisations are owned by the government for the people.

For example, the civil service is responsible for carrying out work for central government, such as collecting taxes (the Inland Revenue, Customs and Excise) and managing the spending of money by the government (the Treasury). The armed forces (navy, air force and army) are also responsible to a government department (the Ministry of Defence). These government organisations do not operate as 'for-profit' businesses but they have to use the taxpayer's money efficiently, so that there should be no room for waste.

The government also owns a number of organisations which are called **public corporations**, such as the British Broadcasting Corporation (BBC) and the Bank of England. Central government sets out clear aims for these public corporations including making best use of taxpayers' money.

There are also local government organisations responsible for raising local property taxes and making sure that local services such as road repairs, the collection of refuse, the provision of street lighting and grass cutting is done properly in your local area. Local government may also run some **municipal services**, whereby it runs a service and collects money directly for that service – such as maintaining and charging for football pitch hire in the local park.

TASK

What evidence is given in the case study that Oxfam was not making best use of its donations in late 2000?

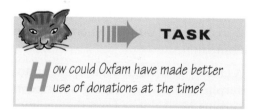

TASK

How could Oxfam have made better use of donations at the time?

'Does government have to make a profit from taxpayers' money in the same way that a business needs to make a profit for shareholders?'

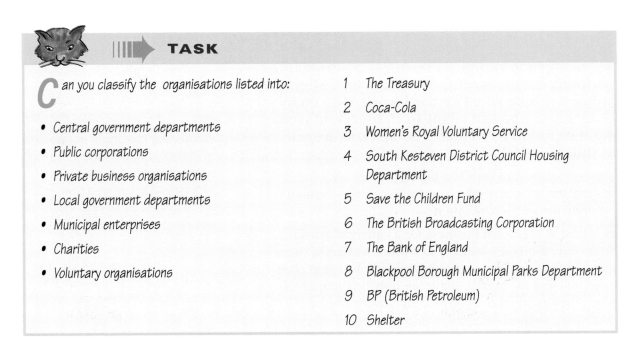

TASK

Can you classify the organisations listed into:

- Central government departments
- Public corporations
- Private business organisations
- Local government departments
- Municipal enterprises
- Charities
- Voluntary organisations

1   The Treasury
2   Coca-Cola
3   Women's Royal Voluntary Service
4   South Kesteven District Council Housing Department
5   Save the Children Fund
6   The British Broadcasting Corporation
7   The Bank of England
8   Blackpool Borough Municipal Parks Department
9   BP (British Petroleum)
10 Shelter

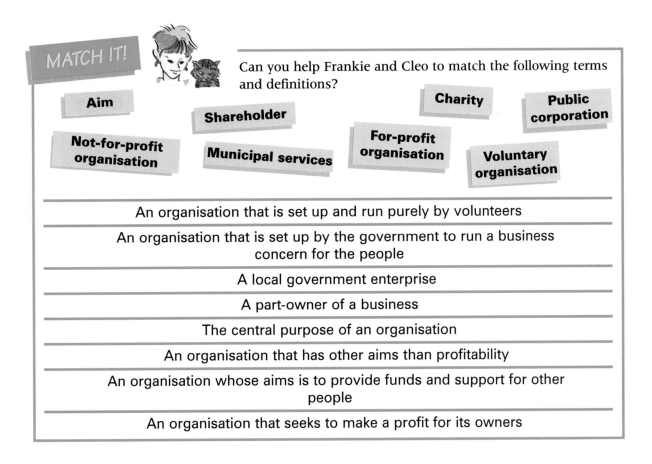

MATCH IT!

Can you help Frankie and Cleo to match the following terms and definitions?

Aim

Shareholder

Charity

Public corporation

Not-for-profit organisation

Municipal services

For-profit organisation

Voluntary organisation

An organisation that is set up and run purely by volunteers
An organisation that is set up by the government to run a business concern for the people
A local government enterprise
A part-owner of a business
The central purpose of an organisation
An organisation that has other aims than profitability
An organisation whose aims is to provide funds and support for other people
An organisation that seeks to make a profit for its owners

17 Starting a Business

Have you got what it takes?

Setting up and running a business is something that only energetic, enthusiastic people should tackle – people who like hard work, who enjoy challenges, who can adapt to change, and who are not put off by failure. Perhaps you are one of those people!

Starting up on your own is a big step. It is always vital to carry out a lot of research and think things through carefully before rushing into it.

People start their own business for a variety of reasons. Some have a bright idea that they think will make them rich. Others find themselves unemployed and start their own business to survive. Some can only be themselves when they are their own boss. Others want to give something to their community and can see no other way of doing it except by setting up on their own.

Business ideas

Of course, an important starting point for a business is the business idea. Most people at some time or another have said things like: *'If only someone sold x here they could make a fortune…'* Or: *'I have a great idea for a new product.'*

There are many ways of coming up with a bright idea. The table below shows a few examples. Try to add two suggestions of your own for each example given.

'This is an important chapter for me. I am keen to start up my own business making biscuits. I find it really useful to find out about other small businesses and how they have been set up.'

Source of idea	Example
Developing a hobby	Making wooden toys
Using your skills	Plastering/painting
A chance idea	A musical toothbrush
Spotting a gap in the market	A home hairdresser
Improving a product or service	A better restaurant
Combining two existing ideas	Coffee shop/bookshop
Solving problems for people	Financial adviser
Listening to people	Teenagers want a mobile disco

Above: Big businesses can start with bright ideas…

LATEST NEWS

Identify your Hot Zone

The American online magazine Entrepreneur.com argues that in seeking a business opportunity you need to identify your 'hot zone' – opportunities that dovetail with your natural strengths. It says: 'The hot zone is the place where your skills, contacts, and personality make a sweet collision with a real marketplace need.'

Sally makes a start

Frankie's friend Sally has set up her own sandwich-making business.

Frankie has been asking Sally what was involved in setting up the sandwich business.

Sally says:

'The sandwich business is booming. Supermarkets are increasing their range and many large cities have phone-in sandwich delivery services.'

But how do you start up a sandwich business?

Sally decided to set up a small sandwich delivery business to earn money and have some fun. First, she carried out research in the area where she planned to deliver...

Checking out the competition

'I thought busy people in the area where I lived needed better-quality lunches. I looked around the local lunchtime places and asked people what was on offer. The choice was very limited, so I thought there would be no difficulty improving on that.'

Bread research

'I wanted to make unusual sandwiches, and I needed a variety of good-quality breads. I visited the local supermarket and bought their range of breads. I tested them for taste and texture. Bread has to be the right shape and size, and go well with the fillings.'

Refining the recipe

'I couldn't find a pitta bread that was the right shape or size. So I have invented my own using dried yeast, strong white flour with wheatgerm, water and a little olive oil. The bread is rolled out in stone-ground flour from a country flour mill. This gives a nutty flavour.'

Fillings

'I chose fillings using flavours from around the world, such as the Greek sandwich with feta cheese and olives. There is also a vegetarian choice, with avocado, tomato and alfalfa sprouts. All the fillings were tested on friends before I made my menu choice.'

CASE STUDY (CONTD.)

Costing it out

Banks may lend money to help small businesses to get started. Some banks have special offers such as free printing of menus and business cards.

For her small business, Sally had to buy special catering equipment. She also needed a basket with a tablecloth, napkins, plates and containers for the delivery round.

The selling price of each sandwich was costed according to the bread used, the price of the filling and the packaging. Then this sum was doubled to cover labour and other expenses.

Starting off

Sally couldn't afford promotion or advertising. So she just set off with a basket full of sandwiches, fruit, cakes, crisps and drinks. Her efforts were rewarded the next day when a satisfied customer remarked: 'Thank you for making such decent sandwiches.'

What changes had to be made?

'The weather affects what people choose. If it's sunny, they prefer salads, but the weather can suddenly change and the salads I have made remain unsold. Shop assistants don't like eating raw onions as it can make their breath smell – and that's no good for customers.'

Customer tastes

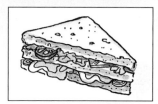

'People turned out to be very adventurous in the choice of sandwiches. Club sandwiches and avocado, bacon, lettuce and tomato are the two bestsellers. I've stopped making plain ham and beef sandwiches."

The future

'I'd really like to open a shop or get a helper, since the delivery takes up so much time. But that all costs money, so we will have to wait and see.'

LATEST NEWS

Many of you will be familiar with Parisa, which is the quickest growing off-licence chain in Britain. Not many of you will know that the chain is owned by Nader Haghighi, who came to this country as a penniless refugee. In the early 1970s as a child from an impoverished family Nader set up a street kiosk (in Shiraz in Iran) selling bric-a-brac, becoming the family's sole breadwinner. In 1980 he came to Britain with no money and speaking no English. He worked as a kitchen porter in a local Pizzaland. Today he has more than 500 shops, cafes and bars across Britain and employs over 4,000 people.

TASK

The Case Study on pages 63–64 highlights some important areas that need to be thought about in setting up a small business. These are:

- *Coming up with an idea*
- *Finding out if there is a market*
- *Looking at the competition*
- *Product research*
- *Costing it out*
- *Pricing*
- *Promotion and advertising*
- *Looking to the future*

Task 1

Working in small groups, study a small local business. Find out what was done under each of the above headings when it was set up.

Prepare a group presentation for the rest of the class. The presentation should be 20 minutes long. Use visual aids - diagrams and charts, examples of products, illustrations, etc.

Task 2

Identify an opportunity for setting up a small business of your own to provide a product or service to be sold in your local area. Carry out some research using each of the headings outlined above. Look at possible competitors, different ways of providing the product or service, etc. Produce your findings in the form of a 1,000-word report supported by charts and diagrams.

MATCH IT! Can you help Frankie and Cleo to match the following terms and definitions?

Bright idea **Costing** **Product research** **Pricing** **Gap in the market**

A novel idea for a product or service
An opportunity that has not already been filled by an existing business
Studying appropriate ways of making goods or developing services to meet consumer needs
Studying the various costs of producing a good or service
Deciding how much and how to charge for goods or services

18 Sole Traders

What is a sole trader?

A sole trader is the most common form of business ownership and the easiest to set up. A sole trader is a business owned by one person – though this business may employ a large number of people. Many new sole trader businesses are currently being set up by young people.

The table below shows some of the advantages and disadvantages of setting up as a sole trader rather than as a larger business.

Unlimited liability

When you set up in business you will need **capital** to run the business. For example, you will need premises to work in, machinery and equipment, and you will need to buy supplies.

'If a business is a sole trader, does this mean that there is only one person working in that business?'

Below: Advantages and disadvantages of being a sole trader

Advantages	Disadvantages
Easy to set up as no special paper work is required	Having unlimited liability endangers personal possessions
Generally these are small businesses, so less capital required	Finance can be difficult to raise
Speedy decisions can be made as few people are involved	Small scale limits discounts and other benefits of large-scale production
Personal attention is given to business affairs	Prices are often higher than those of larger organisations
Special services can be offered to customers	Ill-health/holidays, etc., may affect the running of the business
Can cater for the needs of local people	–
Profits do not have to be shared	–
Business affairs can be kept private	–

Jenny Prescott, signwriter

Jenny Prescott is a sole trader. After leaving art college in 1997, she worked for a signwriting firm and gradually built up her skills and speed. In 2000 Jenny felt that she had developed her abilities and understanding to the stage where she could start her own signwriting company. So she did a business course at college and learnt about the problems and pitfalls of setting up on her own.

Her first task was to find out, by producing a business plan, whether it was worth setting up at all. The business plan covered costs and receipts. **Costs** included paint, labour, heating and lighting, telephone, materials, publicity material, running a van, etc. **Receipts** were based on the number of hours worked and the hourly rate she could charge.

Jenny had decided to operate from home using a shed next to the house for her carpentry and artwork. This reduced her overhead costs considerably.

Businesses need time to get established, and Jenny calculated that at first she would only be working for 5–10 chargeable hours a week. By the end of the first year, she estimated that this would rise to 25 hours.

Taking into account the costs of her materials, she calculated that if she charged £12 an hour, she could make a **reasonable return**. This means that her revenue would more than cover her costs, leaving room for profit.

 TASK

1   Do you think that being a sole trader is a suitable type of business for Jenny's signwriting enterprise?

2   What would be the main advantages and disadvantages to Jenny of this type of business organisation?

3   Give six examples of businesses that might suitably operate as sole traders. Explain why in each case.

4   Cynics might argue that: 'In making and selling clothes there is no room for sole traders. Producing clothing is for people with big ideas and plenty of money! Sole traders haven't a chance!' Do you agree?

Sole traders have only their own resources to draw on, because nobody else is an owner of their business. The sole trader therefore has to use past savings and will usually need to borrow money – probably from a bank.

Sole traders hope to make a profit. However, if a sole trader runs into debt, they will have to pay the money they owe from their own pocket.

The business term we use to describe this position is **unlimited liability.**

For example, if a sole trader has business and equipment worth £10,000, and they run up debts of £50,000, the debt is not limited to the £10,000 which they have already put into the business. This means they may have to sell their house and any other possessions they have to meet the debts. The answer to Frankie's question *(right)* is: 'Yes, running a sole trader business carries a high risk, but the rewards can also be great.'

"Isn't it a bit risky being a sole trader when you hear that two out of three sole-trader start-ups fail their first year?'

'If you don't take risks, you don't make profits!'

MATCH IT!

Can you help Frankie and Cleo to match the following terms and definitions?

Sole trader	Unlimited liability	Capital	Reasonable return

Finance available for running a business

Situation in which there is no restriction to the debts that owners of a business run up

A form of business where there is a single owner

A situation in which revenues more than match costs with a cushion of profit

19 Partnerships

What is a partnership?

A partnership is a business association between two or more owners of an enterprise. Partnerships usually have between 2 and 20 members, though there are some exceptions.

Partnerships are common in many types of business. They are usually found in shop ownership and in professional practices such as vets, doctors, solicitors and dentists.

'A partnership sounds as if it should have just two people in it. Is that right?'

How is a partnership formed?

The usual way to start a partnership is to ask a solicitor to draw up a **Deed of Partnership**. This lays down how profits and losses are to be shared and sets out the duties of each partner – for example, how much capital they should contribute, their roles and responsibilities, how profits will be taken out of the business, and procedures for introducing new partners and settling disputes.

The **Partnership Act of 1890** sets out rules which partners can refer to if they are not already covered in the Deed of Partnership (or if a Deed has not been drawn up).

Limited or **'sleeping' partners** can be introduced to a partnership. They have **limited liability** as long as they take no active part in the running of the business. However, there must always be at least one partner with unlimited liability.

Limited liability

Limited liability means that if a partnership runs into debt the maximum amount in law that they are expected to lose is what they put into the business. In other words, the limited partner is not expected to sell off their house and possessions to meet the business debts.

TASK

Set out a Deed of Partnership between yourself and a friend for a small enterprise that you could set up, such as washing cars, making toffee, etc.

The agreement should cover these topics:

- Who will provide the capital?
- Share-out of profits and losses
- Duties of partners
- How profits will be taken out of business (e.g. weekly, monthly)
- Procedures for bringing in new partners and settling disputes

The advantages and disadvantages of a partnership

Advantages	Disadvantages
Capital from partners	Unlimited liability (except for sleeping partners)
Larger scale than sole trader	Disagreements between partners
Members of family can join	Limitation on number of partners
Affairs can be kept private	Partnership needs to be re-formed if a partner dies
Risks and responsibilities spread among partners	

CASE STUDY

Zara and Rupinder

Zara and Rupinder set up their own website design partnership called 'Ruby WebDesign.com'. Rupinder does most of the page layouts, while Zara deals with clients, mainly over the phone. The good thing about having a partnership is that only one of them needs to be in the office. The other one can go out to meet clients or even have time to play badminton or go for a swim. They both draw a salary from the business and profits are shared 50:50. A disadvantage is that they sometimes argue.

MATCH IT!

Can you help Frankie and Cleo to match the following terms and definitions?

Deed of partnership	Sleeping partner	Limited liability	Partnership Act, 1890

Partnership

A formal agreement setting out the legal details of a partnership

A business association of between 2 and 20 owners who have clear rights and responsibilities to each other

A partner who is not involved in the day-to-day running of a partnership

An arrangement whereby the debts of a part-owner of an organisation are restricted to how much they have put into the organisation

Law introduced in 1890 governing how partnerships can and should be set up

20 Limited Companies

What is a company?

The word 'company' suggests a group of companions who have come together to set up a business. In practice, many companies are not like this today because the owners (share-holders) may be quite far removed from the decision-making.

Private limited companies (Ltd)

The owners of limited companies are called **shareholders**. This is because they each own a share in the business. Private limited companies must have at least two shareholders. There is no upper limit to the number of shareholders they can have, and companies can grow by selling more shares.

The shares of private limited companies are not quoted on the Stock Exchange. Private limited companies are also not allowed to advertise the sale of shares publicly.

Private limited companies face the danger of issuing too many shares and so having to divide the profits between too great a number of shareholders. The liability of shareholders is limited to the value of their shareholding. To warn creditors about the dangers of dealing with these companies, the word **Limited** (or **Ltd**) appears after their name.

All private limited companies must comply with the **Companies Acts** of 1948 and 1980 and register with the Registrar of Companies. In order to register a company, two documents have to be completed. These are the **Memorandum of Association** and the **Articles of Association**.

◆ The Memorandum of Association outlines the relationship of the company with the outside world. For example, it states the name of the company, the purpose of the company and what the company actually does.

◆ The Articles of Association state the internal rules governing the company's organisation, including rules about meetings and the voting rights of shareholders. Also included is a list of directors and information on other internal matters. Shareholders can vote to change the articles.

Once the articles and memorandum have been received by the Registrar of Companies, together with some other paperwork, he or she will provide a **Certificate of Incorporation** and the private limited company can start trading.

'In sole trader businesses and partnerships the owners of the company also make the decisions about how the business is run. The owners are the controllers.
However, in many large companies this is not the case – the shareholders are the owners, but many decisions are made by managers. Is it better therefore to stay as a small business?'

Advantages	Disadvantages
Money from shares	Cannot sell shares on the Stock Market
Firm grows bigger	Accounts not private
Limited liability	Limitations on capital
Specialist managers can be employed	A lot of administrative work is required

Above: The advantages and disadvantages of being a private limited company

TASK

1 Why might a shareholder be interested to read the Articles of Association of a company that they have shares in?

2 Why might a supplier to a company be interested to see its Memorandum of Association?

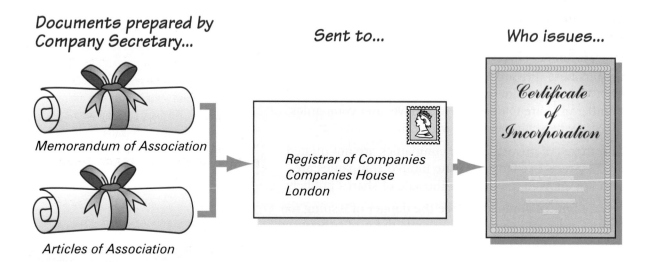

Documents prepared by Company Secretary...

Memorandum of Association

Articles of Association

Sent to...

Registrar of Companies
Companies House
London

Who issues...

Certificate of Incorporation

Above: The process of setting up a private limited company

Buying and selling shares at the Stock Exchange in London

Public limited companies (PLCs)

PLCs have the chance to become larger than private business organisations. They are allowed to raise capital through the Stock Exchange, where shares are bought and sold.

Only two people are needed to form a public limited company, and there is no legal limit on the number of shareholders.

Forming a public company is very similar to forming a private company.

A Memorandum of Association and Articles of Association, as well as a number of other legal documents, have to be approved by the Registrar of Companies. The Registrar issues a Certificate of Incorporation as evidence that the company is registered.

The public company then issues a **prospectus**. This is an advertisement or invitation to the public to buy shares. The issuing of shares then takes place, and the Registrar of Companies issues a Certificate of Trading. Business can then start, and share prices will be quoted on the stock market.

MARKS & SPENCER

Some well known PLCs

TASK

*R*ead the Case Study on the next page then complete the following tasks:

1   List the four main stages in the growth of Marks & Spencer.

2   Explain why Marks & Spencer went through these four stages of growth. (For example, why did Michael Marks need to take on a partner? Why did the business need to become a private company and later a public company?)

3   What are the advantages and disadvantages of bringing more people into a company?

4   What do the following terms mean?

a)   slogan

b)   hire

c)   specialise

d)   administration

e)   shareholder

f)   executive director

g)   non-executive director

h)   discount

i)   manufacturers

j)   wholesalers

k)   Stock Exchange

CASE STUDY

Marks & Spencer PLC

Michael Marks arrived in the north of England in 1881 as a Jewish immigrant from Russia. He started off as a hawker (a person who sells from door to door), going around mining villages selling buttons, needles, ribbons and other small items. He adopted a slogan which he tied on his tray: 'Don't ask the price, it's a penny.' He used this slogan to avoid complications as he could not speak much English.

An early Marks & Spencer store

The business quickly grew and soon Marks was able to afford a stall at Leeds market. As this brought in profits, Marks started to hire stalls at different markets. He decided that to become more successful, he would have to find a partner. In 1894 he became partners with Tom Spencer. Spencer put in £300 to become a partner.

Soon they had 24 market stalls and 12 shops. They each began to specialise in different jobs. Spencer would mainly work at the warehouse and organise administration. Marks specialised in buying goods and looking for new places from which to sell. Their shops were all 'penny bazaars'.

Unfortunately, Spencer became an alcoholic and less reliable. The partners decided to form the business into a private company, with themselves as the major shareholders. Marks stayed with the business, while Spencer left to run a chicken farm. Marks was, therefore, an executive director and ran the company, while Spencer remained a non-executive director.

Michael Marks and Tom Spencer died and Michael's son Simon and his boyhood friend

Israel Sieff began to play an important part in running the company. Simon married Israel's sister, and Israel married Simon's sister.

In the early 1920s, Simon Marks went to America to learn about retailing. On his return he decided to change the company image, giving it a more up-market look, and to expand by opening a whole chain of stores. Instead of buying from wholesalers, he also started buying in bulk from manufacturers, who gave him a discount.

To raise the capital for doing this, Marks & Spencer became a public company with shares quoted on the Stock Exchange. From here, the company grew to its present size and developed the image and reputation that it enjoys to this day. There are now a large number of shareholders and the company is controlled by a board of directors. In 2000 sales at Marks & Spencer began to slip in a very competitive retail market. There were fears that the company might be taken over by a larger company, such as one of the big supermarket chains.

Type of business	Ownership	Control
One-person business	Michael Marks	Michael Marks
Partnership	Michael Marks and Tom Spencer	Michael Marks and Tom Spencer
Private company	Marks and Spencer and other shareholders	Michael Marks and other executive directors
Public company	Shareholders	Directors, including the Sieff family

The four stages in the growth of Marks & Spencer

Benefits to shareholders

The benefits of being a shareholder include:

1 Possible increases in the share price (a **capital gain**).

2 Dividends received. The **dividend** is the shareholder's share of the company profits which are usually paid at six-monthly intervals (an **interim dividend**) or at the end of the year (a **year-end dividend**).

3 Being a part-owner of a business concern, with the right to attend and vote at shareholders' meetings.

4 Perks associated with some shares, e.g. reduced costs of company goods, travel discounts and so on.

Multinationals

A **multinational** company is one that operates in a number of countries. Most multinationals are public companies but there are also a few large private multinationals, such as Mars. Because of their size and their ability to switch operations between countries, multinationals have great powers to control prices. As major employers they can sometimes influence decision-making at government level.

Advantages	Disadvantages
Limited liability for shareholders	Formation can be expensive
Easy to raise capital	Decisions can be slow. 'Red tape' can be a problem
Operates on a large scale	Problems of being too large
Easy to raise finance from banks	Employees and shareholders distanced from one another
Employs specialists	Affairs are public

The advantages and disadvantages of being a PLC

MATCH IT!

Can you help Frankie and Cleo to match the following terms and definitions?

Articles of Association **Memorandum of Association** **Multinational** **Share**

PLC

Certificate of Incorporation **Private limited company (Ltd)** **Dividend** **Certificate of Trading**

Company whose shares are traded on the Stock Exchange

The return to the shareholder of a company

Part-ownership of a company

Organisation which operates and trades in a number of different countries

Company controlled by individuals and restricted groups

Document confirming that an organisation has company status

Document enabling a PLC to commence trading

Document setting out the internal rules and relationships of an organisation

Document setting out the external rules and relationships of an organisation

21 Franchising

What is a franchise?

A franchise is a 'business marriage' between an existing, proven business and a newcomer. The newcomer (known as the 'franchisee') buys permission to copy the business idea of the established company.

For example Frankie's Auntie Meena franchises her hairdressing business from an established company, 'TopCuts'.

The franchisee (Auntie Meena) commits her capital and effort. The franchisor (TopCuts) commits the trading name and management experience, and often supplies materials and equipment.

For example, TopCuts may help to train Meena's stylists, and sell Meena a range of quality supplies and equipment at a good price.

'You hear a lot of talk about franchising these days. My Auntie Meena franchises her hairdressing business from a well-known hairdressing company, TopCuts. Does this mean that Meena doesn't own the business?'

CASE STUDY

Mary Watson, plumber

Mary Watson had worked for a local builder as a contract plumber for several years. She worked long hours and the work was irregular. Then in September 2000 she saw the newspaper advertisement below for SuperRod, a nationwide plumbing and drain-clearing franchise.

Using her savings and a loan from the bank, Mary was able to buy a franchise and set up in business. SuperRod provided her with a three-week training course, a van and an electronic plumbing device that quickly unblocks drains and pipes. She was given an exclusive right to sell her services within a 10-mile radius, and the right to trade and advertise 24 hours a day. In return, Mary had to hand over 12 per cent of her profits to SuperRod.

The SuperRod franchise advertisement

TASK

1   List six advantages and six disadvantages to Mary of taking on the franchise.

2   List what you consider to be the main advantages and disadvantages for the company granting the franchise.

TASK

1   What lines of business is franchising most suitable for? Why?

2   Are there businesses for which franchising is inappropriate? If so, why?

3   If you needed a plumber in a hurry, how would you go about getting one? What might tempt you to choose a franchise plumber?

4   Identify an area of retailing that would be suitable for franchising. How would you go about organising such an operation?

The franchisee buys a licence to copy the franchisor's business system. In return they promise to pay them a percentage of their sales.

The franchisee needs to work hard, put in long hours and use a lot of initiative to get the business started and develop it. In 2000, there were over 1000 franchise opportunities in the UK.

Where can you find out more about franchise opportunities?

The *UK Franchise Directory* lists and describes all established franchise opportunities in the UK. The *Franchise Magazine* provides up-to-date information about franchising.

Both of these publications are available for reference at all JobCentres. Copies can be obtained from:

The Franchise Development Service Ltd
Castle House
Castle Meadow
Norwich
NR2 1PJ

A useful Internet site to investigate is:

franbus@lds.co.uk

These web pages give details of over 200 UK franchises. For example:

◆ BB's Coffee and Muffins – franchise outlets selling fresh coffee and muffins in large shopping centres

◆ Best Training – one of the UK's largest computer training franchises

◆ Dyno-Rod – a leading drain cleaning franchise, etc.

Franchising is common in the fast-food industry. Examples include Spud-U-Like and Pizza Hut. Further examples are Dyno-Rod in the plumbing business, Tumbletots, Body Shop and Prontaprint.

COURSEWORK ACTIVITIES

Identify a franchise opportunity that you find appealing. Find out:

• How much capital the franchisee would have to put into the business

• What the franchise opportunity involves

• The start-up help provided by the franchisor

• How much the franchisee would need to pay the franchisor on an ongoing basis

A useful starting point for this activity is franbus@lds.

MATCH IT!

Can you help Frankie and Cleo to match the following terms and definitions?

Franchisor   **Franchisee**   **Franchise**

A business marriage between an existing, proven business and a newcomer
The business granting a franchise
An individual or group of individuals benefiting from using someone else's trading name and experience

22 Co-operatives

Defining a co-operative

If you look up the word 'co-operative' in the dictionary, you will find the following:

◆ 'Willing to co-operate; helpful'

◆ 'Acting jointly with others; co-operating'

◆ (Of an enterprise, farm, etc.): 'Owned collectively and managed for joint economic benefit'

SPIX

'The idea of co-operatives is very important in the world today. Co-operation is all about people working together rather than simply trying to make some money just for themselves.'

The weavers were paid in tokens

They pooled money to buy food at wholesale prices

By setting up their own co-operative, they were able to buy food which was sold cheaply to members

Retail co-operatives – the early days

Nowadays people tend to think of 'the Co-op' as just another supermarket chain. In fact, co-operatives are unique businesses which place special emphasis on serving the community or their members.

The co-operative movement began with the Rochdale Pioneers in 1844. Twenty-eight weavers pooled money to buy food at wholesale prices. They did this because they were being paid in tokens (rather than money) by their employer. They then had to spend these tokens in the company shop where prices were high. By setting up their own co-operative they were able to buy food, which was sold cheaply to members. Profits were shared out in the form of a dividend, depending on how much each member had bought.

In the late nineteenth century, co-ops flourished and societies sprang up all over Britain. Co-ops brought in the first supermarkets. However, the multiples like Tesco proved too competitive for the co-ops, which were organised into too many small societies and did not benefit enough from bulk buying. The co-ops also employed inexperienced managers and were not as slick as the new multiples. To fight back, small societies have merged together and the smaller shops have been closed.

The first co-op, situated in Toad Lane, Rochdale, is now a museum

Retail co-ops today

In the twenty-first century the co-ops have their own Leo Hypermarkets which employ specialist managers and bulk-buying techniques, coupled with all the latest hypermarket technology. However, they continue to have small supermarkets, many of which help people in poorer communities where there are few local shops.

To become a shareholder in a retail co-op you need only buy a £1 share. Co-ops sometimes give stamps which can be collected and used in payment for goods. Other co-ops give benefits to customers by using profits to cut prices. Many co-ops aim to plough some of their profits back into the local community.

A modern co-operative superstore

In recent years the co-ops have realised the importance of making their customers aware of what makes co-op shopping different. A major part of the co-op difference is their emphasis on ethical business. This means making sure that they buy items like coffee and tea only from suppliers that are not exploiting coffee growers or employing child labour.

Producer co-operatives

Producer co-operatives are groups which combine to produce a good or service.

They are usually registered as companies 'limited by guarantee'. This means that each member undertakes to fund any losses up to a certain amount. There are many types. A **workers' co-operative**, for example, is one that employs all or most of its members. In a workers' co-operative, members:

◆ share responsibility for the business

◆ work together

◆ take decisions together

◆ share the profits

Other examples of producer co-operatives are groups which grow fruit and vegetables, make furniture or organise child-minding.

The main problems that such co-operatives face are finance and organisation. Co-operatives sometimes find it difficult to raise capital from banks because they are not set up with the main aim of making a profit.

TASK

Rank these factors in order of importance, in terms of why a shopper should support their local co-op:

1 The co-op offers goods at low prices.

2 The co-ops have a history of serving the community

3 The co-ops offer a good selection of goods

4 The co-ops ensure ethical trading

5 Co-ops are found at convenient locations

6 Co-ops share profits out among their shoppers

Marketing co-operatives

Marketing co-operatives are most frequently found in farming areas. The farmers set up a **marketing board** to take care of, among other things, grading, packaging, distributing, advertising and selling their products.

Mutuals

Mutual societies share a lot of similarities with co-operatives. A mutual is set up by a group of people for a joint purpose. Many building societies and insurance companies were set up in this way. The members of the society would club together by putting funds into a pool – for example, to build houses or to share the benefits of insurance. The members were thus the owners and they shared any profits that the society made.

TASK

1   Who owned the mutuals, and who owned these organisations when they became PLCs?

2   Why might a member of a mutual be keen to see it become a PLC?

3   Why might a member of a mutual be opposed to his or her society converting to a PLC?

CASE STUDY

Mutuals become PLCs

In the 1990s a number of well known mutuals such as the Halifax and the Abbey National building societies became PLCs (public limited companies). The argument put forward was that as PLCs they would be able to raise far more capital by selling shares on the Stock Exchange. This extra capital would enable them to compete with other major banks and building societies in a competitive market place. Members of these mutuals were asked to vote on whether they were in favour of the conversion to PLC. As an incentive they were offered a windfall of cash or shares if the society converted to a PLC. In most cases the members voted to allow their society to become a PLC. Once these organisations became PLCs they no longer were run for their members but for their shareholders.

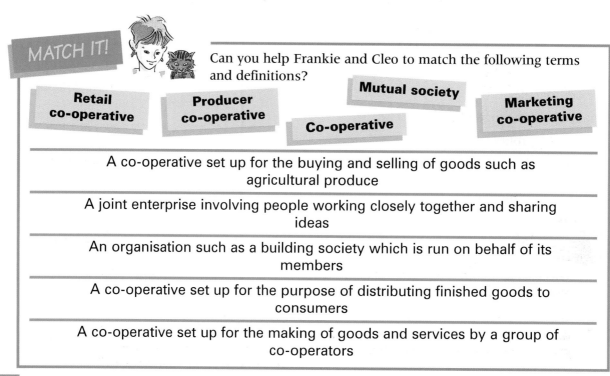

MATCH IT!

Can you help Frankie and Cleo to match the following terms and definitions?

Retail co-operative

Producer co-operative

Mutual society

Co-operative

Marketing co-operative

A co-operative set up for the buying and selling of goods such as agricultural produce

A joint enterprise involving people working closely together and sharing ideas

An organisation such as a building society which is run on behalf of its members

A co-operative set up for the purpose of distributing finished goods to consumers

A co-operative set up for the making of goods and services by a group of co-operators

23 Public Sector Organisations

What is the public sector?

The UK has a mixed economy. This means that, as well as many businesses being privately owned, there are others which are run by the state.

These state-controlled enterprises make up what is known as the public sector.

Public corporations

In the UK the government still owns a number of industries and businesses on behalf of the people.

Examples of **public corporations** include the Bank of England and the British Broadcasting Corporation (BBC). Once a public corporation has been set up, the government appoints a chairperson to be responsible for its day-to-day running.

'I sometimes get confused between the terms "public sector" and "public companies". I know that public companies are owned by people who are called shareholders. But who owns the public sector?'

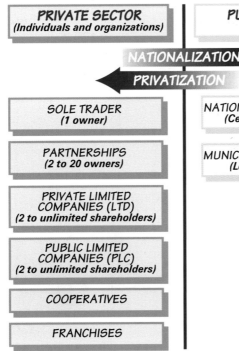

PRIVATE SECTOR (Individuals and organizations)	PUBLIC SECTOR (State)
NATIONALIZATION →	
← PRIVATIZATION	
SOLE TRADER (1 owner)	NATIONALIZED INDUSTRIES (Central government)
PARTNERSHIPS (2 to 20 owners)	MUNICIPAL UNDERTAKINGS (Local government)
PRIVATE LIMITED COMPANIES (LTD) (2 to unlimited shareholders)	
PUBLIC LIMITED COMPANIES (PLC) (2 to unlimited shareholders)	
COOPERATIVES	
FRANCHISES	

The different types of private and public enterprise

The Chairperson of the BBC is accountable to the Home Office

The BBC receives its revenue from TV licences, and sale and production of programmes, for other TV broadcasters

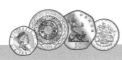

Bank of England

The Chairperson of the Bank of England is accountable to the chancellor of the Exchequer

Became publicly owned in 1946

Power to set interest rates given to its Monetary Policy Committee in 1997

Why a public corporation?

There are a number of reasons why public corporations have been set up:

1 **To avoid wasteful duplication and confusion**

For example, just imagine if more than one bank was allowed to print notes and coins in England and Wales. It would be difficult to control how much money each bank printed, so that the government might lose control over the money supply.

2 **To set up and run important but non-profitable services**

For example, although the BBC makes sure that most of its programmes are profitable and popular, it also operates a loss-making service in some areas, e.g. producing special programmes for deaf people and for minority groups.

3 **To prevent exploitation of consumers**

When there is only one enterprise providing a good or a service, it is sometimes better for it to be a government enterprise rather than a private one. Private firms will want to make a profit, while a government enterprise can make sure that consumers are treated fairly. For example, the Post Office makes sure that deliveries are made to remote parts of the UK at a fair price.

4 **To protect jobs and key industries**

Many people feel that the government has a responsibility to protect jobs, even if this means lower profits. Government may also want to take steps to protect industries which are important to the UK economy.

Once a public corporation has been set up, a government minister is made responsible for the industry concerned. However, the minister chooses a **chairperson** to run the industry on a day-to-day basis.

The government sets targets for the industry to meet, and the chairperson and managers must then decide on the best way to meet them.

Privatisation

Since 1979, a number of public corporations have been privatised. This means that they have been sold from the public sector to the private sector, where they are owned by shareholders. (The latest privatisation is of air traffic control.)

Public corporation	Public company
Set up by Act of Parliament	Set up by issuing prospectus and inviting public to buy shares
Owned by the government	Owned by shareholders
Run by chairperson and managers appointed by government	Run by management team chosen by directors representing shareholders
Aims to provide a public service as well as having commercial goals	Commercial goals

Differences between a public corporation and a public company

TASK

1 Can you identify the government ministers responsible for the Bank of England and the BBC?

2 Who are the current chairpersons of the Bank of England and the BBC?

Why privatise?

There are a number of reasons for privatisation:

1 Some people argue that state-run firms are not efficient because they do not have any real competition. They are also protected from bankruptcy, because the government always pays their debts.

2 It is argued that in a modern society as many people as possible should have shares in businesses. The idea is that everyone – not just the very rich – should become shareholders in enterprises such as British Telecom and Railtrack. In 1979, when Margaret Thatcher became Prime Minister, there were 3 million shareholders in the UK; when she left office in 1990, there were 11 million.

'I think that privatisation is a jolly good idea. It is only when firms are owned by private individuals like me that the best interests of all consumers will be served!'

Do you agree with Ron?

Mrs Thatcher wins the election and becomes conservative Prime Minister. There are 3m shareholders

Many industries were public corporations

The Conservatives sold off many of these industries to private shareholders

When Mrs Thatcher left office, there were 11m shareholders. Tony Blair's Labour government has kept these industries in the private sector

3 Privatising industries raises large sums of money for the government *(see table below)*. This reduces the government's need to tax people and to borrow money.

Company	Date of sale	Proceeds (£m)
BP	1979-1990	5,273
Cable and Wireless	1981,1983,1985	1,021
British Telecommunications	1984,1991,1993	17,604
British Gas	1986,1990	7,793
British Steel	1988	2,425
Regional Water Authorities	1989-1992	3,468
Regional Electricity Companies	1990	7,997
Electricity Generating Companies	1991	2,969

Left: Some of Britain's main privatisations

Regulating privatised industries

When industries are privatised the government appoints a body called a **Regulatory Authority**, headed by a **Regulator** who is responsible for making sure that the industry runs in the public interest – for example, by not charging too much and running an efficient service.

CASE STUDY

Railtrack

The 1993 Railways Act paved the way for the process of rail privatisation, which rapidly reformed Britain's railways. The aim of this privatisation was to improve the quality and efficiency of rail services by introducing private-sector investment and management.

Privatisation in the railway industry involved the creation of nearly 100 different business units, the most significant of which was Railtrack. Railtrack was released from the public sector when it was floated on the Stock Exchange in May 1996 to become Railtrack Group Plc – a privately owned company.

Railtrack owns almost all of Britain's railway infrastructure, including tracks, signalling, bridges, tunnels, stations and depots.

Railtrack plays a key part in the provision of rail services. It is a purchaser of services, such as maintenance and track renewal, and a seller of access to the UK's rail infrastructure. Railtrack's main customers are train operating and freight operating companies – not the general public and rail travellers.

In 2000 the chairman of Railtrack resigned following problems for the company, including serious rail accidents and problems with the quality of the maintenance of track. He defended Railtrack by saying that the Regulator had been putting on too much pressure to make sure that trains ran on time, and not enough emphasis on safety.

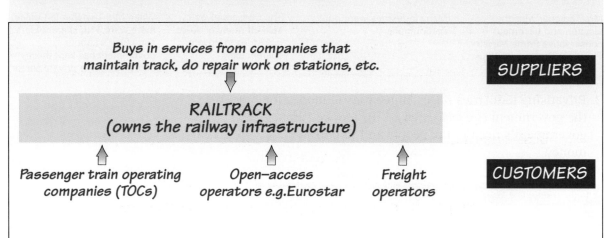

TASK

1   Before privatisation Railtrack was part of the nationalised industry called British Rail. What do you think would be the differences in emphasis between a government-run Railtrack and a privatised one?

2   What do you think should be the priorities of Railtrack?

3   What part do you think the Regulator should play in safeguarding the interests of rail users?

Can you help Frankie and Cleo to match the following terms and definitions?

Regulator   **Public sector**   **Public corporation**   **Private sector**

Chairperson   **Privatisation**

Individual appointed by a government minister to take responsibility for running a nationalised industry
That part of the economy which is run and controlled by the government
Independent official appointed to check on the workings of a privatised industry
Businesses and enterprises owned and run by individuals working in their own interests
A body set up to run a state-owned business
Selling off government industries to private shareholders

24 Business Growth

From tiny acorns...

Most of the giant businesses that we know in the world today had very humble origins. Many products started off as homemade efforts. Coca-Cola was originally brewed up on a kitchen stove, and many mechanical goods were first hammered together in a garden shed.

Many business ideas started off as the brainchild of one person. The creator then brought a partner into the business, and eventually went on to bring in other part-owners by forming a company.

The size of the business

Business owners must choose the scale of production which suits the business best. Many businesses thrive as they become larger. The benefits they gain from growth are called **economies of scale**.

Internal economies of scale

The most obvious benefit of growth is the ability to produce units of output more cheaply. For example, the cost of serving a customer with a pint of beer will be a lot lower in a busy pub than in a pub with very few customers.

'It's all very well setting up a small business. But at what stage should we try and grow bigger? What are the dangers of growth?'

'Many young people who start up in business think they are the next Richard Branson or Anita Roddick. They expand their business too quickly – and then can't cope!'
Can you think of examples that support Ron's argument?

Below: The economies of scale that come into play as a result of growth

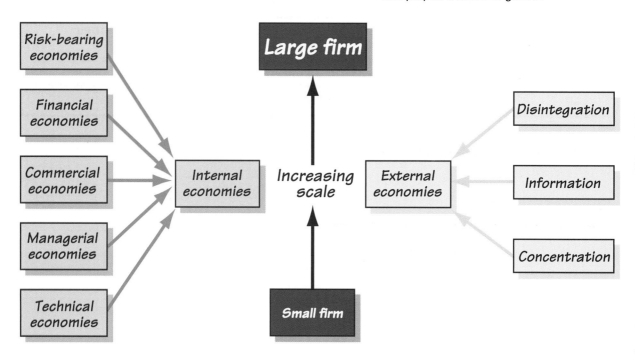

CASE STUDY

The web page designer

In 1999 Adam graduated from University with a degree in Business and Information Technology. At university he had learnt a lot about web page design as well as how to set up and market a business.

Adam realised that there were a lot of businesses in his home city of Nottingham that wanted to rapidly increase the size of their business by engaging in e-commerce. He realised that there was a lot more work to be won than he could handle on his own.

He therefore decided to set up a private company which would enable him to sell shares and raise enough capital to operate from premises in the middle of Nottingham and to employ up to 20 web page designers. At the time investors were very excited about e-commerce and its potential. As a result he was able to raise £200,000 in start-up capital.

Adam quickly found that customers were queuing up to have web sites created for them. He realised that if he could get advertisers to advertise on these sites then he could bring in a lot more revenue to the company. He therefore employed an extra ten people to sell advertising space. He borrowed £100,000 from the bank to finance this expansion.

Unfortunately, while business boomed, cash payments into the business were slow. After six months Adam was forced to close down his business – even though he had full order books, and everyone felt that the business was a great success.

  TASK

1   Do you think that Adam's new business venture was based on a good idea?

2   What factors would have helped the business to take off and win new business?

3   What factors led to the fall of the business?

4   What do you think were Adam's biggest mistakes?

5   What does the case study tell us about the difficulties of business growth?

TASK

Ritz Palace

- *300 beds*
- *Open all year*
- *Offers a range of entertainment*
- *Employs 6 managers, 3 chefs, 5 bar people, 15 waiters, 20 room attendants, 10 general staff*

New Sea Breezes

- *20 beds*
- *Open Spring and Summer*
- *Offers entertainment from the same stand-up comic every evening*
- *Employs 1 manager and*
- *3 cooks/cleaners/waiters*

Explain how The Ritz Palace may benefit from economies of scale relative to the New Sea Breezes Hotel.

Technical economies

Large-scale producers can employ techniques and equipment that cannot be used by small-scale producers. For example, a bakery may have two ovens producing 1,000 loaves a day. As the firm gets larger, these two ovens could be replaced by one oven producing 2,500 loaves a day at half the cost. This means less labour, lower energy costs – and higher profits for the owner.

Labour and managerial economies

Large organisations can employ specialist staff such as accountants and researchers. Such expertise will help to increase output and lower costs. The ratio of managers to staff is also likely to be lower in a large organisation because each manager is responsible for more staff.

Commercial economies

Commerce is concerned with the buying and selling of things. As firms grow larger they are able to buy their inputs such as raw materials or finished goods in bulk. When you buy in bulk, you can negotiate discounts. The cost of transport per unit will be much lower with larger loads. Larger firms are also able to organise the selling of their products more effectively. For example, if you can sell all your output to one or a few buyers, the cost of making the sale will be a lot lower than if you are dealing with thousands of separate customers.

Financial economies

Large firms tend to be a more secure investment than smaller firms and find it easier to borrow money. Their reputation and reliability can often help them to borrow money at lower rates of interest.

Risk-bearing economies

Large firms have the possibility of carrying out a range of activities, rather than 'putting all their eggs in one basket'. We call this **diversification**. They may decide to produce several products rather than one, or they may sell goods in different markets, e.g. France, Spain, Greece, and India as well as the UK. Or, instead of just selling goods to one age range, they may produce products which appeal to different age-ranges – for example, one breakfast cereal for young children, another aimed at teenagers, a third aimed at the weight-conscious middle-aged.

External economies of scale

External economies of scale are those shared by a number of firms in the same industry in a particular area. Examples are:

Economies of concentration

As firms within an industry grow larger in a locality, a concentration of special services develops. These may include local college courses, a skilled workforce and a growing reputation for the area's products.

Economies of information

Larger industries can set up special information services to benefit producers, e.g. by setting up a research unit such as The Chemical Research Unit, or by creating a specialist publication such as *The Building Trade Journal*.

TASK

*C*an you help Frankie and Cleo to classify the following as **internal** or **external** economies of scale?

Can you also say what **type** of economies are involved in each case (e.g. technical economies, economies of information, etc.)?

- A tin box factory makes use of a new automated production line.

- A new university opens in Lincoln, offering courses for local business people.

- Shell UK is able to borrow millions of pounds for a short period from a British bank at a low rate of interest.

- A food processing firm is able to sell all of its output to Marks & Spencer.

- Several new journals are published, providing details of the latest developments in computing.

- A number of new companies start to locate close to the terminals for the Channel Tunnel.

- The growth of an insurance company enables it to attract top specialist managers.

- Virgin starts to move into a number of new product lines such as insurance and cola drinks as well as its traditional lines.

- An airline purchases some jumbo-sized new aeroplanes.

- Component manufacturers set up in the areas where new port construction work is taking place.

- Existing firms increasingly starting to adopt e-commerce as a way of doing business.

Economies of disintegration

Other firms may be attracted to areas where specialised industries already exist – for example, firms producing components or offering help with maintenance and processes. Examples are the many software houses supplying the big computer companies in the Thames Valley.

Integration

Organisations can take advantage of economies of scale by ploughing back profits and gradually expanding their operations. Organic growth of this kind is, however, often a slow process.

A quicker and more dynamic route is through **mergers** or **take-overs.** These involve combining a number of businesses under a single organisation. Merging increases size and enables companies to benefit from economies of large-scale production. Some firms merge in order to increase the benefits of specialisation. Others do so in order to diversify and so cut down risk.

Horizontal integration

A company may take over another which produces similar goods and which is involved at the same stage of production. An example of **horizontal integration** is shown below.

Horizontal integration

Vertical integration

Some products are made in stages which may be carried out by separate firms. **Vertical integration** therefore involves the joining together of firms at different stages of production.

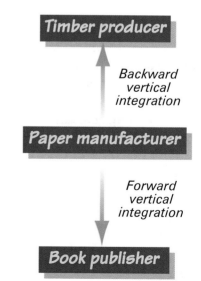

Vertical integration

Backward vertical integration would be the take-over of a supplier, and **forward vertical integration** would be the take-over of a firm at a later stage of production.

Lateral integration

This is a merger between two businesses that produce similar products. For example, a book publisher might acquire magazine and newspaper publishers, or even television and other media products *(below)*. The reasons might be to spread risk or to allow products to share the same channels of distribution.

Left: Lateral integration

Conglomerate integration

Another way of maximising risk-bearing economies is for a firm to acquire businesses that are not connected in any way with its present activities. A conglomerate integration *(below)* can provide wide diversification.

Multinationals

Large companies will seek to expand their markets overseas, and this often leads them to manufacture or assemble goods abroad. In many cases they will develop by taking over companies in other countries.

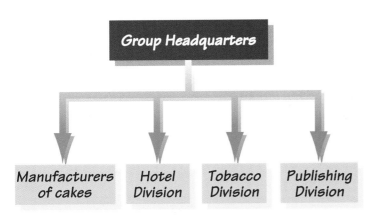

Left: Conglomerate integration

Diseconomies of scale

However, there are some drawbacks to being big. These are called **diseconomies of scale**. Alongside the enormous advantages associated with being large, weaknesses of large firms include:

◆ **Human relations.** Large numbers of employees are often more difficult to organise. Contact between management and shopfloor will be reduced, and this can lead to industrial relations problems.

◆ **Decisions and co-ordination.** The size of a firm may limit the management's ability to make changes quickly in order to maximise sales. Improving products may involve delay and costs. Decision-making may be hampered by excessive paperwork and meetings. It is also difficult for large organisations to take a personal interest in the needs of customers.

◆ **External diseconomies.** If an organisation is big enough to affect whole marketplaces, public opinion may turn against it. Examples include boycotting goods from Indonesia following widely publicised human rights abuses; the campaign for 'dolphin-friendly' tuna, and the campaign for real ale (CAMRA).

Downsizing

The 1990s was the decade of **downsizing**, when many of the UK's big companies such as Shell UK, British Gas, ICI and the high-street banks downsized. We can see the continuation of this trend in areas like banking and insurance, which are increasingly being carried out 'online'.

A major reason for downsizing was that large companies recognised that employing too many people made them inefficient and less competitive. Downsizing led to **delayering**. This means the loss of layers of managers and supervisors whose services are no longer required.

One of the most important reasons for downsizing has been the spread of information technology in the workplace. Another has been competition from the Pacific Rim and other groups of countries. Companies which are very large tend to be slow moving. Decisions are made at the top and slowly filter down. In the world of the electronic marketplace, this is unacceptable.

In small organisations where employees are allowed to make decisions for themselves, changes can be put into place quickly. Giving power to people to make decisions is called **empowerment**. Downsized companies are often described as being 'leaner and fitter' than old-fashioned 'top-down' companies.

'When you downsize an organisation, does that always mean that the organisation becomes more effective?'

MATCH IT!

Can you help Frankie and Cleo to match the following terms and definitions?

Commercial economies

Internal economies

Technical economies

Empowerment

External economies

Risk-spreading economies

Managerial economies

Conglomerate integration

Vertical integration

Horizontal integration

Lateral integration

Downsizing

Diseconomies

Companies reducing in size in order to become more competitive

The advantages a large firm has in buying and selling operations

Firms at different stages of production of the same product joining together

Diversifying into a range of products so as not to be disadvantaged by over-specialisation

The advantages enjoyed by all firms in an industry or region from the growth of that industry or region

Firms joining together which are at the same stage of production of a particular product

Spreading out the responsibility for decision-making to lower levels in an organisation

The joining together of firms producing similar and in some ways related goods and services

The internal benefits to an organisation resulting from the growth of that organisation

The advantages resulting from employing specialist managers in larger firms

The negative effects resulting from being too large an organisation

The benefits which large firms are able to enjoy from using better techniques and equipment

The joining together of firms producing a range of quite different products

3 25 Business Organisation

What is a business organisation?

It is not easy to come up with an exact definition of the word 'organisation' that will fit all organisations. However, the following features help us to arrive at a working definition of the word.

'If the running of a business is disorganised can you still call it a business organisation?'

Organisations are:

◆ Made up of several people, who see themselves as being members of the organisation and who generally are willing to co-operate

◆ Mainly long-term. New people come into the organisation, and other members leave the organisation

◆ Made up of different people who do different tasks

◆ Run and organised according to some basic rules and procedures

Features of business organisations

We have already seen that business organisations take a number of forms, from sole traders through to multinational companies. Below *(left)* is one possible description of a business organisation. The diagram on the right shows the same definition applied to an actual company, Marks & Spencer:

TASK

*D*o the following have the features of an organisation described on the left?

• Your school or college

• A church

• Manchester United Football Club

• Marks & Spencer

• A street corner gang

• Your local cinema

• Passengers on a railway train

A group of people	Shareholders, directors, managers and employees of Marks & Spencer
form	*form*
A structure with rules and authority	The public limited company Marks & Spencer in which there are rules and people holding posts and offices
pursuing	*pursuing*
An objective or set of objectives	Customer satisfaction; quality products; profits for shareholders; and challenging, enjoyable jobs for employees
using	*using*
Resources	Many different types of inputs such as bought-in foodstuffs and clothes
to meet	*to meet*
Customers' needs and wants in exchange for monetary reward	The wants and needs of Marks & Spencer customers

Senior accountant

Junior accountant 1   Junior accountant 2   Junior accountant 3

A simple organisation chart

Organisation charts

An **organisation chart** is a drawing to show the roles of various individuals in an organisation, and the relationships between them. For example, the diagram above shows that a senior accountant has three junior accountants working for her.

Every organisational structure can be charted in this way, to show the departments, how they link together and the main lines of authority between them. This gives us a 'snapshot' view of how the organisation is made up. It shows lines of decision-making and tiers of responsibility. Looking at an organisation chart may also help us to see any weaknesses in the organisation.

 TASK

Read the case study on the following page.

1 Is the organisation of Oxfam different from what you might expect in a for-profit organisation?

2 Why do you think that each division has a finance and human resources team in addition to the whole organisation's Finance and Information Systems Division and Corporate Human Resources Division?

3 Can you suggest ways in which Oxfam might be able to re-organise its organisational structure to create a more efficient structure.

To find out more about Oxfam you can find its website on www.oxfam.org.uk.

 TASK

1 Why do you think Oxfam has organised itself into the various divisions shown in the organisation chart?

2 Who is the main official in the organisation? What is their title?

CASE STUDY

The Organisation of Oxfam GB

Oxfam GB is a charity whose trustees are legally responsible for all the organisation's activities under the charities acts. Oxfam GB is also incorporated as a registered limited company and must comply with the requirements of the Companies Act 1985.

There are approximately 23,000 Oxfam volunteers in Great Britain, working in roles throughout the organisation. About 1,300 staff are employed by Oxfam in Great Britain, including staff with UK citizenship on contracts overseas. Of this number, about 700 are based at Oxfam House in Oxford. There are about 1,500 locally recruited staff working overseas.

The Director of Oxfam is the Chief Executive of the charity. He is responsible to Trustees for the management of Oxfam. Reporting to him are the five deputy directors, each responsible for one of the five divisions.

The Marketing Division is responsible for fund-raising, communications, campaigns, and work to raise awareness of development issues in formal education in Great Britain, and for Oxfam's work in Europe.

The International Division is responsible for implementing Oxfam's relief and development programme overseas, for the GB Poverty Programme and for research, lobbying and publications about the causes of relief of poverty.

The Trading Division is responsible for shops and recycling in Great Britain and the Fair Trade operation, which buys crafts and foods overseas and sells them in Great Britain.

The Finance and Information Systems Division is responsible for organisation-wide finance and information systems matters, such as standards, systems and reporting.

The Corporate Human Resources (CHR) Division leads work with human resources teams in all divisions on delivering Oxfam's human resources strategies. It has specific responsibilities for employee relations, compensation and benefits, human resources management information, and corporate learning and development.

Each division has its own finance and human resources teams, responsible for accounting and personnel matters.

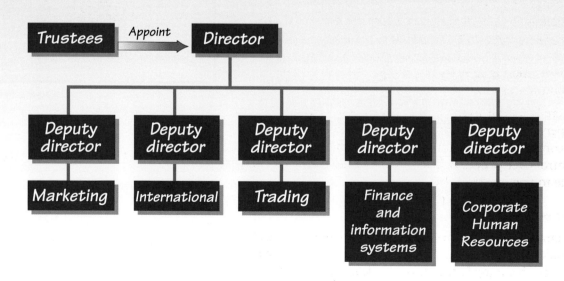

Levels within an organisation

When drawing an organisation chart, it is usual to show posts that have roughly equal amounts of responsibility on the same level. In the example below, the managing director and the senior management team are at the top level. At the next level are the middle managers. Then there are junior managers, supervisors, and finally operatives at the bottom level.

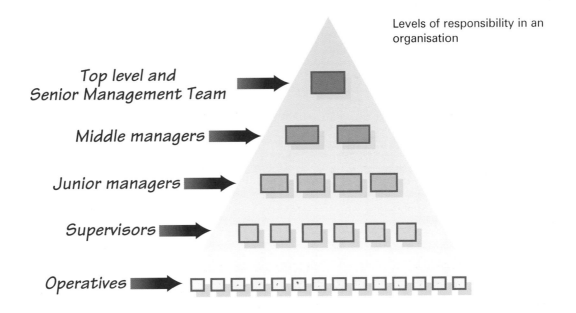

Levels of responsibility in an organisation

Top level and
Senior Management Team

Middle managers

Junior managers

Supervisors

Operatives

Span of control

The **span of control** of an individual is the number of people he or she manages or supervises directly. The diagram on the right shows an organisation with a narrow span of control. No one member of this organisation is directly responsible for more than two subordinates.

There is a limit to the number of people who can be supervised well by one person. Choosing the best span of control means striking a balance between having control over people below you (subordinates) and being able to trust them.

Tall and flat organisations

A narrow span of control makes it possible to control people and to communicate with them closely. However, the disadvantage is that this may lead to too many levels of management. This kind of **tall organisation**, as it is called, can be difficult to run.

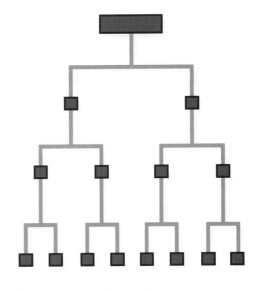

A narrow span of control

Having a wider span means managers must have far more trust in subordinate staff. Fewer managers are needed, and this gives a hierarchy with fewer levels, i.e. a **flat organisation**.

How many people should managers have within their span of control? It is hard to say. Generally speaking, the higher up an organisation an individual is, the fewer people he or she should have in their direct span of control.

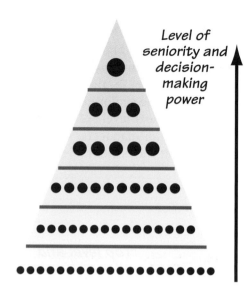

Level of seniority and decision-making power

A tall organisation

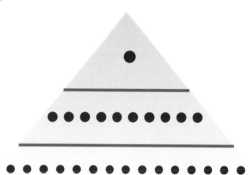

A flat organisation

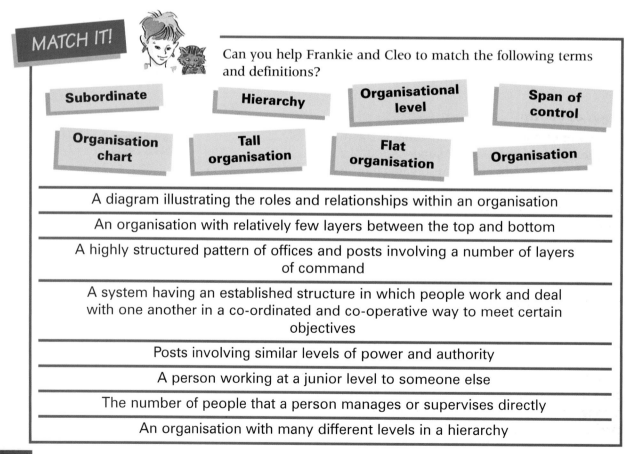

MATCH IT!

Can you help Frankie and Cleo to match the following terms and definitions?

Subordinate	Hierarchy	Organisational level	Span of control
Organisation chart	Tall organisation	Flat organisation	Organisation

A diagram illustrating the roles and relationships within an organisation

An organisation with relatively few layers between the top and bottom

A highly structured pattern of offices and posts involving a number of layers of command

A system having an established structure in which people work and deal with one another in a co-ordinated and co-operative way to meet certain objectives

Posts involving similar levels of power and authority

A person working at a junior level to someone else

The number of people that a person manages or supervises directly

An organisation with many different levels in a hierarchy

26 Post-Fordist Business Organisations

Fordism

Henry Ford created the Ford Motor Company in the early years of the twentieth century. The organisation came to be regarded as the model for many other business organisations during the first three-quarters of the twentieth century, and the word 'Fordism' entered the English language.

'Can the Ford Motor Company today be described as Fordist?'

Henry Ford famously remarked that 'you can have any colour of motor car you like as long as it is black'. He was referring to the Model T cars that his company produced and sold to millions of ordinary Americans, and which were exported across the world.

The Model T Ford was based on standard (identical) parts. A worker did not have to be skilled to work in a Fordist organisation. They simply had to follow instructions – repeating tasks over and over again.

Henry Ford argued that his car-making machinery was farm machinery. Ford had grown up on a farm and he developed machinery that could be used by unskilled young men who had come straight from American farms with very few mechanical skills.

A hierarchical organisation

Fordist **organisations** are hierarchical, with clear layers of command. At the top of the Ford Motor Company was Henry Ford, then layers of managers and supervisors who gave the instructions to the ground-level workers. These workers did not have to think, just follow instructions. There were detailed instructions for everything and it was the managers that gave these instructions.

W. Edwards Deming

The Ford Motor Company went from strength to strength. However, change was taking place.

After the Second World War Japanese industry listened to the ideas of an American business specialist who had new ideas about how industry should be organised. This man was **W. Edwards Deming.**

Deming argued that the best people for improving working practices were the people that made the products – the front-line production workers. His idea was that ground-level production workers should be encouraged to meet regularly with supervisors and managers to discuss ways of improving work. **Quality circles** were formed to identify these improvements.

The quality circle approach was adopted widely by Japanese industry – e.g. in car production and in the manufacture of consumer electronics such as televisions, DVD players and computers.

Quality circles give far more responsibility to the ground-level worker to make decisions. This sharing of power and decision making is called **empowerment**.

'Can you name five well known Japanese companies? You can be sure that all of these were influenced by the ideas of W. Edwards Deming.'

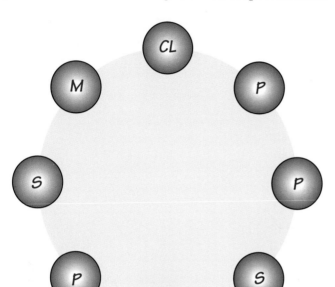

CL = Circle Leader
M = Manager
S = Supervisor
P = Production
    line worker

A quality circle

The Japanese success story

During the 1980s European and American companies felt the full weight of Japanese competition. By emphasising **quality** – i.e. improving the production of products at every stage and making sure that these products met customer requirements – the Japanese were becoming very competitive.

Companies like Ford were finding that they were losing a lot of sales to Japanese products. They were faced with a decision – should they continue with the old Fordist way of organisation or should they create teams working in flatter organisations? **Team working** involves having small teams of employees working together to solve work problems.

From the mid-1980s onwards American and European companies began to copy important parts of Japanese ways of working. Today modern companies seek to find out what consumers want and empower their employees to work towards meeting customer needs.

Relics of Fordism

Fordism is not dead. Fordist organisations were all about control from above and we still find this in a number of industries. For example, in a fast-food restaurant the production of burgers and fries is often done along Fordist lines. With a minimum amount of training an employee is able to operate the 'Fast Food Farm Machines': pressing buttons to start a customer's order and finishing the cooking when a buzzer goes. In a supermarket the check-out operators do not have to think when processing customer cheques. They feed them into a machine and then simply follow the instructions – feed in cheque, print cheque, get customer to sign, check signature, etc.

Used for illustrative purposes only

Inverted organisations

One of the most recent changes in organising the organisation has been in the inversion of organisations – literally turning them on their heads.

Modern organisations need to be staffed by thinking people who often have to deal directly with customers – by e-mail, over the phone and in face-to-face interactions – for example in selling insurance and other financial products, in serving customers in a shop, in dealing with students in educational organisations.

An **inverted organisation** is the opposite of a top-down Fordist organisation. An inverted organisation places its customers at the top. Next most important are the organisation's **front-line workers** who deal with these customers, such as lecturers and teachers in schools and colleges, the people answering the telephones in telephone banking operations, the people on the desk in a leisure centre. These people need to have good skills at interacting with others and in communications.

Behind the front-line workers are the **back-up people** such as information technology specialists. Further back are the **managers**, who create the plans and systems that provide the guidelines for running the organisation.

LATEST NEWS

Backlash against fast-food outlets

In France in recent years we have seen a considerable backlash against fast-food outlets. McDonalds has been picked out as an example of Americanisation for the way that it is destroying traditional eating patterns, and for the way it involves part-time labour in carrying out Fordist-type 'McJobs', which do not require a lot of brainpower.

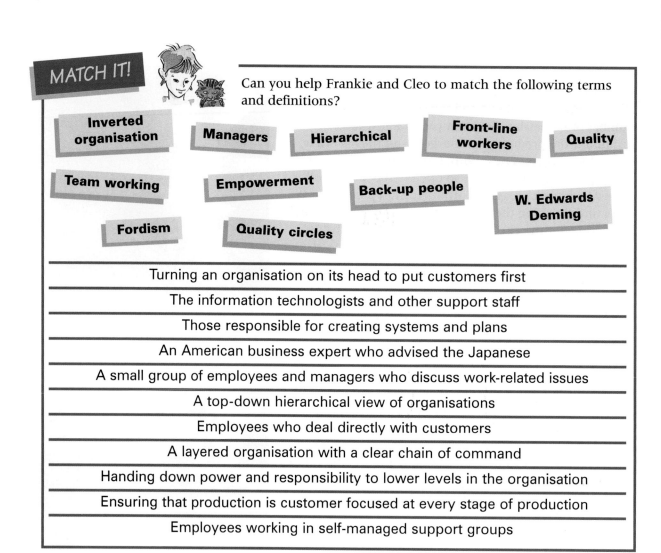

MATCH IT!

Can you help Frankie and Cleo to match the following terms and definitions?

Inverted organisation · Managers · Hierarchical · Front-line workers · Quality · Team working · Empowerment · Back-up people · W. Edwards Deming · Fordism · Quality circles

Turning an organisation on its head to put customers first

The information technologists and other support staff

Those responsible for creating systems and plans

An American business expert who advised the Japanese

A small group of employees and managers who discuss work-related issues

A top-down hierarchical view of organisations

Employees who deal directly with customers

A layered organisation with a clear chain of command

Handing down power and responsibility to lower levels in the organisation

Ensuring that production is customer focused at every stage of production

Employees working in self-managed support groups

27 The Role of Management

What is management?

Every organisation has objectives. Managers are people who help to steer the organisation in the direction of meeting these objectives.

Management has been described as:

'...the process of planning, organising, leading and controlling the efforts of organisation members and of using all organisational resources to achieve stated organisational goals.'

Or, to put it more simply:

'... getting things done by other people.'

A manager's job is to maintain control over the way an organisation does things, and at the same time to lead, inspire and direct the people under them.

'What do managers do? Well, in my business, almost everything!'

POSDCORB

A few years ago, business schools used the mnemonic POSDCORB to help students learn the key elements of management:

'POSDCORB is a useful mnemonic for learning about what a manager does. But does a modern manager need to do more than that?'

P   is for **planning.** Planning involves making decisions today about what you are going to be doing tomorrow.

O   is for **organising.** This means making sure that every last detail is organised, with nothing left to chance.

S   is for **staffing.** This means getting the people to do the jobs that the organisation requires in the best way possible.

D   is for **directing.** Directing involves giving the orders and directions so that things are done in the way that the manager requires.

Co-   is for **co-ordinating.** This means making sure that all the various parts of an organisation pull in the same direction.

R   is for **reporting.** Managers need to produce a lot of verbal and written reports, setting out what is and what should be happening in an organisation.

B   is for **budgeting.** A budget is a future plan, forecasting how resources (particularly financial resources) will be used.

The management of organisations

At one level managers take on a major responsibility for managing organisations. The **Chief Executive** of an organisation and the **Board of Directors** are responsible for making sure that effective plans are made for the whole organisation. We call organisation-wide plans corporate plans.

Managers are responsible for putting these plans into action. Each manager will be responsible for carrying out the plans for their area of responsibility.

The management of resources

A key managerial responsibility is for the **management of resources.** The sorts of resources that a manager will be responsible include:

◆ People – directing the activities and looking after people.

◆ Financial – using financial resources in the best possible way for the organisation in line with profit and sales targets.

◆ Materials – making sure that materials are used in the most productive way with the minimum waste.

◆ Machinery and equipment – using the most appropriate machinery and equipment, and making sure that it is maintained, replaced and updated when necessary.

◆ Time – ensuring the best use of time.

◆ Buildings – making sure that premises are safe and are being used in the best possible way.

◆ Information – in modern organisations it is important to make sure that you have access to the most up-to-date information and that you have the right people with the skills to use this information.

Managers must always make sure that they make best use of resources. If you use resources in one way there is always an **opportunity cost** – i.e. the next-best use of those resources.

Management styles

There are three main types of management style: autocratic, democratic and paternalistic.

Autocratic managers tell others what to do and do not seek the views of others very often. We associate this approach with Fordist management styles. Autocratic managers use a one-way top-down form of communication.

Democratic managers like to involve their employees in decision making. They use a two way-communication process, being prepared to listen to the views of others.

Paternalistic/maternalistic managers act like a caring father or mother. They seek to do what is best for their children/employees. They may use consultation to find out what their employees think and feel but the final decision will be made by the manager.

'I'm a paternalistic manager. I treat my employees like children and give them a good kick up the backside if they misbehave.'
Is Ron a paternalistic manager?

Management and leadership

There is an important difference between management and leadership. **Management** is all about getting things done using the resources available in the organisation, and the organisation's rules and procedures for getting things done. You can thus be a good manager without having to force your will on others in the organisation – you simply manage using the authority that the organisation has given to you.

Leadership, on the other hand, involves driving through change, sometimes against the wishes of others, and pushing through new initiatives. A leader therefore needs to be forceful and to exert some form of power.

The leader may have one or more types of power that enable them to lead. They may have **expert power** because they have more knowledge or skill than others. They may have **personality power** because of the strength of their character and personality. They may have **official power** because they hold an important office or position in an organisation. They may have **political power** because they have formed an alliance with someone who has power in the organisation.

Leadership therefore goes beyond management and it is a quality that is particularly important in organisations where change needs to take place.

MATCH IT!

Can you help Frankie and Cleo to match the following terms and definitions?

Consultative management   **Expert power**   **Democratic management**   **Political power**   **Management of resources**

Co-ordinating   **Directing**   **Autocratic management**   **Opportunity cost**   **Chief Executive**

Leadership   **Management**

Finding out the views of others before taking decisions
Having your decisions accepted because of your knowledge and/or skill
Giving orders to others
Giving responsibility for decision making to others rather than making all the decisions yourself
Planning, controlling and organising the efforts of members of an organisation as well as the use of resources
Being able to instigate and lead change initiatives
Top-down management that doesn't listen to others
Being able to make decisions as a result of alliances with others
Making sure that the parts of an organisation pull in the same direction
The individual with the key decision-making responsibility in an organisation
The next best way of using resources
The management of people, finance, time, etc. in an organisation

CASE STUDY

Managing your boss

In November, 2000 the Institute of Management set out six main types of managers that might exist in the workplace. It also set out a set of strategies that employees could use to cope with their manager.

Dictatorial managers

Such a manager is in charge because they are the best person for the job – so they go round telling everyone what to do and how to do it. They are motivated by the need to win every argument. They get their way through rewards and punishments.

How to cope: Ask their permission before doing anything and show that you are carrying out their orders with enthusiasm.

Bureaucratic managers

They have got to the position they are in by following the rules and see this as the best way of managing. They don't want to take risks and take their work and its responsibilities seriously.

How to cope: By giving them the rules when a decision is necessary and submitting any requests in writing.

Charismatic (strong personality)

Charismatic managers motivate staff by inspiring them to achieve the organisation's goals rather than their own. They lead by personal example and they inspire loyalty. They are driven by the need to act for the company's greater good.

How to cope: Be enthusiastic about their dreams and show that you, too, put the company first.

Consultative

They are very concerned about establishing and keeping close personal and emotional relationships with others. They consult people frequently. They are often afraid to make a decision by themselves and want to share the burden of power.

How to cope: Don't be afraid to give them your opinions, and involve them by socialising with them.

Laissez-faire (leave things alone)

These managers make a conscious decision to leave the staff to get on with things, having observed that they are working well on their own. They assume that people are working because they want to, and are self-motivated.

How to cope: By showing you can be trusted to get on with it and send regular progress memos. Don't bother them with trivial matters.

Abdictatorial (not taking responsibility)

An abdicator does not care enough to get involved with the employees. They 'leave them to it' because they don't like facing up to difficulties. The employees have to make decisions and confront and handle problems which are really the boss's responsibility.

How to cope: By asking for formal meetings to discuss issues and getting permission for projects where possible.

28 Business Decision-making

Who makes the major decisions in a business?

Business decisions can be made and carried out in a number of ways.

Top-down decision-making

In some organisations all major decisions will be taken by senior managers and passed down to junior employees.

This type of organisation is said to be **hierarchical.** Each employee knows who their line manager is and takes commands from them. There may be just a few layers in the hierarchy, or there may be many.

This can be an effective arrangement when work is very routine and easy to predict, but it also has its problems:

1 Lower-level employees may become discontented because they are not allowed to show initiative. They may grumble about the 'hierarchy' (by which they mean people above them) and become unco-operative.

2 When decisions need to be made quickly, junior employees may be unwilling or unable to react. They may say things like, *'I can't do anything about it. It's not my job. You'll have to wait until Mrs X comes back.'*

3 Hierarchical organisations can be costly to run, if there are a lot of people wasting time reporting to each other.

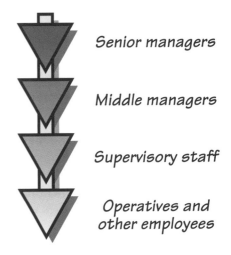

Flow of communication in a hierarchical organisation

'You can't beat a top-down company. The manager needs to be the "gaffer". That way everybody is happy because they know exactly what is expected of them. It works every time. If somebody doesn't like it they can always be replaced by someone better!'

What weaknesses can you see in Ron's argument?

Democratic decision-making

In contrast to a hierarchical system, an organisation may be arranged on more **democratic** lines. Here, individuals are appointed to carry out tasks according to their skills and experience. They are expected to think and act for themselves. One way of representing an organisation like this would be as a circle. Each member is an independent decision-maker, but consults regularly with the others. An example might be a group of vets working as a partnership.

Centralisation and decentralisation

Centralisation

Centralisation means keeping major responsibilities in a business at the centre of the organisation, e.g. at head office. With this system, you have a big head office with small branches and other operating units. This was the picture in many UK companies until recently.

Decentralisation

Decentralisation involves giving decision-making power to an organisation's operating units, e.g. regional offices, factories, retailing units and plants. Today, most large companies are shedding a lot of staff from their central offices.

To make decentralisation possible, operational units must be linked by modern communications facilities such as networked computers, organisation-wide databases, fax communication systems, and so on.

The illustration *(below right)* shows a much smaller head office with relatively bigger branches.

Reasons for decentralisation

There are a number of reasons for decentralisation:

1 People at the top of an organisation cannot be expected to know everything. It may be helpful therefore to give more responsibility to experts lower down the organisation, who can see the picture 'on the ground'.

2 Decentralisation makes possible a quick response to local needs and conditions.

3 Decentralisation may help to motivate employees to make decisions for themselves.

4 Decentralisation can reduce costs, making an organisation more competitive.

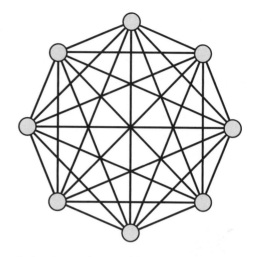

A circular or democratic network

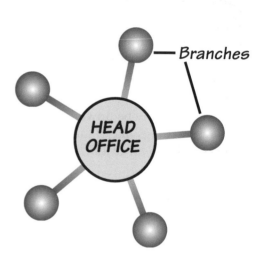

A centralised structure

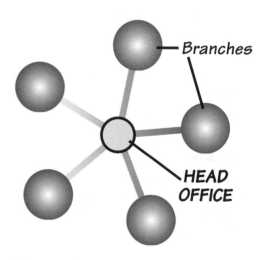

A decentralised structure

Strategic and tactical decision-making

Strategy

Every company should be clear about its **strategy**.

Strategies are the major plans that an organisation develops concerning the whole organisation. For example, a UK retailing organisation may have a strategy of spreading its operations into the European Union. An organisation like Richard Branson's Virgin may have a strategy of moving into new product areas when opportunities arise – Virgin Airways, Virgin Cola, Virgin Rail, etc.

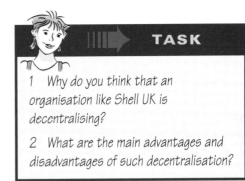

You can see that strategic plans involve large quantities of resources. For example, when Virgin decided to branch into cola this involved building new plant and equipment, and carrying out major advertising and marketing campaigns.

Tactics

Having established its basic strategy, an organisation will need to operate on a day-to-day **tactical** basis to deliver the chosen strategy. For example, for the strategy of branching into Virgin Cola, tactical plans needed to be created for:

◆ Arranging promotions for the new cola, e.g. in-store taste tests

◆ Arranging local advertising campaigns for the product

◆ Arranging ways of distributing the product to retail outlets

The day-to-day tactics therefore support the strategic plan and are concerned with the day-to-day details of delivering the strategy. Tactical decisions are easier to adjust than strategies.

TASK

1 Why do you think that an organisation like Shell UK is decentralising?

2 What are the main advantages and disadvantages of such decentralisation?

CASE STUDY

Decentralisation at Shell

One form of decentralisation is shown by recent developments at Shell UK. The organisational hierarchy of the company has been 'flattened' by removing layers, so that each divisional head now reports directly to the managing director, rather than via other directors.

Another way has been to create separate profit centres: sections of the overall business are given the responsibility and resources to operate as if they were independent. For example, Shell's bitumen business is now run by Shell Bitumen UK, a separate profit centre within Shell Oil UK.

TASK

Strategy or tactics?

Which of the following decisions by a supermarket chain are strategic in nature and which are tactical?

- *The decision to commit 20% of the organisation's budget to introducing a major new product*
- *The decision to postpone an advertising campaign by a day because of a strike by TV camera operators*
- *The decision to shut down the European operations of the company*
- *The decision to create a global brand image for all of a company's products*
- *The decision to adjust advertising for a product in a particular television region*
- *The decision to decentralise the activities of the whole organisation in order to make it less centralised*

 **MATCH IT!**

Can you help Frankie and Cleo to match the following terms and definitions?

Tactics

Strategy   **Democratic**

Centralisation   **Top-down**

Decentralisation

The big decisions that are made by an organisation
A system whereby decisions feed down from senior managers to the lower levels of an organisation
The day-to-day operational decisions of an organisation
Where decisions tend to be made at head office rather than in the branches of an organisation
Giving decision-making powers to lower levels within an organisation
An organisation in which everyone is involved in the decision-making process

29 Organisational Structures of Large Organisations

Departmental organisation in a large business

Large organisations in the UK are mostly private companies, public companies or public corporations (see Chapter 23). Here we focus on a large public company.

The company will be owned by **shareholders** who appoint a committee known as a **board of directors** to represent their interests. The board of directors then appoints a **managing director**. Like a head teacher in a school or the principal of a college, the **managing director** has the job of making sure that all the various departments are running well.

Every organisation is different and has different needs and objectives. The example set out below may be found in some company structures, but many variations are possible.

Many business organisations are split up into a series of functions – that is, they are divided up into a number of sections with different purposes.

'Does the organisation of an organisation depend more on its size or the type of goods and services that it produces?'

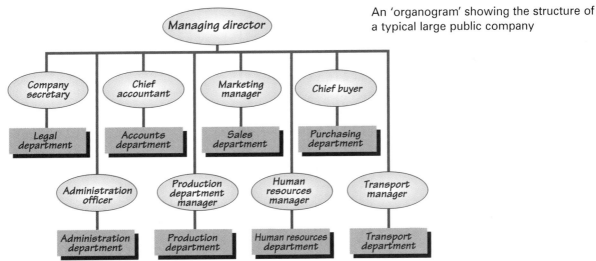

An 'organogram' showing the structure of a typical large public company

In addition to organising the business on functional lines it could be organised:
◆ Geographically into areas – e.g. north, south, east and west
◆ By product – e.g. confectionery division, soft drinks division, crisps division

A **matrix structure** (right) combines two or more different forms of organisation. For example, teams within an organisation could be in the soft drinks division north, the crisps division west, etc.

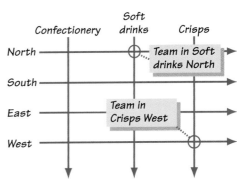

Create an organogram to show the various functions of a local company that you have access to, or draw an organogram to show the functional organisation of your school or college.

Management responsibilities

The company secretary and the legal department

The **company secretary** is responsible for all the legal affairs of the company. If paperwork is not done properly, he or she could end up in court. He or she must fill in and periodically amend official company records and documents such as the Memorandum and Articles of Association. He or she must also keep the share register. Departmental managers may consult the company secretary on legal matters.

The administration department

Many large firms have a central office which is responsible for controlling the general paperwork of the firm. This department may handle the filing of materials, the sorting of the company's mail, word-processing and data-handling facilities. Modern offices use information technology to service all these key areas.

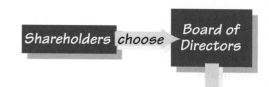

The control structure of a large public company

The chief accountant and the accounts office

The **chief accountant** is responsible for running the accounts department. The accounts section must keep a detailed record of all money paid in and out, and present the final balance sheet at the end of the year. Modern accounts are stored on computer files, and procedures are greatly simplified by the use of computers.

The production department

The **production manager** is responsible for making sure that raw materials are provided and made into finished goods as cost-effectively as possible. He or she must make sure that work is carried out smoothly and supervise procedures for maximising efficiency.

The marketing manager and the marketing/sales department

Marketing may be combined with sales, or the two functions may be separate.

◆ Marketing is concerned with finding out what people want and then meeting their wants and needs at a profit.

◆ Sales is concerned with all aspects of selling to customers.

In a combined sales/marketing department, the manager will be responsible for market research, promotions, advertising, distribution and organising product sales.

The human resources manager and the human resources department

The **human resources department** (sometimes called the **personnel department**) is responsible for the recruitment and training of staff. It is also responsible for health and safety at work, trade union negotiation and staff welfare. It also makes sure that the organisation focuses on meeting the needs of its human resources.

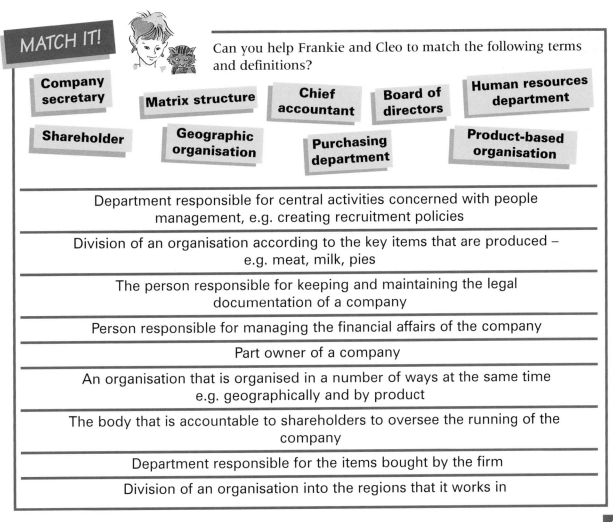

MATCH IT!   Can you help Frankie and Cleo to match the following terms and definitions?

Company secretary   Matrix structure   Chief accountant   Board of directors   Human resources department

Shareholder   Geographic organisation   Purchasing department   Product-based organisation

Department responsible for central activities concerned with people management, e.g. creating recruitment policies
Division of an organisation according to the key items that are produced – e.g. meat, milk, pies
The person responsible for keeping and maintaining the legal documentation of a company
Person responsible for managing the financial affairs of the company
Part owner of a company
An organisation that is organised in a number of ways at the same time e.g. geographically and by product
The body that is accountable to shareholders to oversee the running of the company
Department responsible for the items bought by the firm
Division of an organisation into the regions that it works in

30 Business Objectives

The nature of objectives

A business organisation sets out to achieve certain goals. In doing so, it must balance the needs of its customers and the people involved in the organisation. It is like making sure that your snooker balls go into the right pockets.

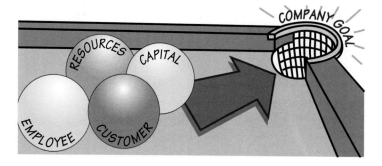

The goals of a business are the future state of affairs that it is working towards.

'Who decides on the aim of an organisation?'

'Me! I decide what I want and how I am going to get it!'

A mission for an organisation

Many large organisations today set out a mission for the total organisation. The mission is a general aim that the organisation is working towards and will usually be set out in a short statement.

For example, here are the **mission statements** of Levi's (jeans) and Ford (cars).

"We all want a company that our people are proud of and committed to, where all employees have an opportunity to contribute, learn, grow and advance based on merit, not politics or background. We want our people to feel respected, treated fairly, listened to and involved. Above all, we want satisfaction from accomplishments and friendships, balanced personal and professional lives, and to have fun in our endeavours…"

"Ford Motor Company is a worldwide leader in automotive and automotive-related products and services as well as in new industries such as aerospace, communications and financial services. Our mission is to improve continually our products and services to meet our customers' needs, allowing us to prosper as a business and to provide a reasonable return for our shareholders, the owners of our business."

Objectives

If the mission provides a general aim for an organisation, then it is important to follow it up with a series of more specific **objectives**.

Objectives are the ends that a person or organisation sets out to achieve. Objectives need to be:

- Measurable
- Time limited
- Attainable
- Relevant

For example, an appropriate objective for you might be to achieve an A* grade for Business Studies in the summer that you take your exam. This objective is measurable (an A*), it is time limited (e.g. the summer of 2003), it is attainable if you are capable of achieving it (if not you might set yourself the objective of a B, C, etc.) and it is relevant because it is the course that you are currently working on.

Given Newcastle United's mission (*right*), some of their objectives might be:

- To get into the top five in the Premier Division by 2004
- To increase ground capacity by 5,000 by 2005
- To increase revenues from the sale of club merchandise by 5% per year over the next five years

Types of business objective

In the long run most firms need to make a profit. People will only invest their money in a business if they are satisfied with the returns from it. But although profit is a major business objective, it is not the only one.

Some individuals set up in business because of the freedom it gives them to make decisions for themselves. Other motivations for running a business might include:

- Market share: To win a certain quantified share of the market by a certain date.
- Maximisation of sales: Sales maximisation is quite a sensible business objective. If you increase your sales then you take them away from rivals. Large sales often generate higher profits – although this is not always the case.
- Building a reputation: The image and reputation of a company can be very important. A good reputation wins custom, which in turn wins profit. The reputation of a company can be measured by

TASK

The mission statement of Newcastle United PLC is:

'The business of Newcastle United is football – our aim is to play attractive football, to win trophies, to satisfy our supporters and shareholders and to continually improve our position as a top European club.'

Do you think that this mission statement gives a clear indicator to people involved at the club of what the club is aiming to achieve?

TASK

Which of the following objectives are primarily concerned with profit and which are more concerned with the market?

- To make an annual profit of £100,000
- To be the market leader by 2005
- To increase sales by 10% per year
- To increase market share

customer surveys. An organisation could set itself the objective of becoming recognised as one of the ten most reputable companies in its industry by 2005.

◆ Survival: In some businesses, the objective may just be to survive. For instance, an old-established company may have the objective of staying under the control of the original family owners.

◆ Pleasure or interest: Some small businesses are run for pleasure rather than profit. Their owners keep them going mainly because they enjoy it. This form of objective is more difficult to quantify.

Setting objectives

An organisation's objectives are usually set as part of the strategic planning process. The objectives provide something for the organisation to work towards. The strategy is the means by which the objectives are met.

For example, if the organisation has the objective of becoming the market leader in production of dog food in Europe, then the strategy might involve opening up new factories in new European countries and carrying out a Europe-wide advertising campaign.

Stakeholders

Organisations usually involve a number of interested parties. Take a school, for example. If you look at the diagram below, you can see that there are a number of people with a stake in the running of a school.

Clearly these stakeholders will have different views about how the school should be run. They may agree on some of the goals of the school, but disagree on others. In the end, the goals that are chosen depend on who has most power to make decisions.

End	Objective: No 1 Dog food producer in Europe
Means to achieve the end	Strategy: Open up new plant in Europe and advertise Europe wide

TASK

Who are the main stakeholders in an organisation that you are familiar with? Set out a diagram to show this. Who do you think will have most power to decide the goals of the organisation?

Rank the stakeholders in terms of what you see as being their power to influence the organisation's objectives.

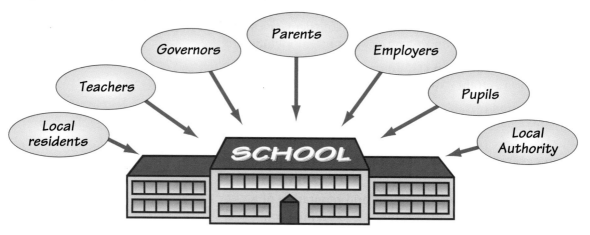

Stakeholders in a school

The same applies to any organisation. There are a number of stakeholders with different views about what the goals should be. Those with most power will determine the main goals.

For example, a mining company might be able to get away with extracting ores that harm the environment because the shareholder grouping in the company (seeking profits) may have more power than the local community grouping (which wants to protect the environment).

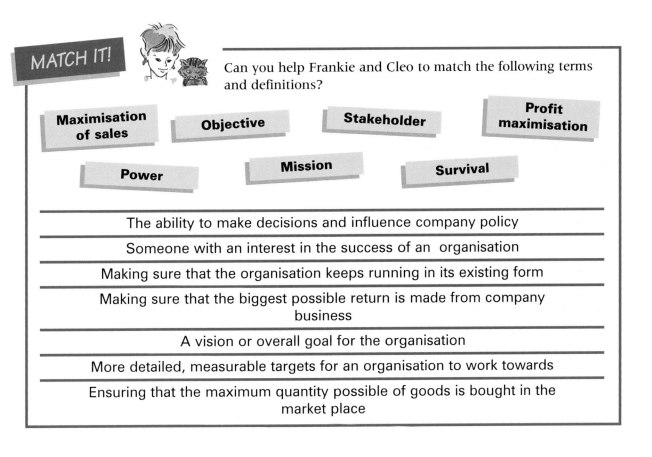

MATCH IT!

Can you help Frankie and Cleo to match the following terms and definitions?

Maximisation of sales   Objective   Stakeholder   Profit maximisation

Power   Mission   Survival

The ability to make decisions and influence company policy
Someone with an interest in the success of an organisation
Making sure that the organisation keeps running in its existing form
Making sure that the biggest possible return is made from company business
A vision or overall goal for the organisation
More detailed, measurable targets for an organisation to work towards
Ensuring that the maximum quantity possible of goods is bought in the market place

4 ⟩ 31 Market Research

The importance of marketing

Many companies today claim that their main aim is to satisfy consumer needs. Instead of having to use hard-selling techniques to persuade customers to buy, these market-led companies sell goods easily because they produce what consumers want.

In its simplest form marketing answers the question:

'What does the customer want to buy?'

A definition of marketing which you should learn is:

'Marketing is the anticipation and identification of consumer wants and needs in order to meet these needs, and to make a profit.'

Researching the market

Market research means systematically gathering, recording and analysing data about the market for goods and services.

To find out what the customer wants, a wide variety of market research techniques are used. These involve asking the kind of questions shown in the diagram below.

CASE STUDY

A bright idea

Frankie and Cleo have come up with a bright idea. They have produced a new kind of shortbread which is very popular with their friends. Their plan is to sell the shortbread to the people of Midtown in packets that Frankie is designing. However, they are not sure whether the shortbread will be bought by enough people, or what price to charge or where to sell from.

They want some evidence to prove that their shortbread will be a success. This means carrying out some market research!

MARKET RESEARCH QUESTIONS

What is the target market?	Where are they?	What do they want?	When do they want it?	Can we satisfy them?	How can we improve it for them?

↓ ↓ ↓ ↓ ↓ ↓

MARKET INFORMATION

TRENDS

CUSTOMER PROFILES

TASK

What information do you think that Frankie and Cleo will need before they start producing shortbread for sale?

Can you think of any ways in which Frankie and Cleo might collect the information they need?

Methods of market research

A firm can employ either its own (in-house) marketing department or an outside specialist organisation. Market research can be classed under two headings:

◆ **Desk research.** This involves using existing sources of information to research the market. It is sometimes called **secondary research.**

◆ **Field research.** This is the process of gathering new information about the market by going into the 'field' (e.g. house-to-house or street surveys). It is sometimes called **primary research.**

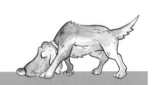

LATEST NEWS

'Fit and Fifty'

In November 2000 the Economic and Social Research Council (www.esrc.ac.uk) published some of the their research findings in a report called 'Fit and Fifty?' This research showed that men and women in their 50s are breaking out of the stereotypes of typical middle age. As life expectancy increases people are thinking differently about what it means to get older. The study used current trends to forecast what it will mean to be fit and 50 years old in a decade's time. The report stated that 'more will see themselves as young, and engage in a diversity of active, creative leisure pursuits. Reaching 50 will no longer be a predictor of changes in spending, saving and buying patterns.'

Retailers will have to think carefully about how they respond to this research. Age will increasingly become less relevant for advertising, and marketing. People in their 50s will be more similar to those in their 30s and 40s than to those in their 60s.

TASK

*W*hich of the following activities do you think would best be carried out by desk research, and which by field research?

• *Finding out about the age structure of the population in the UK*

• *Finding out what people think of a new type of wine*

• *Investigating the public's view on changing the opening hours of a supermarket*

• *Examining circulation figures for different national newspapers*

'Market research is a waste of time. It is a costly business, and by the time you have collected your information, it is out of date!'

Do you think Ron Rust might be making a mistake?

Desk research

A popular form of desk research is for a company to study its own sales figures for trends. Or it may analyse requests from customers for changes in existing products. It may also explore customer requests for new models or lines.

An organisation can also investigate its competitors' products to find out their popular and unpopular points. This can help them develop new and improved products of their own at a competitive price.

For example, Frankie and Cleo might go to another town to investigate sales of shortbread by a rival firm.

An organisation can also study published sources of information. These include:

1 Government statistics

Useful sources of information include census data produced by the Office of Population Censuses and Surveys. A full census is carried out every ten years. The most recent national survey took place in 2001. It shows numbers of people in different age groups, where they live, gender breakdown, ethnic breakdown, etc.

Social Trends provides detailed information about typical social behaviour patterns in different parts of the country – e.g. numbers with access to the Internet, numbers owning their own homes.

Business Monitor, published quarterly, provides a lot of useful information about different markets.

2 Published market research information

Today there are a number of market research organisations such as Mintel, which work full-time to produce statistics about different markets. In return for a fee, Mintel provides a monthly journal. This contains reports on consumer markets ranging from bread and alcoholic drinks to insurance.

3 Quality newspapers and magazines

Papers like *The Independent* and specialist marketing magazines provide a lot of useful information about market trends.

Desk research has two key advantages over field research:

◆ It is cheaper

◆ The information already exists, so it is quicker and easier to obtain.

Field research

There are several field research methods which are used by businesses. Each method involves using one or more of the following:

TASK

Which of the following are primary and which secondary market research sources?

• Conducting a survey of every fifth person who passes you in the street

• Looking up information about people buying different types of insurance in a Mintel survey

• Asking each of your classmates 20 questions

• Copying out information from your local evening newspaper

• Interviewing people through a phone survey

• Sending a questionnaire through the post

1 Questionnaires

These are lists of questions designed specifically for a task. Questionnaires can be completed by holding an interview. This can take place face-to-face, over the telephone, or through the post.

2 Test marketing

This is when a product is marketed to just a small part of a total market to see if it is suitable for wider release.

3 Consumer panels

This is where a selected group of people are given a product and asked to comment in detail.

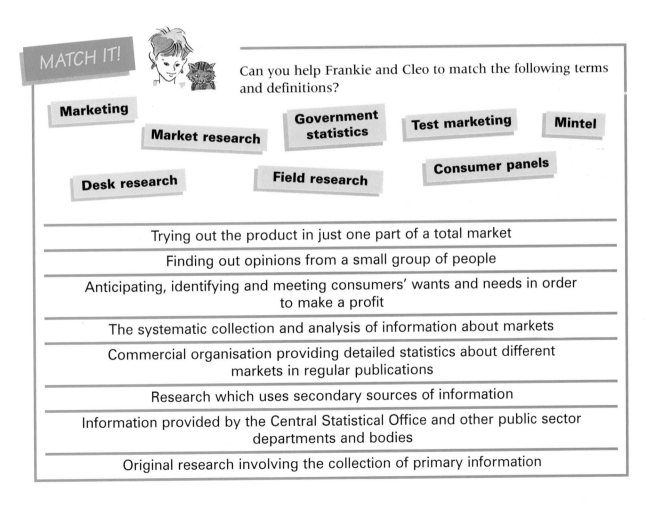

MATCH IT!

Can you help Frankie and Cleo to match the following terms and definitions?

Marketing

Market research

Government statistics

Test marketing

Mintel

Desk research

Field research

Consumer panels

Trying out the product in just one part of a total market

Finding out opinions from a small group of people

Anticipating, identifying and meeting consumers' wants and needs in order to make a profit

The systematic collection and analysis of information about markets

Commercial organisation providing detailed statistics about different markets in regular publications

Research which uses secondary sources of information

Information provided by the Central Statistical Office and other public sector departments and bodies

Original research involving the collection of primary information

32 Consumer Behaviour

What makes people buy?

In business it is important to have a clear idea of why consumers buy goods. This is an important part of marketing. Find out what drives consumer buying decisions and you will be well placed to meet consumer needs.

The buying decision can be broken down into a number of stages:

1 A consumer recognises that there is a problem, e.g.:

   'We're running out of breakfast cereal, so we will have to buy some more soon'.

   Or the consumer identifies an opportunity, e.g.:

   'It's time for the January sales. If we look carefully we may be able to buy some electrical goods at bargain prices.'

2 The consumer will then search for information enabling them to make a good buy. For example, they may go round several shops comparing prices, looking in catalogues, etc.

3 The consumer then weighs up the alternatives, e.g.:

   'Coca-Cola costs 45 pence in a garage, 30 pence in the corner shop, and only 25p in a supermarket.'

4 The consumer then decides what to buy and where, and purchases the item.

5 After buying, the consumer reviews the purchase, e.g.:

   'I thought I was getting a bargain when I bought that Hoover in the discount store. But the problem is, there's no after-sales service. Next time I may buy from a more expensive shop which offers after-sales service.'

This simple model can be set out in a diagram, showing that there is feedback between each of the stages in the decision process:

'How do people go about making a buying decision?'

Below: The purchasing process

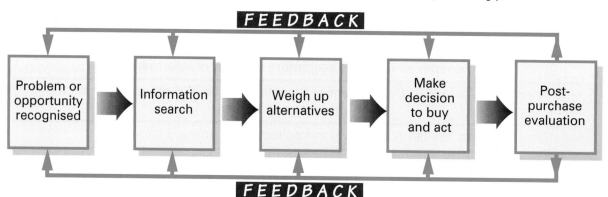

TASK

*T*hink of an item that you have recently bought. Draw a flow chart showing each of the stages involved in making the buying decision. For example, in the first box of the flow chart you might write:

'I needed to buy a new pair of jeans to go to a party!'

Individual consumer requirements

Because consumers are human, they are all different. Only a few companies (for example, made-to-measure tailors and hairdressers) can provide products designed specifically for each individual customer.

But there are two ways in which a business can get as close as possible to meeting the individual needs of its customers:

◆ Market segmentation

◆ Customer service

1   Market segmentation

Market segmentation is the process of dividing a market up into different groups of customers, in order to create different products to meet their specific needs.

Primary segmentation

The most obvious type of segmentation is between customers who buy entirely different products. For example, a firm like Colgate-Palmolive will make toothpaste and soap to meet quite different customer needs. There are not many people who clean their teeth with soap!

Segmentation by demographics and psychographics

Further segmentation can be based on **demographic** and **psychographic** factors:

◆ Demographics segments people according to facts about them as members of the population, e.g. their sex, their age, the size of their family, their income, where they live, the type of work they do, etc.

◆ Psychographics segments people according to their **lifestyle.** A person's lifestyle is their individual pattern of behaviour, made up of their attitudes, beliefs, interests and habits.

'Segmentation sounds as if the market is being divided into segments – just like an orange.'

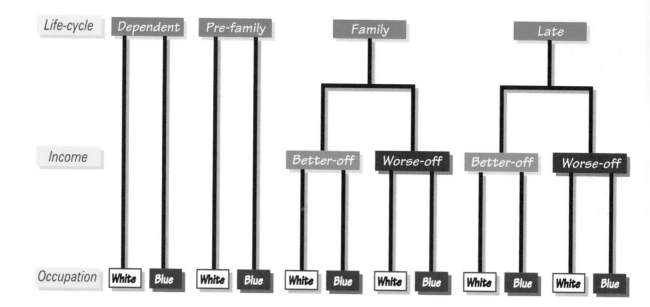

Above: Segmentation by life-cycle, income and occupation

◆ **Sagacity lifestyle grouping** combines psychographic and demographic segmentation. This approach works on the principle that people behave in different ways as they go through life. Four main stages of the life-cycle are identified, and these are sub-divided according to income and occupation groups (white-collar and blue-collar occupations).

The life-cycle stages can be grouped in the following way:

◆ **Dependent** – mainly under-24s, living at home or full-time students

◆ **Pre-family** – under-35s who have established their own household but have no children

◆ **Family** – parents under 65 with one or more children in the household

◆ **Late** – includes all adults whose children have left home, or who are over 35 and childless

The occupation groups are:

◆ **White** – head of household in the ABC1 occupation group where A is upper/upper middle class, B is middle class, C is lower middle class.

◆ **Blue** – head of household in the C2DE occupation group, where C2 is skilled working class, D is working class, E is the lowest level of subsistence

COURSEWORK ACTIVITIES

If you live near a multi-screen cinema, carry out some research to find out what type of people watch the films that are showing at the moment.

Group the audiences by age and sex, and present your results in the form of graphs and charts, using a computer package.

2   Customer service

The second technique used by companies aiming to achieve a 'one-to-one' relationship with customers is **customer service**.

Customer service describes the way a customer is treated by sales staff on the telephone, in the shop and at the check-out. It covers the way queries and complaints are handled, and the use of the latest technology to personalise even the most large-scale promotional campaign letters. All these affect the relationship between customer and business.

Types of purchases

We can identify a number of purchases that people make which involve different levels of decision-making.

1   Routine purchases

These are everyday purchases that do not require much thought. For example, a routine purchase will be the bread and butter that goes into a family's sandwiches. Every six months the family will need to renew the car tax licence and every year the television licence – again these are routine purchases.

2   Limited-decision purchases

These are purchases that are less routine and involve more careful thought.

For example, if a new flavour of crisps becomes available, a purchaser will carry out a limited amount of research before deciding whether or not to buy it. Once they are familiar with the product, it may then become a routine purchase.

3   Extensive decision-making

These are purchases which involve considerable thought or prior research – for example, buying a new car or computer. The buyer will want to have a lot of information before committing themselves to a decision.

4   Impulse purchases

These are purchases made on the spur of the moment. For example, while paying for petrol at a service station shop, a customer may notice a magazine, some attractive sandwiches, and a packet of sweets which are all temptingly displayed. On impulse, they may buy far more than they had originally intended.

'The problem with internet marketing is that it doesn't really create a one-to-one relationship.'

Do you agree with Frankie?

Making the buying decisions

When planning an advertising campaign, it is important for businesses to know who has most influence over the buying decision, as well as who actually makes the purchase.

For example, in a family, children may not spend much money themselves, but they can still have a considerable influence over what their parents buy. Similarly, in a typical household, women often have a considerable influence over the choice of the family car, tending to value environmental factors, design qualities and safety. Manufacturers need to bear this in mind.

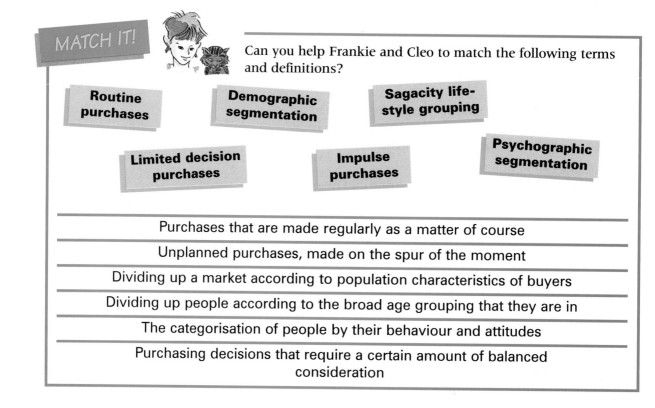

MATCH IT!

Can you help Frankie and Cleo to match the following terms and definitions?

Routine purchases

Demographic segmentation

Sagacity life-style grouping

Limited decision purchases

Impulse purchases

Psychographic segmentation

Purchases that are made regularly as a matter of course

Unplanned purchases, made on the spur of the moment

Dividing up a market according to population characteristics of buyers

Dividing up people according to the broad age grouping that they are in

The categorisation of people by their behaviour and attitudes

Purchasing decisions that require a certain amount of balanced consideration

33 The Marketing Mix

Creating the right mix

When marketing their products, firms need to create a successful mix of:

◆ **The right product**

◆ **Sold at the right price**

◆ **In the right place**

◆ **Using the most suitable promotion**

The 'Four Ps'

The ingredients of the marketing mix are often referred to as the **Four Ps:** PRODUCT, PRICE, PLACE and PROMOTION.

A mix is made of ingredients that are blended together to meet a common purpose. As with a cake, no ingredient is enough on its own: it has to be blended together to produce something very special. In the same way that there are a many cakes to suit all tastes, a marketing mix can be designed to suit the precise requirements of the market.

'Successful marketing involves creating the right mix of marketing ingredients to meet your customer's needs.

'All this talk about a "marketing mix" is nonsense. There is only one factor that makes products sell, and that's price. If you charge the lowest price, then none of the other things matter!'

Do you agree with Ron?

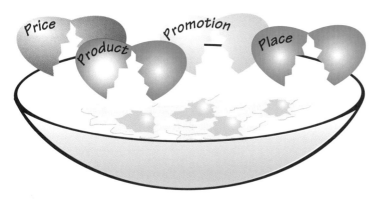

A perfect mix

To create the right marketing mix, businesses have to meet the following conditions:

◆ The **product** has to have the right features – for example, it must look good and work well.

◆ The **price** must be right. Consumers will need to buy in large numbers to produce a healthy profit.

◆ The goods must be in the right **place** at the right time. Making sure that the goods arrive when and where they are wanted is an important operation.

◆ The target group needs to be made aware of the existence and availability of the product through **promotion.** Successful promotion helps a firm to spread costs over a larger output.

TASK

What do you think are the key features of the marketing mix for Coca-Cola?

COURSEWORK ACTIVITIES

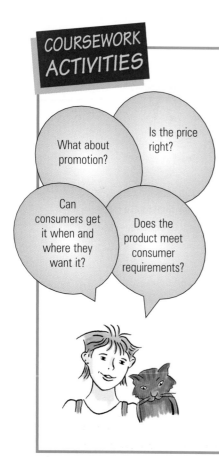

What about promotion?

Is the price right?

Can consumers get it when and where they want it?

Does the product meet consumer requirements?

Think of a product that you buy regularly, such as an item of confectionery or a teenage magazine. How effective is the marketing mix for this product?

Before you start, make sure you know who the product is supposed to sell to (the target market). Is the product aimed at teenagers? Male or female?

Now choose a sample of 30 people to interview from the appropriate group, e.g. females in the age range 13–18. Ask your sample to compare your selected product with three or four rival products. Rule up a table similar to the one below and then compare the brand you use with its competitors.

Now suggest how the marketing mix could be improved for the product you buy.

Product A	Very good	Good	Average	Poor	Very poor	Comment
Place						
Promotion						
Price						
Product						

TASK

Identify the key ingredients of the marketing mix of a company engaging in e-commerce (e.g. one selling wine, foodstuffs or books over the Internet). Examine the website of the company to identify the chief features of its marketing mix. Compare the marketing mix of the e-trader with that of a conventional shop-based trader selling the same type of items.

MATCH IT!

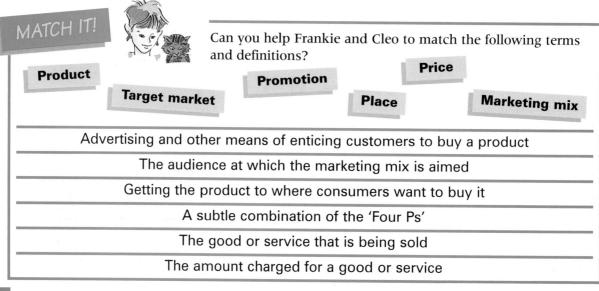

Can you help Frankie and Cleo to match the following terms and definitions?

Product

Target market

Promotion

Price

Place

Marketing mix

Advertising and other means of enticing customers to buy a product

The audience at which the marketing mix is aimed

Getting the product to where consumers want to buy it

A subtle combination of the 'Four Ps'

The good or service that is being sold

The amount charged for a good or service

34 Product Life-cycles

What is a product life-cycle?

During its life, every plant and animal goes through a series of stages, involving birth, growth, maturity and eventually decay. In the same way, products have a life-cycle, although the pattern varies.

The life of a product is the period over which it appeals to customers. We can all think of goods that everyone wanted at one time but which have now gone out of fashion. Obvious examples are drainpipe trousers and winklepicker shoes.

'The life-cycle of a person involves a series of ages. Is it the same for a product?'

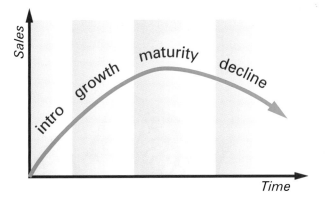

Left: The classic product life-cycle

Sales performance and profitability

The sales performance of any product rises when the product is introduced to the market, reaches a peak and then goes into decline. Most products have a limited life-cycle. Initially the product may flourish and grow, but eventually the market will mature and the product will move towards decline.

At each stage in the product life-cycle, there is a close relationship between sales and profits, so that as organisations or brands go into decline, their profitability decreases.

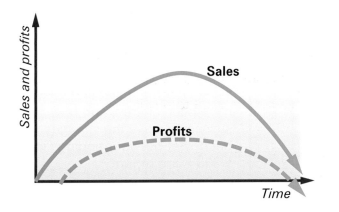

Amazon.com

Amazon is the best known example of an Internet bookseller in the UK, although other established organisations such as WH Smith have followed suit on-line.

The chart below shows how Amazon was introduced to the market in 1997 and how its sales have grown over time. Amazon's success has been based on its widescale advertising over the Internet and the speed with which it gets books to customers. However, Amazon has not as yet (early 2001) broken even.

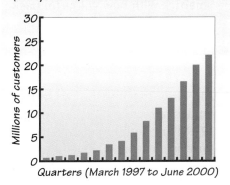

Number of customers – Amazon (source: company annual report)

129

Injecting life into the product life-cycle

The product life-cycle may last for a few months or for hundreds of years. To prolong the life-cycle of a product, an organisation may inject new life into the growth period of the product by adjusting the ingredients of its marketing mix.

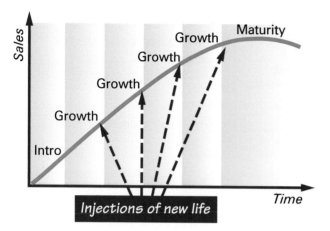

Periodic injections of new life

Ways of altering the marketing mix to inject new life into the product might include:

1 **Changing or modifying the product** to keep ahead of the competition. For example, Nestlé Rowntree, makers of Smarties, responded to competition from other brands of sweets by introducing a number of improvements to Smarties.

◆ In 1989 they brought out a blue Smartie

◆ In 1991 they introduced printing on sweets

◆ In 1992 they introduced green-coloured chocolate

◆ In 1995 they relaunched the standard range of Smarties with new colourful packets

◆ In 1999 they introduced Smarties ice cream

◆ In 2001 they introduced mini Smarties

2 **Altering distribution patterns** to create more attractive retail outlets for consumers. For example, in 1989, the clothing retailers Next introduced *Next Directory*, a catalogue enabling shoppers to buy Next goods by mail order from their own home.

TASK

How would you place each of the items below in terms of product life-cycle?

The Smarties range

COURSEWORK ACTIVITIES

Frankie needs your help with some research.

Identify an example where the marketing mix has been altered to inject new life into a product. What aspects of the marketing mix have been altered, and how successful have the changes been? Set out your findings in a 300-word report.

3 **Changing prices to become more competitive.**
   During the 1990s, sales of national newspapers have
   fallen as people have switched to alternative sources
   of information. This has led to a price war as
   newspaper companies have competed for greater
   market share.

4 **Promotional campaigns.** Another way to inject new
   life into a product is by promoting the product
   through methods such as advertising, special offers,
   'Buy one, get one free' promotions, trial offers, etc.

TASK

What would the life-cycle for each of the following products look like?

The VW Beetle, cat and dog food, Action Man toys, Lee and Perrins sauce, stiletto heels, sledges, body piercing, National Lottery tickets , Easter eggs, the TV programme East Enders, condoms, bicycles, rave Music, Lo-Lo balls, the Bible, Pretty Polly tights, shell suits, mobile phones.

MATCH IT!

Can you help Frankie and Cleo to match the following terms
and definitions?

Maturity   **Life-cycle**   **Injecting new life**   **Introduction**

Relaunch

| Stimulating fresh demand for a product |
| Redesigning or substantially altering a product |
| The stage at which the product has settled into a regular sales pattern |
| The period in which a product is brought out in its market |
| The period over which a product appeals to customers |

35 Products, Brands and Packaging

Meeting consumer needs

The most important part of the marketing mix is the product itself. The product must meet an identified consumer need.

There is no point in spending a fortune on promoting, charging a competitive price and getting your product to a good selling place unless people want to buy it.

Before launching a product, you must make sure it has the right **benefits** that consumers require.

Product benefits

Benefits are the advantages gained by buyers from the goods or services that they buy.

For example, on a hot day you receive the benefit of refreshment from a long cool drink. At the end of a long week, you get the benefit of entertainment from going to the cinema on a Friday night. In the same way, your milkman gives you the benefit of convenient, reliable doorstep delivery. The benefits offered by a product or service can include:

'What are the most important aspects of a product – the product itself, or the way that it is branded and packaged?'

◆ Convenience and accessibility

◆ Good after-sales technical support and advice

◆ Reliability

◆ Comfort and ease of use

◆ Accountability – the knowledge that if things go wrong, the manufacturer will put them right

◆ Courtesy and helpfulness of staff

◆ Attractive, appropriate and efficient design and packaging

◆ Peace of mind – the knowledge that you can trust the company, that your needs are understood and the good or service you have purchased will not let you down

The more benefits that you can provide for customers, the more likely you are to be able to sell your product and get a 'good price' for it. Competition is all about creating more benefits than rival products.

The product mix

Many organisations produce more than one product. The **product mix** is the complete range of items made by the organisation. For example, the Boots organisation makes a range of products which fall under a number of headings:

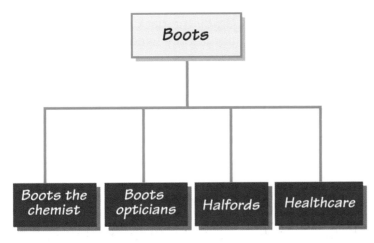

The full Boots product mix would consist of the range of products that falls under each of the above headings – cough syrups, eye drops, car batteries, health supplements, etc.

Branding

A **brand** is a product with a unique, consistent and easily recognisable character. For example, we all recognise the Coca-Cola brand, not only by its logo but by the shape of its bottles, the colour of its cans, the taste of the product and other features.

The uniqueness of a brand comes from its physical characteristics (e.g. the taste and unique ingredients of Coca-Cola), plus its image (i.e. its logo, advertising, etc.) – which are usually created by the manufacturer through advertising and packaging.

The importance of image

Our **image** is the way that others see us. Whether we like it or not, it is our public face. People quickly form opinions about us from the way we dress, walk and talk, from where we live and work, and our interests.

In the same way, every product conveys an image to the consumer. This can be a positive or a negative image, depending largely on how the product is designed and presented.

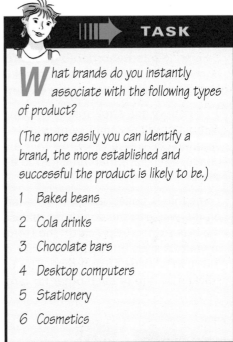

TASK

What brands do you instantly associate with the following types of product?

(The more easily you can identify a brand, the more established and successful the product is likely to be.)

1 *Baked beans*

2 *Cola drinks*

3 *Chocolate bars*

4 *Desktop computers*

5 *Stationery*

6 *Cosmetics*

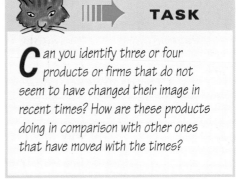

TASK

Can you identify three or four products or firms that do not seem to have changed their image in recent times? How are these products doing in comparison with other ones that have moved with the times?

Packaging

Packaging is the way that goods and services are presented to the customer. It can give added benefits to a product, such as an attractive design, protection during transport, ease of access and so on.

However, packaging can also add considerably to the cost of production. The heavier and bulkier the packaging, the higher the cost of moving the goods around. The more packaging you use, the more material that needs to go into the packets, etc. And of course, the more packaging you create, the greater the environmental cost of disposing of it. Firms therefore need to think very carefully about the advantages and disadvantages of packaging.

COURSEWORK ACTIVITIES

Study the packaging of five commonly used products.

Analyse ways in which the manufacturer could reduce the cost of packaging whilst continuing to make the package look attractive.

CASE STUDY

Solving the home delivery problem

Delivering Internet-ordered goods to customers' homes when they are out is one of the chief problems facing business-to-consumer e-commerce companies.

J Sainsbury, the supermarket group, has linked up with a company called Homeport to use a system that involves delivering groceries in secure aluminium boxes, which are then attached to a wall by a steel cable.

The cable is bolted into a small intercom-style console on the wall and the customer releases the cable and the box using a wipe card. The Homeport boxes come in various sizes but a standard size can take around four carrier bags of shopping. The boxes can also be stacked on top of each other for larger orders.

TASK

1   How does the system outlined on the left improve the value of Sainsbury's retail service?

2   Why is delivery such a stumbling block for e-commerce?

3   How can this stumbling block be overcome?

Can you help Frankie and Cleo to match the following terms and definitions?

Packaging	Product mix	Branding	Image	Benefits

The diversified range of goods and services made by an organisation
The way in which a product is presented
The way in which someone or something is perceived
The range of advantages to consumers provided in a good
Giving a product a unique, consistent and easily recognisable character

36 Pricing

What is the best price for a product?

Charging the right price is a very important part of the marketing mix. In setting a price for your product you will almost certainly want to cover your costs and make a profit as well.

The pricing decision

The actual price that a business charges for its products will depend on whether they are trying to win a massive share of the market or whether they want consumers to buy their product because it is different and better than rival products. The main pricing decision for a firm, therefore, is whether to charge:

◆ A **low price** in order to attract sales. This makes it possible to sell large quantities at a low average cost.

◆ An **average price**. If you charge an average price, you will need to compete with your rivals by other means, e.g. by having a better-quality product, better promotion and advertising, etc.

◆ A **higher price**. Firms can charge a high, or **premium, price** if they are seen as being better than their rivals in meeting the needs of a chosen group of customers.

'You should always charge a little less than your competitors. Then you wipe them out and rule the market!'

Do you think that Ron will always be right in this opinion about pricing?

Different pricing positions

Pricing techniques

1 Cost-plus pricing

A common way to make pricing decisions is to calculate how much it costs to do a particular job or activity, and then add on a given percentage as a return for the job or activity. This is sometimes known as a **mark-up**.

For example, a business may decide that it will cost £100 to do a small repair job on a car, including parts, labour, use of premises and equipment, etc. The business works on the basis of making a 20% return on all the work that it does. It therefore charges the customer £120.

2 Hour-based pricing

Many small businesses are able to work out what their typical costs are for every hour of work they do, e.g. for gardening, signwriting, photography, etc. The business owner is then able to charge a standard charge per hour.

3 Penetration pricing

When a firm brings out a new product into a new or existing market, it may feel that it needs to make a lot of sales very quickly in order to establish itself and to make it possible to produce larger quantities. It may therefore start off by offering the product at quite a low price. When market penetration has been achieved, prices can be raised.

4 Skimming

When you bring out a new product, you may be able to start off by charging quite a high price. Some customers may want to be the first to buy your product because of the prestige of being seen with it, or because they want to be associated with your product before anyone else.

The word **skimming** comes from the idea of skimming the top layer of cream first, allowing the cream to build up again, skimming off the second layer, and so on.

For example, you could sell an exclusive dress at an exclusive price to wealthier customers. The next season, you could lower the price, making it accessible to a less wealthy group of customers. Later on, you could mass-produce the dress so that it is available at a low price to the mass market.

5 Destroyer pricing

Destroyer pricing involves selling your good at a very low price in order to destroy new competitors or existing competitors. For example, in the mid-1990s *The Times* newspaper engaged in a price-cutting campaign to take sales away from rivals. Other newspapers followed suit, and the eventual result was that in November 1995 the *Today* newspaper went out of business.

TASK

For each of the following brands, try to explain whether the manufacturer/retailer is going for a low price, an average price, or a high price. Explain why you think they have chosen the price that they have:

- Chanel No. 5 perfume
- Charlie perfume
- Rolls Royce motor cars
- Ford Ka motor cars
- Dime bars
- Mars bars
- Mars ice cream
- Freezepops
- Own-brand supermarket goods
- Heinz baked beans
- Market stall clothes
- Etam clothes
- Benetton clothes

TASK

Read the Case Study on Ryanair on the next page.

1 Why do you think Ryanair uses a low fare strategy?

2 What would be the benefits of operating this pricing strategy?

3 What might be the dangers?

CASE STUDY

Ryanair soars away with 500,000 fares at £5

In October 2000 the short-haul airline Ryanair offered nearly half a million return flights to Europe for just £5 each.

The price applied to every seat on the Irish operator's 180 daily flights from Stansted, Essex to its 28 destinations, including France, Germany, Italy and Sweden over a two-week period for the middle of October.

The Chief Executive of Ryanair, Michael O'Leary, stated that this was a response to the way in which big airlines such as KLM and British Airways had recently raised their fares. He went on to say 'we see a future where the only markets where air fares will be falling will be those where Ryanair will be offering low-fare competition to the high-fare alliances all over Europe. If our main competitors continue to raise prices as they are doing then the prospects for strong growth of the Ryanair "low fares" formula in Europe remains bright.'

Frankie is carrying out some research to compare different types of teenage magazines Four of the key teenage magazines are *Sugar, Mizz, Just Seventeen* and *Shout*.

* *Sugar*
  Published: monthly
  Target age group: 13–18-year-old girls
  Typical features: Interviews with pop and soap stars, fashion and real-life stories

* *Mizz*
  Published: fortnightly
  Target age group: older teenagers
  Typical features: Fashion and pop news, plus a regular column which explains slang terms

* *Just Seventeen*
  Published: weekly
  Target age group: 13–17-year-old girls
  Typical features: Fashion and pop news, plus environmental features

* *Shout*
  Published: fortnightly
  Target age group: 12–15-year old girls
  Typical features: Adopts the safe approach. Gossip on television and pop stars, real-life stories

Frankie is trying to assess why these magazines choose to sell at different prices. Carry out some further research into these teenage magazines to find out why they price in the way they do. First find out the prices. You will also need to compare the style of the magazines, as well as finding out some typical readers' views about the prices charged.

Alternatively, choose another market and analyse price differences of similar products.

TASK

What type of pricing is involved in each of the following examples?

- Frankie and Cleo have decided to work out how much it costs them to produce their biscuits per hour. They will then add 10% to this cost in order to make a reasonable return.

- Ron Rust has managed to wipe out some of his rivals who have tried to set up in local towns. As soon as a new scrapyard opened up, Ron started selling scrap at a much lower price than these yards could afford to sell at.

- Suzanne is a signwriter. She charges her clients according to the time it takes her to do a job.

- When Honton Winrab brought out his book about the life of the well-known aristocrat Lady Ophelia McStarkers, the original edition was in hardback and sold at £25 per copy. A second Christmas edition of the book was brought out at £20 per copy. Then the book was brought out in paperback at £10 a copy.

- A Belgian company introduced a new breakfast cereal in the UK originally selling at 50p less than similar brands. Once the new cereal had developed a good hold on the market, prices were raised to comparable levels with rival cereals.

MATCH IT!

Can you help Frankie and Cleo to match the following terms and definitions?

Destroyer pricing

Cost leadership

Penetration pricing

Market share

Cost-plus pricing

Hour-based pricing

Charging customers according to the time it takes to do a job
Producing large outputs cheaper than your rivals
Adding a percentage on to your costs in order to make a reasonable return
Initially charging a low price in order to establish a good position in a market
Undercutting rivals in order to force them out of business
The percentage of the overall market in the hands of a particular firm

37 Reaching the Market

What is meant by distribution?

Delivery, or distribution as it is commonly called, makes products available to customers where and when they want them. Place is a very important part of the marketing mix.

Something like 20% of the total production cost of a product is taken up with **freight charges**. These are the costs of moving the raw materials to the producer and then transporting 'finished' products to the end-user.

Transport

Different forms of transport have their own advantages and disadvantages.

1 **Pipelines** are expensive to construct and repair, but are a cheap way to transport oil and gas.

2 **Roads** give door-to-door delivery, are fast over short and some long distances, and make it possible for firms to use their own fleet of vehicles relatively cheaply.

   However, road travel is also subject to traffic delays and breakdowns, and drivers may drive their vehicles for only a certain number of hours in a day.

3 **Rail transport** is relatively cheap and quick over long distances, particularly between major cities.

   However, rail is not always a good way of reaching out-of-the-way destinations. Guaranteed speedy deliveries by rail can also be costly.

4 **Air transport** is very fast between countries, as long as the destination is not too far from a major city. Air is generally used for carrying important, urgent, relatively light and valuable loads.

5 **Sea transport** is a cheap way of carrying heavy and bulky loads when speed is not a factor.

Place

In marketing terms, the **place** is where the final exchange occurs between the seller and the customer. An important marketing decision is where this exchange takes place and how. For example, at one time, all bank services were provided 'across the counter', but in recent years banks have moved to cashpoints and increasingly towards telephone banking.

SPIX

'In the modern global economy distribution has become a real problem. Every day we consume products from the far-flung corners of the globe. Transporting them here uses scarce energy resources and can contribute to pollution. For example, airlines flying high above the Earth's surface emit pollution-creating gases, which affect the ozone layer far more quickly than surface transport.'

Below: Changing place for banking activities

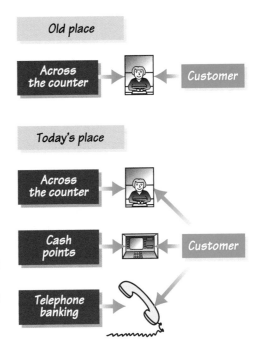

Old place

Across the counter → ← Customer

Today's place

Across the counter →

Cash points → ← Customer

Telephone banking →

Where place is the fast-food outlet

Market research indicates that in the first decade of the twenty-first century most people make use of fast-food outlets. In a world in which more people than ever before are working or studying at school, college or university, there is an increasing demand for fast food as an alternative to cooking meals at home or visiting restaurants. Increasingly consumers want convenience. The customer wants a combination of value for money and quality. The usual place for fast-food outlets is on the high street, or in other busy urban areas with easy access to transport links.

Of course, fast food has a long history. In the sixteenth century, poorer Londoners ate stale bread and cheese or a minced ox tongue pie from local 'cookshops'.

Our love affair with fish and chips began in the 1830s with Jewish traders in London's East End.

But the gambling habits of John Montagu, the fourth Earl of Sandwich, provided our most enduring fast food. The earl invented the sandwich when he refused to break from the card table for a meal and simply snatched a slice of cold beef from a passing footman to slip it between two pieces of toast.

Though the hamburger rocketed to fame in the US at the 1904 St Louis World Fair; the British were more reluctant to fall for its charms. In 1962, a London restaurant was banned from using the word because it was considered fraudulent.

All that changed with the opening of the first McDonald's in Woolwich in south-east London in 1974, 34 years after Dick McDonald and his brother, Mac, opened their original American fast food joint and six years after the first Big Mac (or Big Boy as it was originally called) was produced. A hamburger cost just 18p.

An increasing awareness of food led to chains such as Pret A Manger peppering our high streets, and by the late 1990s sales of sandwiches were up 45%. Despite the foreign pretenders, the British sandwich has held its own.

TASK

1   Do you think that the success of fast-food restaurants in this country is mostly a result of (a) place, (b) price, (c) product or (d) promotion?

2   What are the main ingredients of 'place' that make fast-food restaurants so successful?

Channels of distribution

A **distribution channel** is the means by which an organisation and its customers are brought together at a particular place and time for the purpose of buying and selling goods. This may be in a shop, office, via a computer link, or by television shopping.

The organisations that are involved in the distribution chain are:

◆ **Manufacturers** – i.e. the firms that make products.

◆ **Wholesalers** – i.e. the firms that store goods in bulk which they purchase from manufacturers before selling them on to retailers

◆ **Retailers** – i.e. the firms that sell goods to final consumers

The diagram on the right shows a traditional distribution channel from the manufacturer to the final consumer.

The diagram on the next page shows how there can be a number of different types of channels of distribution between the manufacturer and the eventual consumer.

◆ In **Channel A**, the manufacturer sells direct to consumers by mail order. Examples are clothing manufacturers like Racing Green and Next, who have their own mail order networks.

◆ In **Channel B**, the manufacturer distributes direct to their own warehouses and company shops which supply consumers. Examples are products that are produced directly by large supermarket chains in their own factories. Here, the manufacturer is entirely responsible for the distribution of their own products.

◆ **Channel C** is sometimes called the 'traditional channel of distribution': a manufacturer makes goods; a wholesaler buys lots of different goods from several manufacturers. The wholesaler sells on to retailers. The manufacturer, wholesaler and retailer are all independent organisations. This was the pattern for most goods in the UK until the 1960s.

◆ In **Channel D**, retailers buy directly from manufacturers. This is easiest when the retailers have a very large storage area, or when goods can be bought in bulk.

COURSEWORK ACTIVITIES

Interview people and use your own personal experience to identify three products for which the 'place' has changed in recent times.

Why do you think these changes in place have occurred? (Show how the place has changed.)

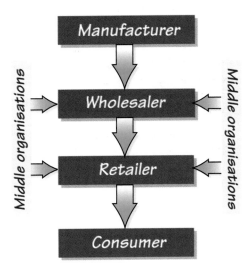

A distribution channel

◆ **Channel E** has become particularly important in the last five years as more and more households become linked up to the Internet, through televisions and computers. The e-tailer is the organisation that deals with the customer through an interactive website, which enables the customer to buy goods online.

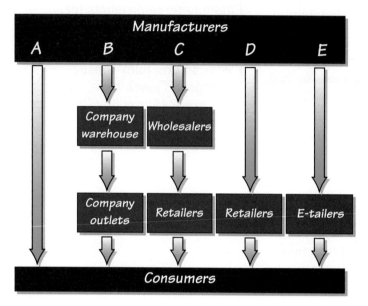

Examples of distribution channels

COURSEWORK ACTIVITIES

Interview the owner of a retail outlet to find out what channels of distribution they use for the various items they stock. (You will normally find that they use more than one channel of distribution).

MATCH IT!

Can you help Frankie and Cleo to match the following terms and definitions?

Place

Manufacturer

Retailer

Wholesaler

Distribution

Consumer

| The person who enjoys the final good or service |
| Organisation that makes goods |
| Where the final exchange takes place between the seller and buyer |
| A middle organisation that is responsible for storing goods in bulk before selling them on in smaller quantities |
| Making products available to consumers where and when they want them |
| Person or organisation who sells finished products to end-users |

38 Electronic Commerce

E-commerce (buying and selling over the Internet) has transformed the way that a lot of buying and selling is done in this country in recent years.

There are two main types of e-commerce:

◆ B2B (business-to-business) buying and selling, and

◆ B2C (business-to-consumer) selling

From the mid-1990s onwards businesses increasingly began to realise that they could sell directly into a consumer's home – through television shopping and through computer-based Internet shopping.

Today nearly all young people, and many older people, are comfortable with using the Internet. Consumers spend many hours browsing the Internet, and many will use the Internet as a means of buying goods and services.

'Is e-commerce a good way for a food company to reduce its costs?'

B2B buying and selling

Most large businesses have realised the importance of the Internet in trading with other businesses. The Internet has helped to slash the costs of ordering new components, parts and stocks of goods. The Internet makes it possible for buyers to interrogate databases to find information about items which are for sale – not just in this country but also in other parts of the world. The Internet has enabled companies to reduce their buying costs because it has increased the level of competition between firms.

Major companies such as car producers have pooled together to create databases of supplies and suppliers of car components. This procedure is estimated to have reduced car production costs by as much as 20%.

SPIX

'Unfortunately not everyone has access to the Internet. So in some ways e-commerce is creating a bigger divide between the "haves" and "have-nots"!'

B2C buying and selling

However, it is in the area of B2C links that electronic commerce is having its greatest impact. Businesses have realised that the Internet provides them with a way of developing a relationship with customers.

A **website** is an organisation's electronic shop window. However, it is more powerful as a sales and marketing tool than the traditional shop window, because once set up.

The main marketing and selling tool is the website. For example, a customer wanting to buy wine can search the Net for sites selling wine. The customer can browse through the details of the different types of wine on offer, and then order wine directly over the Internet or using phone or mail links.

Once the electronic wine seller has details of the customer they are able to follow up with special offers aimed at tempting that particular customer.

Pressure for the adoption of e-commerce

In business it is always important to keep up with the latest changes in technology in your industry. If you don't there is a good chance that your competitors will steal a march on you.

In recent years we have seen the potential of e-commerce to cut costs and to increase an organisation's ability to sell into a larger market place. For example, football clubs like Manchester United have their own extensive websites, which enable them to sell merchandise directly to the end consumer (cutting out the middleman). Using the Internet gives the club the ability to sell into a global market.

CASE STUDY

Bryant Homes

Bryant Homes have constructed an interactive website. The site enables Bryant Homes to find out what type of properties individual customers are looking for and then to follow up leads (initial enquiries) by supplying potential customers with the right sort of sales information.

Put yourself in the position of someone wanting to buy a new home, perhaps someone who is relocating to another part of the country. Imagine the frustration involved in having to make the journey to visit a house hundreds of miles away only to find that it does not quite meet your requirements.

The website's main dedicated system for customers is named 'Homefinder'. Homefinder is a system that will perform a search against consumer needs and requirements to locate a house type and location to suit their lifestyle. It contains images and floor plans of the entire Bryant Homes product portfolio. The information on Homefinder comes directly from a central database and is updated every 24 hours. Prices and build-by dates are published on the website. 'Homefinder' enables the prospective buyer to view and compare properties, to note their locations and the features offered. If the viewer wishes to find out more

information they can request general or specific details, and can take the first steps towards making a purchase.

One of the benefits of 'surfing the web' for customers is that *they* drive the information. Bryant Homes doesn't tell the user what to look for. The prospective buyer is able to tour the property at leisure. From the sales and marketing perspective the website is also a good way of issuing press releases. Bryant Homes' website is also advertising space and is capable of reaching an international audience. This is particularly useful for attracting people to relocate to the UK from overseas as such comprehensive information would be difficult to obtain otherwise.

Difficulties in the development of e-commerce

There are a number of difficulties in setting up an effective website and using e-commerce. The first problem is to make sure that the website is good enough to attract and maintain the interest of customers. Most firms today will contract the services of an experienced web design firm that already has experience of setting up similar sites.

The website needs to be easy for the user to find their way around. It also needs to be interactive so that the customer can look up and search those bits of information that interest them, and interact with the site (by, for example, ordering goods). If a site is difficult to navigate a potential customer will switch off within a few seconds.

Another major problem in developing e-commerce is that building an Internet presence requires a lot of investment. This is costly. It takes a long time for an Internet venture to repay the initial investment and hard work. This is why a number of Internet sites have run into financial difficulties and closed down. The idea may be a good one, but not enough cash might come in in the early days to pay back the investment.

A further difficulty is that of payment. Most customers are reluctant to give their credit card and bank details over the Internet because of the widescale existence of Internet fraud. This continues to be a major hurdle to the success of e-commerce.

Delivery is another major problem. Most households in the UK are only designed to receive deliveries through their letter box. It is likely that over the next few years we are going to see a host of new types of delivery boxes to accommodate for Internet deliveries.

Benefits to business of e-commerce

Most large British businesses (and many medium and small companies) have moved into e-commerce. For large companies the benefits include:

◆ Selling to larger markets

◆ Attracting new customers

◆ Using websites to advertise more widely

◆ Using the interactivity provided by the Internet to gather information about customers, which can then be used to make new offers to them

◆ Reduction in costs of premises, distribution, purchasing, etc.

TASK

Why is the Internet a good way of selling houses?

2   Why would customers be pleased to browse the Net to search for property?

3   What other firms in the building and property market would benefit from selling over the Internet? How would they benefit?

'Can you design a new type of delivery box for deliveries of goods ordered over the Internet?'

For companies like banks and insurance companies developing an Internet presence (coupled with telephone banking and insurance operations) has enabled them to slash costs and reduce the number of employees.

Smaller businesses have been able to benefit by developing 'cottage industries' with a national market. For example, a small producer of ceramics or honey can now sell their product in a very large market place.

Benefits to consumers of e-commerce

Consumers are now able to choose products from a much wider range of outlets, and can purchase from low-cost sellers – e.g. buying books from Amazon.com.

The consumer is able to browse the Internet from their own home, and to choose goods at leisure rather than being rushed into a purchase. The consumer is able to navigate a site to search for relevant details.

Using the Internet, consumers can choose goods at leisure in their own home

Disadvantages of e-commerce

The disadvantages of e-commerce are:

◆ What the consumer sees on the screen is not necessarily what they get through the post. The website may make goods and services appear more attractive than they really are.

◆ There may be considerable delays in delivery.

◆ Often the distribution and handling costs are quite high, so the buyer may find that they have to pay more than they expected.

Although many consumers have been excited about the prospects of buying from across the globe using the Internet, many have also been disappointed.

The large companies that are now investing heavily in Internet shopping such as supermarket chains have to make a lot of improvements in terms of:

◆ Delivery, getting goods to consumers in a convenient form, and at appropriate times.

◆ Developing safe and reliable methods of payment.

◆ Ensuring that customers don't have to pay more than they expect.

'Do you think that customers really benefit from the replacement of counter banking by telephone and Internet banking?'

CASE STUDY

Complaints soar as switch to Internet and call centres gathers pace

In November 2000 a study provided by the Forum of Private Businesses reported that the quality of service provided by banks had worsened with the shift to Internet and telephone banking operations.

Hundreds of branch closures, coupled with the loss of face-to-face contact, mean that customers' needs are taking second place to cost-cutting and profits. Banks have rushed to join the Internet revolution, claiming that customers prefer the convenience of 24-hour banking via personal computer or telephone to high-street banking. Mass branch closures and a shift to computer banking are designed to cut costs.

But customers have not seen benefits in terms of cheaper banking, the report argued.

Some 89.5% of Clydesdale customers felt they had suffered higher charges, as did 83.3% of Lloyds TSB customers, 75% of Barclays' customers and 73.3% NatWest's customers.

Bank	Service rating	
	2000	1998
Clydesdale	47.8	59.3
Bank of Scotland	52.9	59.1
NatWest	53.2	56.3
Lloyds TSB	54.1	59.4
Barclays	54.1	57.4
Co-op	54.3	55.1
Yorkshire	54.5	57.9
HSBC	57.6	60.7
Royal Bank of Scotland	57.8	58.5

Customer satisfaction in banks (source *Forum of Private Business*, November 2000)

Many small business owners feel unhappy at the loss of personal contact with bank staff. The increasingly distant relationship, mainly via unhelpful call centres, means that businesses find it difficult to get quick decisions.

The table on the left shows how customer confidence in banks generally has been falling. The index (out of 100) rates customer satisfaction: the lower the figure the poorer the service.

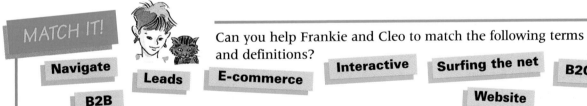

MATCH IT!

Can you help Frankie and Cleo to match the following terms and definitions?

Navigate Leads E-commerce Interactive Surfing the net B2C B2B Website

Finding your way around the Internet
Enabling the user of the Net to find their own way round a website and to input information and decisions involving that site
Initial enquiries from customers, which can then be followed up
Searching the Internet for relevant sites and information
Links between one business organisation and another, often involving buying and selling
Trading over the Internet and through other electronic forms of communication
An Internet address and pages belonging to an individual or organisation
Links between a business and potential consumers/customers

39 Advertising and Publicity

The role of advertising

There are many parts of the promotional mix. In this chapter we deal with advertising and publicity. In the next chapter we deal with selling and sales promotion.

One of the best forms of advertising is the product itself. But advertising still plays a very important role. Advertising is the presenting or promoting of a product to the public to encourage sales.

It can have spectacular results. For example, in 1996 jeans manufacturer Levis suddenly switched to using female models in their television adverts. Jean sales shot through the roof.

Adverts don't always have to be popular to be successful. For example, in the second half of the 1990s one advert sent TV viewers into a frenzy. The zany commercial for 'Chicken Tonight' was listed as the 'most irritating advert on the box'! Viewers' love–hate relationship with a TV advert can mean that the product sticks in their mind. Advertisers know this, and often go out of their way to make an advertisement 'daft but memorable'.

Publicity means any technique or process used to attract public attention to people and products. Unlike advertising, however, publicity is usually free. Any type of publicity is advertising.

'But surely if a product is good enough then you won't need to advertise it?'

CASE STUDY

Using sex to promote ice cream

Contestants in Europe's $7 billion-a-year ice cream market are using sex to turn on the public. The use of naked flesh to advertise products is nothing new, but fierce competition in the 'adult' market is inspiring advertisers to new heights. In the UK, campaigns by two manufacturers in the gourmet market have raised eyebrows as well as brand awareness.

The UK's television watchdog, the Independent Television Commission, banned a series of erotic advertisements for ice cream, saying they were 'too hot' for British viewers. The Advertising Standards Authority has also received complaints about the use of sex in ice cream adverts.

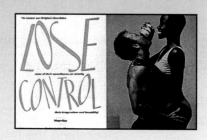

Haagen-Dazs advertisement

Unilever's best-known adverts featured the pan-European Cornetto gondola. It, too, has recently turned to sex appeal with the 'girl-licks-lolly' formula to help it to double the sales of Magnum, the chocolate-covered ice cream on a stick. With predicted sales of £300 million-plus in Europe each year in the late 1990s, it shows that the proof of the pudding is in the eating!

TASK

1   Why might the use of sex to sell ice cream be considered against the public interest?

2   Outline the benefits of using such methods to (a) sellers of ice cream and (b) consumers.

3   What other methods of promoting ice cream might also be successful? Working in groups, consider what themes you would emphasise if you had to promote a new ice cream product in the luxury 'after-dinner' segment of the adult market.

Informative advertising

In the UK, the highest spender on advertising is the government. Most government advertising is aimed at giving information to the public. This passing on of information is a very important part of advertising.

Persuasive advertising

Most adverts, however, try to do more than just inform the public. The soap-powder manufacturers spend almost as much money on advertising as the government, and their advertisements are blatantly designed to attract people to buy their products.

A **persuasive** selling message is one that promises a desirable and believable benefit to the people to whom it is addressed. There are many different types of advert that can be used to persuade, including the following:

A government health warning

◆ Adverts showing a 'personality' using the product

◆ Adverts comparing one product with other products

◆ Adverts using sex appeal

Many firms aim to develop strong **brand images** for their products. If people associate a brand name with a product, then this will help create loyalty for the brand.

TASK

Examine the advert below, which outlined the changes in London's phone codes in October 2000.

1   Who paid for and thus placed the advert shown?

2   Is it mainly informative or persuasive?

3   Who would stand to gain from the public reading the advert?

4   Why are adverts like this one good as a 'public relations' exercise?

Still using London's old phone codes? Your times's up.

	CODE	LOCAL NUMBER
Old	0171	123 5467
New	(020) 7	123 4567

Make sure you update the numbers stored in your fax machines, mobiles and alarms.

On October 14th all of London's old numbers will be turned off. The Capitals code becomes 020. Inner London numbers will need a 7 added to the front of them and all Outer London numbers need an 8 at the start of them. It's all part of The Big Number. For help call free on 0808 22 4 2000 or visit www.numberchange.org

The Big Number

All The Phone Companies Together

Public relations

The aim of public relations is to create, promote or maintain goodwill and a favourable image of a company or institution among the public.

Advertising agencies

Running an advertising campaign is very expensive, and firms need to make sure that their money is well spent. Generally firms will use an advertising agency to carry out the campaign. For advertising to be successful it must:

◆ Reach the right audience

◆ Be attractive and appealing

◆ Be cost-effective in relation to the extra sales

Control over advertising in the UK

Advertisers cannot just say anything they like when preparing an advert.

1 They must keep within the law. For instance, the **Trades Descriptions Act** lays down that goods advertised for sale must be as they are described (e.g. a 'waterproof' watch must be waterproof).

2 The advertising industry has its own **Code of Practice,** which advertisers must obey.

The British Code of Advertising and Sales Promotion

This is a voluntary agreement by firms in the advertising industry to keep their adverts up to certain standards. It covers newspapers, magazines, cinema adverts, leaflets, brochures, posters and commercials on videotape, but not TV or radio advertising.

The Advertising Standards Authority (ASA)

The ASA is responsible for ensuring the standards of non-broadcast advertisements in the UK. You may have seen the advert on the right in national newspapers and magazines.

The advert goes on to say that if you have any complaints about adverts in the paper, you should write to the ASA, who will take up your complaint and force the advertiser to make changes if necessary.

Of course, some of the complaints received by the ASA are frivolous, like the man who complained that he had poured Heineken lager over his pot plant and it had died!

COURSEWORK ACTIVITIES

Watch television commercials and list six examples of what you consider to be 'sit-up-and-notice' commercials. Then survey 20 people to find out if they can remember the advertisement and what it is advertising.

Find out what people's views are of the advertisement and whether they have actually purchased the article recently.

Are you:

Legal ✓

Decent ✓

Honest ✓

Truthful ✓

Advertisers have to be.

ASA press advertisement

The Independent Television Commission

Following the 1990 Broadcasting Act, the Independent Television Commission (ITC) was set up to replace the Independent Broadcasting Authority (IBA). It now exercises control over television advertising.

CASE STUDY

Captive View

The washrooms of pubs and clubs might not be everybody's idea of the perfect place to advertise. However, one technology company is so convinced of the potential that it has launched a joint venture with a firm making lavatory equipment.

Captive View is installing 'Viewrinals', and their female equivalent 'Viewloos', in high-profile London attractions such as the Hammersmith Palais and the Aquarium. The firm claims the response to the innovation – video screens in the washroom that can play anything from music videos to TV-quality advertisements – has been so positive that by the end of 2000 it had 100 of these facilities installed and 1,000 planned for the end of 2001.

The total market consists of 125,000 publicly accessible washrooms in the UK, all of which provide advertising opportunities. It is thought that at the moment there are only 30,000 posters in 5,000 facilities.

LATEST NEWS

In May 2001, ITV came under fire for using 'subliminal advertising' tp promote a new reality programme, *Survivor*.

Many ITV programmes were followed by a fleeting image of the *Survivor* logo. A number of viewers complained to the ITC.

TASK

1 What do you see as the benefits of viewrinals and viewloos?

2 What is the main competition for this form of advertising?

3 What would be the drawbacks of this new form of advertising?

MATCH IT!

Can you help Frankie and Cleo to match the following terms and definitions?

Advertising

British Code of Advertising Practice

Persuasive advertising

Informative advertising

ASA

Public relations

Projecting a positive image of an organisation

Body responsible for making sure that adverts are legal, decent, honest and truthful

Voluntary agreement regulating behaviour in the advertising industry

Presenting or promoting a product to the public

Setting out basic factual information about a product or service

Enticing consumers to buy a product through advertising techniques

40 Selling and Sales Promotion

Selling v. marketing

It is important to understand the difference between selling and marketing.

◆ **Marketing** begins by identifying and anticipating what consumers want and need. Once these wants and needs have been identified, products or services can be developed to meet them.

◆ **Selling** and **sales promotion** are concerned with persuading potential customers that your solution is the best one to fulfil their needs.

For example, market research might indicate that there is a big market made up of households that want to buy a computer that gives them access to the Internet. It is the job of the salesperson to convince potential customers that your particular PC and Internet connection is the best way of meeting their needs.

Stages in selling

The diagram on the right shows the various stages involved in the selling process.

Making sales

At the point of sale, the aim is to persuade the customer to take the step from wanting a product or service to actually buying it. The more closely the product matches their needs, the easier this will be. The key thing for the seller to remember is that customers are not so much looking for particular products or services as for the **benefits** those products or services will bring.

Sales promotion

Sales promotion refers to a set of methods used to encourage customers to buy a product, usually at the point of sale.

Sales promotion is used along with advertising, personal selling and publicity. It can include the use of point-of-sale materials (e.g. leaflets and brochures), competitions, offers, product demonstrations and exhibitions.

A distinction is often made between promotion into the pipeline and promotions out of the pipeline:

◆ **Promotions into the pipeline** are methods which are used to sell more products into the distribution system – i.e. they are aimed at wholesalers and retailers rather than final consumers. Examples are

THE SELLING PROCESS

Preparing to make the sale
The salesperson needs to know everything possible about a particular product and how it can meet different customer needs.

Contacting and meeting customers
Choose a moment when the customer has plenty of time to discuss their problem and will be receptive.

Finding out the problem/need
If you sell the customer a product which does not really meet their needs, you are unlikely to make a repeat sale.

Providing the solutions
This should meet all the customer's needs.

Closing the sale
This should be done in a business-like and friendly way.

Dealing with objections
Unless objections are dealt with in a systematic way the customer may go away to 'think about it' and never return.

After-sales service
This can include a service and repair agreement.

'dealer loaders', such as thirteen for the price of twelve, point-of-sale materials, dealer competitions, extended credit to dealers, sale-or-return and promotional gifts.

COURSEWORK ACTIVITIES

When you visit a supermarket, you will often find sales representatives encouraging you to taste or try a product (wine, cheese, biscuits, etc.) as part of a sales promotion.

List and describe five other types of sales promotion that you have seen in a supermarket recently.

◆ **Promotions out of the pipeline** help in promoting and selling products to the final consumer. These include free samples, trial packs, coupon offers, price reductions, competitions, demonstrations, charity promotions and point-of-sale materials.

TASK

What do you see as being the strengths and weaknesses of the following sales promotions?

- A manufacturer of a new type of disposable razor advertises the product on television and then gives out thousands of free razors to people visiting the cricket Test matches in a series against the Australians.

- To boost falling sales, the manufacturer of an exclusive brand of perfume offers free sample bottles of the perfume nationwide in a chain of well-known chemists.

- The manufacturer of a new type of cheese runs a 'free' promotion one week before the cheese goes on sale nationwide. Taster pieces of the cheese are given away free in supermarkets for one week before the national launch.

- A national newspaper runs its own 'lottery-style' promotion for five weeks. Every week there is an expensive car as first prize in the competition, which is only open to purchasers of the newspaper.

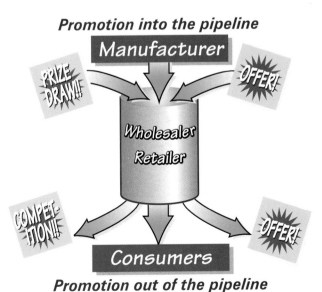

Promotion into and out of the pipeline

'Sales promotion is a complete waste of time. Whoever heard of someone buying a good because they were given a free sample? If people want to try a good, they should pay for it!'

Do you agree with Ron?

The effectiveness of promotions

The effect of sales promotions varies widely. Though most promotions using free samples lead to an immediate (if temporary) increase in sales, sales promotions are a short-term measure on the whole and have little effect on brand loyalty over a longer period.

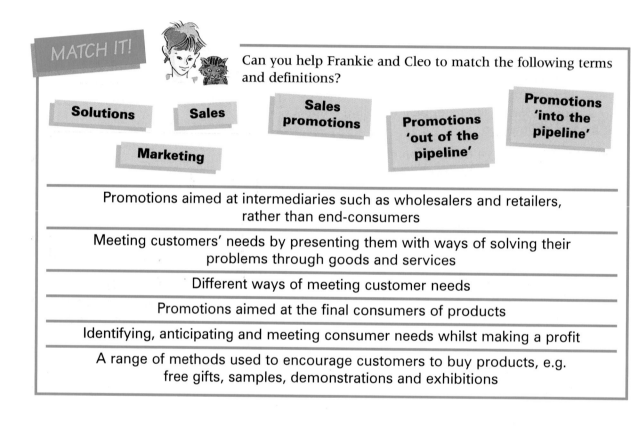

MATCH IT!

Can you help Frankie and Cleo to match the following terms and definitions?

Solutions   Sales   Sales promotions   Promotions 'out of the pipeline'   Promotions 'into the pipeline'   Marketing

Promotions aimed at intermediaries such as wholesalers and retailers, rather than end-consumers

Meeting customers' needs by presenting them with ways of solving their problems through goods and services

Different ways of meeting customer needs

Promotions aimed at the final consumers of products

Identifying, anticipating and meeting consumer needs whilst making a profit

A range of methods used to encourage customers to buy products, e.g. free gifts, samples, demonstrations and exhibitions

41 Protecting the Consumer

Meeting standards

Every good or service that is bought or sold must meet certain standards. Some of these standards are laid down in law, some in voluntary codes of practice within an industry, and others are set by individual businesses.

Businesses supply goods or services for consumers in return for payment. The legal system sets out a fair framework for trading, and to help to settle disputes that may arise.

'In my business it's a case of "let the buyer beware!"'
Do you think that Ron will be able to get away with this sort of attitude?

Buying goods

The **Sale of Goods Acts 1979 and 1994** says that goods must be:

◆ 'Of satisfactory quality' – i.e. free from significant faults, except defects that are drawn to your attention by the seller (for instance, if goods are declared to be 'shop-soiled').

◆ 'Fit for the purpose' – including any particular purpose mentioned by you to the seller. For example, if you ask for a jumper that is machine-washable, you should *not* be sold one that has to be hand-washed.

◆ 'As described' – i.e. on the package or sales literature, or verbally by the seller. If you are told that a shirt is 100% cotton, then it should not turn out to be a mixture of cotton and polyester.

Any good that you buy from any sort of trader (e.g. shop, street market, mail order, or door-to-door salesperson) should meet these basic requirements. They also apply to food and goods bought in sales.

What to do if things go wrong

If there is something wrong with what you buy, you should tell the seller as soon as possible. Exactly what you are entitled to depends on how serious the fault is and how soon the goods are returned.

If you take faulty goods back straight away, you should be able to get your money back. You have not legally 'accepted' the goods, and this means you can 'reject' them (i.e. refuse to accept them). You can still reject goods even if you have taken them home, provided that you examine and try them out as soon as possible, and then take them back at once (or within a few days of purchase).

What is acceptance?

When you take faulty goods back to the seller you may be offered a replacement or a free repair. You do not have to agree to this. You can insist on having your money back. If you agree to a repair, you may have problems getting all your money back later if the fault is not sorted out, because, in law, you will have **accepted** the goods. If you accept a credit note, you will not usually be able to exchange it for cash later on.

Once you have 'accepted goods' in the legal sense, you lose your right to a full refund. You can only claim compensation.

TASK

Frankie wonders whether the Sale of Goods Act has been broken in the following cases. Can you help her?

'Last year was a bit of a disaster for my Christmas shopping. First of all I bought my Auntie Amber a beautiful micro dress. The first time she washed it, it shrank so she couldn't wear it again. The label said "guaranteed shrinkproof"…

'…Then I bought my sister Juniper a pair of gloves which had one of the fingers missing. I think we should have taken that back to the shop…'

'…Then I bought my brother Ossie a multi-purpose football pump adaptor, but it wouldn't fit any of his footballs.'

'Acceptance' normally happens when you have kept the goods beyond a reasonable time. The law does not lay down any fixed periods for what is considered 'reasonable' – it depends on the goods and the circumstances. But you would generally be expected to make it clear to the seller that you are rejecting the goods as soon as possible after purchase.

Buyers' rights

Buyers should not be put off by traders trying to talk their way out of their legal responsibilities. The law says that it is up to the seller to deal with complaints about defective goods, so the seller should not try and lay the blame on the manufacturer.

As a buyer, you have the same rights even if you lose your receipt. A receipt, however, is useful evidence of where and when you bought the goods.

You may be able to claim compensation if you suffer loss because of faulty goods – for example, if a faulty iron ruins your shirt or trousers.

Buying a service

When you pay for a service – for example, from a dry cleaner, travel agent, car mechanic, hairdresser or builder – you are entitled to certain standards.

A service should be carried out:

◆ **With reasonable care and skill.** The job should be done to a proper standard of workmanship. If you have a dress made for a special occasion, it should not fray or come apart at the seams for no reason.

◆ **Within a reasonable time.** If you have to have your hi-fi system repaired, it should not take weeks and weeks. You can always agree upon a definite completion time with the supplier of the service.

◆ **At a reasonable charge**, if no price has been fixed in advance. However, if the price is fixed at the outset, or you have agreed some other way of working out the charge, you cannot complain later that it was unreasonable.

Always ask a trader how much a particular job will cost. The trader may only be able to make an informed guess at the cost and give you an estimate. If you agree a fixed cost, it is usually called a **quotation.** A fixed price is always binding.

'I frequently get asked to pick up cars which have been smashed up in accidents. I never quote a price to the customer at the time, just in case they think it's too high. When they get my bill, they have a bit of a shock, but then they can't do anything about it!'

Is Ron Rust keeping within the law? What do you think?

Other consumer laws

1 The Trades Descriptions Act 1968

The description given of the goods forms part of the contract between the buyer and the seller. This Act makes it a criminal offence for a trader to describe goods falsely. A type of case frequently prosecuted under this Act is the turning back of the 'clock' on a used car to disguise the mileage.

2 The Weights and Measures Act 1985

This Act aims to ensure that consumers receive the actual quantity of a product that they believe they are buying. For example, pre-packed items must have a declaration of the quantity contained within the pack. It is an offence to give 'short weight'.

3 The Food Safety Act 1990

This act prohibits the sale of unfit food and controls the standards of food. It also controls the description, advertising and labelling of food. This area is particularly important because safe food is so important to our well being.

4 The Consumer Protection Act 1987

This Act provides for liability for damage caused by defective products – if goods do not meet the required standards and cause harm to people then they can sue for compensation. The Act bans the supply of unsafe goods and sets out that suppliers of goods that are found to be harmful must warn the public of the dangers.

5 The Protection of Children (Tobacco) Act 1986 and the Children and Young Persons (protection from tobacco) Act 1991

These Acts prohibit the sale of tobacco to children and control the siting of cigarette vending machines so that children can not gain easy access to them.

6 The Clean Air Act 1993

This Act controls the lead content of petrol and the sulphur content of diesel fuel in order to reduce air pollution.

7 The Knives Act, 1997

This act prevents the marketing of dangerous knives and their sales to minors.

'Can you find a recent example from a newspaper where a firm that has supplied a good which has been found to be unsafe is warning the public of the possible dangers?'

TASK

What do you think the legal situation would be in the following cases?

1 Frankie's mum buys her a new school blazer in a department store on a Saturday afternoon. When she gets the blazer home, she realises that it is black, not dark blue as required. On Monday Frankie's mum takes the blazer back to the store.

2 Instead of returning the blazer straight away, Frankie's mum lets Ossie wear it for a few days. However, it is too large for him, so the next week she takes it back.

Find out about three other pieces of interesting consumer protection legislation by accessing the Trading Standards website (Trading Standards Central – Trading Standards and consumer Protection Information for the UK – legislation).

LATEST NEWS

Ultimate designer perfume: an eau de toilette by Jimmy Riddle

The story leaked out from the Trading Standards Authority in early December 2000 that the bottles of something labelled 'Chanel No 5' and going cheap in an Oxfordshire market were not what they seemed. The description on the box of eau de toilette was, for once, more or less what it said on the label.

A trading standards officer who raided a market stall at Finmere sent the 'perfume' to a laboratory for tests, and later confirmed that what was claimed to be the classic French scent was indeed diluted with urine. It seems that human pee has many of the same properties as perfume – it has a straw colour, and produces a mildly astringent sensation on the skin – and its odour is initially masked by the fumes of whatever else has been put into the bottle, whether it is a little of the real thing or some other product.

Help and advice for consumers

There are a number of bodies providing advice and help to consumers:

1 **Trading Standards** departments of local authorities have powers to investigate complaints about false or misleading descriptions or prices, inaccurate weights and measures, consumer credit and the safety of consumer goods. They will often advise on everyday shopping problems.

2 **Environmental Health** departments deal with health matters such as sub-standard food and drink, and dirty shops and restaurants.

3 **Citizens' Advice Bureaux** offer help with many consumer problems, including shopping complaints.

4 **Trade Associations** often have written codes of practice. A code of practice is not legally binding, but it can be a guide to whether traders have broken their own rules. The trade association can put the case before an independent person who will decide in favour of either the seller or the buyer.

TASK

How have the suppliers of the liquid described in the case study fallen foul of consumer protection legislation?

5 **Utilities watchdogs.** If you have a complaint about gas, water, electricity or telephones, you can call a customer service helpline (the telephone number will be on your bill). In addition, the four utilities each have a regulator who has the power to investigate complaints brought by consumers.

6 **The Consumers' Association** is a well known and powerful consumer group. It produces the monthly consumer magazine *Which?*, and is funded by subscriptions from members who buy the magazine. The Consumers' Association uses its funds to test a wide variety of products, which are then reported in the magazine. It also produces books on consumer-related matters.

MATCH IT!

Can you help Frankie and Cleo to match the following terms and definitions?

'Fit for the purpose'	Trade Association	'Of satisfactory quality'	Consumer Protection Act
'Acceptance'	Trading Standards Department	Weights and Measures Act	Trades Descriptions Act

Bans the supply of unsafe goods
Group set up by commercial organisations to set their own codes and standards
Of goods: free of significant faults
Legal consequence of having kept goods beyond a certain time
Body having powers to investigate complaints about false or misleading descriptions or prices, inaccurate weights and other matters
Law stating that adverts and labelling of goods must be accurate
Of goods: able to serve the purpose which the seller has mentioned in any way to the buyer
Act setting out requirements for the contents of foodstuffs and medicines

5 42 Production and Marketing

Understanding customer needs

The production and marketing of products should be seen as two parts of the same important process.

An organisation's **product** is the good or service it offers to consumers. The goods and services that firms produce must meet consumers' needs. They can only meet these needs if the manufacturer or producer first finds out what consumers want.

Product-led or market-led?

A criticism of many UK firms until the late 1980s and 1990s was that they were **product-led**. People in organisations came up with good ideas or carried on with existing ideas without finding out what the consumer wanted. Not surprisingly, many products flopped.

Today, far more companies are **market-led**. They first identify what consumers want, then set about trying to create the kind of benefits that will satisfy them.

Frankie says:

'We first find out what benefits our customers want and need. We then set out to make sure that we provide these benefits.'

Above: a market-led approach

CASE STUDY

Tesco develops the consumer-led pea

Millions of leftover peas are being thrown into the bin by exasperated parents every day, according to Tesco.

Youngsters are eating fewer and fewer peas as a staple part of their diet, research carried out by Tesco has shown.

The company set its food scientists to work with a brief to reinvent the pea in an easier-to-handle form. As a result, the elusive petit pois is to be relaunched as the grand pois, a larger and firmer variety that will taste just as sweet but be easier to scoop up with a fork.

Tesco's research found that many children want finger food, like burgers, chips and pizza or food they can eat using just a fork:

chasing peas around a plate is too much hassle. The fast-food culture doesn't help because it encourages young people to eat using only their hands. Correct use of a knife and fork is seen by young children as uncool and is in danger of falling out of fashion. Many adults have given up trying to encourage children to eat peas. The research showed that children often prefer cauliflower and broccoli because they find them easier to pick up.

Tesco's move is the latest in a string of initiatives in which food retailers have attempted to make vegetables more attractive to youngsters – e.g. carrots in chocolate sauce and pizza-flavoured sweetcorn.

The importance of meeting consumer needs

When you produce a product or service, you must make sure that it genuinely meets consumer needs. You are unlikely to be successful if you try to persuade customers to buy a product that fails to meet their needs. You 'may fool some of the people some of the time, but you can't fool all of the people all of the time'.

The message is clear: produce a real product that provides the benefits that consumers require, and then promote those benefits in a genuine way.

TASK

1   Do you think that Tesco is right to be seeking to create peas that are more in line with consumer demand?

2   What other examples of products that have been altered to appeal more to customers can you think of?

Above: a product-led approach

Ron Rust says:
'I produce the goods that I'm good at producing, and supply them to the market. I expect customers to buy them because of the knowledge I have about the scrap metal business.'

The production function

Production is the process of using resources to add value to a product or a service and so meet the customers' needs. In a manufacturing company, this will involve buying in raw materials and transforming them through a series of processes and stages into finished products, which can then be distributed to the market.

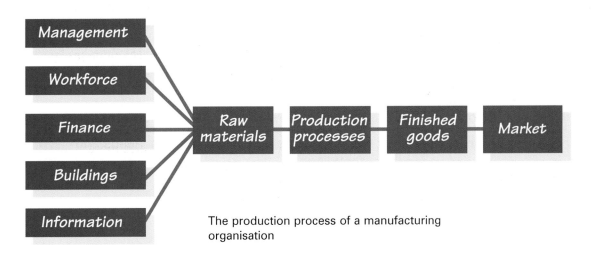

The production process of a manufacturing organisation

In service industries, the production function involves organising resources efficiently to offer the final consumer the best value and quality. The finished good may be a haircut, a night's entertainment, an enjoyable visit to a leisure centre or theme park, or any of a thousand and one other services on offer today.

TASK

1 Which is better for the consumer, the product-led approach, or the market-led approach?

2 How have M&S replaced a product-led focus with a market-led one?

CASE STUDY

Regaining touch with the customer

Marks & Spencer was always thought to be the British company that was best associated with providing quality products for their customers. It therefore came as a shock to the business world when the company's profits tumbled in 1998 and 1999. It quickly became apparent that they had lost touch with what many of their customers were looking for.

Marks & Spencer had been quite happy to produce traditional products that appealed to what they thought of as being their typical customer – 'the middle-aged woman in the twinset with fairly conservative buying patterns'. However, by the millennium this stereotypical customer had largely disappeared. Today, people in their 40s, 50s and 60s are far more adventurous in their tastes than ever before – it was Marks & Spencer that had not moved with the times.

The company has responded by developing a far more market-led approach. At a shop floor level staff are now trained to talk to customers and find out exactly what they want. The company have also hired a team of top fashion designers to produce a range of clothes for them – designers who have a keen eye for what the customer wants. Detailed market research has been carried out to develop a customer focus. Rather than focusing on the 'middle-aged woman in the twinset' they have realised the importance of developing a much more realistic picture of their customers and a much broader appeal.

MATCH IT!

Can you help Frankie and Cleo to match the following terms and definitions?

Product-led	Product	Market-led

Producing a good or service because you are good at making that product
Providing goods and services which genuinely meet consumers' needs and wants
The good or service offered to consumers

43 The Production Function

What is meant by 'value added'?

One of the most important terms in business is 'value added'. All businesses prosper in direct proportion to their ability to add value to their 'input' materials. The more value they add, especially in comparison with competitors, the better they do.

Value is added at each stage of production. A simple example is the carpenter converting relatively inexpensive materials into furniture. The difference between the cost of the wood and the price of the finished article is the wealth which he or she has created. The illustration below shows the simple stages involved:

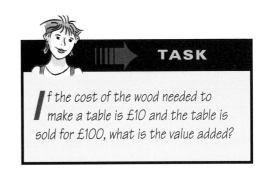

TASK

If the cost of the wood needed to make a table is £10 and the table is sold for £100, what is the value added?

Adding value in making furniture

Forest

Stage 1

Planks

Stage 2

Chairs

Stage 3

At Stage 1 trees are grown in a forest. At Stage 2 they are converted into seasoned wood in a sawmill. At Stage 3 they are converted into finished chairs by a carpenter. At each stage value is added.

◆ Perhaps the forester buys £100,000 worth of small trees from a tree nursery, and they eventually grow into £500,000 worth of trees for sale. The value that is added is £400,000.

◆ The £500,000-worth of trees are seasoned and eventually converted into finished planks by the sawmill. The planks are worth £1 million.

◆ A furniture factory then converts the wood into chairs which are sold in the factory shop for £2 million.

TASK

1   Frankie and Cleo are setting up a biscuit-making business. How can they make sure that they add more value than all their rivals?

2   Think about the way in which a top-quality company works e.g. Cadbury-Schweppes, Unilever or Virgin. Show how this organisation adds value to its products.

We can show value added at each stage of production in the following way:

Stages of production	Input	Output	Value added
Tree nursery	0	£100,000	£100,000
Forestry	£100,000	£500,000	£400,000
Sawmill	£500,000	£1,000,000	£500,000
Furniture factory	£1,000,000	£2,000,000	£1,000,000

You can see that the final value of the chairs is £2,000,000, and that this value has been created to a greater or lesser extent at each stage in the chain of production. We can represent this in another table *(right)*.

Value added and chain of production	
Value added by tree nursery	£100,000
Value added by forestry	£400,000
Value added by sawmill	£500,000
Value added by furniture factory	£1,000,000
Total value added in production	£2,000,000

The importance of adding value

Businesses compete with each other. They are all involved in adding value. However, if your rivals are more successful at adding value than you, then they are more likely to win sales.

Creating consumer benefits

A **benefit** is an advantage gained by a customer from a product or service. Consumers will buy those products that give them the greatest benefit.

Adding value therefore should involve creating and adding benefits which consumers want and then producing them at an acceptable price and in an environmentally acceptable way.

A well-run business will produce the maximum benefits at the lowest possible cost. The way in which value is added is the key to business success.

'The only benefit that I know that customers want is low prices. In business, low price is all that counts. Give customers the lowest price and they will be happy!'

The chain of production

For every product there is a **chain of production**. Some products go through many stages in the chain of production, while for others the chain is a lot shorter.

In tea production, for example, we can identify a number of clear stages, as shown in the diagram on the right.

At each stage, value is added. The stages need to be very closely linked together to avoid wastage and ensure that maximum value is added.

Other products may have a much shorter chain of production – for example, when fresh vegetables are grown by a farmer and sold over the garden gate.

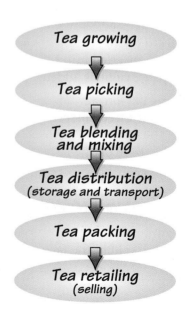

Chain of production for tea

Links in the chain of production

A crucial part of adding value successfully is the way in which each stage in the chain is linked. If we look at how a business operates we can see that it requires:

◆ Excellent links with suppliers

◆ Excellent internal links between activities inside the company

◆ Excellent links with customers

Links with suppliers

A business needs to make sure that it gets inputs of the right quality, at the right price, and at the right time. For example, a company like Marks & Spencer will insist that the goods it buys from outside sources meet very high standards. If suppliers cannot meet these standards, it will no longer buy from them.

Internal links

Within a company there need to be very good links between each activity involved in a production process.

Links with customers

Finally, there needs to be very close liaison with customers, so that the goods can be transferred smoothly to the next stage in the chain with no hold-ups or complications. There also needs to be a very good relationship with firms later on in the chain of production, so that everybody involved works together to create maximum consumer benefits.

Links in the chain of production can be illustrated as a **value chain**, as in the illustration on the right.

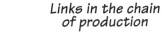

Links in the chain of production

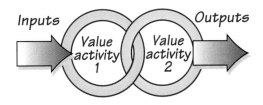

A value chain

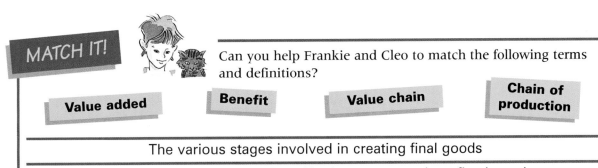

MATCH IT!

Can you help Frankie and Cleo to match the following terms and definitions?

Value added	Benefit	Value chain	Chain of production

The various stages involved in creating final goods

The links involved in creating effective consumer benefits through production

Advantages gained by consumers from goods and services

The increase in the benefits of a good which are created at each stage of production

44 Methods of Production

Maximising efficiency

All businesses need to organise their methods of production efficiently so as to meet the needs of their customers.

The key to doing this successfully is through **operations** or **production**. Operations or production are the processes and methods an organisation uses to produce something or to make a service.

Although operations vary between one organisation (and between products) and another there are a lot of similarities in the management of operations – e.g. between the operations of getting a smooth flow of cars into and out of a supermarket car park and getting a smooth flow of biscuits down a biscuit factory's production line. Both of these sets of operations involve careful planning and layout of the steps in the process, and making adjustments to avoid bottlenecks.

'Are the operations involved in producing services different from the operations involved in manufacturing goods?'

Sequenced operations: booking a haircut, having it washed, cut and dried

The methods of production

Most businesses use one of the following methods of production:

◆ Project production

◆ Job production

◆ Batch production

◆ Line production

◆ Continuous flow production

It is easiest to relate these methods to manufacturing operations, but the same classifications can quite easily be used for services.

1 Project production

A **project** involves bringing together a number of people and resources to complete one product, e.g. building a new hotel or motorway, making a Hollywood movie, developing a new CD-ROM and so on.

When you do a GCSE project, you will look at it as a 'one-off' assignment. You will need to carry out operations in a set order, e.g.:

◆ Choose a project title

◆ Decide how to collect the information

◆ Start collecting information by interviewing and writing letters

◆ Start to assemble and make sense of information

◆ Design front cover for project

◆ Write up introduction, etc.

Project production works in exactly the same way. For example, a project may be to produce a film for a television company. There will be a sequence of steps that need to be followed. The success of the operation depends on:

◆ Planning the tasks

◆ Carrying them out in the right sequence

◆ Making sure that all the steps in the project fit together closely

◆ Ensuring that the steps are carried out successfully

The term we use to describe this is **project management**.

TASK

*I*magine that you are a project manager employed in creating a new pop video.

List six groups of people that you would need to bring together to create the video. Set out a series of steps showing the most important operations that would need to be carried out to create the video. Set these steps out in the form of a flow chart.

2 Job production

Job production is the term we use to describe a situation where an organisation produces one or a small number of items – for example, a designer dress or hand-made suit. Many products produced using this method will be made on the producer's premises and then delivered to the purchaser – or the purchaser may come to pick up the item – e.g. a painted or photograph portrait.

The producer might work on several jobs at the same time for different groups of customers. Firms operating in this way need to make sure that they keep having orders for new jobs to replace the ones that are nearly completed.

3 Batch production

This is where a number of identical or similar items are produced in a set or **batch**. The items need not be for any specific customer but are made at regular intervals in specific quantities.

Batch production involves work being passed from one stage to another. Each stage of production is highly planned.

A simple example would be the production of loaves of bread in a bakery. Every day 200 brown loaves, 100 white loaves, and 500 small buns are produced. First the dough is made for the brown loaves. While this rises, the dough is made for the white loaves. While this is rising, the dough for the brown loaves is kneaded – and so on.

A key feature of batch production is that every now and then you have to stop the production process and reset it for a different product.

Most manufacturing companies work in this way, as do most service organisations. For example, a cinema attendant at a multiplex cinema checks the tickets of a batch of cinema-goers waiting to see *Captain Corelli's Mandolin*; he or she then checks the tickets of a batch going to see *Charlie's Angels* – and so on.

4 Line production

This involves products or services passing down a **line of production**. The production process is a repeating one, with identical products going through the same sequence of operations. Car assembly lines are a classic example of line production. The work comes down the line to the worker, who carries out a set operation. Nowadays humans have been replaced by robots on many production lines. Examples of line production can also be found in fast-food outlets.

Line production produces identical products. The disadvantage of this is that many customers (e.g. car buyers) want their purchase to be made different or distinctive in some way.

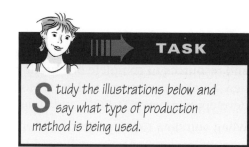

TASK

Study the illustrations below and say what type of production method is being used.

5   Continuous flow production

Continuous flow production takes line production one step further. Today, it is an advantage to be able to mass-produce standard items like Mars bars and cans of beer. Continuous flow involves producing for 24 hours a day, using automatic equipment in a standardised way.

An oil refinery, for example, works on a continuous flow basis, with petrol being refined around the clock. Modern breweries, paper mills and chocolate factories also use the continuous flow method.

In continuous flow, the whole operation is handled by machinery controlled by computers. Human labour does not touch the product. Continuous flow therefore does not apply in the service industries, which depend more on human labour.

TASK

1   Why is Coca-Cola a suitable product for mass production?

2   What other production lines can you think of that are suitable for continuous flow production?

3   Why is it that these products are suitable for continuous flow?

4   What types of products would be unsuitable for continuous flow?

5   Why is accuracy so important in the production of Coca-Cola?

6   How does computer technology help with the continuous flow of Coca-Cola?

CASE STUDY

Coca-Cola manufacture

Cans delivered to a Coca-Cola canning plant are delivered in bulk by lorry. At this stage the cans are not fully formed as the ring pull end has yet to be fitted and each can is shaped like an open cup ready to receive the drink. First, cans will be inspected to check that there are no faults. They are then individually run through a rinser to make sure that they are clean and ready for the filling process.

To form the syrup which lies at the heart of the final drink a liquid sweetener and a concentrated beverage base are combined. Metering of the syrup added to the drink is monitored by computer, improving the accuracy and consistency of syrup manufacturing. Water, which provides the main part of any drink, will be taken from local water supplies, but will first be treated to ensure absolute purity. Carbon dioxide is also delivered to the canning plant, where it is stored and then piped into the manufacturing process.

The syrup needs to be combined in exactly the right proportions with water and carbonated (to create the fizzy effect). A key process in the manufacture of Coca-Cola is that of getting the proportions right to ensure the right combination of ingredients. The latest techniques in computer technology are used to guarantee this mixing process is accurate.

It is now the time to combine the packaging preparation with the finished drink product. This process is managed by a rapid filling process, with hundreds of cans passing along an automated production line each minute to be filled with Coca-Cola. The filler injects a precise amount of product. As the cans run along the production line they are seamed to include the ring pull end and create the finished can. Can ends are inspected for smooth, uniform application without gaps or leaks. As the cans run off the line they have an individual code stamped on them so that every one can be traced back to the point and time of production. The date code ensures product freshness.

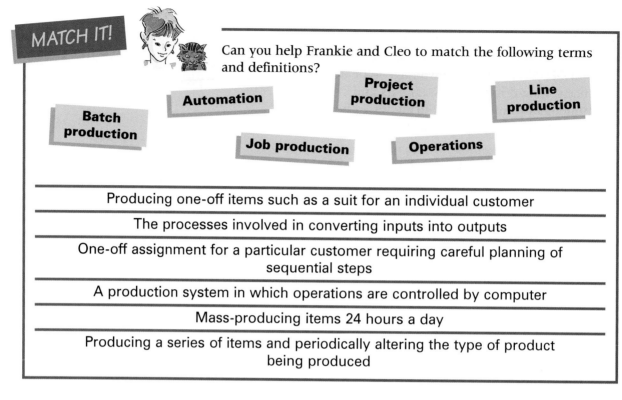

MATCH IT!

Can you help Frankie and Cleo to match the following terms and definitions?

Batch production　Automation　Project production　Line production　Job production　Operations

Producing one-off items such as a suit for an individual customer
The processes involved in converting inputs into outputs
One-off assignment for a particular customer requiring careful planning of sequential steps
A production system in which operations are controlled by computer
Mass-producing items 24 hours a day
Producing a series of items and periodically altering the type of product being produced

45 The Importance of Quality

What is quality?

Today the emphasis in most modern industrialised countries is on quality. This emphasis has largely been copied from Japanese businesses such as Toyota, Nissan and Sony, which have built quality into their production methods for many years. It was the success of the Japanese in car manufacture and consumer electronics that made American and European industry realise that they would be left behind if they did not build quality into their production methods.

Quality is defined as consistently providing what customers want. In other words, it means seeing things from a customer's point of view. The involves the whole organisation in understanding the central importance of customers to its success and even to its survival.

This is why, for example, when Marks & Spencer seemed to have lost touch with its customers at the turn of the millennium it developed a new quality initiative based on making sure that everyone in the organisation was trained to understand the importance of meeting the needs of the customer.

'Does quality mean providing the most upmarket products or the ones which meet customer requirements?'

A consumer's perception of the quality of a product or service is perhaps the most important factor in determining its success. Consumers will be prepared to pay for the best quality. Value is thus added by creating those quality standards required by consumers.

In UK business there have been three stages involved in moving towards quality: quality control, quality assurance and Total Quality Management (TQM).

1   Quality control
    Quality control is an old idea. It involves inspectors checking finished goods and detecting and cutting out components or final products which do not meet the required standard. It can involve considerable waste as sub-standard products have to be scrapped.

2   Quality assurance
    This is less wasteful than quality control. **Quality assurance** occurs both during and after production, and seeks to stop faults happening in the first place. Quality assurance aims to make sure that products are produced to pre-set standards. It is the responsibility of the workforce rather than of inspectors.

3   Total Quality Management (TQM)
    This is the most complete form of operations management. It encourages everyone in the workplace to think about quality in everything they do. Every employee sets out to satisfy customers, placing them at the heart of the production process.

Three stages in the move towards quality

Just-in-time production
'Just-in-time' production is another key element in the Japanese manufacturing success story, which has now been successfully copied in leading industrial countries.

LATEST NEWS

The importance of the internal customer

The idea of the 'internal customer' is an important part of TQM. Everyone in an organisation does work which helps other people in their own organisation (internal customers). The best way to meet the needs of the external customer is to also meet the needs of all internal customers.

For an organisation to be truly effective, every single part of it, each department, each activity, and each person and each level, must work properly together, because every person and every activity affects and in turn is affected by the others. This is the recognition that everyone is a customer within the organisation and consumers goods or services provided by other initial suppliers, and everyone, is also an internal supplier of good and services for other internal customers.

CASE STUDY

'Kaizen' at Jaguar

Jaguar is one of the most famous British products which we associate with high-performance cars at the top end of the price range. Today Jaguar is part of the American Ford motor company.

During the 1980s Ford lost a lot of its market share to Japanese car producers. It therefore decided to employ a group of advisers who had worked for Toyota to help it to develop new quality initiatives. These new initiatives were introduced to Jaguar manufacturing plant in the UK at the turn of the millennium and have proved to be highly successful. 'Kaizen', or 'continuous improvement', lies at the heart of the Japanese quality idea of TQM.

'Kaizen' requires the total involvement of all employees. It is based on the idea that in order for people to want to create quality they must feel part of the team. Jaguar believe that:

- All employees have a valuable contribution to make as individuals, and this contribution is most effective when they work together as a team.

- Working in teams, members contribute ideas to improve working processes to serve the internal and external customer.

Team members discuss ways of improving quality on a regular basis. The purpose is to provide the best possible cars to satisfy customers.

The idea is very simple: to cut costs by reducing the amount of goods and materials a firm holds in stock. It involves producing and delivering finished goods 'just in time' to be sold, partly finished goods 'just in time' to be assembled into finished goods, parts 'just in time' to go into partly finished goods, and materials 'just in time' to be made into parts.

For just in time to work successfully it is important to have **flexible workers** who are trained to do a range of tasks. Another aspect of 'just in time' is the control of quality. Products and parts also need to be produced right first time. This is where worker participation and suggestions are important. Workers need to be encouraged to come up with good ideas and to help pinpoint any production problems. An environment of **participation** (joining in and making suggestions) must be created to get all employees to contribute to problem solving in team meetings.

When it works well, it is a very efficient method. However, in a mass production plant it requires a constant delivery of new parts, and employees therefore need to be highly skilled and flexible. Other disadvantages are:

TASK

1   What do you understand by the term 'quality'?

2   Why is 'quality' so important to business?

3   How is 'Kaizen' at Jaguar likely to encourage quality production?

◆ If you run out of stock the plant cannot function.

◆ The workforce must be flexible or the system becomes difficult to run.

◆ The organisation is at the mercy of the quality standards of its suppliers.

The Kanban system

The **Kanban** system is an essential part of just-in-time manufacture in a company. 'Kanban' is the Japanese word for a card or signal. The Kanban is used in a factory to show that a customer (the next stage in a production process) requires more parts, components or materials. In its simplest form, it is a card used by a customer stage to instruct its supplier stage to send materials. Kanbans can also take other forms. In some Japanese companies they are solid plastic markers or even coloured ping-pong balls, the different colours representing different parts.

'This is the Kanban. When I hold it up, you pass me some more biscuits.'

Just in case and just in time

Japanese manufacturing systems have transformed the way in which production takes place in the twenty-first century.

In the past, European and American companies always carried extra stocks and supplies 'just in case' they were needed to produce goods. An old-fashioned car factory in the UK would have had lots of spare parts, tools and equipment blocking up the factory floor. 'Just in time' involves getting rid of all the clutter – having just enough equipment and stock to meet current orders. If orders build up then more components and parts are called up just before they are needed.

A factory operating using just in time is much tidier, much more organised and usually much more efficient than the old-fashioned just-in-case factory. In the just-in-time factory the production line operatives are trained to think and to work together to solve problems (in just in case operatives simply follow instructions).

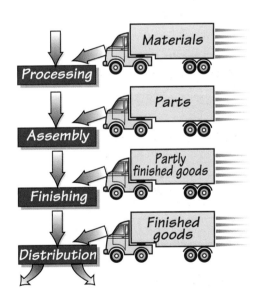

Just-in-time production

Mass production

The twentieth century saw the development of **mass production** of many products, from Coca-Cola to contraceptives, Mars bars to medicines.

Mass production has been made possible through the development of mass markets. Firms are able to produce standard products using standard parts, built on standard machines.

The greater the volume of mass production, the easier it is for a firm to cut costs. Mass production can also lead to better quality, particularly where computers and robots are involved in the process.

Today, many manufacturers have gone beyond mass production to **mass customisation.**

This is where goods are produced in very large quantities, but can be customised (produced specially for a particular customer). In Japan, in particular, machinery can be programmed to make a specific product such as a car for a specific customer almost as quickly as it makes a standard car.

This is possible because of the sophistication and flexibility of computer-driven equipment. Mass customisation makes it possible to produce individual items at almost the same cost as mass-produced ones.

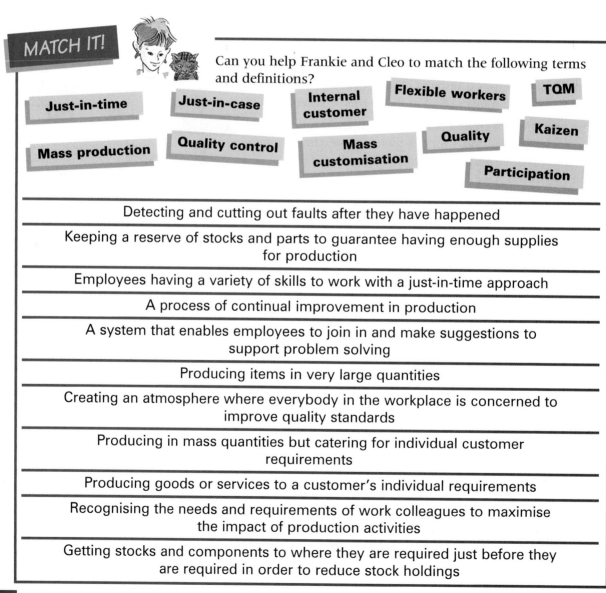

MATCH IT!

Can you help Frankie and Cleo to match the following terms and definitions?

Just-in-time   Just-in-case   Internal customer   Flexible workers   TQM

Mass production   Quality control   Mass customisation   Quality   Kaizen   Participation

Detecting and cutting out faults after they have happened

Keeping a reserve of stocks and parts to guarantee having enough supplies for production

Employees having a variety of skills to work with a just-in-time approach

A process of continual improvement in production

A system that enables employees to join in and make suggestions to support problem solving

Producing items in very large quantities

Creating an atmosphere where everybody in the workplace is concerned to improve quality standards

Producing in mass quantities but catering for individual customer requirements

Producing goods or services to a customer's individual requirements

Recognising the needs and requirements of work colleagues to maximise the impact of production activities

Getting stocks and components to where they are required just before they are required in order to reduce stock holdings

46 The Importance of Stock Control

Types of stock

Most businesses hold stock because demand for their product varies and because suppliers are often late – so stocks act as a protection against unpredictable events.

There are a number of different types of stocks that a business will hold:

◆ **Raw materials and components** – stocks that the business has bought from outside suppliers, and which are waiting to be processed

◆ **Work-in-progress** – work that is currently in the process of being carried out but is not yet complete

◆ **Finished goods** – items that are waiting to be sold. The firm may hold onto them to await demand to pick up, or because it delivers the goods in batches.

◆ **Consumables** (e.g. stationery)

◆ **Plant and machinery spares**

'It is always best to have surplus stocks because you can not be sure when you are going to need them. Too much stock is better than too little.'

Do you agree with Ron?

Stock control

The chart below illustrates the problems caused by having the 'wrong' stock levels.

Problem of low stocks	Problem of high stocks
1 It may be difficult to meet customer demand	1 There is an increased risk of stock becoming obsolete (out of date).
2 It can lead to a loss of business - the customer buys from someone else	2 The risk of stock waste is increased
3 It can lead to a loss of goodwill as customers get fed up with waiting	3 The costs of storage are high
4 Ordering needs to be frequent and handling costs are higher	4 Stocks can tie up a company's working capital

Buffer stocks (reserves) can be built up to prevent against running out of stock due to changes in demand. A minimum stock level will be set, below which it will be hoped that stocks will not fall, though this may depend upon the **lead time** between placing an order and receiving the goods.

Stock rotation

Most firms will seek to **rotate** their stock. This usually means getting rid of the oldest stock first so that stocks do not go off or out of date. The principle behind stock rotation is First In First Out (FIFO). For example, in a supermarket it is common practice to put new stock at the back of a shelf so that the old stock gets used up first.

Stock control charts

A stock control chart sets out details of stocks as a line graph. There are a number of parts to the graph:

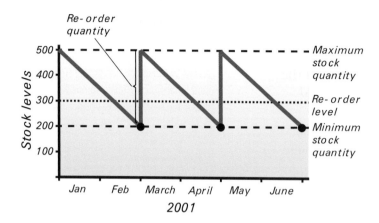

Control of stocks of tomato soup at a local supermarket

1 Stock level

This shows how stock levels have changed over the time period in the graph. As stock is used up this level will fall. When new stock arrives this line will pick up again. In the graph the stock of tomato soup at a local supermarket starts at 500 cans at the beginning of January 2001 and falls to 200 by the end of February, when it is built up to 500 again – falling to 200 by the end of April, etc.

2 Maximum stock

The most stock that the firm is willing or able to hold. In this case this is 500 cans of tomato soup.

3 Re-order level

This is the point at which a firm will re-order stock because levels have fallen far enough that it is felt necessary to prepare to rebuild the stock. In the example the re-order level is 300 tins of tomato soup.

4 Minimum stock

This is the stock below which it is felt to be unsafe for the firm to operate. Below this level the firm may not be able to meet customer orders, or may have to shut down some of its operations. In the example this is at 200 tins of tomato soup.

5 Re-order quantity

This is the number of new items that will be bought in when stocks fall to the re-order level. In the example, this is 300 tins of soup.

CASE STUDY

Stock control at the Choc Shop

The Choc Shop sells a variety of different types of chocolate. One of the products it buys in for resale is SuperChoc boxes.

The diagram below shows the Choc Shop's stock control diagram for SuperChoc boxes.

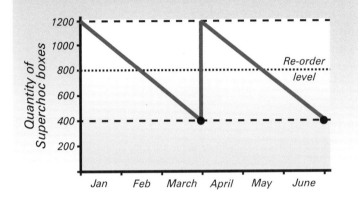

Stock control at the Choc Shop

TASK

1 What is the re-order level? At what times is this re-order level reached in the six months shown in the diagram?

2 What is the re-order quantity?

3 What are the minimum and the maximum stock levels?

4 How will setting out a stock control diagram help the Choc Shop to keep good control over its stock?

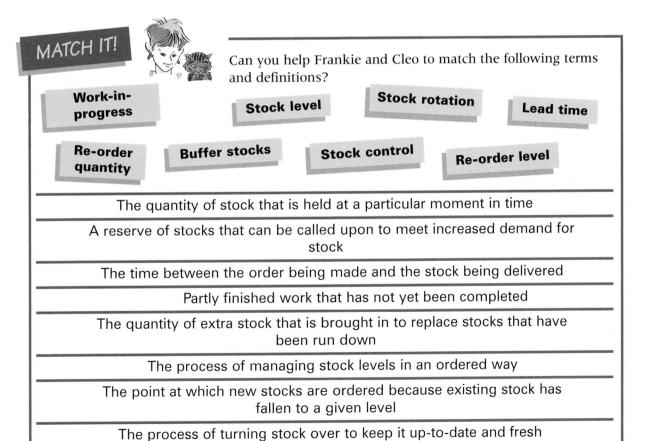

MATCH IT!

Can you help Frankie and Cleo to match the following terms and definitions?

Work-in-progress   Stock level   Stock rotation   Lead time

Re-order quantity   Buffer stocks   Stock control   Re-order level

The quantity of stock that is held at a particular moment in time

A reserve of stocks that can be called upon to meet increased demand for stock

The time between the order being made and the stock being delivered

Partly finished work that has not yet been completed

The quantity of extra stock that is brought in to replace stocks that have been run down

The process of managing stock levels in an ordered way

The point at which new stocks are ordered because existing stock has fallen to a given level

The process of turning stock over to keep it up-to-date and fresh

47 New Products

The changing marketplace

In today's marketplace it is essential for companies to create new products to meet the needs of consumers, whose wants and needs are changing all the time.

We can illustrate this by looking at the activities of British pharmaceutical companies (i.e. firms that make medicines and drugs).

When you produce a new drug or medicine you only have the patent for that medicine for a limited amount of time. A **patent** is a government licence to an inventor assigning her or him the sole right to make, use and sell the invention for a given period of time.

Once the patent runs out, anyone can copy the product. When pharmaceutical companies carry out research into a new product, such as a cure for AIDS, a cure for the common cold or a cure for cancer, these research projects will take decades and may never yield results. And a rival may come up with another discovery any time. The research and development of new products is a highly risky business.

'One of the problems today is that people constantly want new products. Investment in new products reduces profit margins for people like me!'

'What new products can you think of that have made a big impact recently?'

Testing the market

A lot of planning needs to take place before a good or service is launched. Firms need to study the market and the way it is changing. **Research and development (R & D)** is a very important business process that relies on market research information.

TASK

Can you think of any medicines or drugs that have recently come onto the British market which have taken a long time to research and develop?

Below: Planning a new product

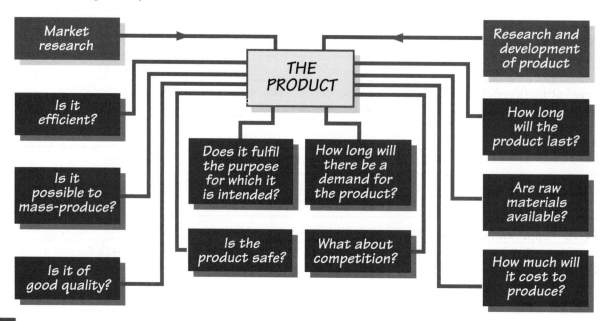

Setting up a production line can be very expensive. You need to make sure that you have got everything right before you start. Careful work in the early stages will help to ensure that the launch will be successful and that consumers get the benefits they want.

Research and development

Once a firm is sure there is a suitable market for a product, then research and development must find out the best way of meeting demand. The product must be attractively designed to appeal to consumers and to meet their needs. The researchers need to answer many questions, including those shown on the illustration on the previous page.

An organisation may be reluctant to change an earlier design, particularly if it is distinctive or helps to give a good image of the organisation, such as the radiator grille of a BMW, or the lettering on a Coca-Cola can. Designers need also to think about the way the product will be handled. For example, consumer goods need to be easy to use, especially products for the elderly; children's toys must be safe and able to stand up to wear and tear, and so on.

TASK

*R*ead the Case Study below, then answer the following questions.

1   When was the ballpoint pen patented?

2   List two advantages the Biro has over the fountain pen.

3   What mistake did Laszlo Biro make?

4   How did Marcel Bich take the ballpoint pen forward?

The Bic Cristal – the largest-selling pen in the world

CASE STUDY

The ballpoint pen

The ballpoint pen was patented in 1938 by a Hungarian journalist, Laszlo Biro. Unlike a fountain pen, it used a runny, jelly-like ink.

A British entrepreneur, Henry Martin, spotted the potential of the invention. He bought the patents to sell the product in the UK and many other countries. Martin realised that the great strength of the ballpoint pen was that it was unaffected by changes in air pressure, so it could be used by aeroplane pilots and navigators for making calculations. The Biro Pen Manufacturing Company was set up near Reading and 30,000 pens were produced for use by the RAF during the war.

In 1945, the Biro pen cost the equivalent of £2.75 – approximately the weekly wage for a secretary. Within four years it was outselling the fountain pen.

The launch in the USA in October 1945 was equally spectacular. The New York department store Gimbells sold 10,000 Biros at $12.50 each. Unfortunately, Laszlo Biro failed to register his invention and it was soon copied.

In France, another entrepreneur, Baron Marcel Bich, took the ballpoint even further. He created the Bic Cristal, a simple plastic ballpoint which is now one of the best-known trademarks in the world. In 1957 Bich's Société Bic SA took over the Biro company. As time went on, more and more products were sold under the Bic name and fewer and fewer under the Biro brand.

Today 15 million Bic ballpoints are sold every day, making the Bic Cristal the best-selling pen in the world. When Marcel Bich died in 1994 he was the fifth richest man in France.

Today designers often allow for **planned obsolescence**, so that the product will need replacing after a time. For example, many cars are only built to last a limited number of years, and today we even have 'throw-away' cameras.

Testing and trialling

Once a design has been developed, the researchers will either build a **prototype** that can be tested or trial the service on offer. Many prototypes will be tried and then discarded, while others may be altered and improved *(see right)*.

It is essential to look at the profits that a new product is likely to generate. This involves estimating how many it is likely to sell in a given time period, and how much costs will be during this period.

Sometimes the product or prototypes are **test-marketed** with a representative sample of consumers. This provides useful feedback and reduces the risk of a failure when the product is officially launched.

The **launch** is the final stage. This involves presenting the product to the market for the first time.

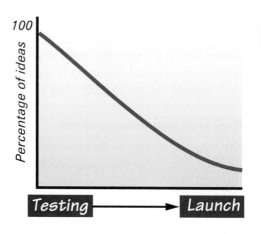

Many ideas will be discarded during the testing process

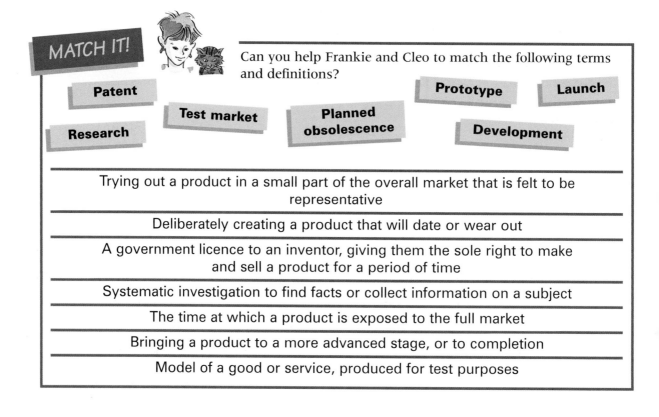

MATCH IT!

Can you help Frankie and Cleo to match the following terms and definitions?

Patent · Test market · Planned obsolescence · Prototype · Launch · Research · Development

Trying out a product in a small part of the overall market that is felt to be representative

Deliberately creating a product that will date or wear out

A government licence to an inventor, giving them the sole right to make and sell a product for a period of time

Systematic investigation to find facts or collect information on a subject

The time at which a product is exposed to the full market

Bringing a product to a more advanced stage, or to completion

Model of a good or service, produced for test purposes

48 Production Technologies

Keeping pace with changing technology

We live in an age of rapid progress in production technology. In the past, firms struggled because they were twenty years out of date. Today firms can struggle because they are a year or even a few months out of date.

The new economy

The millennium saw a major change in business in the USA, Europe and many other advanced economies. During the 1990s the American economy had grown at a faster rate than ever before, driven by companies like Microsoft (the computing and information technology giant). Information technology was driving down costs of production – not just for a few firms but for most businesses. Key elements of this revolution were the development of new Internet and telephone-based developments (e.g. Internet and phone banking, insurance, booking of holidays). Businesses are now able to buy supplies over the Internet from around the globe rather than having to depend on face-to-face interactions with suppliers. The term **new economy** has been coined to describe a new set of relationships between businesses and customers based on information technology and the Internet.

Companies like Marks & Spencer have now developed their own websites, and this new way of dealing with customers (termed e-commerce) has helped to vastly reduce the costs of running a business.

'Advanced technology is a waste of time. It is always expensive to buy and rarely lowers costs. Firms are more likely to go out of business than gain an advantage from using new technology!'

Do you agree with Ron?

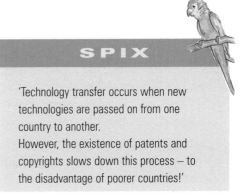

SPIX

'Technology transfer occurs when new technologies are passed on from one country to another.
However, the existence of patents and copyrights slows down this process – to the disadvantage of poorer countries!'

Advantage through technology

If we look at the development of production technology in many fields, we can see that progress often takes the form of a major breakthrough, followed by a series of less spectacular improvements. This pattern will then be repeated at regular intervals, as shown below:

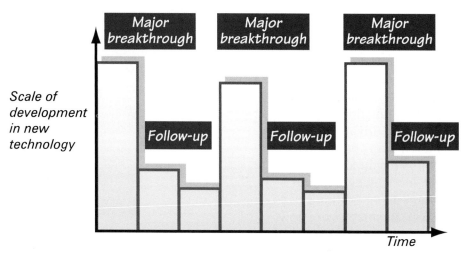

The pattern of progress in production technology

Many businesses expect to replace their plant and equipment every few years, and allow for this in their forward plans. The best time to buy new technology is immediately after a 'giant step', rather than just before one. The firm that buys plant and equipment just as it is becoming out of date may be left with old-fashioned plant while rivals are leaping forward.

LATEST NEWS

M & S is tops for online buying

A report published by the research company Vanson Bourne and commissioned by the Computer Sciences Corporation in December 2000 showed that J Sainsbury needed to improve their website provision while Marks & Spencer came top of the list. The report stated that the process of making a purchase from the Sainsbury's site is too cumbersome.

The report was designed to report the experience of first-time users. The sites were rated on characteristics such as accessibility, the ease of making a purchase, the delivery service and the returns policy.

The report stated that it was difficult to navigate the Sainsbury's site because it kept freezing and losing the contents of an order. However, Sainsbury's delivery was good.

In contrast, the Marks & Spencer site was described as generally very good with particular praise being given to its clear and simple design, goods delivery and returns policy.

The report also revealed that around a third of British consumers with Internet access have made a purchase online, and over 70% of shoppers rated the experience as good.

Examples of recent technologies

Computer-aided design (CAD)

Computer-aided design has improved the reliability and speed with which complex structures such as aeroplanes, cars and bridges can be designed. These computer applications are also of value in a wide range of industries that involve an important design component, such as clothes and fashion design. The system works like an electronic drawing board, allowing complex two- and three-dimensional shapes to be modelled quickly and accurately on-screen, stored conveniently and copied when needed. CAD drawings can be altered without needing to start again – and can be stored on computer and changed easily to meet new customer specifications.

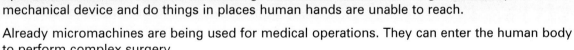

CASE STUDY

Micromachines

Micromachines are the newest success story in production technology. The Japanese have developed this project, which has involved massive sponsorship from the Japanese government.

Micromachines are tiny intelligent machines powered by the latest laser technology. They can be programmed to perform a number of key operations. Their greatest use is when they are put to work inside other machines.

For example, until recently, when you wanted to clean a nuclear reactor you had to close it down and strip it out. A micromachine is able to climb through the pipes of the reactor and carry out cleaning operations while the reactor is still running. Micromachines are able to get inside any mechanical device and do things in places human hands are unable to reach.

Already micromachines are being used for medical operations. They can enter the human body to perform complex surgery.

Machine tool developments

As well as CAD, developments have also taken place in machine tools. Many are now controlled numerically **(numerical control – NC)** or controlled numerically by a computer **(computer numerical control – CNC).**

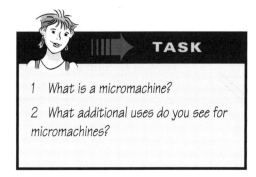

TASK

1   What is a micromachine?

2   What additional uses do you see for micromachines?

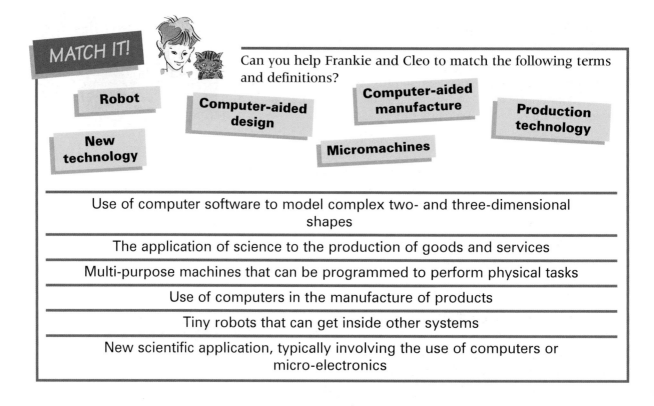

CAD/CAM (computer-aided design/computer-aided manufacturing) refers to the use of data from a CAD system to drive machines as part of the manufacturing process. A more recent development in this process is **computer-integrated manufacturing (CIM).** Here, the CAD system not only designs the product but also orders materials, drives CNC machine tools and has its own control system which provides data for purchasing, accounts, sales and other functions.

Robots

Robots are multi-purpose machines that can be programmed and re-programmed to perform physical tasks. An industrial robot in a car factory may be programmed to paint and then re-programmed to weld pieces together or to assemble parts.

Robots in industry now use vision and touch recognition systems. These make it possible for them to recognise objects by their shape and size, and to fit items like car windscreens by measuring up and centring the screen.

MATCH IT!

Can you help Frankie and Cleo to match the following terms and definitions?

Robot | Computer-aided design | Computer-aided manufacture | Production technology

New technology | Micromachines

Use of computer software to model complex two- and three-dimensional shapes

The application of science to the production of goods and services

Multi-purpose machines that can be programmed to perform physical tasks

Use of computers in the manufacture of products

Tiny robots that can get inside other systems

New scientific application, typically involving the use of computers or micro-electronics

49 Specialisation

The growth of specialisation

Very early on in the history of the human race, people discovered that, rather than everyone meeting their own needs for food, clothing and shelter, it made sense for some tasks to be performed by specialists.

Some people could specialise in hunting, others could go and gather berries, while others built shelters or made weapons.

In this country until fairly recent times you would have found a blacksmith, baker, butcher and many other specialist trades in every village.

As the economy became more developed, individuals were able to sell their specialist skills in return for money or a salary or wage. They could then use their income to buy items or services produced by other specialists. If we concentrate on what we do best, we can all gain from this process of specialisation.

The division of labour

The **division of labour** is one example of specialisation that is very important in modern economies. Division of labour involves breaking down a production process into a number of clearly defined specialist tasks. The reason for doing this is that the total output of a group can be increased, if, instead of each person trying to do everything, each one specialises in a particular skill or activity.

The most famous early example of division of labour was in a pin factory, described by Adam Smith in his book *The Wealth of Nations* (see Case Study opposite). Smith noted that where operations were divided and where workers specialised, output was far greater than it would otherwise have been.

Other forms of specialisation

◆ Specialisation of **equipment** – e.g. specialist machines performing specialist tasks and processes

◆ Specialisation of **plant** – e.g. different factories specialising in making different things

◆ Specialisation by **firms** – different firms concentrating on different lines, e.g. Shell on oil, gas and chemical products, Virgin on air travel, contraceptives, soft drinks, credit cards, rail travel, etc.

TASK

Frankie and Cleo are making a quick list of 10 specialist jobs involved in bringing tinned fruit to people in supermarkets. Help them to list the specialists.

'There are the lorry drivers that bring the products to the supermarket... And of course the people that pick the fruit in the first place... Who else is there?'

◆ Specialisation by **region** and by **nation.** Many regions still specialise in producing certain products. For example, Scotland is famous for whisky; parts of France, Germany, Spain, Australia and South Africa focus on wine; coastal areas of Portugal on fishing, Nigeria on oil production, Uganda on sisal, etc.

Comparative advantage

Specialisation is often explained in terms of the theory of **comparative advantage.** This states that resources are used in the best (most cost-effective) way when they are used in areas where they are most efficient.

For example, a golf professional may be good not only at her sport but also at being a solicitor. However, she will be well advised to concentrate on her golf, because golf is her **best line**, i.e. the area in which she is most talented.

As a solicitor, she may be able to earn £40 an hour. But as a golf professional, she can earn £50 an hour. She can then pay a solicitor to handle her legal business and pay the solicitor out of her golf earnings. For every hour that she hires a web page designer at £40 an hour, she is making a £10 profit from concentrating on what she does best.

The same rule applies to any form of specialisation. For example, it makes sense for countries to use their land to grow crops which earn them the most revenue, rather than things which they can import cheaply.

The advantages of specialisation

The advantages of specialisation are:

1 Resources can be concentrated where they are most productive.

2 Factors of production become more efficient if they are concentrated on a set task. For example, the more skilled the worker becomes at a particular task, the more they produce.

3 Specialisation allows a larger output to be produced at a lower unit cost.

4 Concentrations of specialists can lead to sharing of skills and experience. This is why footballers will improve their game far quicker when they play for a top Premier League club rather than playing in a low-level league!

CASE STUDY

Pin-making in Adam Smith's day

'...To take an example from a very trifling manufacture... the trade of pinmaker. An inexperienced workman, unfamiliar with this business, could scarce, with his utmost effort make one pin in an entire day. But in the way in which this business is now organised, not only is the whole work in a particular trade, but it is divided into a number of individual branches, each of which can be considered as a particular trade of its own. One man draws out the wire, another straightens it, a third cuts it, a fourth points it, a fifth grinds it at the top in preparation for the head; to make the head requires two or three distinct operations; to put it on is a peculiar business; to whiten the pins is another; it is even a trade by itself to put them into the paper; and the important business of making a pin is, in this manner, divided into about eighteen distinct operations, which in some manufactories, are all undertaken by separate people.'

From *The Wealth of Nations* by Adam Smith, 1776

TASK

1   How was it possible to produce pins using lots of specialists?

2   What examples of division of labour can you think of today?

The disadvantages of specialisation

There are also several drawbacks to specialisation:

1 Specialisation can lead to monotony. Repeating a task over and over again can be boring and demotivating.

2 Where tasks are closely linked, delays or hold-ups in one area can disrupt the whole production process.

3 Specialisation may lead to workers becoming little more than machine operators. This can lead to a loss of skills over time.

4 Narrow specialism makes it difficult for factors of production to respond to change. An employee who has done the same task for ten years will have problems if suddenly required to do a different task.

5 **Multiskilling** is often more useful than specialism. Someone with many skills may be in a position to look at the parts of an organisation and develop good ideas for change and improvement.

'Specialisation is the way forward! There's no point in people being able to do a lot of different tasks and trades. They should specialise in what they do best, just like in Adam Smith's day! Good old Adam!'

Do you agree with Ron?

Multiskilling in the modern workplace

In the modern workplace employees are expected to carry out a range of tasks rather than simply repeat the same operation over and over. Modern employees are given the training for multiskilling – and are encouraged to make decisions rather than to be told what to do.

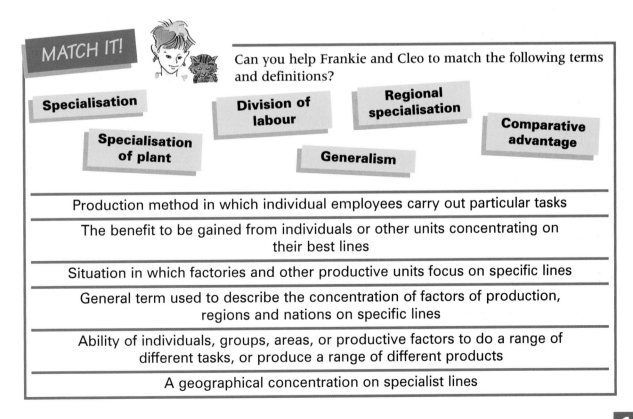

MATCH IT!

Can you help Frankie and Cleo to match the following terms and definitions?

Specialisation

Division of labour

Regional specialisation

Comparative advantage

Specialisation of plant

Generalism

Production method in which individual employees carry out particular tasks

The benefit to be gained from individuals or other units concentrating on their best lines

Situation in which factories and other productive units focus on specific lines

General term used to describe the concentration of factors of production, regions and nations on specific lines

Ability of individuals, groups, areas, or productive factors to do a range of different tasks, or produce a range of different products

A geographical concentration on specialist lines

6 | 50 Accounting Processes

Monitoring performance

Whether you are at college, school or at work, you will naturally be concerned about how you are getting on. The likelihood is that you will measure your success with information or feedback.

For example, your exam results will tell you how you have performed. If you are at work, a positive word from a supervisor may be very helpful.

In the same way, business organisations need **financial information** in order to measure their performance. This information may help them to judge how successful they are in achieving their objectives.

'I now understand all about marketing and production, but I have not yet come across many figures. How do I know if my business is doing well?'

Why do we need accountants?

Different businesses have different objectives, but every business owner needs to keep an eye on the firm's finances.

The job of an **accountant** is to answer crucial questions about the financial health of the organisation, such as:

'Excuse me. You know your business is doing well when you can afford to buy a large flash car with alloy wheels and have an impressive home like mine.'

◆ How are we doing?

◆ What sort of return are we going to get?

◆ Can we meet our debts?

◆ Should we expand?

◆ What about taxation?

◆ Where does our future lie?

As well as helping managers to manage the business more efficiently, information supplied by accountants can help:

◆ Shareholders to assess the value of the money they invest in a business

◆ Suppliers to assess whether a company can pay its debts

◆ Providers of finance to know whether repayments are possible

◆ Employees to know how a company is performing

◆ The Inland Revenue to make an accurate tax assessment

These individuals or organisations are known as **stakeholders,** as they have a 'stake' or interest in the way the organisation is run. Some of the stakeholders

Stakeholders in a business

are within the organisation – such as managers and employees. Others are from outside the organisation. For example, providers of finance and suppliers will want the business to do well so that they can be paid for their products and financial services.

Accounting data prepared by accountants can therefore be used by a variety of different groups of people to help them make decisions.

The accounting process

An **accounting system** consists of methods and procedures that are used to keep track of financial activities, and to summarise information for managers.

Accounting therefore acts as an information system, so that groups of individuals can understand how well or badly the organisation is performing.

The three steps in the accounting process are:

1 **Recording financial activities.** This means having an organised record of financial activities. For example, whenever a transaction takes place, even if it involves credit, it has to be recorded.

2 **Classifying information.** A jumbled list of business transactions would be too large, diverse and unwieldy for decision-makers. It needs to be classified into a series of groups and categories.

3 **Summarising data.** For accounting information to be useful, it must be summarised.

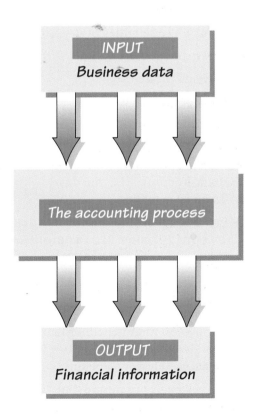

The accounting process

TASK

*R*ead the Case Study, then answer the following questions:

1   What is a chartered accountant?

2   Why are accountants required to take difficult examinations?

3   How can accountants help business organisations?

Management and financial accounting

The process of accounting falls into two broad areas:

1   Management accounting

2   Financial accounting

Management accounting is concerned with giving managers information from within the business so that they can plan, control and make decisions. Management accounting may help a business to:

◆ Control its costs

◆ Monitor its operations and make day-to-day decisions

◆ Control the activities of departments

◆ Create budgets for various parts of the business

◆ Forecast future events

◆ Manage its activities efficiently

Financial accounting is primarily about recording transactions and extracting information from them. It involves:

◆ **Book-keeping** – i.e. the day-to-day recording of financial activities

◆ Preparation of **final accounts** such as the **trading account** (Chapter 54), the **profit and loss account** (Chapter 55) and the **balance sheet** (Chapter 56)

Final accounts are **summary statements** prepared at the end of a certain period. By studying these, shareholders know how the directors or managers have performed on their behalf. From the final accounts, **ratios** (see Chapter 58) can be extracted. These show fairly accurately how a business is performing.

A financial accountant must also ensure that a business's accounts provide a **true and fair** view of its activities and that they comply with the provisions of the Companies Acts.

8The Institute of Chartered Accountants in England and Wales

The Institute of Chartered Accountants in England and Wales has over 119,000 members. Qualifying as a chartered accountant requires individuals to take difficult examinations, while also completing a training contract. 'Chartered' accountants use the letters ACA or FCA, and work in all areas of business. Chartered accountants are necessary for all types of business organisations. Some specialise in tax returns, while others may focus upon business accounts or helping business people make financial decisions. They have a wide breadth of experience that can help business organisations to meet the needs of all of their stakeholders, while at the same time helping them to achieve their business goals.

'Who needs paperwork? I'm so good at running my business that paperwork is not that important.'

TASK

R on Rust has been told by the Inland Revenue that he must keep a better set of financial records. He looks in the drawers in his desk and finds lots of different types of information (see below). Which of this information might the tax inspectors want to see?

MATCH IT!

Can you help Frankie and Cleo to match the following terms and definitions?

Shareholders	Accounting process	Inland Revenue	Financial accounting
Management accounting	Stakeholders	Classifying information	Book-keeping

Government department to which taxes are paid

Methods and procedures to keep track of financial activities

People or organisations who own a financial stake in a business

The grouping of business transactions

The recording of financial activities

The providing of information for managers so that they can make decisions

The recording and summarising of financial information for management

People with a 'stake' or interest in the successful running of an organisation

51 Sources of Finance

Understanding cashflow

Within all organisations, money comes in and flows out. This is called the organisation's cashflow.

From time to time, business managers may pose questions such as:

◆ *'Can we afford to buy x?'*

◆ *'Are we going to be able to pay that bill?'*

◆ *'Wouldn't it be nice if we could develop y?'*

To answer such questions, they will often have to carry out some form of financial planning – and often to seek additional finance from outside the company. The key issues are:

◆ What is the finance for?

◆ How long will it be needed?

◆ Is it affordable, i.e. can the firm keep up with the repayments?

'I suppose it is a bit like organising your personal finances. I often used to run out of cash when I did not plan ahead. In fact, I remember receiving my first student loan when I was at university. I received it as a lump sum instead of by terms. I thought that I was rich, but then, after a few weeks and a few calculations, I worked out that I would not be able to survive the year if I did not plan exactly what I had to spend on a week-by-week basis.'

Common methods of finance

Sources of finance fall into two main categories. **Short-term** finance is designed to be paid back quickly, while **long-term** loans may be paid back over many years. Below are some of the different types of finance available:

1 Trade credit

This is a useful source of finance provided by suppliers. With trade credit, a business can use the goods or service provided by suppliers before they are paid for.

The **credit period** is simply the period between receiving a good or service and paying for it. Although no charge or rate of interest is attached to trade credit, cash discounts may be lost if payments are not made within the agreed time.

2 Overdraft

An overdraft is probably the most frequently used solution to cashflow problems. The bank sets an agreed limit on the customer's bank account, beyond which they will not draw. This is called an **overdraft facility**. The amount the customer borrows is called an **overdraft**.

Below: Short-term and long-term sources of finance

SHORT TERM
Trade credit
Overdraft
Factoring
Leasing and hire purchase
Loans

LONG TERM
Mortgages
Profit retention
Government grants
Venture capital
Equity

A special charge is made for setting up the overdraft facility, and interest is calculated on the level of the overdraft on a daily basis. Businesses often depend on customers paying bills promptly. Given that customers like Ron Rust may delay payment as long as possible, an overdraft can be a useful form of short-term business finance.

3   Factoring

Trade debts mean that money can often be tied up for as much as six months. For a business requiring cash quickly this can be a real problem. A **factoring** company may offer immediate payment of part of the amount owed to a business – normally around 80% – with the balance being paid when the debt is settled. This provides an immediate way for a business to improve its cashflow. In return, the factoring company will charge a fee, which includes interest and administration charges.

4   Leasing and hire purchase

There are many different ways for customers to receive goods and make payments over time.

Goods on **hire purchase** remain the property of the finance company until the customer has made all the payments. Other **credit purchasing** schemes enable the goods to belong to the customer from the first payment.

With **leasing,** the lessee uses the asset while making regular payments to the lessor, who owns it. An **operating lease** is for a small amount, and a **capital** or **finance lease** is for a large item over an extended period.

TASK

*R*on sometimes has problems getting suppliers to provide him with the goods he wants. Everybody in the scrap metal trade knows how he does business. Because of this, he gets no cash discounts, smaller trade discounts that other customers, and suppliers tend to charge him higher-than-average prices anyway!

Name two advantages which Ron would receive if he made his business practices more efficient.

'I never pay bills until the last possible moment. In fact I am notorious for it. If people want my business, they have to accept my rules. After all, I am their customer. I want the goods now and I will pay them in three months.'

CASE STUDY

Ark Geophysics Ltd

When Ark Geophysics, a software company in the geophysics industry, was first established, its founders Richard Gleave, Kitty Hall and Andy McGrandle had to ask themselves a number of questions:

- What equipment would they need?

- Would there be enough work to generate the income they required?

- Could they meet a repayment schedule?

- How would they be affected by their competitors?

- What were their financial needs?

They began by carefully researching their **revenue expenditure**, i.e. the day-to-day running expenses of their business, such as rent, office expenses, electricity, telephone, etc. They also looked at their **capital expenditure** on large or fixed items such as computers and office equipment. They tried to work out what they would have to pay out and when their income would come in. Next they drew up projections of cashflow in a **business plan**. This outlined how their proposals would work. It was shown to several banks. Soon they were being offered help in the form of loans and leasing facilities.

Today Ark Geophysics Ltd is a successful company with a reputation throughout the industry.

TASK

1 Explain the difference between revenue expenditure and capital expenditure.

2 Why was it necessary for Richard, Kitty and Andy to draw up a business plan?

5 Loans

Most businesses need to borrow in order to trade successfully. The charge for borrowing is called **interest**. The key to calculating interest is usually the risk involved. For example, a longer-term loan or a loan to a business with no track record may carry higher rates of interest.

Banks may offer a variety of types of loans. These include business starter loans, franchise finance and the Small Firms Guarantee Scheme, offered by banks and supported by the DTI.

Large public limited companies may issue **debentures**. A debenture is an acknowledgement of a debt made to a company for a fixed rate of interest which specifies the terms of repayment at the end of a period. Debentures are bought and sold on the Stock Exchange.

6 Mortgages

A mortgage is a loan secured on a property. The size of the mortgage payment will depend upon factors such as the amount of the loan, the age of the property and the income of the borrowers.

7 Profit retention

Probably the most important source of finance for many businesses is profit which is ploughed back from one year to the next. Although managers must first satisfy shareholders, they will also be conscious of the need to put some of their profits back into the business.

8 Government grants

Important sources of finance for many businesses are **soft loans** and **subsidies** from the EU or from central or local government. Soft loans are loans at lower rates of interest. Subsidies help to reduce the price of products and encourage producers to produce more.

9 Venture capital

A **venture capital company** may help small firms to get established by providing investment capital in return for a shareholding in the business. 3i is the largest venture capital company of this type.

10 Equity

This means finance provided by the owners of the business. How easily equity can be raised will depend upon the type of business. For example, a sole trader may rely on personal sources, and extra sums of money may be difficult to raise. Sole traders may even take in partners to inject some capital into the business.

A private limited company has certain restrictions on the rights of members to transfer shares, and there are limits on their ability to extend share ownership.

A fully listed public limited company may have many different opportunities to raise fresh capital from the financial markets. However, the problem with issuing more shares is that it dilutes the control of the original shareholders.

CASE STUDY

The problem of late payment

A recent survey by a firm of accountants revealed that:

- 76% of firms wait 3 months or more for their bills to be paid
- Only 14% receive their money within the contractual limit of 30 days
- 8 out of 10 manufacturers have to wait up to 3 months for payment
- 96% of businesses say it adds to their problems, and 30% say it seriously affects their business!

Most businesses feel they are in a difficult situation. They want payment for the goods and services they provide, but they do not want to have to take their customers to court in order to get it.

 TASK

1 Why do organisations delay paying their bills?

2 How might delayed payment affect the cashflow of the supplier and the customer?

3 What would you consider to be a reasonable credit period?

4 Work in a small group to discuss what action could be taken to stop late payment.

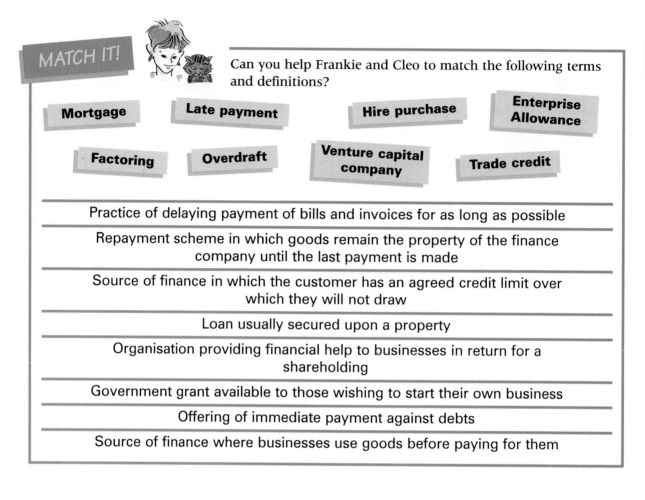

MATCH IT!

Can you help Frankie and Cleo to match the following terms and definitions?

Mortgage	Late payment	Hire purchase	Enterprise Allowance

Factoring	Overdraft	Venture capital company	Trade credit

Practice of delaying payment of bills and invoices for as long as possible

Repayment scheme in which goods remain the property of the finance company until the last payment is made

Source of finance in which the customer has an agreed credit limit over which they will not draw

Loan usually secured upon a property

Organisation providing financial help to businesses in return for a shareholding

Government grant available to those wishing to start their own business

Offering of immediate payment against debts

Source of finance where businesses use goods before paying for them

52 Liquidity and Cashflow

Organising our own finances

When it comes to looking after our own finances, we all know that we have to take some form of responsibility.

If we spend too much, we will soon run out of money. We will then either have to go without things that we need, or borrow in order to get them. But if we borrow, can we pay back the lender?

One way to predict if we are able to meet our financial commitments as and when they arise is to draw up a **cash** or **cashflow budget** showing our income and expenditure. **Cashflow forecasts** are statements which enable us to analyse our proposed expenditure and income over a period of time.

'I try wherever possible to plan my finances by working out what spending I will have to commit myself to in future months and then matching this to my forecast income. If I didn't do this, I would not be able to meet all of my financial commitments.'

'Forecasting sounds good in theory, particularly if you are working for somebody else, but for businesses like mine it just doesn't work. I have good months and bad months and I just cannot predict when the good months are likely to occur.'

'Do you set money aside for the bad months, so that you can pay your bills?'

Just imagine the problems that face Ron Rust when he can't pay his bills *(above and right)*. You'll notice he doesn't say how he copes with not having enough money to pay his bills. Perhaps he visits his bank manager to arrange an overdraft or sells off his debts to a factoring company. Whatever solution he chooses, it can only be a short-term answer. One day there will be a crisis and he won't be able to raise enough cash to sort out his problems.

'But how do you cope if you can't pay the bills?!'

Financial forecasting and liquidity

Looking into the future will help all organisations to plan their activities so that things can happen in the way they want.

The process of financial forward planning using techniques such as cashflow forecasting is known as **budgeting.** We all budget to a greater or lesser extent. Our short-term budget may relate to how we are going to get through the next week and do all of the things we want to do. In the longer term we may be thinking about Christmas, buying a car or splashing out on a special birthday present for someone. In exactly the same way, businesses try to look into the future.

The **cashflow forecast** is a financial plan or budget which tries to anticipate money coming into and going out of the business over a future period.

CASE STUDY

Planning your cashflow

Imagine that you have left school and started work. You earn £80 a week and out of this you have certain fixed weekly expenses *(below)*.

Expenditure	£
Rent to parents	20
Daily fares	5
Lunches	10
Weekends	12
Records, magazines, etc.	10
TOTAL	57

On 2nd of January you receive your wages of £80. You owe your father £40 from December. There are some clothes that you want to buy costing £15 in a sale that ends on 6th January. A deposit of £30 for a holiday must be paid during the second week. This week you are taking three friends to a cinema which will cost you £9 and you have to pay a dry-cleaning bill of £2. There are four weeks in January, and in the third week you will economise and not buy any records and magazines.

Week	1	2	3	4
Income	80	80	80	80
Expenditure				
Rent	20	20	20	20
Fares	5	5	5	5
Lunch	10	10	10	10
Weekends	12	12	12	12
Records, magazines, etc.	10	10	-	10
Clothes	15	-	-	-
Cinema	9	-	-	-
Dry cleaning	2	-	-	-
Holiday	-	30	-	-
TOTAL	83	87	47	57
NET	(3)	(7)	33	23
Loan from mother	(3) B	(7) B	(10) R	-
Loan from father	-	-	(23) R	(17) R
TOTAL	-	-	-	6

B = Borrowing   R = Repayment

A cashflow forecast will enable you to see if you can afford to do all of these things and predict how soon you can pay back the loan from your father.

Look carefully at the cashflow forecast on the left and analyse all of the different expenditures.

The cashflow forecast indicates that you need to borrow from your mother in Week 1 and 2, but you can pay her back in Week 3, and that you can finish paying your father back in the last week of the month.

Cashflow has, therefore, provided the planning necessary to cope with the timing of your various financial commitments – and the same principle applies in business.

TASK

1 Using a similar format to the one above, produce a cashflow forecast of your income and expenditure for the next month.

2 What sort of benefits would you gain if you regularly used this sort of technique for monitoring your finances?

Profit and cash

Whereas **profit** is a surplus from trading activities, **cash** is money a business can use to pay its debts. It is thus a **liquid asset** which enables an organisation to buy the goods and services it needs in order to add value to them, to trade and make profits.

However, a business can trade and appear to be profitable, but at the same time not have enough money flowing in to pay its bills. All businesses must therefore ensure that cash coming in is enough to cover cash going out.

By budgeting, a firm can forecast the flows into and out of its bank account, so that surpluses or deficits can be highlighted. By doing this, any necessary action such as arranging an overdraft facility can be taken beforehand.

SPIX

'The problem is that businesses are so concerned about profit, profit and more profit that they forget about the environment! What about *my* future?'

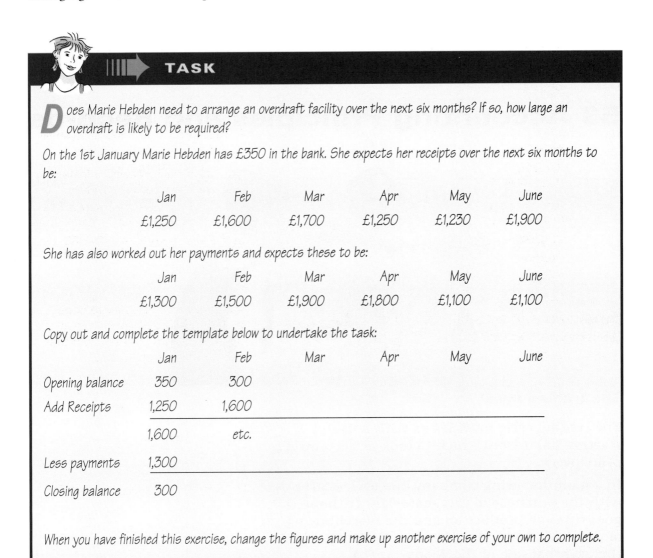

TASK

*D*oes Marie Hebden need to arrange an overdraft facility over the next six months? If so, how large an overdraft is likely to be required?

On the 1st January Marie Hebden has £350 in the bank. She expects her receipts over the next six months to be:

Jan	Feb	Mar	Apr	May	June
£1,250	£1,600	£1,700	£1,250	£1,230	£1,900

She has also worked out her payments and expects these to be:

Jan	Feb	Mar	Apr	May	June
£1,300	£1,500	£1,900	£1,800	£1,100	£1,100

Copy out and complete the template below to undertake the task:

	Jan	Feb	Mar	Apr	May	June
Opening balance	350	300				
Add Receipts	1,250	1,600				
	1,600	etc.				
Less payments	1,300					
Closing balance	300					

When you have finished this exercise, change the figures and make up another exercise of your own to complete.

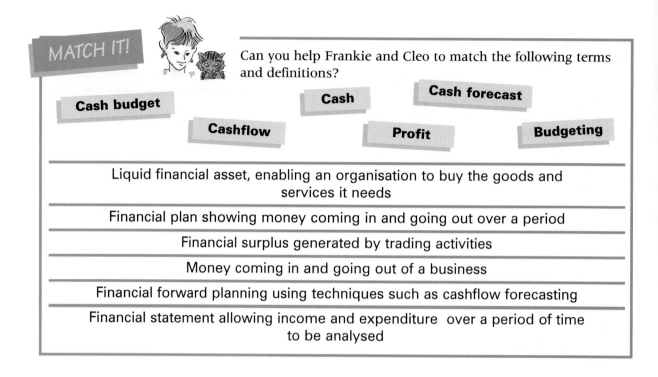

Can you help Frankie and Cleo to match the following terms and definitions?

Cash budget   **Cash**   **Cash forecast**

Cashflow   **Profit**   **Budgeting**

Liquid financial asset, enabling an organisation to buy the goods and services it needs
Financial plan showing money coming in and going out over a period
Financial surplus generated by trading activities
Money coming in and going out of a business
Financial forward planning using techniques such as cashflow forecasting
Financial statement allowing income and expenditure over a period of time to be analysed

53 Accounting Principles and Records

'I am beginning to understand why I need to look after my finances. What I do not understand is how I go about doing this.'

'Ah, now I can tell you all about this. You need to set up a book-keeping system.'

The trading cycle

The trading cycle provides us with a useful starting point from which to look at accounting principles.

In a manufacturing company, the cycle starts with the purchase of raw materials. It then goes through production and the warehousing of finished goods ready for sale, finishing with the eventual sale of the goods.

The diagram on the right shows what the trading cycle might be like for a manufacturer of food products.

Of course, not all organisations manufacture products. Some provide services. The trading cycle for a service organisation will be very similar (see diagram below right), except that the business may be purchasing goods which are then offered for resale, or providing a service such as gardening. When payments are made, further stock can be purchased.

The trading cycle provides a useful and easy way of thinking about how businesses operate and trade. The ultimate purpose is to meet customer requirements. But at the same time, organisations have to meet their business objectives – for example, making a profit. That is why organisations need to keep records of all the trading activities that take place. By keeping records of their activities, they can measure their performance, improve their overall financial control and take action when problems arise.

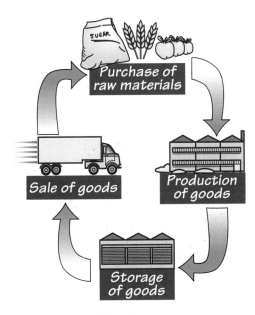

The trading cycle for a food manufacturing business

A basic accounting system

A useful definition of accounting is: *'the art of preparing accounting reports from book-keeping records in accordance with acknowledged methods and conventions.'*

Let us look more closely at this definition:

◆ **Book-keeping records.** In the past, records of account were kept in books or ledgers. These records were continually updated as transactions took place. Today most businesses – except of course Ron Rust's – record their transactions on computer.

◆ **Preparing accounting reports.** In order to be understood and analysed, entries from the book-keeping records have to be presented in a clear way.

This is done by preparing **trading** and **profit and loss accounts** and **balance sheets** based on information collected via the book-keeping system.

◆ **Acknowledged methods and conventions.** There are certain set ways of recording accounts which have grown up over a period of time. Records need to be set out according to these conventions.

Imagine the confusion if everybody presented information in a different way. It would be nearly impossible to make comparisons between one business and the next.

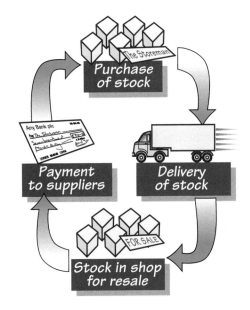

The trading cycle for a retailing organisation

Frankie and Cleo visit their bank manager

Frankie's bank manager has been providing her with advice about how to run her business. She says:

- *Keep all of your records up to date. Write them up promptly and regularly.*

- *Get professional advice if you are in any doubt about your records.*

- *Remember that the Inland Revenue and Customs & Excise will be interested in your records.*

- *Accurate and up-to-date records will help you to manage your business, as well as saving money with your accountant.*

The accounting process

There are a number of stages involved in putting together a basic accounting system:

1 Preparing, keeping and using documents

2 Transferring information from documents to records in books or on computer

3 Setting out a **trial balance** (a list of balances for all accounts)

4 Producing financial statements known as **final accounts**

We will look briefly at each of these stages in turn.

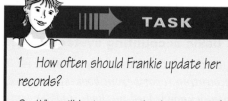

TASK

1 How often should Frankie update her records?

2 Who will be interested in her records? Why will they show such interest?

1   Business documents

When we go into a shop to buy a newspaper or magazine there is little need for documentation. Organisations, however, will usually require a lot more documentation to record each transaction. This is because:

◆ Most organisations buy goods or pay for services on credit (i.e. buy now and pay later). Documents help to record what is happening.

◆ Documents help to create records which meet the legal requirements of the Inland Revenue and Customs & Excise.

◆ Documents provide source data which forms the basis for detailed accounting records.

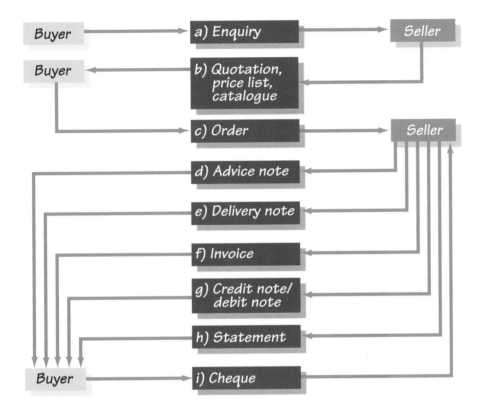

Documents produced during a typical business transaction

The diagram above shows the various documents produced during a typical business transaction:

a **A letter of enquiry** will be sent to suppliers to find out what they can offer

b The buyer will then receive several **quotations, price lists** or **catalogues**.

c The buyer will then send out an **order** specifying their requirements.

d Before sending the goods, the seller may send an **advice note** to say that the goods are being sent and that they will arrive shortly.

e A **delivery note** is often sent with the goods.

f The **invoice** shows the details of the transaction.

g A **credit note** or **debit note** may be used to change amounts appearing on an invoice. The credit note will reduce the invoice price, while the debit note may increase the invoice amount.

h A **statement** is simply a copy of the customer's account in the sales ledger. It is usually sent to remind them to pay their bill.

i A **cheque** is sent by the buyer to the seller to settle the account.

COURSEWORK ACTIVITIES

Talk to somebody who either owns or works for a local business. Find out more about their accounting systems. For example, are records kept manually or by computer? How often are entries made? How is the system used? What information does it generate?

Provide a full description of their accounting procedures and record-keeping processes.

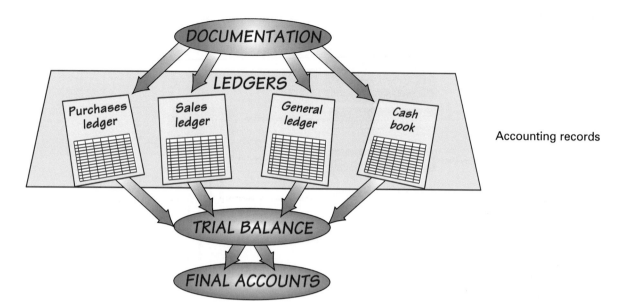

Accounting records

2 Accounting records

Book-keeping records are kept in **ledgers**. These are often referred to as **books of prime entry** as they are the first place where information is recorded. There are four main types of ledger:

a The **purchases** ledger records purchases and includes the accounts of creditors (i.e. people the business owes money to).

b The **sales** ledger records all the sales transactions carried out by the business. It contains the accounts of debtors – customers to whom goods or services have been supplied on credit.

c The **cash book** records all the cash or bank transactions within the business.

d The **general** or **nominal** ledger contains all the other records of the business.

3 Trial balance

In ledgers, transactions are recorded using the **double-entry system.** This means that for each transaction one account is debited and another is credited. This system reflects a process of exchange.

The **trial balance** is a list of all of the accounts from all the ledgers. It should balance, because for every debit entry into one account there should have been a corresponding credit entry into another. This list provides the raw material for accountants to draw up the final accounts.

LATEST NEWS

The Institute of Chartered Accountants for England and Wales objects to the limited amount of the time given to debating the government's Finance Bill. See www.icaew.co.uk for more.

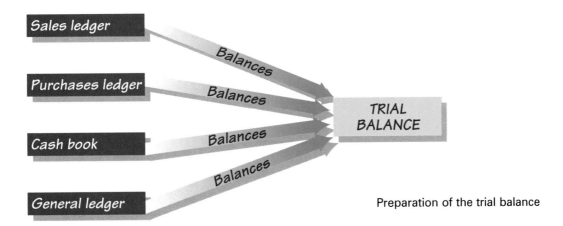

Preparation of the trial balance

4   Final accounts

Final accounts are financial statements drawn up at regular intervals by a business's auditors. They provide valuable information about the business and will help to answer many questions. They include:

◆ The trading account

◆ The profit and loss account

◆ The balance sheet

We will look at each of these in more detail in later chapters.

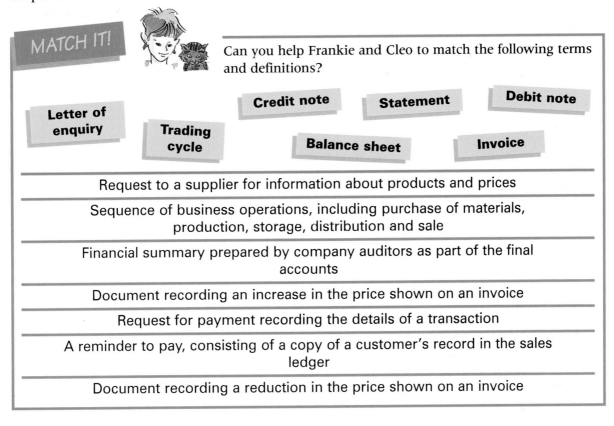

MATCH IT!

Can you help Frankie and Cleo to match the following terms and definitions?

Letter of enquiry   **Trading cycle**   **Credit note**   **Statement**   **Debit note**   **Balance sheet**   **Invoice**

Request to a supplier for information about products and prices

Sequence of business operations, including purchase of materials, production, storage, distribution and sale

Financial summary prepared by company auditors as part of the final accounts

Document recording an increase in the price shown on an invoice

Request for payment recording the details of a transaction

A reminder to pay, consisting of a copy of a customer's record in the sales ledger

Document recording a reduction in the price shown on an invoice

54 The Trading Account

What is the trading account?

In the previous chapter, we saw that accountants use information from the ledger accounts and the trial balance to draw up the organisation's final accounts. Final accounts are the summary financial statements produced at the end of each year's trading.

There are three basic types of financial statements:

◆ The trading account

◆ The profit and loss account

◆ The balance sheet

Calculating profit

In the example of Kim Hughes *(opposite page)*, profit is simply the difference between the overall cost of all of the stock bought and the income generated through sales. Though there are one or two further complications, this simple principle works in the same way in business.

The trading account is rather like a video giving ongoing pictures of an organisation's trading activities. For many businesses, such as that of Kim Hughes, trading involves buying and selling stock. The difference between the value of the stock sold (sales) and the cost of producing those sales – which may be the production costs of manufactured goods for a manufacturing company, or the cost of purchasing supplies for a trading company – is known as the **gross profit**. The trading account simply shows how gross profit is arrived at, i.e.:

Sales – Cost of sales = Gross profit

Remember that gross profit is NOT the final profit. It is simply the profit made from trading or from selling goods, before all of the overheads and expenses have been taken into consideration.

In the Case Study, Kim starts business with no stocks and, at the end of the year, has sold all of the football kits. In practice this is clearly unrealistic. Cost of sales has to take into account the value of stocks. Opening stocks is effectively a purchase, as these goods will be sold in the current trading period. On the other hand, closing stocks must be deducted from purchases as these will be sold next year. The true cost of sales is therefore found by applying the following formula:

Opening stocks + Purchases – Closing stocks

'What sort of information do you want to find from your accounts, Ron?'

'As far as I am concerned, the only purpose of my accounting system is to tell me how much profit I am making.'

CASE STUDY

Working out profit

Kim Hughes has a small part-time business buying and selling sports wear. He works from home and his business has no costs of operation.

He started his business on 1st April when he bought 165 football kits for £23 each. During the year he bought a further 83 kits for £25. All the kits were sold during his first year of operation at an average selling price of £40. By the end of the year he had no kits left in stock and decided to close his business.

Let us imagine that Brenda Cross sells or has a turnover of £15,000-worth of widgets, from the beginning of January to the end of December 2001. At the beginning of January her opening stock was £4,500. During the year her purchases were £9,000 and at the end of the year her closing stock was £6,400. From this basic information we can draw up her trading account as shown below:

The Trading Account of B. Cross for the year ended 31/12/01

	£	£
SALES		15,000
Less Cost of sales		
Opening stock	4,500	
Add Purchases	9,000	
	13,500	
Less Closing stock	6,400	7,100
GROSS PROFIT		£7,900

*R*ead the Case Study on the left then complete the following tasks:

1   Work out Kim's profit for the year. (Make sure that you show all of your calculations)

2   Explain how you worked it out.

3   Kim's profits did not take into account any costs. If he had incurred £5,000 of costs such as transport and warehousing, how might this have affected his profits?

'I know I shouldn't boast, but see if you can work out my gross profit. During 1996 my turnover – or sales – was £87,000. My closing stock was £15,000 and my opening stock was £35,000. During the year I purchased £65,000 of stock.'

'You mean – that's all I've made!???? How can I afford the school fees????'

Returns

If a firm buys goods that are faulty, these goods should be returned to the supplier and recorded as **returns outwards**. For the purpose of the trading account they are deducted from the purchases figure. Similarly, if a firm sells goods that are returned by the customer these are also known as returns, but this time as **returns inwards**. These are then deducted from the sales figure in the trading account.

TASK

Complete the following examples from the information provided:

1 At the end of 2001, A. Tree had a sales figure of £23,200. His opening stock was £3,760 and his closing stock £8,564. During the year he purchased £14,530 of goods. Draw up his trading account and calculate his gross profit.

2 R. Terry runs a manufacturing business. At the end of 2001, her turnover for the year was £34,532. Her opening stock of finished goods was £3,456 and at the end of the year a stock check of finished goods revealed a cost value of £4,553. The production cost of manufacture was £18,767. Draw up her trading account and calculate her gross profit.

(Remember that the cost of manufacture will effectively appear in the same place as purchases.)

The Trading Account of H. Ogden for the year ended 31/12/01

	£	£	£
SALES			20,000
Less Returns inwards			2,000
			18,000
Less Cost of sales			
Opening stock		3,000	
Add Purchases	14,000		
Less Returns outwards	1,000	13,000	
		16,000	
Less Closing stock		3,000	13,000
GROSS PROFIT			£5,000

MATCH IT!

Can you help Frankie and Cleo to match the following terms and definitions?

Returns inwards   Gross profit   Trading account

Cost of sales   Closing stocks   Opening stocks   Returns outwards

Financial statement showing sales revenues for the year, less the cost of those sales
Value of stocks held at the end of the year
Goods returned by customers (and deducted from sales)
Opening stocks plus purchases less closing stocks
Sales revenue less cost of sales
Goods returned to suppliers (and deducted from purchases)
Value of stocks held at the start of the year

55 The Profit and Loss Account

What is net profit?

The profit and loss account is usually drawn up beneath the trading account and covers the same period of trading. The gross profit from the trading account becomes the starting point for the profit and loss account.

> Net profit = Gross profit + Income from other sources – Expenses

Net profit is the final profit of the business. It is the amount of profit made by the owners of the business at the end of the period.

Some organisations receive income from sources other than sales. This can take the form of rent, commission, discounts received, profits on the sale of assets, etc. As these are considered to be extra income, but not from trading, they are added to the gross profit.

In addition, every organisation incurs **expenses** and a range of **overheads,** and these are deducted to show the true net profit of the business.

For example, the expenses might include:

◆ Rent of premises

◆ Depreciation

◆ Gas

◆ Bad debts

◆ Electricity

◆ Interest on loans

◆ Stationery

◆ Advertising costs

◆ Cleaning costs

◆ Sundry expenses

◆ Insurances

◆ Motor expenses

◆ Business rates

◆ Accountancy and legal fees

'I now understand about trading profit. But surely it can't be my final profit – it doesn't take into account my expenses.'

'If I only made £2,000 gross profit, what am I going to have left after I deduct all my expenses…? Ah…how will I afford my season ticket at the Villa?'

Calculating net profit

In the previous chapter we looked at the example of Brenda Cross. Brenda made a gross profit of £7,900. Let us now have a look at her other income and expenses so that we can work out her net profit.

During the same year Brenda received £500 rent from a tenant. She then had to pay a range of expenses. These included electricity (£455), administration expenses (£509), insurance (£45), salaries (£3,400), advertising (£45), and interest (£55). From this information, we can draw up her profit and loss account below:

The Profit and Loss account of B. Cross for the year ended 31/12/01

	£	£
GROSS PROFIT		7,900
Add other income:		
Rent received		500
		8,400
Less Expenses:		
Electricity	455	
Administration expenses	509	
Insurance	45	
Salaries	3,400	
Advertising	45	
Interest paid	55	4,509
NET PROFIT		3,891

Bad debts

Not everybody pays their bills on time. We have seen how long it takes Ron Rust to pay his bills! Some businesses are not just late paying their bills, they are not able to pay their bills at all.

Imagine if you sold £5,000 of goods to a small business on credit and it went bankrupt. Though you might get some of that debt back, the chances are that you would not get all of your money back. If this happens the debt is declared 'bad' and entered in your accounts. **Bad debts** are simply treated as an expense and written off through your profit and loss account.

Depreciation

The things we own do not last for ever. Assets wear out for a number of reasons. For example,

◆ Consumption (they get used up)

◆ Changes in techniques and fashions

◆ Obsolescence (they no longer work)

Most businesses are realistic about the lifespan of their assets. They therefore 'write them off' over many years. This means that their value is gradually reduced to

TASK

Complete the following tasks from the information provided:

1 At the end of 2001, A. Daley has a gross profit of £17,110. During the year he incurred the following expenses: Rates £1,140, rent £861, advertising £432, salaries £4,953, light and heat £639, bad debts £45 and sundry expenses £55. Draw up his profit and loss account and calculate his net profit.

2 Copy out the following trading and profit and loss account and insert the missing figures:

The Trading and Profit and Loss Account of D. Boy for the year ended 31/12/01

	£	£
SALES		XXXX
Less COST OF SALES		
Opening stock	3,100	
Add Purchases	4,215	
	XXXX	
Less Closing stock	1,218	6,097
GROSS PROFIT		12,058
Less Expenses:		
Rent	132	
Rates	85	
Salaries	XXXX	
Advertising	327	
Interest paid	95	
Light and heat	41	2,136
NET PROFIT		£XXXX

nothing over the period of their use. This is called **depreciation.** Depreciation is charged as an expense in the profit and loss account.

There are two main methods of working out how much an asset has depreciated and what to charge to the profit and loss account.

The **straight-line** or **equal instalment method** charges an equal amount of depreciation to each accounting period for the life of an asset. The instalment to be charged to the profit and loss account is calculated by:

$$\frac{\text{Cost of asset} - \text{Residual value}}{\text{Expected useful life of asset}}$$

For example, a machine which is expected to last five years costs £20,000. At the end of its life its residual value will be £5,000.

$$\text{Depreciation charge} = \frac{£20,000 - £5,000}{5 \text{ years}} = £3,000$$

TASK

Ron Rust made a gross profit of only £2,000 last year. His expenses were: administration £1,100, rent £350, salaries £4,400, advertising £600, interest charges £1,200, electricity £660 and sundry expenses £245.

Produce a profit and loss account for Ron and tell him whether or not he has made a net profit.

	Year 1 £	Year 2 £	Year 3 £	Year 4 £	Year 5 £
Cost	20,000	20,000	20,000	20,000	20,000
Accumulated depreciation	3,000	6,000	9,000	12,000	15,000
Net book value	17,000	14,000	11,000	8,000	5,000

The **reducing balance** method calculates the depreciation charge as a fixed percentage of net book value from the previous accounting period. This method, therefore, allocates a higher depreciation charge to the earlier years of the asset's life.

For example, a machine is purchased by a business for £20,000 and its expected useful life is 3 years. The business expects that its residual value will be £4,320 and thus wishes to depreciate it at 40%:

'Should we have a whip round for Ron's season ticket?'

Accumulated depreciation	£	£
Machine at cost	20,000	
Depreciation Year 1	8,000	8,000
Net book value		12,000
Depreciation Year 2	4,800	12,800
Net book value		7,200
Depreciation Year 3	2,880	15,680
Residual value		£4,320

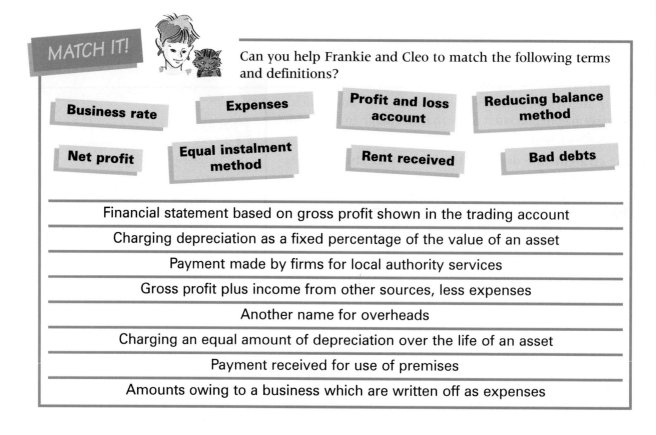

MATCH IT!

Can you help Frankie and Cleo to match the following terms and definitions?

| Business rate | Expenses | Profit and loss account | Reducing balance method |

| Net profit | Equal instalment method | Rent received | Bad debts |

| Financial statement based on gross profit shown in the trading account |
| Charging depreciation as a fixed percentage of the value of an asset |
| Payment made by firms for local authority services |
| Gross profit plus income from other sources, less expenses |
| Another name for overheads |
| Charging an equal amount of depreciation over the life of an asset |
| Payment received for use of premises |
| Amounts owing to a business which are written off as expenses |

56 The Balance Sheet

What is a balance sheet?

In the last two chapters we saw that the trading and profit and loss accounts provide an ongoing picture of how a business is performing in terms of profitability – a bit like a video. A balance sheet is a snapshot of what a business owns and owes on a particular date.

'The balance sheet is an important statement. It shows what you've got, and who you owe things to.'

Why does a balance sheet balance?

A balance sheet is a clear statement of the assets, liabilities and capital of a business at a particular moment in time – normally the end of an accounting period.

The balance sheet balances simply because in book-keeping you record everything twice.

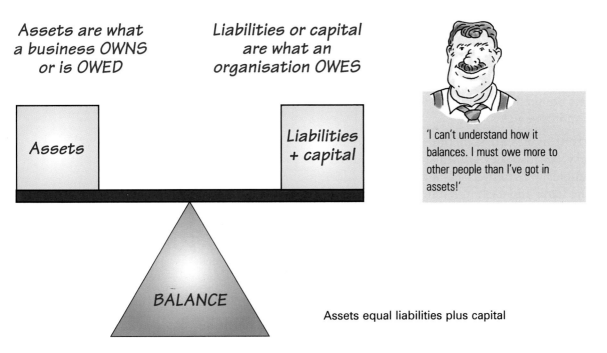

Assets are what a business OWNS or is OWED

Liabilities or capital are what an organisation OWES

'I can't understand how it balances. I must owe more to other people than I've got in assets!'

BALANCE

Assets equal liabilities plus capital

For example, if you lent me £100 we can say that:

1 I owe you £100 (a *liability*)

2 I own £100 (an *asset*)

My balance sheet is therefore:

Asset	Liability
£100	£100

At the end of a period, a business will have a number of **assets** and **liabilities**. Whatever the nature of the individual assets and liabilities, the balance sheet will always balance.

The parts of a balance sheet

Every balance sheet has a heading, which will contain the name of the organisation and the date at which the 'snapshot' is taken.

Assets

The asset side of the balance sheet is normally set out in what is called an **inverse order of liquidity**. This means that items which may be difficult to convert to cash quickly and are therefore **illiquid,** appear at the top of the list of assets. Those which are easy to convert to cash appear further down the list of assets. At the bottom is the most liquid asset of all – **cash.**

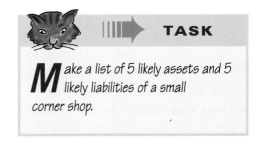

TASK

Make a list of 5 likely assets and 5 likely liabilities of a small corner shop.

Assets can be divided into **fixed** and **current**.

◆ **Fixed assets** tend to have a lifespan of more than one year. They are items that are purchased and generally kept for a long period of time. Examples of fixed assets are premises, fixtures and fittings, machinery and motor vehicles.

◆ **Current assets** are sometimes called 'circulating assets' because they are constantly changing. Examples of current assets are stocks, debtors, money in the bank and cash in hand.

Perhaps the best way of describing how current assets circulate is to refer to the **cash cycle**. A manufacturing business holds **stocks** of finished goods so that it can be ready to satisfy the demands of the market. When a credit transaction takes place, stocks are reduced and the business gains debtors. These debtors have bought goods on credit and therefore owe the business money. After a reasonable credit period, payment will be expected. Once payment is made by debtors, the business will be able to pay for further stocks. 'Cash' or 'bank' changes to 'stock', then to 'debtors', back to 'cash' or 'bank', and then to 'stock' again.

Liabilities

Liabilities can be divided into **current** and **long-term**.

◆ **Current liabilities** are debts which a business needs to repay within a short period of time (normally a year).

Current liabilities may include trade creditors, who are the suppliers of goods on credit for the business. They may also include the bank (for an overdraft) or any unpaid taxes or short-term loans.

◆ **Long-term liabilities** are not due for payment until some time in the future, normally longer than one year. Examples might be a bank loan or a mortgage on a business property.

Capital

Capital is provided by the owner of the business and is therefore treated as being something owed to the owner of the business. The balance shows an updated record of this amount.

During a year's trading the owner's capital may be increased by flows of **profits** and decreased by **drawings** (money or assets taken out of the business for

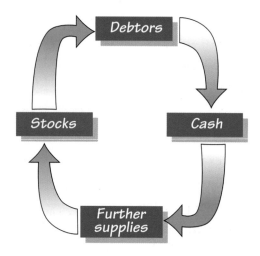

The cash cycle

the owner's personal use). After these have been taken into consideration, a new capital figure is calculated at the end of an accounting period.

Let us now finish the final accounts of Brenda Cross by completing her balance sheet:

The Balance Sheet of B. Cross as at 31/12/01

	£	£			£
Fixed assets				**Capital**	15,935
Property	25,000			*Add* Net profit	3,891
Motor vehicles	3,000	28,000			19,826
Current assets				*Less* Drawings	5,510
Closing stock	6,400				14,316
Debtors	2,300			**Long-term liabilities**	
Bank	325	9,025		Mortgage	20,000
				Current liabilities	
				Creditors	2,709
		£37,025			£37,025

Meanwhile we cannot ignore the plight of Ron Rust. Earlier in the chapter, Ron thought that he probably owed people more than he owned. Let's have a quick look at his balance sheet. Can you advise Ron upon the strengths (if any) and weaknesses of his financial position as shown by his balance sheet?

The Balance Sheet of Ron Rust as at 31/12/01

	£	£			£
Fixed assets				**Capital**	25,000
Property	30,000			*Less* Net loss	6,555
Fixtures and fittings	1,000				18,445
Motor vehicles	10,000	41,000		*Less* Drawings	10,000
Current assets					8,445
Closing stock	15,000			**Long-term liabilities**	
Debtors	2,500	17,500		Mortgage	40,000
				Current liabilities	
				Bank overdraft	10,055
		£58,500			£58,500

TASK

Philip Brown is in a dilemma and has asked you for help. He understands how to work out his profit and has calculated that he has made £2,000 net profit during 2001. But he needs to draw up his balance sheet – and that's where he's asked for your help.

1 Briefly explain to Philip the importance of drawing up a balance sheet and how a balance sheet is organised.

2 Draw up his balance sheet as at 31/12/01 from the following information: land and buildings £8,150, motor vehicles £2,000, machinery £6,000, closing stock £850, debtors £400, bank £20, creditors £1,200, bank loan £6,000, capital £10,000 and drawings £1,780.

3 Philip is worried he may not be able to pay his debts. What figures from the balance sheet indicate that he has cause for concern?

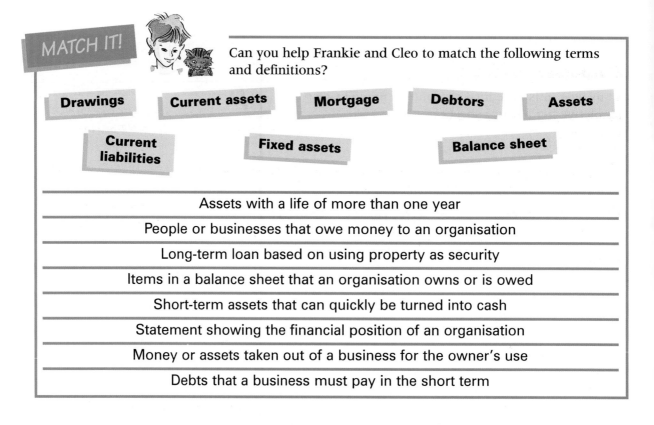

MATCH IT!

Can you help Frankie and Cleo to match the following terms and definitions?

Drawings   Current assets   Mortgage   Debtors   Assets

Current liabilities   Fixed assets   Balance sheet

Assets with a life of more than one year
People or businesses that owe money to an organisation
Long-term loan based on using property as security
Items in a balance sheet that an organisation owns or is owed
Short-term assets that can quickly be turned into cash
Statement showing the financial position of an organisation
Money or assets taken out of a business for the owner's use
Debts that a business must pay in the short term

57 Company Balance Sheets

Meeting legal requirements

Companies must comply with the Companies Act and the Companies Registration Office. This means that information in their annual report and accounts must be presented in a special way. Company accounts therefore differ slightly from the accounts of a sole trader.

Remember that:

◆ The company has a legal identity which is separate from that of its owners

◆ The owners of a company are known as **shareholders** and have certain rights and responsibilities

◆ Shareholders have limited liability

◆ Management is delegated to a board of directors who may not be shareholders (*see Case Study on opposite page*)

◆ Corporation tax must be paid on profits made

'When we set up our business, I am not sure whether we are going to be sole traders. If we become a company, will our accounts be very different?'

'I wouldn't set up as a company. Too much paperwork!'

Corporate governance

The owners of companies are known as **shareholders.** In many instances, particularly in the case of larger companies, shareholders will not be directly involved in running the business which they part-own. This task is undertaken by professional managers, some of whom may even be shareholders themselves.

This process whereby managers take responsibility for the running of the company on behalf of shareholders is known as **corporate governance.**

One of the main aims of the many different Companies Acts is to ensure that managers carry out their responsibilities properly. For example, the shareholders will want to know 'who holds the reins' in the business in which they have invested, and what decisions the managers are making.

Horizontal and vertical balance sheets

In the previous chapters, the balance sheet of the sole trader was presented 'horizontally', with assets on one side of the equation and liabilities and capital on the other. Most businesses today, and particularly companies, will want to present their information in a balance sheet which is displayed vertically *(see Case Study on page 218).*

The main reason for this is that the vertical balance sheet shows **working capital.** As we will soon see, this is a useful indicator of how easily a business can pay its short-term debts.

TASK

1 What responsibilities do professional managers have to shareholders?

2 Why will shareholders want plenty of information about the activities of the company in which they have invested?

Assets

In the balance sheet of a company, the fixed and current assets are presented in the same way as in any other form of balance sheet. In the vertical style, however, current liabilities are deducted from current assets in order to show working capital.

Working capital

When drawing up a vertical balance sheet, **working capital** is a very important calculation. Working capital is simply current assets less current liabilities. Having too much working capital means that the business is not using its resources well. If it has too little, it may not be able to pay its short-term debts.

A vertical balance sheet

Fixed assets		xxxx
Current assets	xxxx	
Less Current liabilities	xxxx	
= Working capital		xxxx
		xxxx
Less Long-term liabilities		xxxx
Capital employed		xxxx
Financed by:		
Authorised share capital		xxxx
Issued share capital		xxxx
Reserves		xxxx
		xxxx

The Balance Sheet of Stilton Sandwiches Ltd as at 31/12/01

	£	£	£
Fixed assets			
Land and buildings			22,000
Machinery			10,000
Motor vehicles			10,000
			42,000
Current assets			
Stocks		5,000	
Debtors		4,500	
Bank		2,000	
Cash		1,000	
		12,500	
Less **Current liabilities**			
Creditors	2,000		
Proposed dividends	4,000		
Corporation tax	2,000	8,000	
Working capital			4,500
			46,500
Less **Long-term liabilities**			
Bank loan		10,000	
Debentures		3,500	13,500
			33,000
FINANCED BY:			
Authorised share capital			
20,000 ordinary shares of £1			20,000
			20,000
Issued share capital			
20,000 ordinary shares of £1			20,000
Reserves			
Retained profit			13,000
			33,000

Working capital is important because it keeps 'the wolf from the door'. It is the amount of money a company has available to meet its immediate liabilities. Many businesses have suffered the consequences of having too many of their assets tied up as illiquid assets.

Liabilities

The **current liabilities** of a company are similar to those of a sole trader, except that limited companies also have to show **corporation tax** due to be paid to the Inland Revenue, as well as any **dividends** (shares of profit) to shareholders. Long-term liabilities may include long-term loans raised through the financial markets such as debentures.

The 'Financed by' section

The second part of the vertical balance sheet is known as the **'Financed by'** section. This displays the capital of the company and reflects the company's relationship with shareholders.

At the top of the 'Financed by' section are details of the **authorised capital.** This will show the value and number of shares a company's shareholders have authorised managers to issue. These are in the balance sheet for interest only and their value is excluded from totals. **Issued capital** shows details of shares actually issued. **Reserves** appear below the capital and are **retained profits** *(see Chapter 51, 'Sources of finance', page 195)* that the directors and shareholders decide to keep.

Keeping the wolf from the door

'I'm beginning to understand now. Though my working capital ratio appears OK, all of my current assets are tied up in stock, which means that I have to use a bank overdraft in order to pay the bills!'

COURSEWORK ACTIVITIES

Write to a public limited company to obtain a copy of their annual report and accounts. Within an annual report there will appear a set of accounts. Describe the statements accompanying the report. Comment on other information and indicate what these statements try to show. Explain why they are important for shareholders.

MATCH IT!

Can you help Frankie and Cleo to match the following terms and definitions?

Corporate governance

Debenture

Companies Acts

Shareholder

Corporation Tax

Limited liability

Authorised capital

Part-owner of a company
Capital which a company has been authorised to issue
Shareholders' liability for debts
Long-term liability of a company
Process of management on behalf of shareholders
Set of laws within which companies must operate
Tax paid on company profits

58 Business Ratios

Picking out useful information

Taken on their own, figures from final accounts can be confusing. But when financial ratios are used to analyse the information more closely, it becomes more meaningful.

A number of people might be interested in a business's accounts. For example:

◆ The **owner(s)** will want to know if the business is profitable

◆ **Employees** will want to know how the business is doing and whether their job is secure

◆ **Managers** will want to use information from the records to make business decisions

◆ **Creditors** and providers of loans will want to know if the business can afford to repay them.

All these groups of people can use business ratios to pick out the information they need.

'Looking at all these financial statements is very interesting. But how do I know what all the figures in the statements mean?'

Types of business ratio

Financial ratios are an arithmetical way of comparing different figures within a set of accounts. Using ratios helps you to answer key questions about a business organisation. But you must be clear why you are using the ratio and what it can tell you. Properly used, ratios can tell us about three main areas:

◆ Profitability

◆ Liquidity

◆ Asset usage

Profitability

1 Return on capital employed (ROCE)

If you invest £100 in a business, you will be looking at the return and comparing it with other investments. For example, if you received £30 back, you would probably be quite pleased as this would be significantly higher than any investment in a building society. But if you only received £2 from the business, you might think about putting your money elsewhere.

The **return on capital employed** simply relates profitability to an investment in a business. The ratio is expressed as:

$$\text{Percentage return on capital employed} = \frac{\text{Net profit for year}}{\text{Capital employed}} \times 100\%$$

The figure for capital is usually taken at the beginning of the year, as this is the capital generating profit for the following year. ROCE is a good measure of how effective an investment is and how it compares with others.

2 Gross profit percentage

This ratio is extracted from the trading account. It simply relates gross profit to sales revenue:

$$\text{Gross profit percentage} = \frac{\text{Gross profit}}{\text{Sales revenue}} \times 100\%$$

For example, if sales of £100,000 produce a gross profit of £50,000, then the gross profit percentage is 50%. In other words, every £1 of sales generates 50p of profit.

The gross profit percentage should be calculated at regular intervals and any rise or fall investigated. For example, if the ratio falls, it may simply mean that the price of raw materials has gone up. However, it might also mean that stocks have been stolen or damaged.

'Figures, figures and figures. There is no substitute for business acumen ... I wonder what 'acumen' means?'

COURSEWORK ACTIVITIES

Look at the accounts of a business. Use the simple ratios described in this chapter to help you analyse and comment on their performance.

3 Net profit percentage

This is extracted from the profit and loss account and is calculated as follows:

$$\text{Net profit percentage} = \frac{\text{Net profit}}{\text{Sales}} \times 100\%$$

This takes into account any changes in business expenses. For example, if the gross profit percentage is consistent and a change occurs in the net profit percentage, this would indicate an increase in overheads (costs) as a proportion of sales revenue. This may suggest that managers need to reduce overheads.

Liquidity

Liquidity is the ability of an organisation to convert its assets to cash and meet its debts.

1 Working capital ratio

The working capital ratio is the ratio of current assets to current liabilities:

Working capital ratio = Current assets:Current liabilities

It is important for every organisation to maintain a sensible ratio. What this is depends on the type of business, and how quickly funds may be needed to meet liabilities (e.g. creditors demanding repayment quickly).

A prudent ratio is usually 2:1, but this might not necessarily be the case if stocks form the bulk of current assets. Companies have to be aware that bank overdrafts are repayable on demand.

2 Quick ratio/acid test ratio

This ratio takes into account stocks. It is simply:

Current assets less stock:Current liabilities

This is a tougher ratio than the working capital ratio and excludes stocks because they are not immediately available to pay short-term debts. A rule of thumb for this ratio is that it should be greater than 1.

Asset usage

1 Stock turnover

An organisation does not want its stock staying around too long. Stock turnover is the average period of time an item of stock is held before it is used or sold. This ratio usually depends upon the type of business. For example, a fast-food outlet (right) would turn over its stock many more times a year than a furniture business.

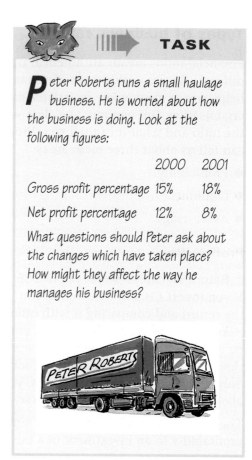

TASK

Peter Roberts runs a small haulage business. He is worried about how the business is doing. Look at the following figures:

	2000	2001
Gross profit percentage	15%	18%
Net profit percentage	12%	8%

What questions should Peter ask about the changes which have taken place? How might they affect the way he manages his business?

Stock turnover can be worked out using the following formula:

$$\text{Stock turnover} = \frac{\text{Cost of sales}}{\text{Average stock}}$$

In this formula the average stock is calculated by adding together the values of the opening stock and the closing stock and dividing the result by 2.

2 Asset utilisation

It is possible to relate the use of other things to sales in order to show how efficient an organisation is in generating sales revenue. For example, how many sales are assets generating? One way to find out is to relate sales to fixed assets. This would be measured by:

$$\text{Asset utilisation} = \frac{\text{Sales}}{\text{Fixed assets}}$$

This would show how well managers are using fixed assets like machinery and equipment to generate sales.

TASK

Help Ron to work out his acid-test ratio. His current assets are £17,500 but his closing stock is £15,000. His only current liability is his overdraft, which is £10,055.

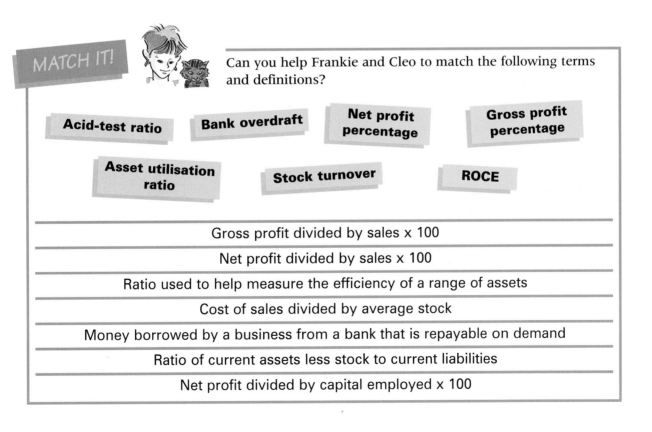

MATCH IT!

Can you help Frankie and Cleo to match the following terms and definitions?

Acid-test ratio   Bank overdraft   Net profit percentage   Gross profit percentage

Asset utilisation ratio   Stock turnover   ROCE

Gross profit divided by sales x 100

Net profit divided by sales x 100

Ratio used to help measure the efficiency of a range of assets

Cost of sales divided by average stock

Money borrowed by a business from a bank that is repayable on demand

Ratio of current assets less stock to current liabilities

Net profit divided by capital employed x 100

59 Making Comparisons

'Now I understand about how to read accounts, let's put these skills to practical use and look at some final accounts. How about looking at your final accounts, Ron?'

'Sorry, not now, can't stop, I have an interview – with my bank manager!'

Analysing accounts

In this chapter we will look at Ice Freeze Ltd, a company owned by a friend of Frankie's *(see Case Study on opposite page)* and make comparisons between two sets of accounts.

Profitability of Ice Freeze Ltd

1 Return on capital employed
Probably the first thing Frankie's friend will want to know is whether her business has become more profitable between the years.

$$2000 \qquad\qquad 2001$$
$$\frac{8,900}{70,000} \times 100 \qquad \frac{4,500}{70,000} \times 100$$
$$= 13\% \qquad\qquad = 6\%$$

Note: For the purpose of this example, we have called the capital employed £70,000 and not taken into account the reserves.

Frankie's friend is worried because the ROCE figure shows that the profitability of the business has halved over the two years.

2 Gross profit percentage

$$2000 \qquad\qquad 2001$$
$$\frac{20,000}{55,000} \times 100 \qquad \frac{25,000}{70,000} \times 100$$
$$= 36\% \qquad\qquad = 35\%$$

Despite the massive increase in turnover, there is virtually no change in the gross profit percentage. Like-for-like, sales seem to be generating the same amount of trading profit.

'Oh well, I have a friend who runs a frozen food business called Ice Freeze. I'll ask her if we can look at her accounts instead.'

SPIX

'Have you heard of an environmental balance sheet?'

CASE STUDY

Analysing the accounts of Ice Freeze Ltd

The Trading and Profit and Loss accounts of Ice Freeze Ltd

	2000		2001	
	£	£	£	£
Sales		55,000		70,000
Less Cost of sales:				
Opening stock	15,000		10,000	
Add purchases	30,000		45,000	
	45,000		55,000	
Less Closing stock	10,000	35,000	10,000	45,000
Gross profit		20,000		25,000
Less Expenses:				
Rent	1,400		1,500	
Rates	300		300	
Salaries	8,000		14,000	
Advertising	1,000		1,500	
Sundry expenses	400	11,100	3,200	20,500
Net profit		8,900		4,500

Balance Sheets of Ice Freeze Ltd

	2000			2001		
	£	£	£	£	£	£
Fixed assets						
Land and buildings			50,000			50,000
Fixtures and fittings			20,000			20,000
Motor vehicles			5,000			5,000
			75,000			75,000
Current assets						
Stocks		10,000			10,000	
Debtors		5,500			9,700	
Bank		3,200				
		18,700			19,700	
Less Current liabilities						
Creditors	3,000			2,000		
Bank overdraft		3,000		1,000	3,000	
Working capital			15,700			16,700
			90,700			91,700
Financed by:						
Authorised share capital						
70,000 ordinary shares of £1			70,000			70,000
			70,000			70,000
Issued share capital						
70,000 ordinary shares of £1			70,000			70,000
Reserves						
Retained profit			20,700			21,700
			£90,700			£91,700

3 Net profit percentage

$$\begin{array}{cc} 2000 & 2001 \\ \dfrac{8,900}{55,000} \times 100 & \dfrac{4,500}{70,000} \times 100 \\ = 16\% & = 6.4\% \end{array}$$

These figures are extremely important and reveal the main cause of the fall in profitability.

Expenses have risen from £11,100 to £20,500 and this ratio has fallen dramatically. To improve this, Frankie's friend may want to look at ways of cutting some of her expenses.

Liquidity of Ice Freeze Ltd

1 Working capital ratio

2000   2001
1:6.2   1:6.5

Ice Freeze has a comfortable working capital position and there are no real liquidity problems revealed by this ratio.

If anything, despite the fall in profitability and the bank overdraft, the ratio has become slightly stronger over the two years.

2 Quick ratio/acid test ratio

2000   2001
2.9:1   3.2:1

Again, despite the bank overdraft, Ice Freeze has more debtors in 2001, so the quick ratio shows a slight increase and no real liquidity problem.

Asset usage by Ice Freeze Ltd

1 Stock turnover

2000   2001
35,000   45,000
12,500   10,000
= 2.8 times   = 4.5 times

There is a clear change in asset usage over the two-year accounting period. Stock turned over much more frequently in 1996 than in 1995.

COURSEWORK ACTIVITIES

Is there a Young Enterprise group at your school or college? Find out how they are operating, about the goods or services they are producing and how successful they have been.

Look at their book-keeping processes and offer to help them produce their financial statements and analyse their final accounts.

2 Asset utilisation

2000	*2001*
55,000	70,000
75,000	75,000
= 1:1.36	= 1:1.07

With this ratio, the same amount of fixed assets are operating more efficiently because they are generating higher levels of sales.

Summary

Overall, there are few major differences over the two years, other than the rise in expenses affecting the profitability ratios. Sales have increased, the company is operating more efficiently and there are no obvious liquidity problems.

60 Classifying Costs

What is cost?

The word 'cost' has several meanings, even in everyday language. The cost of goods in the shops is something we all know about!

Organisations will want to use management accounting to control their costs and forecast future events. This helps managers to make decisions about future activities.

Costing techniques

In organisations managers frequently refer to calculating the cost of, or **costing,** an event or activity.

What they mean by this is that they are using a knowledge of past costs and expected revenues to plan something they hope to achieve. These **costing techniques** are a useful source of data for management accountants.

All businesses incur some form of cost. A sound knowledge of costs and the factors affecting them will help a business to assess its profitability. Remember that profits only begin to be made once costs are met!

'So, we have looked at financial accounting by looking at financial statements and analysing them with ratios. What about management accounting?' Has anyone heard from Ron?

TASK

Some of Ron Rust's costs are shown below. Which of these are going to be his fixed costs and which will be his variable costs?

- Purchases of scrap
- Business rates
- Electricity
- Ron's salary

- Wages to labour in the yard
- Rent
- Telephone bills
- Advertising

CASE STUDY

Johnsons Toy Company

Johnsons Toy Company produces toy trains and sells them at £12 each. Next year it expects to produce 10,000 trains. The fixed costs for the business are £14,000 and the variable cost to produce each train is £8. Below is a table to show how much profit will be made if Johnsons manage to produce and sell the 10,000 they anticipate.

Units of production	Fixed costs £	Variable costs £	Total costs £	Revenue £	Profit/loss £
1,000	14,000	8,000	22,000	12,000	(10,000)
2,000	14,000	16,000	30,000	24,000	(6,000)
3,000	14,000	24,000	38,000	36,000	(2,000)
4,000	14,000	32,000	46,000	48,000	2,000
5,000	14,000	40,000	54,000	60,000	6,000
6,000	14,000	48,000	62,000	72,000	10,000
7,000	14,000	56,000	70,000	84,000	14,000
8,000	14,000	64,000	78,000	96,000	18,000
9,000	14,000	72,000	86,000	108,000	22,000
10,000	14,000	80,000	94,000	120,000	26,000

We can see that if Johnsons Toy Company produces 10,000 toy trains they will make a profit of £26,000. Clearly, analysing costs has helped them to predict the future with more certainty.

Fixed and variable costs

There are two types of costs:

◆ **Fixed** costs

◆ **Variable** costs

Fixed costs are costs that do not increase as output increases, for example, rent, heating bills, mortgage repayments, rates and salaries. An organisation could therefore increase the number of units it produces from 10,000 to 20,000 and incur no increases in these types of costs.

Variable costs are costs that increase as output increases. This is because when more units are produced, more of these costs are incurred. For example, if you produce more items, you might need more workers on the shop floor and more raw materials.

Marginal costing compares fixed and variable costs with sales revenue at different levels of production in order to calculate the profit that will be made.

Contribution

We have seen that fixed costs have to be paid however many units are sold. A management accountant may also want to look at how much each unit sold is contributing to paying off the fixed costs of its production. This **contribution** is calculated by taking the variable cost from the selling price:

Contribution = Selling price – Variable costs per unit

This technique is particularly useful for making short-term decisions – for example, helping to set the selling price of a product, or deciding whether or not to accept an order.

TASK

*R*ead the Case Study on Duvey Duvets Ltd (right).

1 Divide the costs listed into fixed and variable.

2 Draw up a chart to show fixed, variable, total costs and total revenue for each 1,000 units produced up to 12,000 units.

3 Duvey Duvets aim to produce and sell 10,000 duvets this year. How much profit will they make if their plans succeed?

CASE STUDY

Duvey Duvets Ltd

Duvey Duvets is a small business producing low-cost duvets. The company is run by Pauline Smithers. She employs five full-time employees: one production manager and four machine operators who cut out material for sending to part-time workers. The part-time workers then use their own sewing machines to make up the duvets in their own homes.

The costs of the business are as follows:

* Pauline's salary of £500 per week

* Salary of production manager – £200 per week

* Salaries of machine operators – £150 per week each

* Rent and rates – £500 per week

* Electricity – £300 per 3 months

* Sundry overheads – £100 per week

* Material costs for each duvet – £5

* Payment to workers for producing duvets – £3 per duvet.

The duvets are sold for £20 each.

TASK

Scotties Pens hope to sell 2,000 pens next year at £9 per unit. The firm's variable costs are £5 per unit and its fixed costs are £4,000.

Draw up a profit statement to show how much it will make in the year. Also, draw up a table to show how much profit it will make at each 500 units of production up to 3,000 units.

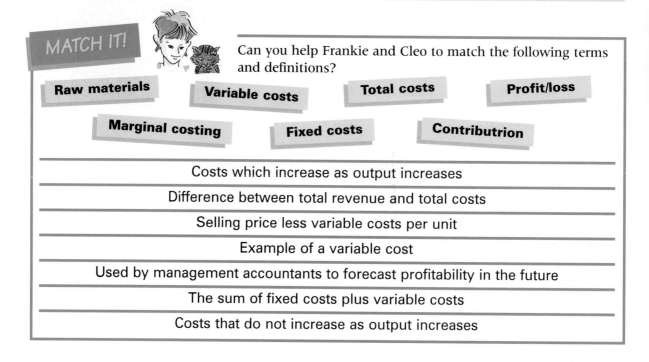

MATCH IT!

Can you help Frankie and Cleo to match the following terms and definitions?

Raw materials   Variable costs   Total costs   Profit/loss

Marginal costing   Fixed costs   Contributrion

Costs which increase as output increases

Difference between total revenue and total costs

Selling price less variable costs per unit

Example of a variable cost

Used by management accountants to forecast profitability in the future

The sum of fixed costs plus variable costs

Costs that do not increase as output increases

61 Break-even Analysis

When does a business break even?

Break-even extends the principles of marginal costs, which we looked at in Chapter 60.

Break-even is the unique point at which an organisation makes neither a profit nor a loss. If sales go beyond the break-even point, profits are made. But if sales have not reached the break-even point, losses are incurred.

'People keep using this term "break even". If I broke even, would that mean that I had covered my costs?'

'Don't get confused by terminology. I've never broken even and it's never bothered me!'

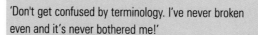

Calculating the break-even point

To calculate the break-even point, there are two stages:

◆ Calculate the unit contribution (selling price less variable costs)

◆ Divide the fixed costs by the unit contribution:

$$\text{Break-even point} = \frac{\text{Fixed costs}}{\text{Contribution}}$$

This shows how many units must be produced to break even at that selling price. The **sales value** of the break-even point is calculated by multiplying the number of units at the break-even point by the selling price.

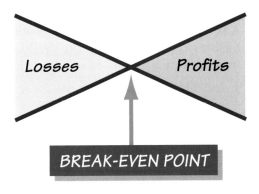

The break-even point

C ASE S TUDY

Trio Toys

Peter Taylor, the dynamic entrepreneurial chairman of Trio Toys, has been carefully monitoring the baby buggy division of his company. Each baby buggy sells for £12 and the variable costs in manufacture include:

* £4 direct labour per unit

* £3 direct materials per unit

* £1 other variable overheads per unit

The fixed costs of the baby buggy division are £80,000.

Peter carefully works out the break-even point for the buggy. The unit contribution for each buggy produced will be:

£12 (Selling price) – £8 (£4 + £3 + £1 Variable costs) = £4

$$\text{Break-even point} = \frac{\text{Fixed costs}}{\text{Unit contribution}}$$

$$= \frac{£80,000}{4} = 20,000 \text{ units to break even}$$

Sales value to break even = 20,000 units x £12 Selling price

= £240,000

Peter hopes to make a profit of £30,000 on his buggies. In other words, he not only has to cover his fixed costs but also to make an extra £30,000. To find out how many units he has to sell to achieve this, he must add a profit target to his fixed costs and divide this by his contribution.

$$\frac{£80,000 \text{ (Fixed costs)} + £30,000 \text{ (Profit target)}}{4} = \frac{110,000}{4}$$

= 27,500 units to achieve this target

The sales value required to make this profit is therefore 27,500 units x £12 selling price

= £330,000.

Producing a break-even chart

A **break-even chart** shows the point at which a business breaks even and the profits and losses it will make at various levels of activity. It is constructed by:

1 Labelling the horizontal axis for units of production and sales.

2 Labelling the vertical axis to represent the value of sales and costs.

3 Plotting fixed costs (this will be a straight line as fixed costs do not rise as more units are produced).

4 Plotting variable costs. These are shown rising from where the fixed cost line touches the vertical axis. This line also therefore represents total costs. It is plotted by calculating total costs at two or three random levels of production (*see table below*).

5 Sales are plotted by taking two or three random levels of turnover. They are shown rising from the intersection of the two axes.

A sample break-even chart based on the Case Study on page 231 is shown below.

TASK

Read the Case Study on page 231 then complete the following tasks:

1 One alternative strategy for Peter Taylor of Trio Toys is to increase the price of the baby buggy to £15. At this price, market research reveals that the company should be able to sell 22,000 units. Find the new break-even point and then find out whether Peter would be able to meet his profit target at this level of production.

2 Describe the benefits of using techniques of break-even analysis.

	10,000 units £	20,000 units £	30,000 units £
Variable costs = £8 per unit	80,000	160,000	240,000
Fixed costs	80,000	80,000	80,000
Total cost	160,000	240,000	320,000
Sales £12 per unit	120,000	240,000	360,000

Left: Table showing total costs and sales for Trio Toys at three random levels of activity *(see Case Study, page 231)*

Below: the same information displayed as a break-even chart

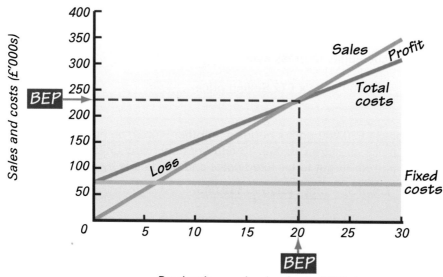

Production and sales (units/'000s)

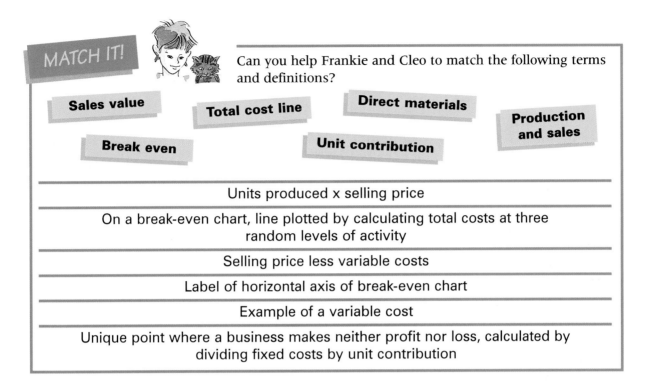

MATCH IT!

Can you help Frankie and Cleo to match the following terms and definitions?

Sales value

Total cost line

Direct materials

Production and sales

Break even

Unit contribution

Units produced x selling price
On a break-even chart, line plotted by calculating total costs at three random levels of activity
Selling price less variable costs
Label of horizontal axis of break-even chart
Example of a variable cost
Unique point where a business makes neither profit nor loss, calculated by dividing fixed costs by unit contribution

7 | 62 Communicating Within a Business

What is communication?

Communication is the passing on or exchange of information, ideas or feelings.

Today there are many ways of communicating. These include writing letters and articles, speaking to people face to face, telephone conversations, sending a fax, sending e-mail and using computer links such as the Internet.

Some of these communications involve written words, some involve spoken words, and others are made up of visual symbols.

Internal communication

Internal communications are those that take place within an organisation – for example, between a manager and a supervisor, between two employees, etc.

It is very important to have good, clear communications so that the organisation can run smoothly.

'Does the rapid speed of modern communications mean that communications today are better than ever?'

Purposes of internal communication

A number of purposes of internal communication are set out in the diagram below:

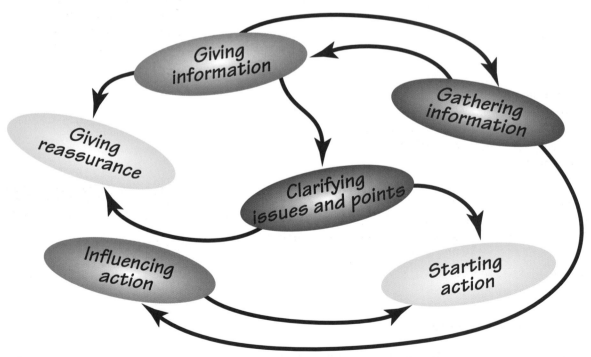

Purposes of internal communication

1 To give information

A common reason for communication is to give information. For example, a manager may want to tell people when a meeting has been arranged, or to inform people of Health and Safety requirements.

2 To gather information

People in organisations need information to help them make decisions. For example, the managing director may ask for sales figures from different regions. Or the personnel manager may want information about accidents and injuries in the workplace. Modern computer-based information systems allow huge amounts of information to be gathered onto shared databases, which can be accessed by relevant people within the organisation.

3 To give reassurance

Information is needed to reassure people that they are doing things correctly, or that things are happening in an organisation. For example, employees may feel better if they are given a written report on their work. A manager may want a report to reassure him or her that safety checks are being carried out properly.

4 To clarify issues and points

Communications are required to clarify anything that may be confusing in an organisation. For example, if employees are not sure who they should report to after being absent from work, then this can be made clear in a written notice.

5 To start action

Communications are important in getting new ideas off the ground. For example, if managers want to introduce a major change in an organisation, they may call everyone together to tell them what will be happening.

6 To influence action

Communications are required to make sure that things happen in a desired way. For example, if output is falling and costs are rising in a company, managers may need to warn staff that if things don't improve the business may fold.

Types of communication

We will now look at a number of ways of communicating within an organisation.

CASE STUDY

Internal communications at Novelty Icecreams

Novelty Icecreams has recently (June 2001) made some changes to their working practices. In particular they have shortened the working day in line with European Union requirements for the 48-hour week. To introduce this change the company held a series of meetings at which employees were briefed by their team leaders. In addition an information sheet was produced on the company website on the pages that are prepared for employee information, and a poster outlining the changes was displayed at prominent parts of the factory. The information made it clear that, although people would work shorter hours, their take-home pay would not be reduced. Some of the employees were worried that they might have to work to a different shift pattern but the information given made it clear that this would not be the case.

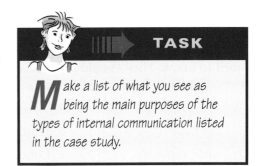

TASK

Make a list of what you see as being the main purposes of the types of internal communication listed in the case study.

1 Written communications

Written communications are used to pass on information and ideas in an organisation. They can also be used to confirm verbal messages.

Memos

One of the most often used forms of internal communication is the **memorandum**, or **memo** for short. The word comes from the Latin meaning 'a thing to be remembered'. Today memos are used to pass on information, instructions and enquiries and are like letters sent within the company. In modern organisations most memos are now sent by e-mail.

The organisation's name does not normally appear on a memo, and there is no need to start with 'Dear Sir', or finish 'Yours faithfully', as with a letter.

Memos are often sent to several people at the same time, although they are also sent to individuals.

Reports

A **report** is a written communication from someone who has collected and studied some facts or issues. It is usually sent to someone who has asked for it for a particular purpose. The report will often form the basis for a decision that needs to be taken.

Typical examples of situations in which reports would be sent include:

♦ to present the results of some research and to recommend action

♦ to supply information for legal purposes, perhaps as a result of an accident

♦ to supply information to shareholders (or other stakeholders, e.g. employees)

♦ to weigh up the possible results of changing a policy.

Reports should be well written, concise and to the point. They should not contain anything the reader does not need to know. They should be clear and arranged in a logical order. A suggested form of presentation for a written report is:

1 Title page	5 Findings
2 List of contents	6 Conclusion
3 Terms of reference	7 Recommendations
4 Procedure	8 Signature

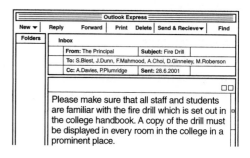

A typical e-mail memo

TASK

*S*end an e-mail memo to other members of your class informing them of the brief details and hand-in dates of a recent assignment, or send an e-mail memo to other members of your class setting out the school or college calendar for the year, i.e. start and finish dates of each term.

SPIX

'The great thing about electronic mailing is that it makes it possible to reduce the use of paper, helping to create more sustainable solutions.'

The **terms of reference** explain why the report is being written, by stating the group or persons for whom it is being prepared. For example:

'This report is being written in response to a request from the owner of the Regal cinema for our business group to carry out some market research to see if there is a demand for a second screen at the cinema.'

The **procedure** section describes how the report has been put together. What letters have been sent? Who has been interviewed? What else has been done?

The **findings** indicate what has been discovered as a result of the investigations that have been carried out.

The **conclusions** contain a summary of the findings. For example:

'There appears to be a strong opportunity for a new cinema screen. Seventy per cent of those interviewed stated that they would visit the cinema more often...'

Recommendations may be included where appropriate. For example, you may be trying to look at ways of solving a problem through your studies. If so, you may want to suggest some form of action as a result of your report.

Agendas and minutes

An **agenda** is a written outline of the issues to be discussed at a meeting. It is set out under a number of headings, and must contain the date, time and place of the meeting. It should be sent in advance to all the people who will attend the meeting so that they have the chance to prepare their contributions.

Minutes are a written record of a meeting. Sometimes they may be placed on a noticeboard so that more people can read them. Minutes should be clear, concise and accurate.

Notices and house publications

Notices are written displays placed in obvious places in order to give out information. They can be used to set out instructions, advertise future events, set out policies and so on. They can be a useful way of motivating staff. Notices should be designed and presented so as to attract people's attention.

House magazines, journals, and company newspapers can be used to share information inside an organisation. Today many of these are being presented as on-line journals and newspapers because it is much cheaper and quicker to do so. They are particularly important in large organisations for communicating information to employees.

HEALTH & SAFETY COMMITTEE
Meeting to be held on
Thursday 21st March 2001
at 10.30 am in the **Committee Room**

AGENDA

1 Apologies for absence
2 Minutes of last meeting
3 Visit by Environmental Health Officer
4 Fire Drill
5 Report on Health & Safety at the Warehouse
6 Any other business
7 Date of next meeting

A typical agenda

2 Verbal communications

Verbal communication involves direct word-of-mouth contact. Much of the time it involves face-to-face exchanges with the aim of giving messages, providing advice, personal discussion, instructions and guidance.

Face-to-face contact enables communicators to get to know each other. It also allows for instant feedback. However, the main disadvantage is that there are no permanent records. It can also lead to confusion when messages are not clear.

Body language is an important part of face-to-face communication *(right)*. It is important to take an honest and open posture when dealing with other people.

Meetings

Nearly all employees at all levels in an organisation will spend some time at meetings. This is particularly true of managers and administrative staff. Meetings are held to discuss issues and problems, to come up with new ideas and to develop plans.

In a meeting you are able to draw on the specialist skills of a group of people, all of whom will be able to make a useful contribution.

A notice of a meeting will be accompanied by an **agenda** setting out the order of the meeting.

Some meetings will be **informal** discussions between groups of people. Other meetings will be more organised or **formal**.

A **chairperson (or 'chair')** has certain duties and powers in a meeting. He or she makes sure that there are enough people at the meeting for decisions to be made. The word **quorum** means the minimum number of people needed before business can be carried out in a meeting.

The chair has the task of making sure that the meeting concentrates on the tasks in hand, and seeking the views of those who are involved. The chair makes sure that votes are taken properly, and corrects anyone who wastes time or disrupts the meeting.

At the start of the meeting, the secretary will say which people have given apologies for not being able to attend, and will read out the minutes of the previous meeting. Members are asked to approve the minutes from the previous meeting as being correct.

The chair then works through the minutes of the meeting in the order that they have been set out in the agenda.

Body language is an important part of everyday communication

What sort of messages do you think Ron Rust is giving in his body language in the situations below?

The final item is called **Any other business (A.O.B.)**. This allows people at the meeting to bring up minor matters for discussion. It should not be allowed to go on for too long.

Committees

Committees are groups of people who come together regularly to take part in decision-making. Most large organisations have committees for dealing with particular aspects of work, e.g. a Health and Safety Committee, a Sports and Recreation Committee, etc.

Teams

Many modern organisations involve a number of self-managing teams, or project teams. Instead of having a 'top-down' communication system within an organisation, decision-making can be put in the hands of these teams. Verbal communication is very important in these teams. Employees need to have excellent communication and interpersonal skills.

Quality circles

Quality circles are small groups of employees who meet regularly to discuss work problems. They are made up of managers, supervisors and employees, all sharing ideas in a democratic way. The aim is to increase communications, motivation and efficiency.

3   Visual communications

Visual communication is often the best way of getting a message across. If people can see what is expected of them, or how something works, they are more likely to remember it. Visual communication techniques are being used more and more within organisations. Examples are the use of overhead projectors, television and multimedia. For instance, medical specialists are able to view a patient's injuries from hundreds or thousands of miles away by means of television screens and virtual reality systems.

Modern companies like Shell UK use visual communications at their annual general meetings. These might include a video showing highlights of the year's performance, or a slide presentation using computer-generated graphics.

Similar techniques are now being used for training and development within organisations. CD-ROM and CD-I have also had a great impact on communication, as has the development of virtual reality. The Internet has led to the creation of many web-based training packages, so today you can do a course in almost any subject you want over the Internet.

LATEST NEWS

Many organisations are reducing the number of formal meetings they hold. It has been found that electronic communication such as e-mail enables the rapid transmission of information within an organisation, reducing the need for meetings.

TASK

*F*rankie is deciding which order the following should go in in a well planned meeting. Can you list them in the correct order?

- Any other business
- Notice of meeting
- Closing of the meeting
- Working through the agenda
- Discussing the minutes of the previous meeting.
- Opening of meeting
- Sending out the agenda to participants in the meeting
- Apologies for absence

4 Information and communication technology

Information technology has revolutionised communications both within and between organisations. Today
many employees are networked together, and are able
to share vast information systems. Increasingly, large
numbers of employees are able to work from home and
many people work with shared information systems
such as the Worldwide Web. We will look in detail at
information technology communications in Chapter 64.

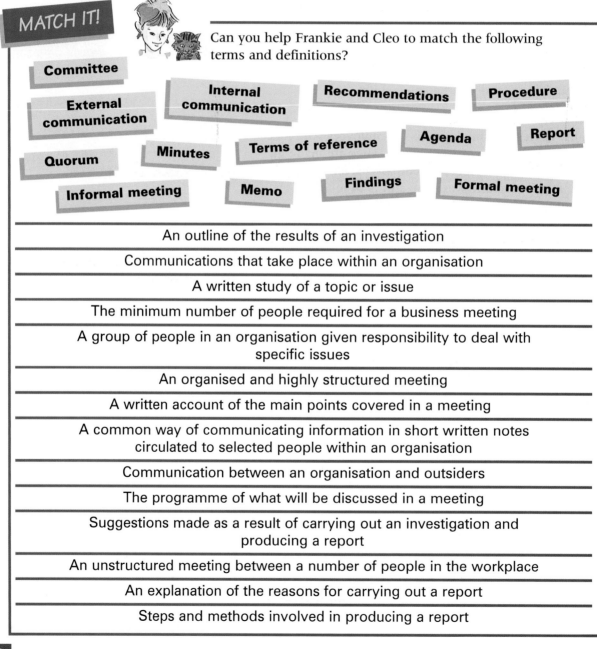

MATCH IT!

Can you help Frankie and Cleo to match the following
terms and definitions?

Committee

External communication

Internal communication

Recommendations

Procedure

Quorum

Minutes

Terms of reference

Agenda

Report

Informal meeting

Memo

Findings

Formal meeting

| An outline of the results of an investigation |
| Communications that take place within an organisation |
| A written study of a topic or issue |
| The minimum number of people required for a business meeting |
| A group of people in an organisation given responsibility to deal with specific issues |
| An organised and highly structured meeting |
| A written account of the main points covered in a meeting |
| A common way of communicating information in short written notes circulated to selected people within an organisation |
| Communication between an organisation and outsiders |
| The programme of what will be discussed in a meeting |
| Suggestions made as a result of carrying out an investigation and producing a report |
| An unstructured meeting between a number of people in the workplace |
| An explanation of the reasons for carrying out a report |
| Steps and methods involved in producing a report |

63 Communicating Outside a Business

Purposes of external communications

External communication is concerned with how an organisation communicates with and is viewed by people and organisations outside the business.

There are a number of purposes of external communications *(see diagram below)*:

1 **Providing information.** For example, railway and bus companies provide their customers with access to timetables, businesses provide annual reports for shareholders, etc. Today much of this information can be accessed on the Internet through a company webpage.

2 **Giving instructions.** For example, telling suppliers where to deliver goods or telling customers to use products in a certain way.

3 **Confirming arrangements.** This may include confirming meetings or conferences or perhaps details of transactions.

4 **Improving customer service.** Good communication can help to reduce errors, provide customers with plenty of feedback and deal more efficiently with enquiries.

5 **Public relations.** Good communication can help to project a more positive image and overcome prejudices that people may have against the company.

'My business provides a valuable environmental service! I reckon local people see me as a sort of successful business entrepreneur.'

'Funny, I'm sure I've seen letters of complaint about Ron's business in the local paper…'

Below: The purposes of external communications

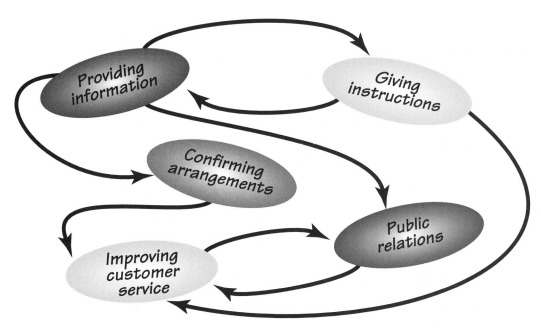

Methods of external communication

There are a number of different methods of external communication:

The business letter

The business letter is probably the most widely used form of external communication. To write an effective letter you need to prepare properly. It may be necessary to investigate the background first by searching through previous correspondence.

A letter may be written to:

◆ Seek information

◆ Place or confirm an order

◆ Deal with a problem

◆ Obtain quotations

◆ Quote a price, etc.

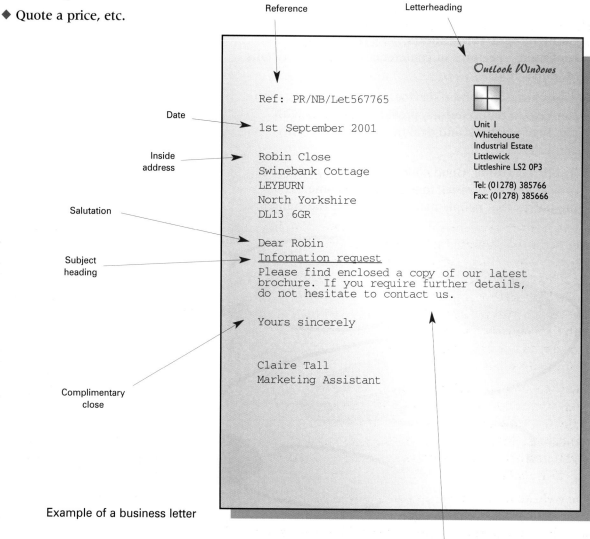

Example of a business letter

The layout, style and appearance of a business letter will vary from one organisation to another. A typical business letter will have the following features *(see example on opposite page)*:

◆ Heading or letterhead

◆ Reference (so that enquiries can be traced)

◆ Date

◆ Inside address

◆ Salutation (e.g. 'Dear Sir')

◆ Subject heading

◆ Body of the letter

◆ Complimentary close (e.g. 'Yours faithfully' or 'Yours sincerely')

Company websites

The most dramatic increase in the use of electronic media for the purpose of external communication is the creation of Internet websites. Most companies have a website they use for all forms of external communications purposes and for public relations activities.

An effective website is one that has a distinctive name – e.g. Coca-Cola.com, manutd.com.

The site should be easy to access and to **navigate** (i.e. to move around). The site needs to be broken down into clear sub-sections, which should be well signposted. Users need to be able to access quickly the part of the site that interests them – research has shown that if a user becomes frustrated with a site they will click off in seconds rather than minutes. The site also needs to have clear links with other parts of the site that will be useful to the browser. For business firms it is also important that the site makes it easy for the user to do business with the company that has the site – for example, simple and easy to use order forms coupled with credit card security mechanisms.

The site should be welcoming and packed with interesting material to encourage the user to re-visit. Many websites also carry advertising for other companies. Shared advertising arrangements are negotiated between companies so that they mutually benefit from links.

The website needs to be supported with other aspects of good customer relations. For example, if someone makes an order through the website this should be backed up by quick, safe, reliable and convenient delivery systems.

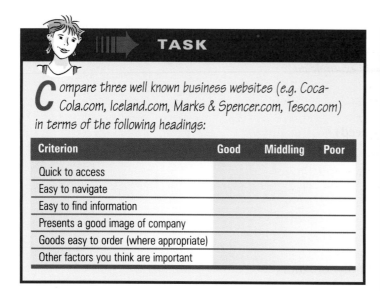

TASK

Compare three well known business websites (e.g. Coca-Cola.com, Iceland.com, Marks & Spencer.com, Tesco.com) in terms of the following headings:

Criterion	Good	Middling	Poor
Quick to access			
Easy to navigate			
Easy to find information			
Presents a good image of company			
Goods easy to order (where appropriate)			
Other factors you think are important			

Customer newsletters

These can be a useful way of communicating product or service changes and developments to different groups of customers (e.g. the leaflet that comes through your door outlining prices in your local supermarket).

Customer newsletters may contain information about offers, new developments in a firm (e.g. a new store opening), or other developments in the firm.

Advertisements

Advertisements are a form of external communication that we are all familiar with. They can be found in various media such as television, the local or national press, magazines or on billboards.

The telephone

The way employees deal with enquiries on the telephone can often have a big influence on the way customers feel about a company. Politeness and efficiency are vital when dealing with telephone enquiries from members of the public.

File transfers

While electronic mail transfers text between computers and is a very important form of external communication, it is quite slow at transferring very large files. Another specialist system (known as **file transfer**) is therefore better for sending files such as computer programs and graphics, using a method that bunches the data into packages. The receiving computer will check each 'bunch' to make sure no errors have been made. If everything is fine, it will confirm this and wait for the next 'bunch'.

CASE STUDY

The virtual Tesco

Tesco has introduced 'virtual' shop assistants to help take some of the stress out of shopping.

Instead of having to hunt down supermarket staff to answer queries, customers will be able to turn to the electronic Omniscan. The high-tech barcode machine provides full information on any item the customer scans. It will expand on the basic list of ingredients shown on labels and describe how certain lines are made. This will help, for example, consumers with allergies to find out more about the potential dangers of products they buy, and will show consumers how products are made.

'It's so much easier when you can scan in the price of goods.

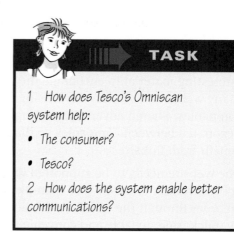

TASK

1 How does Tesco's Omniscan system help:

• The consumer?

• Tesco?

2 How does the system enable better communications?

Electronic data interchange (EDI)

Increasingly, the world's giant food manufacturers and retailers are setting up large-scale systems for purchasing goods electronically. Manufacturers such as Coca-Cola and Heinz have joined together with retailers such as Sainsbury's and Carrefour (of France) to create a company known as GlobalNetExchange. EDI is a network link that allows retailers to pay suppliers electronically, without the need for invoices and cheques, thus dramatically reducing time, paperwork and costs.

Video conferencing

Video conferencing has improved out of all recognition as a result of the development of digital systems. Video conferencing means that people who are geographically separated can hold face-to-face meetings. Desktop systems mean that participants in a conference can communicate with each other without leaving their desks.

Desktop video conferencing requires a powerful PC, a sound card, a video camera and a video compression card.

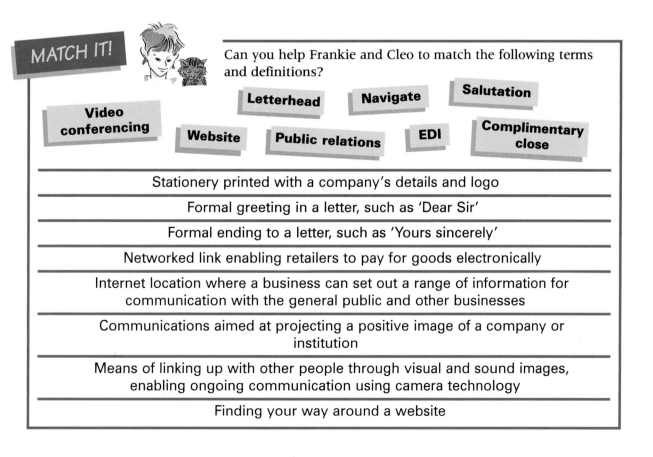

MATCH IT!

Can you help Frankie and Cleo to match the following terms and definitions?

Video conferencing · Letterhead · Navigate · Salutation · Website · Public relations · EDI · Complimentary close

Stationery printed with a company's details and logo
Formal greeting in a letter, such as 'Dear Sir'
Formal ending to a letter, such as 'Yours sincerely'
Networked link enabling retailers to pay for goods electronically
Internet location where a business can set out a range of information for communication with the general public and other businesses
Communications aimed at projecting a positive image of a company or institution
Means of linking up with other people through visual and sound images, enabling ongoing communication using camera technology
Finding your way around a website

64 The Role of Information Technology

The information revolution

In the twenty-first century information and communications technology lies at the heart of the successful business.

One of the fastest growing areas is business-to-business (B2B) communications – i.e. web-based trading networks that enable buyers and sellers to interact. B2B has become very important in most industries enabling suppliers – which sometimes number tens of thousands in a large industry such as chemicals or a multiple chain store – to connect up and enable much better management of supply in all sorts of industries, from textile and clothing to cement.

At the same time most businesses understand the benefits of business-to-consumer (B2C) communication links through the provision of websites to advertise, give information, take orders, and interact with consumers.

At the turn of the millennium many new 'dot com' businesses were set up, but these were not very successful. The problem for these companies was that, although they were able to raise a lot of capital from selling shares, this capital was rapidly used up as the companies made trading losses. If they had had more time they might have been successful but unfortunately in business you need to be able to break even in a relatively short period of time (one to two years).

The main benefit of the **dot com revolution** was that it made existing businesses wake up to the need of rapidly developing an Internet presence, and all of the major companies in the UK now communicate widely through a website.

Modern information technology means that today employees:

◆ have access to more information than before

◆ can carry out a wider variety of tasks

◆ are more efficient

◆ can use data in different ways

◆ can present data in many different forms (tables, charts, diagrams, etc.)

'I enjoy using computers. They help to make you feel in complete control of your business.'

LATEST NEWS

Today most towns have a cybercafé, so business people don't have to carry laptop computers. They can simply pick up their e-mails at the nearest cybercafé.

IT in the office

In a modern office, information is usually processed by means of a **computer system**. This will usually contain the following key elements:

- **Input devices.** These allow information to be fed into the system. Keyboards and scanners are examples of input devices.

- **Storage devices.** These store information and data so that it can be accessed when needed. A computer hard disk or CD-ROM drive is a storage device.

- **Software/programs.** These allow the data or information to be processed or manipulated *(see examples below).*

- **Output devices.** These produce the processed data in the form required by the user. A printer is an example of an output device.

Software for business

There are many different types of program to help business people communicate with each other. Some you will already be familiar with.

Word processing

Word processors enable text to be keyed in, stored, altered easily and printed out.

Desktop publishing

Desktop publishing (DTP) programs make it possible to produce pages of combined text and graphics to a very high standard. DTP is used to produce reports, newsletters, training materials – even books.

Spreadsheets

A spreadsheet is a table of numbers that can be organised and analysed on a computer. A **spreadsheet program** is used when making forecasts and doing calculations – the advantage being that the computer does all the work for you!

Spreadsheets are particularly useful for financial forecasting and 'what if' modelling. For instance, a business may forecast all the money that will come in and go out over a twelve-month period. The figures can then be adjusted to show the effect, for example, of reducing a heating bill by a certain amount each month. The computer automatically recalculates the columns to change the heating figures, total cost figures and cashflow for each month.

Below: Three generations of information processing...

The age of the quill pen

The age of the mechanical typewriter

A modern office with computers and telecommunications equipment

Databases

A database is like an electronic filing system which can be used by, for example, a bank or a building society to store information about its customers' accounts.

A church may keep a database of members of its congregation, or a football club may keep details of tickets sold for matches. The club could then use information from this database to make special offers to people they know have bought tickets (e.g. sending them a catalogue of merchandise and special offers for matches at Christmas time).

Under the Data Protection Act, companies wishing to store any personal information on a computer system must register with the government-appointed Data Processing Officer.

Graphics packages

In recent years there have been a number of developments in the type and range of graphics packages. These enable data to be translated into a graphical form such as charts, pictures and graphs. Presentation graphics can also be used for overhead transparencies (OHTs), high-resolution colour slides or presentations using a computer and projector.

Project planning

Project planning packages may be used for planning a complex project with a series of interrelated activities.

Expert systems

These are programs consisting of a set of rules based on the knowledge of experts. These rules can be used to help users find answers to problems that the program works on when it is given information.

The Internet

The Internet, or Worldwide Web, is currently transforming global communications. It is a global 'network of networks' that can be accessed from a personal computer by means of a modem or telephone link. It enables users from anywhere in the world to communicate and share information quickly and easily.

The Internet has revolutionised the business world by slashing costs and by rapidly increasing the quantity and speed at which information can be communicated and manipulated.

COURSEWORK ACTIVITIES

Find out about the use of information technology in your school or college office.

Present a report to show how this technology is used.

LATEST NEWS

The sales of dedicated hand-held games such as Nintendo have been dramatically hit by the growth of mobile phones, which increasingly are enabling users to download new games from the Internet.

Controlling access to information on the Internet is a serious problem for governments and politicians. There are all sorts of abuses including credit card fraud, the rapid spread of computer viruses, the sale of prohibited substances (drugs, pornography, etc.) and other associated problems involving criminal activity.

TASK

1   Why do you think people buy books and travel tickets using the Internet?

2   How is the Internet a good medium of communication for sellers of books and travel tickets?

3   What other services would benefit from using websites to communicate with customers?

CASE STUDY

On-line shopping

The following table shows the percentage of Internet users who bought the following items:

Item	1998	2000
Books	17%	65%
Travel tickets	20%	40%
Entertainment tickets	22%	25%
Financial products/services	4%	16%
Clothes	12%	22%

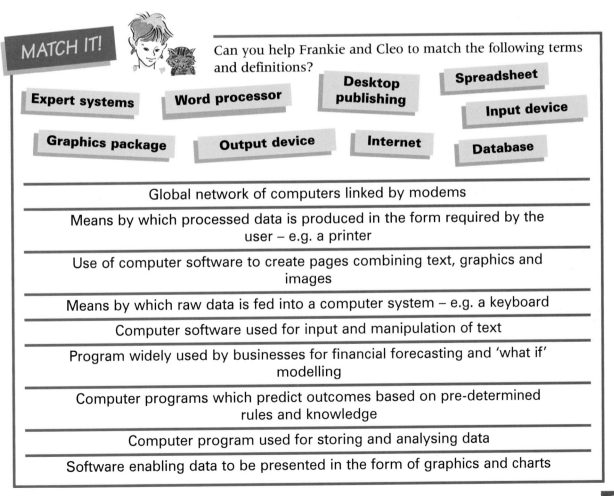

MATCH IT!   Can you help Frankie and Cleo to match the following terms and definitions?

Expert systems   Word processor   Desktop publishing   Spreadsheet   Input device   Graphics package   Output device   Internet   Database

Global network of computers linked by modems

Means by which processed data is produced in the form required by the user – e.g. a printer

Use of computer software to create pages combining text, graphics and images

Means by which raw data is fed into a computer system – e.g. a keyboard

Computer software used for input and manipulation of text

Program widely used by businesses for financial forecasting and 'what if' modelling

Computer programs which predict outcomes based on pre-determined rules and knowledge

Computer program used for storing and analysing data

Software enabling data to be presented in the form of graphics and charts

8 65 Human Needs at Work

Job satisfaction

Many people spend a considerable part of their lives at work. So it is not surprising that they expect to be rewarded and satisfied with the job they do.

To some people, work is a great pleasure, giving them a sense of personal fulfilment, but for others it is just a necessary way to make a living.

'What do you think? Should work be a pleasure, or simply a way of making money to buy pleasure?'

Motivation

Motivation is what causes people to act or do something in a positive way. By understanding why people behave in the way they do, managers can make work more fulfilling for people, and thus **motivate** them. A well motivated workforce will work harder and contribute more to the success of a business.

We all have different motives for the things that we do. For example, some people strive to be successful and powerful. Others strive for money. Others just want to be liked or to help other people. What drives us depends on our personality, our background and other important factors.

Satisfying needs

A lot of research has gone into finding out what motivates people at work. One of the leading theories is that of **Abraham Maslow.**

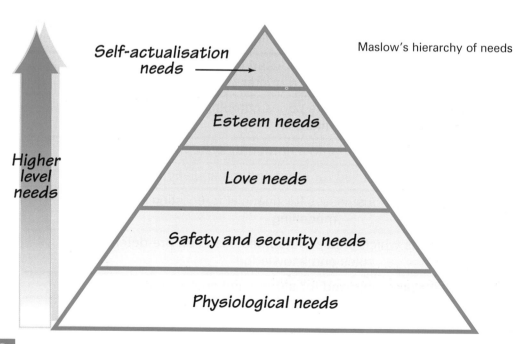

Maslow's hierarchy of needs

From his research Maslow drew up what he called a **hierarchy of needs**, with basic needs at the bottom and higher needs at the top *(see diagram on opposite page)*.

Maslow claimed that people must satisfy their lower-level needs before moving on to a higher level.

1 Physiological needs

Physiological needs are for basics such as food, shelter and clothing. These basic needs must be met in order to keep the body functioning. Some sections of our society, such as people sleeping under railway arches in London, are not even satisfying these basic needs.

At work, the basic level of need is for employees to receive payment for their work. The workplace also needs to be safe from accidents and danger.

2 Safety and security needs

In order to be safe from danger, people need to be able to work in a clean and orderly workspace. The job itself needs to be secure, and employees should have the right to take part in pension and sick-pay schemes.

Today, many jobs are under threat – so again, there are many people for whom this need is not being met.

3 Love needs

Love needs arise because we all need to be able to give and receive love. This involves building up good relationships and a feeling of belonging.

In the workplace these needs can be satisfied by the companionship of fellow employees, the pleasure of working in a group or team and company social activities.

4 Esteem needs

Esteem needs are based on our desire for self-respect and the respect of others. Employees have a need to be recognised as individuals, to have a job title or some form of status or prestige, and to have their efforts noticed.

5 Self-actualisation needs

Self-actualisation is about our need to develop our skills and creativity and achieve our full potential as individuals.

In order to meet these needs at work, we need to have the chance to progress and develop through training, and to use our creative talents and abilities to the full.

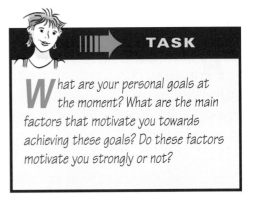

TASK

What are your personal goals at the moment? What are the main factors that motivate you towards achieving these goals? Do these factors motivate you strongly or not?

Everyone has a basic need for food and shelter

TASK

How do each of the following individuals fit against Maslow's hierarchy of needs?

1 Joseph (right) is a talented violinist who has dedicated his life to music. He plays first violin in one of the top orchestras in the UK. Frequently he plays solo pieces, and is always being allowed to develop new ideas. However, there is some uncertainty about the future funding of the orchestra.

2 Maria (left) is a children's book illustrator. Her work is nationally recognised and she always has a string of projects on the go at the same time. She is able to pick and choose the work she does, and can work on her own ideas.

3 Ben (right) left school with no formal qualifications. He expected to get a job as an electrician in the factory where his father worked. However, the factory closed and he now has little prospect of getting a job. He has barely enough food to live on and has recently been made homeless.

4 Stephanie (left) works as a nursery nurse. The pay is not very good but she has enough to make ends meet. She loves working with children and the work gives her tremendous satisfaction. However, she sometimes finds it frustrating that there is little opportunity to develop her managerial skills. Sometimes she also feels a bit undervalued.

Human Resource Management

In modern businesses we use the term **Human Resource Management** to describe the way in which people should be looked after at work.

The idea of Human Resource Management contrasts with the way in which people were treated in the early part of the twentieth century, when employers like Henry Ford used an approach based on what was known as **Scientific Management**.

CASE STUDY

Finding the motivation

A senior manager in a company was surprised at the performance of an employee who had only been in the post for three years.

The employee had the right qualities for the job, as well as the skills, but was not doing as well as expected. He was running a department with 30 highly skilled people working under him. His role was to lead and motivate the team in order to get things done. Despite a generous salary, health insurance, company car and pension scheme, his heart just did not seem to be in the job. Instead of taking pride in running the department, he busied himself in technical work.

After talking with this employee, the senior manager found that the role was no longer challenging enough for him. He had been chosen on the basis of his technical ability and management potential. But what management failed to realise was that he also needed to be constantly involved in projects that required skill and imagination.

This case is not uncommon. Attitudes to work often depend on how much chance individuals have to express their talents and skills. Although the individual in this case was being well paid, he was not being **motivated**. The solution in this case was to move him to a job at a similar level which enabled him to use his skills to the full.

Scientific Management involved treating employees as if they were a resource no different from a machine. Employers worked out the best way of using their human 'machines' to get the most output from them. They reduced the movements that workers needed to make to a minimum and made them repeat the same movement over and over again.

Of course, if they worked hard and productively, they were well paid. But this approach did not meet the higher needs of employees.

Human Resource Management involves humanising work. It involves finding out how to motivate people by treating them as human beings with their own dreams and aspirations.

This often means organising people in teams, encouraging them to solve problems, make decisions and set their own targets.

Human Resource Management also requires organisations to communicate their objectives to people at work. In return employees are encouraged to communicate their hopes and dreams to managers in personal interviews called **appraisals** *(see page 280)*.

Human Resource Management is the best way of meeting people's needs at work.

 **TASK**

1   Explain why material rewards are not the only things that people look for in a job.

2   What are the things that would make a job satisfying for you?

3   What do you understand by the term 'motivation'?

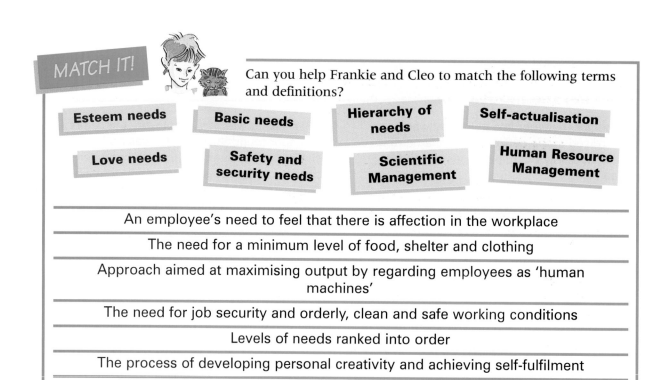

MATCH IT!

Can you help Frankie and Cleo to match the following terms and definitions?

Esteem needs

Basic needs

Hierarchy of needs

Self-actualisation

Love needs

Safety and security needs

Scientific Management

Human Resource Management

| An employee's need to feel that there is affection in the workplace |
| The need for a minimum level of food, shelter and clothing |
| Approach aimed at maximising output by regarding employees as 'human machines' |
| The need for job security and orderly, clean and safe working conditions |
| Levels of needs ranked into order |
| The process of developing personal creativity and achieving self-fulfilment |
| The need for self-respect and the respect of others |
| Treating people as people, in order to enable them to achieve fulfilment and satisfaction and at the same time maximise their contribution to the company |

66 Roles Within the Workplace

Who does what in an organisation?

Some organisations are very small while others are very large. On the whole, the larger an organisation, the more complicated its organisational structure.

Large organisations often have several 'layers' of command (see Chapter 28). Some people spend a lot of time making important decisions while others are mainly involved in carrying out routine tasks.

'How are responsibilities shared in organisations?'

This chapter examines 'who does what' in an organisation. It looks at three different layers of responsibility: managers, supervisors and operatives.

1 Management

Managers have the job of managing the other resources in the workplace, including other people. It is the manager's job to develop systems for 'organising the organisation'.

Strategic-level managers

Top-level decisions concerning the organisation are made by **strategic managers**. These include what range of products to concentrate on, what markets to sell in, what new investments to make, and so on.

'What do strategic-level managers do?'

Middle managers

Middle managers organise and control the resources of an organisation within the guidelines set out from above. Middle managers often have considerable scope for using their own judgement and for bringing in new ideas after consultation with senior management. Examples of middle management decisions include setting and controlling a departmental budget, organising a salesforce, and changing the price of some products.

Junior/supervisory management

Junior/supervisory managers are usually concerned with short-term and routine decisions.

These generally involve areas that are predictable and straightforward. Examples include managing stock, arranging the delivery of goods, organising hours worked by staff, etc.

Unfortunately, because the title 'manager' has a certain status, companies often advertise jobs for 'junior' or 'trainee' managers in the hope of attracting people who will work hard for relatively low pay. If you apply for this kind of job, be sure to check that it really does offer opportunities for promotion.

'That is our new junior supermarket cleaning manager.'

2   Supervisors

Supervisors are often the backbone of an organisation. These are people who know how things should be done at ground level. They work with middle and junior managers to put plans into practice.

Below are some of the typical duties of a supervisor:

◆ Set daily schedules

◆ Oversee work being carried out

◆ Identify and sort out operational problems

◆ Introduce new staff to work tasks

◆ Give advice and guidance

◆ Keep check on levels of stock

◆ Apply expert knowledge of production

◆ Liaise with management

'The best supervisors are the ones that bark! Their job is to be ruthless and to rule the people under them with a rod of iron!'

Do you agree with Ron?

Supervisors know the capabilities of all the resources (machines, people and materials) because they work alongside them every day.

Supervision is a skilled and demanding job. The supervisor is like a sergeant major in the army giving orders to the ground troops. He or she will be first in line to deal with day-to-day problems as and when they occur.

TASK

Which of the following decisions or activities in a supermarket chain would you expect to be carried out by (i) strategic (ii) middle, and (iii) junior managers?

• The decision to move nationally into more organic products

• The decision in a supermarket branch to change the procedure for opening the store in the morning

• The decision to bring in a new system of electronic stock control which will cover the whole supermarket chain

• The decision to open up three new stores per year until the year 2010

• The decision to discount a series of items in a store which are nearing their sell-by date

• Scheduling the hours which staff will work in a given week

• Opening up new tills when existing tills become overloaded

• Designing a training programme for new staff in a particular supermarket

• Making sure that safety notices are put up after spillages

Organisations therefore look for people with good qualifications to become supervisors. They are likely to have mathematical and communication skills as well as a good knowledge of the technology of their industry. Supervisors may have 'risen through the ranks' of their organisation by hard work and the ability to cope with responsibility, so they need to upgrade their skills periodically through training courses.

3 Operatives

Whilst operational activities may be routine, they need to be done with great care and precision. There are many different types of operatives.

In a supermarket there are shelf-fillers and checkout staff; in a textile company there are cutters, stitchers and packers. Operatives need to feel that they are valued, and there should be opportunities for them to learn new skills, so that they can move on to higher-grade work.

COURSEWORK ACTIVITIES

Interview three people – one at management, one at supervisory and one at operational level. Compare the qualifications, knowledge and skills required by each.

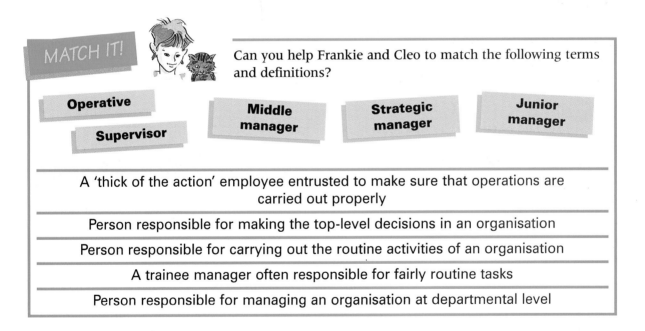

MATCH IT!

Can you help Frankie and Cleo to match the following terms and definitions?

Operative	Middle manager	Strategic manager	Junior manager

Supervisor

A 'thick of the action' employee entrusted to make sure that operations are carried out properly

Person responsible for making the top-level decisions in an organisation

Person responsible for carrying out the routine activities of an organisation

A trainee manager often responsible for fairly routine tasks

Person responsible for managing an organisation at departmental level

67 Wages and Salaries

Methods of payment

Staff workers – usually office workers – are paid an annual salary. This is divided into twelve equal parts and normally paid directly into the employee's bank account each month by credit transfer.

The amount paid each month does not usually vary a great deal because staff workers do not tend to receive overtime or piece-rate payments.

Non-staff employees such as machine operatives are paid weekly **wages**. Usually employees receiving wages will be asked to work for a week in advance before they are paid.

'I wonder what the difference is between a wage and a salary...'

Calculating pay

The sum paid for a normal working week is referred to as a **basic wage** or **salary**. Many employees receive extra benefits on top of their basic wage, either in money or some other form.

Not all employees receive a wage or salary. For example, salespeople may be paid on a **commission** basis, i.e. according to their success in selling the firm's products. The main ways of calculating pay are described below.

Flat rate

This is a set rate of pay, based on a set number of hours – for example, £120 for a 20-hour week. This is easy to calculate and administer, but it does not give the employee any incentive to work harder.

Time rate

Under this scheme, the worker receives a set rate per hour. Any hours worked above a set number are paid at an **overtime** rate.

Piece rate

This system is sometimes used in the textile and electronics industries, among others. Payment is made for each item produced which meets a given quality standard.

The advantage of such a scheme is that it encourages effort. However, it is not suitable for jobs which require time and care. Also, the output of many jobs in service industries is impossible to measure accurately. For example, how could you measure the output of a teacher, bus driver or doctor?

TASK

*P*eter works in an office and is paid £500 per month.

Emma makes sandwiches and earns £80. She is paid weekly.

Does Peter or Emma earn a salary?

COURSEWORK ACTIVITIES

Study the job advertisements in a national newspaper. Make a list of the non-money benefits offered with different jobs.

Bonus

A bonus is paid as an additional encouragement to employees. It can be paid out of additional profits earned by the company as a result of the employee's effort and hard work. Bonuses may also be used as an incentive to workers around Christmas or at times when they might be inclined to slacken effort.

Commission

This is a payment made as a percentage of the sales a salesperson has made.

LATEST NEWS

A report produced by Incomes Data Services (IDS) in January 2001 showed that bar staff, hairdressers and many similar workers earn less than £200 a week. In the health service some pay is only a little higher – hospital porters are on £237. Primary school teachers earn £479 a week, a touch above the average.

The report, which looks at full-time work, says almost two-thirds of staff have weekly earnings before tax of less than £411 (£21,370 a year). Although this figure is the official national average, it is boosted by a small number of high earners – such as MPs on £930 a week and doctors on £964 – and is well above the typical level.

Attendance records

In order to make up pay packets, it is necessary to keep a fair record of how much work is being done. Today, most large employers pay their employees' wages by bank **multiple giro (credit transfer)**.

With a credit transfer system, the firm's payroll department has a record of the bank and bank account number of each of its employees. A wages clerk then simply fills in a multiple giro form authorising the firm's bank to make payments to its employees' bank accounts. Most firms today operate this system through computer records.

There are several ways in which a record can be kept of attendance at work.

Clock-cards (swipe cards)

Large firms will often have a **clocking** system so that the employee 'clocks on and off'. Each employee runs their personal swipe card into a machine on arriving at work. Employees may have to clock off and on again when they take a lunch break and then off again when they finish work.

Using computerised systems, wages can be automatically calculated at the end of the week.

Time-sheets

This method is often used for employees who do not always work at the same place each day, e.g. contract workers such as painters and decorators, film crews, road builders, etc. The sheet is filled in each day and is signed by the supervisor to prove accuracy.

Flexitime

Flexible working time (FWT) is increasingly used in the modern workplace. At 'peak' times all members of staff will be at work. Outside these 'core' hours, there is more flexibility and staff have a certain amount of choice about when they work, provided they work a minimum number of hours.

The advantages of flexitime are:

1 It gives employees more control over when they work. Employees may enjoy this type of freedom. It also makes it easier for them to fit in private engagements such as hair and dental appointments and to take their children to and from school.

2 At least for the basic core time, all the workforce are operating together.

Shift work

In many industries it is important to have machinery working all the time in order to make the most efficient and profitable use of resources. This is true of industries such as textiles, chemicals, steel, coal-mining, food processing and many others.

There are a number of ways of doing this. In some textile businesses, for example, there are distinct day and night shifts. In the North Sea oil industry, production workers may work on a rig for two weeks and then take a two-week break. In the chemical industry, employees sometimes work the day shift for one week, followed by a week on the night shift – and so on.

Employees will be paid higher rewards to make up for having to work unsocial hours.

'Flexitime sounds barmy to me. It is a shirker's charter! The best workers are those that work to a company's hours, not pick and choose their own!'

Is Ron right that the best workers do not need flexibility?

LATEST NEWS

Currently the issue of whether women should be given the legal right to work flexible hours is being debated. What do you think?

CASE STUDY

A typical pay slip

The pay slip below belongs to Milorad Rajic who works in the accounts department of Tasty Sweets PLC. Let us look at the pay slip one column at a time.

Column 1	Column 2	Column 3	Column 4
PAY ADVICE	NAME	Ref No (Quote on any query)	27 Nov 01
① TASTY SWEET PLC	⑤ M Rajic	27 2687 2017	
Basic Pay/Additions	**Deductions**	**Pay Cumulatives**	Your net pay has been credited to your account as stated below:
② Basic pay 1052.25	⑥ Tax Code: 0450H 209.96	This year	⑰
③ Overtime 40.50	⑦ Nat. Insurance 78.41		Bank Nat. Westminster
	⑧ Superannuation 63.13		
	⑨ Union 4.00		Sorting code 06 17 25
			Account Number 76256905
	⑩ Nat. Insurance no YT82034B		
	⑪ Date of payment 28 Nov 01		
	⑫ Income Tax Year 01/02		
	⑬ Pay period 08		MR M RAJIC
	⑭ Enter 'X' if final pay period in tax year ☐		
④ TOTAL PAY £1092.75 ADDITIONS	⑮ TOTAL DEDUCTIONS £355.50	⑯ NET PAY £737.25	

Column 1

1 The name of the company
2 The employee's basic month's pay
3 Milorad has worked some overtime.
4 If we add (2) and (3), we get Milorad's gross pay.

Column 2

5 The employee's name
6 Milorad is a married man with a mortgage. He is entitled to some tax-free pay as an allowance each month. He pays income tax on any earnings above this allowance each month.
7 As well as income tax, employees have to pay a compulsory National Insurance contribution. This money goes towards providing benefits like pensions and unemployment benefit.
8 Milorad also contributed £63.13 towards his company's pension scheme.

Column 2 (Contd.)

9 This is Milorad's trade union membership subscription
10 This is Milorad's national insurance number
11 The date on which money will be transferred to Milorad's bank account by giro payment.
12 The tax year runs from 1st April 2001 to 31st March 2002
13 The pay period is for the eighth month, i.e. November.
14 An 'X' would appear in this box in March.
15 This is the total value of deductions.

Column 3

16 Net pay, i.e. gross pay minus deductions.

Column 4

17 This statement shows that the money is being paid by BACS into Milorad's bank account.

In addition to the above details, the pay slip would typically show the overall amount of gross pay, tax, superannuation and national insurance paid in the financial year up to that date.

Gross and net pay

Gross pay is the total amount of money earned by an employee before any deductions have been taken off. It includes the basic pay, plus any additional payments such as bonuses and overtime.

Net pay is the total amount of money received by an employee after deductions – i.e. an employee's take-home pay:

Net pay = Gross pay – deductions

The difference can be shown by examining a typical pay slip – see the example in the Case Study on page 261.

Statutory deductions from pay

Income tax

This is paid through the **pay-as-you-earn** system **(PAYE)**. People of working age will have income tax deducted from their pay by their employer.

The amount of income tax a person pays depends on their income and **tax allowances**. These will depend on their marital status, whether they have dependent relatives at home, etc. Each employee is given a **tax code** by the Inland Revenue. By looking at the 'free-pay' table issued by the Inland Revenue, the wages department knows how much to deduct.

Self-assessment

A number of people have to fill in their own tax form using a self-assessment method. These people include:

◆ self-employed people

◆ company directors

◆ business partners

These people have to fill in an eight-page tax form and return it by 31 January (to cover the previous tax year). The tax bill they receive will be based on these figures. The amount of tax that needs to be paid is based on all the person's taxable income and gains received (taking away allowances). The Inland Revenue will then work out how much tax needs to be paid (it can be paid in two six-month instalments).

'What do you see as being the good and bad points of asking people to assess their own tax payments?'

Changing job

When an employee leaves his or her job, the employer completes a form **P45.** The P45 must be given to the new employer, who can then continue tax deductions without complications.

At the end of the tax year, an employee receives a form **P60,** which is a summary of their gross and net pay during the year. It must be kept safely because they may need it in order to apply for a mortgage, or claim sickness or unemployment benefit in the coming year. These benefits are **earnings related**.

A person taking up work for the first time will probably not have a tax code or P45. To begin with, they are normally taxed on an emergency code. If they are over-taxed they will be entitled to a **rebate**.

National Insurance contributions

These are paid to the government jointly by the employer and the employee. Contributions from National insurance go into the National Insurance Fund, the National Health Service and the Redundancy Fund. These contributions pay for sickness and unemployment benefit, old age pensions and the National Health Service. The employer's contribution makes up the greater part of the overall contribution. Contributions are not made by the unemployed or when an employee is claiming sickness benefit, provided a doctor's certificate is obtained.

'I think it is outrageous that the unemployed don't have to pay National Insurance!'

Do you agree with Ron?

'In 1998, 16% of the population was over 65. By 2010 this will be 17%. Will we have to pay more National Insurance for pensions?'

LATEST NEWS

Can National Insurance contributions pay for pensions?

A major problem facing the government today is that of the ageing population. With greater numbers of people being in retirement it has become more difficult for the working population to pay for the pensions of retired people. Our own state pensions will be paid for through the National Insurance contributions paid by people who are working when we retire.

The government therefore has suggested that people should look to buying private pension schemes to support their state pensions.

Voluntary deductions from pay

1 Superannuation/private pension schemes

Many employees nowadays choose to pay money into a private pension scheme to supplement their state pensions. For some employees this is a condition of employment. The pension paid depends on how much the employee contributes to the fund.

2 Savings

Some employees contract to pay a certain amount each month into a fund such as the government's **Save-As-You-Earn (SAYE)** scheme. By saving regular sums, the employee is entitled to a lump sum with interest after a given period of time.

3 Trade union contributions

These can also be paid directly from wages.

4 Private medical scheme contributions

An increasing number of people contract to make payments into private medical schemes.

Other voluntary contributions include contributions to the company social club and donations to charity.

'I'm all in favour of people standing on their own feet. They should save for their own pensions rather than relying on the state.'

Do you agree with Ron?

Statutory sick pay (SSP)

The government has now made businesses largely responsible for paying sick pay to employees. This is called **statutory sick pay (SSP)**. These payments are made if a worker is sick on normal working days.

Computerisation of wages

Today much routine payroll work is done by computers. This includes the calculation of wages, the printing of pay slips and the production of payment instructions to the bank. Computers are able to handle a lot of work quickly and accurately. As with any other computer work, it is essential to take a back-up copy.

'I run my car and mobile phone on the business!'

Fringe benefits

Many jobs include a wide range of **perks** or benefits that do not appear directly in the pay packet. Railway employees and their families, for example, may be allowed free rail travel. Managerial jobs often include perks such as subsidised company cars and phone bills. Other fringe benefits include subsidised canteen facilities, free training courses, or the right to buy the firm's products at discount prices.

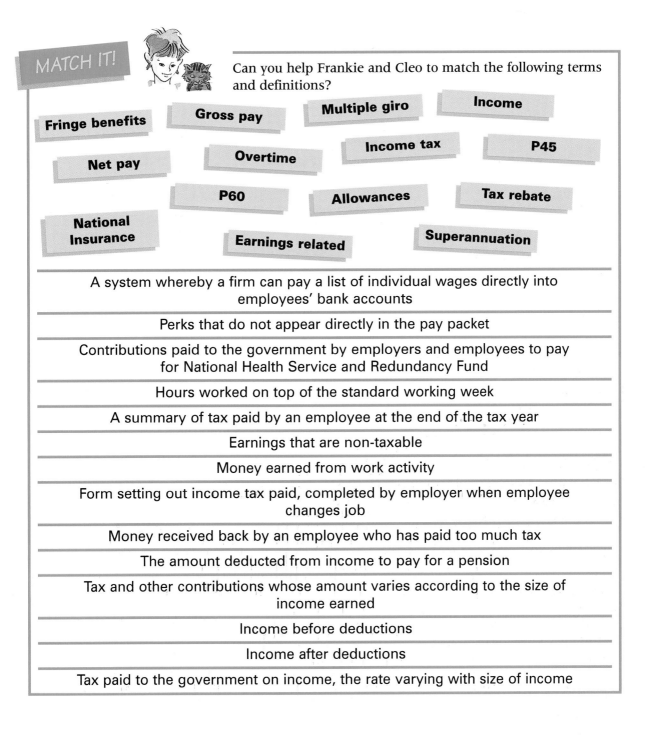

MATCH IT! Can you help Frankie and Cleo to match the following terms and definitions?

Fringe benefits | Gross pay | Multiple giro | Income | Income tax | P45 | Net pay | Overtime | P60 | Allowances | Tax rebate | National Insurance | Earnings related | Superannuation

A system whereby a firm can pay a list of individual wages directly into employees' bank accounts

Perks that do not appear directly in the pay packet

Contributions paid to the government by employers and employees to pay for National Health Service and Redundancy Fund

Hours worked on top of the standard working week

A summary of tax paid by an employee at the end of the tax year

Earnings that are non-taxable

Money earned from work activity

Form setting out income tax paid, completed by employer when employee changes job

Money received back by an employee who has paid too much tax

The amount deducted from income to pay for a pension

Tax and other contributions whose amount varies according to the size of income earned

Income before deductions

Income after deductions

Tax paid to the government on income, the rate varying with size of income

68 The Employment Contract

What is a contract?

A contract is an agreement between people or organisations to deliver goods or services, or to do something on jointly agreed terms.

Although a contract of employment does not have to be made out in writing the law requires a summary of the most important terms in the contract to be given to the employee.

The **Employment Rights Act 1996** dictates that the **terms** and **conditions** that must be set out in writing are:

♦ The names of the employer and the employee

♦ The date when employment began

♦ The scale or rate of pay and the method of calculating pay where the employee is paid by commission or bonus

♦ When payment is made (i.e. weekly or monthly), and the day or date of payment

♦ The hours to be worked, including any compulsory overtime

♦ Holiday entitlement and holiday pay

♦ Sick pay and injury arrangements

♦ Entitlements to a pension scheme

♦ The length of notice of termination an employee must receive or give

♦ The job title

♦ The duration of temporary contracts

♦ The work location or locations

♦ Grievance procedures

♦ Disciplinary procedures

The case study opposite outlines what a contract of employment might look like.

'If you are working have you received a summary of your terms and conditions of work?

COURSEWORK ACTIVITIES

Study the contract of employment of someone you know. Identify each of the features listed on the left on their contract of employment.

A typical contract of employment

Contract of employment for restaurant employees

This document sets out the terms and conditions for kitchen staff at JOLLY RESTAURANTS. It is drawn up in accordance with the Employment Rights Act, 1996.

Employee: Sally Davies

Address.   314 The Laurels, Grantham, NG31 9HL

Job title   Kitchen porter

This contract takes effect as at: 8.00.a.m.

Your employment with JOLLY RESTAURANTS starts on:

1st January, 2002.

1. Pay

Your rate of pay and overtime has been established nationally by the Trade Union and the Hotel Employers' Association. A copy of this agreement is available for reference from the personnel manager.

Your current rate of pay is £5.60 per hour for a 34-hour working week, and is paid in arrears normally on a Friday.

Each payment will be accompanied by an itemised pay statement. In addition to the above rate of pay, the company operates a bonus scheme depending on the number of customers using the restaurants. A copy of this scheme is available from the personnel manager for reference.

1

  TASK

1   How clear do you find the above introduction to a contract of employment?

2   Why is it set out so precisely?

3   What details have been included so far in the contract which must be there by law? (Note that employers must provide an itemised pay statement!)

Dismissal

Over the years, the rules for dismissing employees have become more and more complicated. The heart of the matter lies in the difference between what the courts regard to be 'fair' and 'unfair' dismissal.

Fair dismissal can take place when an employee can be shown to be guilty of:

♦ Wilful destruction of company property

♦ Sexual or racial harassment

♦ Continuous bad timekeeping

♦ A negative attitude at work

♦ Inability to do the job

♦ Sleeping on the job

In some cases (e.g. for bad time keeping) employees would normally receive oral warnings, written warnings and even suspensions before dismissal. **Unfair dismissal** would almost certainly be deemed to have occurred in any of the following circumstances:

♦ **Pregnancy:** An employee can be sacked only if she is unable to do her job properly as a result of being pregnant (e.g. stacking shelves).

♦ **Race:** A worker cannot be sacked on grounds of race.

♦ **Homosexuality:** A person should not be sacked on grounds of their sexual orientation.

♦ **Union membership:** An employer cannot sack a worker for belonging to a trade union.

♦ **Criminal record:** If an employer does not find out about an employee's criminal record until some time after employment starts, they cannot sack them unless they were convicted of a 'relevant' crime (e.g. a cashier who has a record of stealing petty cash).

TASK

*L*ook at the following examples. What do you think the legal position would be in each case (i.e. would it be fair or unfair dismissal)?

1 A taxi firm dismisses one of their drivers after a tabloid newspaper identifies him as a homosexual. The taxi firm argues that this will lose them business.

2 An employee is caught on the firm's security cameras writing graffiti about the chairman on a wall in front of the company headquarters.

3 A senior manager of a company is reported to the managing director for persistently pinching the bottom of one of the junior employees and making lewd comments.

4 An employee of the firm persistently sets out to recruit other members of a company to a trade union during breaks and lunch hours.

5 A new employee of a firm reports an existing employee for being involved in an assault charge 20 years ago.

'I often take people on to see what they're like. However, if they don't come up to scratch during the first thirteen weeks I get rid of them!'

Is Ron keeping within the letter of the law?

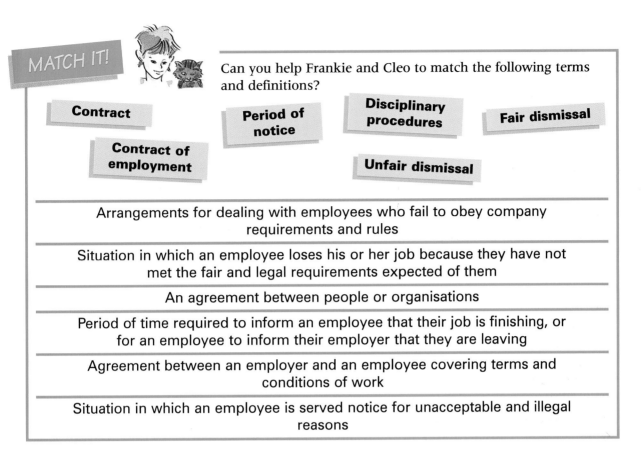

MATCH IT! Can you help Frankie and Cleo to match the following terms and definitions?

Contract

Period of notice

Disciplinary procedures

Fair dismissal

Contract of employment

Unfair dismissal

Arrangements for dealing with employees who fail to obey company requirements and rules
Situation in which an employee loses his or her job because they have not met the fair and legal requirements expected of them
An agreement between people or organisations
Period of time required to inform an employee that their job is finishing, or for an employee to inform their employer that they are leaving
Agreement between an employer and an employee covering terms and conditions of work
Situation in which an employee is served notice for unacceptable and illegal reasons

69 Personnel

What do we mean by 'personnel'?

The word 'personnel' means the people employed in an organisation or a service. Within an organisation, the personnel department interviews, appoints, keeps records of employees, and carries out other tasks shown below.

The important responsibilities of a personnel department

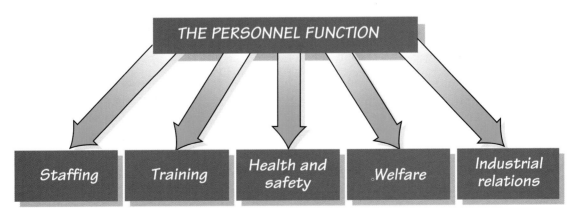

THE PERSONNEL FUNCTION

Staffing

Training

Health and safety

Welfare

Industrial relations

Managing human resources

Today, organisations depend on the individual qualities of people more than ever before. This is particularly true in service industries, where employees are usually involved in frequent direct relationships with customers – e.g. in talking to them over the phone or in face-to-face customer service relationships. Human Resource Management is therefore very important. Good human relations at work is one of the best ways of adding value to output.

Personnel management is concerned with all aspects of developing interpersonal relationships within a firm. This includes recruitment and selection, dismissal, training, discipline, pensions, wage negotiations and other matters.

The employment procession

One way to remember what personnel work involves is to think about what is called the **employment procession**.

This involves looking after the needs of employees from the time they are chosen to work in an organisation to the time they retire.

The employment procession starts with the **recruitment** process – finding new recruits and choosing who to take on. New staff then need to be helped to 'fit in', so they go through a period of **induction**.

During their employment they will need to be **trained** to upgrade their skills and knowledge. Then, when the need arises, they can be **transferred** to other jobs or areas.

When they finish working for the organisation they need to have their jobs **terminated** in a satisfactory way. This includes making sure that pension and other matters are dealt with according to the law.

Other personnel functions

The personnel department is also responsible for:

◆ Health and safety

◆ Equal opportunities

◆ Pay bargaining

◆ Appraisals

◆ Discipline

◆ Payment systems

'The employment procession can be very quick for some people I employ. If they don't meet my requirements I soon kick them out by the seat of their pants!'

Has Ron fully understood the nature of human resource management?

 **TASK**

Read the Case Study on the following page, then answer the questions below:

1 How many stages are there in the employment procession?

2 If Tommy started work at 16 and retired at 63, how many years did he spend at work?

  TASK

Examine each of the stages in Tommy's employment procession. How might each of these stages be different for a young person starting working today and following their career through to the middle of the twenty-first century?

The employment procession

We can see the employment procession more clearly by looking at the cartoon strip below which shows stages in the working life of Frankie's grandad, Tommy.

1 Recruitment

On leaving school at 16, Tommy went for an interview at a local engineering works along with 100 other boys. He was lucky to be one of 20 taken on as an apprentice.

2 Induction

For his first month at work, Tommy sat alongside a more experienced worker, Frank, who taught him how to work a lathe, and generally 'showed him the ropes'.

3 Training

Tommy worked four days a week learning his work 'on the job'. He also went to the local technical college for one day a week – learning 'off the job'.

4 Transfer

Later on, Tommy became a skilled engineer. He was transferred to another section of the company as a foreman in a plant producing racing cars.

5 Termination

In 2000 Tommy took early retirement at the age of 63. In return for his loyalty, he was presented with a two-week holiday in Bermuda, a gold watch, and a miniature replica of the first racing car he produced.

All of the above stages in Tommy's career path had been planned and prepared for him in discussion with the personnel department of his company.

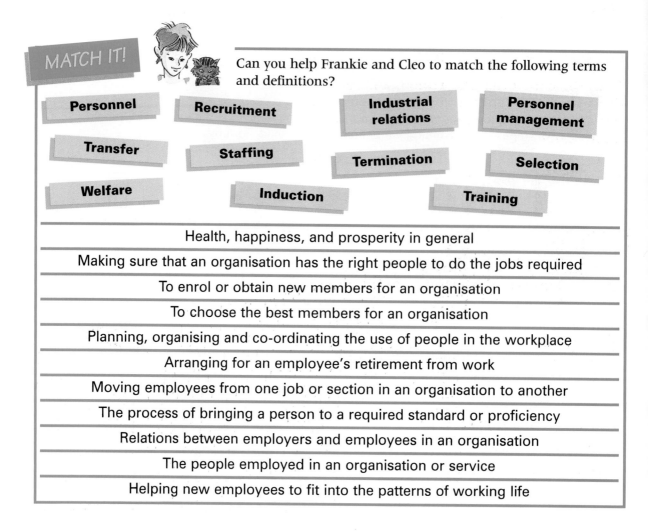

MATCH IT! Can you help Frankie and Cleo to match the following terms and definitions?

Personnel   Recruitment   Industrial relations   Personnel management

Transfer   Staffing   Termination   Selection

Welfare   Induction   Training

Health, happiness, and prosperity in general
Making sure that an organisation has the right people to do the jobs required
To enrol or obtain new members for an organisation
To choose the best members for an organisation
Planning, organising and co-ordinating the use of people in the workplace
Arranging for an employee's retirement from work
Moving employees from one job or section in an organisation to another
The process of bringing a person to a required standard or proficiency
Relations between employers and employees in an organisation
The people employed in an organisation or service
Helping new employees to fit into the patterns of working life

70 Recruitment and Selection

The purpose of recruitment

From the personnel department's point of view, the purpose of recruitment is to buy in and keep the best people to work for the organisation.

The first step in the process is to set out clearly what the particular job involves.

'How much planning goes into making sure that you recruit and select the right person for the job?'

Job analysis

Before advertising a job, the personnel department need to think clearly about what the duties and responsibilities of the job-holder will be. Once they have analysed what they are looking for, they can make out a **job description**.

A job description is a written statement setting out how a particular employee is to fit into an organisation. For example, the job of a trainee manager in a supermarket could be described under the following headings:

◆ Title of post

◆ The main purposes of the job

◆ Supervisory/management responsibilities

◆ The sort of decisions he or she will need to make

◆ Responsibility for assets, materials, etc.

A job/personnel specification

A **job** or **personnel specification** is more than a simple description of the job. It describes the mental and physical requirements of the job-holder. The layout of a personnel specification may look something like this:

Personnel specification for a shop assistant

Attributes	Essential	Desirable
Physical	–	To be healthy, and able to lift packages, and stack shelves
Qualifications	Maths, English	NVQ Intermediate equivalent GCSEs (A–C)
Experience	–	Previous experience of working as a shop assistant
Etc.		

Having drawn up a job/personnel specification, the personnel department can use it to:

◆ Make sure that a job advertisement covers the qualities that a new job-holder will need to have

◆ Enable interviewers to check that candidates for a job have the right qualities

◆ Check from time to time that people who have been appointed to a job are doing what is required of them

The recruitment process

Organisations can recruit **internally** or **externally**, i.e. they can choose people from inside the organisation or widen the field to outsiders.

Advantages of internal recruitment are:

1 There is less risk involved, because the employer already knows the person who will be filling the vacancy.

2 It saves the cost of press advertising and is therefore cheaper.

3 It saves on induction costs.

4 The opportunity for promotion in the organisation encourages people to work hard.

Disadvantages of internal recruitment are:

1 No new ideas are brought into the organisation from outside.

2 There is no 'buzz' that follows when a new person joins the organisation.

3 Appointing from within the organisation may cause jealousy and resentment among other staff, who may feel they have been 'passed over' for promotion.

'Isn't it better to promote people from within an organisation? You already know whether or not they can do a job!'

Do you agree with Frankie?

COURSEWORK ACTIVITIES

Study the job description of someone you know who is currently working. If you are working part-time, you may like to use your own job description.

Set out a brief report for other students showing how each section of the job description works in practice. How accurately does it describe the tasks and responsibilities the job-holder actually performs?

EMPLOYMENT SERVICE
Serving People through Jobcentres

Above: The government Employment Service provides help for firms and job-seekers.

External recruitment

There are a number of ways of recruiting externally.

1 Placing a newspaper advertisement

Newspaper advertising is a very important form of recruitment. Local newspapers will be used for jobs that can be filled within a locality, e.g. work in a local supermarket or service station. Major companies, however, will seek to advertise nationally when seeking recruits to fill important jobs. The advert on the right sets out a humorous view of what a national advert for the England football manager might look like (although the layout is typical of national newspaper advertisements).

2 Advertising in a Jobcentre

Jobcentres can be found in most towns. They are run by the Employment Service, which is part of the Department for Education and Employment. They are used by job-seekers and employers.

Jobcentres display details of vacancies on cards in their window *(see example, right)*. Job-seekers can apply for jobs locally and further afield. They can also get information about training opportunities which will help them get back into work.

3 Commercial employment/recruitment agencies

There are many commercial employment agencies that help businesses to recruit staff. Fields in which these agencies often specialise are professional, secretarial, high technology, nursing and casual work.

Selection

Selection is all about choosing the best person to do a job. Methods vary according to how the job has been advertised, and the experience, skills and expertise required.

Methods of application

Sometimes employers will ask candidates to apply by letter. A good letter of application will tell them whether the candidate is worthy of an interview *(see next page)*.

England Manager
£1 MILLION + UNLIMITED ABUSE

The job: The football association is seeking a manager to lead the England team to glorious victory in the World Cup.

The manager will work for 16 weeks in each year, getting up early on Saturdays, standing in the rain, shouting, swearing, disciplining players for non-appearance, and looking sad in newspaper photographs.

He or she will be expected to pontificate on television before, during and after every match, using a selection of approved phrases, for example "The lads gave it one hundred and ten per cent".

The person: The successful candidate will be motivated, patriotic, self-starting, enthusiastic, unafraid of confrontation, criticism and personal abuse. Being German, French, Scandinavian or Italian is not necessarily a disadvantage.

Salary: £1,000,000 a year.

Fringe benefits: Chauffeur driven car, luxury apartment Wembley area, opportunities to meet Posh Spice, Baby Beckham, Des Lynam, Tony Blair and other famous people. Luncheon Vouchers, monogrammed track suit.

The Football Association, Lancaster Gate, London W1 NEX.

We are an equal opportunities employer, and we are desperate.

Ref 4-4-2

EMPLOYMENT
Man or Woman

JOB	Full-time sales assistant
DISTRICT	Central Northampton
WAGE	£5 per hour. Annual staff bonus. Fringe benefits
HOURS	36-hour wk. 6-day flexible work pattern
DURATION	Permanent
DETAILS	Ladies fashion dept. Age 25-45. Experience essential.
JOB NO.	15

Ask for COR: 12345

A vacancy advertised in a government Jobcentre

```
                                              Nina Mistry
                                            20 Belton Lane
                                                  Grantham
      10th September 2001                     Lincolnshire
                                                NG31 9HL

      Dear Ms Stevens

      I am writing to apply for the position of Design Engineer
      which I saw advertised in the Grantham Jobcentre (COR: 7547).

      My last job was in a small electronics company who were
      involved in making electronic equipment for refrigeration.
      The company, Whitegoods International, made energy-saving
      motor controllers enabling reductions in the cost of
      refrigeration in an environmentally-friendly way. I worked
      for the company for three years, and this enabled me to build
      up an extensive understanding of refrigeration equipment. I
      enjoyed working for the company but am now looking for a post
      with more responsibility.

      As you can see from my CV, I am 25 years of age and my
      qualifications are of a high standard in both electronics and
      programming. Recently I have learnt to use a variety of
      programming languages to a good level of competence.

      I hope my application is of interest to you and I look
      forward to hearing from you in the near future.

      Yours sincerely,

      Nina Mistry

      Nina Mistry
```

Above: A typical letter of application

In other cases candidates will be asked to fill in a printed **application form**. This enables them to set out information about themselves in a standardised way, which helps firms to choose candidates for interview later on.

The interview

The interview is the most common method of selection. This is a face-to-face meeting between the candidate and the employer to find out whether the applicant will be suitable for the job, and vice versa. Sometimes an organisation will ask for **references** before interviewing. However, often they will interview first and then make a job offer, 'subject to suitable references'.

TASK

Working in groups of four (two pairs), complete the following tasks using a word processing package, and e-mail facilities. Transfer each of the documents outlined as an attachment.

1   Pair A should prepare a job advertisement for a hotel porter in a firm called Jolly Hotels. Meanwhile Pair B should prepare an advertisement for a receptionist at Jolly Hotels. Make up details where necessary.

2   Each pair sends a letter of application for the job advertised by the other pair.

3   Each pair writes to the other pair inviting them for interview.

4   Interviews are held with all four candidates. If possible, make a video.

5   Analyse the performance of both interviewers and candidates. Then make a list of interviewing techniques for interviewers, as well as a list of interviewing techniques for applicants.

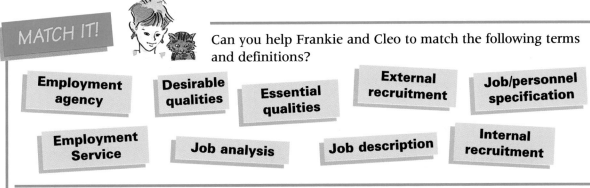

MATCH IT!   Can you help Frankie and Cleo to match the following terms and definitions?

| Employment agency | Desirable qualities | Essential qualities | External recruitment | Job/personnel specification |

| Employment Service | Job analysis | Job description | Internal recruitment |

| A commercial organisation which helps firms to fill job vacancies |
| The key requirements looked for in an applicant for a job |
| Where a firm recruits from people already working within the organisation |
| Studying the requirements for a job before creating a job description |
| Written statement of how a particular job will fit into an organisation |
| A government-run service to help firms and job-seekers to fill vacancies |
| Choosing new employees from outside an organisation |
| A detailed list of the mental and physical requirements of a job-holder |
| A list of requirements of a job-holder which may be desirable but are not essential |

277

71 Training and Development

What is training?

Training involves guiding or teaching someone to do something by providing them with a planned programme of exercises and activities. Training develops the skills and knowledge of employees to help them to do their jobs better, and prepares them for more demanding jobs in the future.

'What are the advantages to a firm of training its people? After all, it is costly.'

An organisation will carry out a Training Needs Analysis (TNA) to find out what extra skills, knowledge and abilities are required by employees that work for the organisation. It is then possible to create a training plan based on the TNA.

Development is not the same as training. Development is more concerned with the personal development needs of individuals that work for an organisation. Individual Development Plans (IDPs) can then be created to help individuals to develop themselves.

While training focuses on the needs of the organisation, development planning also helps the organisation – because individual employees who feel that their development needs are being met are far more likely to be motivated to work hard for the organisation.

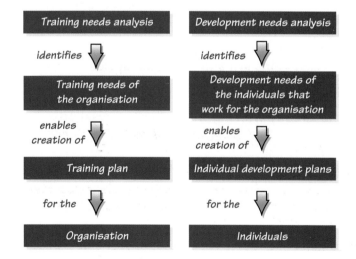

Training and development plans

Training costs money

A business needs well-trained employees if it is to be competitive. But training costs money. Special instructors may have to be employed; courses need to be paid for and will require materials, equipment, space and time.

A business therefore has to decide how much money it wants to spend on training, what sort of training should be given, and to whom.

How much should be spent on training?

How and when is the training to be carried out?

What sort of training?

Who gets trained?

Training issues for the employer

Training – a two-way process

Training helps those being trained *and* the organisation they work for. Training can therefore be one of the most effective ways for an organisation to add value.

◆ **Benefits to individuals** include greater skills, more knowledge, confidence, better career prospects, etc.

◆ **Benefits to the organisation** include more productive employees, better-quality work, more job satisfaction leading to lower absenteeism and staff turnover, greater ability to use the latest technology, etc.

CASE STUDY

Training opportunities in a biscuit factory

The following is a short extract from an employee's handbook in a biscuit factory:

'This company values training and development for all our employees, in order to widen your experience and help you to gain promotion.

'Your most important contact is your line supervisor or manager (the person directly above you). This person will help you to deal with any immediate problems.

'In your first six months there will be opportunities to discuss your training needs with your immediate superior. The training needs of all employees are constantly examined. Together with your supervisor, line leader and training instructors, we will teach you the skills you require, including the importance of safety at work.

'The company also encourages you to continue with education courses in your spare time. If you choose an appropriate course we will refund your tuition and exam fees.'

Types of training

There are a number of different types of training:

1 Induction

Induction training is given to new employees. Its aim is to familiarise them with the organisation and its rules.

It can also be used to show the new employee particular job skills. For example, as part of the induction process, a supermarket cashier may be trained to use electronic scanning equipment and follow other checkout procedures.

2 Upgrading skills

Work changes all the time. This is particularly true in organisations that rely on new technology. It is therefore essential for businesses to **upgrade** the skills of their employees. For example, in the UK today many employees still lack important information technology skills.

3 Retraining

As time moves on, some jobs change or disappear. As a result the employees who previously did these jobs may need to **retrain** to do something else.

4 Multi-skilling

Multi-skilling is the process of training employees to do a number of different tasks. Today's employees need to have different skills and be able to turn their hand to a variety of tasks. We also call this **flexibility**. Work flexibility can be developed through training.

Training methods

Training methods can be split into two main types:

◆ On-the-job training

◆ Off-the-job training

On-the-job training

On-the-job training involves learning new skills through experience at work. A new employee may observe a more experienced worker and copy the methods they use. This is a cheap and often an effective method of training.

Off-the-job training

This involves taking employees away from their jobs to be trained. It can be done within a company, or employees may be sent outside to courses run by educational and training groups.

Appraisal

Many organisations today run **appraisal schemes**. The scheme usually requires individual job-holders to collect and record, in a set way, their impressions of the people working under them. They can then assess strengths and weaknesses in the employees' performance and identify suitable training and development to meet their needs.

Appraisal also helps the employee by allowing them to identify and work towards their chosen career path.

TASK

1 Why does the company in the Case Study on page 279 train its employees?

2 Who benefits from training?

3 What evidence is given in the case study that the biscuit firm is interested in the development of its employees as well as in training?

'Appraisal is a good idea. It helps managers to find out who's causing problems in an organisation! It is a good way of getting rid of bad workers!'

Do you think that Ron understands the real purpose of appraisal?

The appraisal interview

Appraisal interviews are held at regular intervals – say, once a year. The **appraisor** (the superior who carries out the appraisal) will usually ask the **appraisee** (the employee being appraised) to fill in a questionnaire before the interview. This form then becomes a basis for discussion. Typical questions will include:

◆ What were your most important targets/achievements this year?

◆ How successful were you in meeting those targets?

◆ What do you feel are your current strengths?

◆ What do you feel are your current weaknesses?

Often appraisal is linked to pay. Targets are set during the appraisal interview. If the target is met or exceeded then the employee may receive performance-related pay.

COURSEWORK ACTIVITIES

Interview somebody who has recently had an appraisal interview. What was the format of the interview? What sort of questions were they asked? How useful did they find the appraisal process?

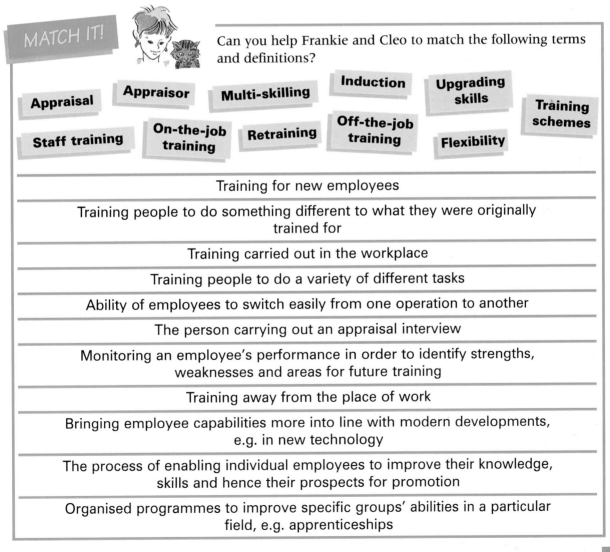

MATCH IT!

Can you help Frankie and Cleo to match the following terms and definitions?

Appraisal · Appraisor · Multi-skilling · Induction · Upgrading skills · Training schemes · Staff training · On-the-job training · Retraining · Off-the-job training · Flexibility

Training for new employees
Training people to do something different to what they were originally trained for
Training carried out in the workplace
Training people to do a variety of different tasks
Ability of employees to switch easily from one operation to another
The person carrying out an appraisal interview
Monitoring an employee's performance in order to identify strengths, weaknesses and areas for future training
Training away from the place of work
Bringing employee capabilities more into line with modern developments, e.g. in new technology
The process of enabling individual employees to improve their knowledge, skills and hence their prospects for promotion
Organised programmes to improve specific groups' abilities in a particular field, e.g. apprenticeships

72 Health and Safety

Accidents in the workplace

Over 350 people die each year as a result of accident or injury in the workplace. Over 10,000 early deaths occur as a result of past exposure to hazardous material and substances such as asbestos. 29 million working days are lost as a result of injuries and accidents at work.

'Why is health and safety at work such an important issue?'

These statistics immediately show the importance of health and safety – and why organisations need to take health and safety very seriously.

The Health and Safety at Work Act, 1974

The Health and Safety at Work Act 1974 is the most important law governing issues related to health and safety. This Act is supervised by the Health and Safety Commission. More recently, Health and Safety requirements have been updated by a series of European Union Directives, which have been agreed by Member States and have become law in this country.

Most importantly, Health and Safety regulations were set out in 1992 in a series of measures known as the **'six pack'**. These regulations set out the general duties that employers have to their employees and members of the public, as well as obligations that employees have to each other.

The Management of Health and Safety Regulations 1997 set out clearly what managers have to do in relation to every work activity.

Risk assessment

The main requirements of Health and Safety regulations in this country are that:

◆ Every employer with five or more employees must carry out a 'risk assessment'

◆ The employer must then take health and safety measures in line with the risk assessment

◆ The employer must appoint competent people to help carry out the health and safety arrangements

◆ Employers must set up emergency procedures

◆ Employers must provide clear information and training to employees

◆ They must work jointly with other employees sharing the same premises

The Health and Safety Executive provides guidance to help people interpret and comply with the law. The Health and Safety Executive also creates codes of practice, which have legal status.

A written safety policy

In law, if an organisation employs five or more people, it must have a written **safety policy**. This must set out:

◆ Who is responsible for workplace health and safety

◆ The arrangements that have been made for health and safety

This policy must also be communicated to everyone in the workplace. All employees should be given the training and information they need in order to work safely. There should be regular safety inspections, and large organisations should also have an active Health and Safety committee.

CASE STUDY

Safety in the modern workplace

One of the major retailing organisations in this country has set out the responsibilities of management for health and safety as being:

• *The provision as far as is reasonably practicable, of safe plant and safe systems of work*

• *Arrangements for ensuring, so far as is practicable, safety in the use, handling, storage and transport of substances*

• *The provision of such information, instruction, training and supervision as is necessary to fulfil the responsibilities for health and safety*

• *The provision, as far as is reasonably practicable, of a workplace and environment which is safe and without risks to health*

• *The reporting of accidents, injuries, reportable illnesses and dangerous occurrences as required by the law*

Providing protective clothing for workers is an important management responsibility

Employee responsibilities

Safety in the workplace is not *just* a management responsibility. It is also up to employees to take steps to ensure their own – and other people's – health and safety. In particular, employees must:

◆ **Comply** with company arrangements and procedures for securing a safe workplace

- ◆ **Report** incidents to management that have led, or may lead, to injury
- ◆ **Co-operate** in the investigation of accidents in order to prevent them happening again

Other health and safety regulations

There are a number of other important health and safety regulations:

Reporting of Injuries, Diseases and Dangerous Occurrences Regulations, 1985 and 1996 ('RIDDOR')
These regulations require that any injuries resulting from accidents at work where the employee is unable to work for three or more days must be reported to the authorities within seven days.

Listed diseases must be reported, and accidents involving work equipment.

COURSEWORK ACTIVITIES

Ask if you can borrow a copy of the safety policy for your school or college. Make a list of the major points of interest that you find in this policy and discuss them with other students.

TASK

Can you help Frankie and Cleo to list all the unsafe working practices shown in the picture?

Control of Substances Hazardous to Health Regulations, 1988 and 1997 ('COSHH')

This states that employers must identify work tasks which are likely to be harmful and take steps to minimise the risks. Workers dealing with hazardous substances must be given detailed information and training.

Noise at Work Regulations, 1989

Employers must reduce the risk of hearing damage to employees to the lowest practical level, for example, by providing ear protectors when noise reaches a certain level.

Workplace Health and Safety at Work Regulations, 1992

These set out requirements for minimum ventilation, heating, lighting, and welfare facilities in the workplace.

Display Screens Regulations, 1992

Sets out requirements for health and safety standards for employees working with visual display units, such as computer screens.

'I can't be bothered with all these laws. At the end of the day it's up to my workers to operate in a safe fashion. The responsibility is basically theirs if something happens. They're the ones that'll be taken to court!'

Is Ron right?

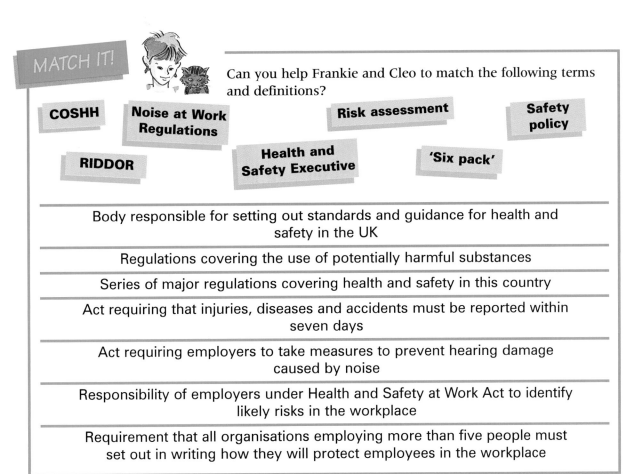

MATCH IT!

Can you help Frankie and Cleo to match the following terms and definitions?

COSHH   Noise at Work Regulations   Risk assessment   Safety policy

RIDDOR   Health and Safety Executive   'Six pack'

Body responsible for setting out standards and guidance for health and safety in the UK

Regulations covering the use of potentially harmful substances

Series of major regulations covering health and safety in this country

Act requiring that injuries, diseases and accidents must be reported within seven days

Act requiring employers to take measures to prevent hearing damage caused by noise

Responsibility of employers under Health and Safety at Work Act to identify likely risks in the workplace

Requirement that all organisations employing more than five people must set out in writing how they will protect employees in the workplace

73 Equal Opportunities

What do we mean by equal opportunities?

Equal opportunities exist when everyone is given the same opportunity with regards to being interviewed for a job, stands an equal chance of being selected, is given equal access to training, promotion, etc. regardless of gender, racial group, age, physical characteristics, sexual orientation or other features.

Many business organisations now realise that it is actually in their own interests to provide equal opportunities *(see Case Study below)*. After all, it is only by offering equal opportunities that they can gain most benefit from all the different people that make up our society.

'Does the fact that there are now more women at work than men mean that we have equal opportunities?'

CASE STUDY

Equal opportunities at Shell and Sainsbury's

Shell

A workplace where all staff are treated as individuals and progression/development is based on merit

Fair and unbiased treatment of all employees

Encouraging and using talent regardless of sex, marital status, ethnic origin or disability

EQUAL OPPORTUNITIES MEAN

Making sure that we observe the spirit as well as the letter of the law

Making sure the policy actually happens in practice

SAINSBURY'S

Our policy is designed:

• To ensure that no employee receives less favourable treatment on the grounds of sex, race, colour, ethnic origin, religion, disability or marital status.

• To ensure fair and equal access to training, career development and promotion through a well established appraisal scheme.

• To promote a positive environment that enables the organisation to tap the widest possible sources of talent.

  TASK

1 What similarities can you see in the two companies' attitudes?

2 How do the two organisations stand to benefit from having such clear equal opportunities policies?

3 Is there anything you would add or change in the statements made by these two organisations?

The Sex Discrimination Acts,1975, 1986

These Act sets out to make sure that both sexes are treated equally in the workplace. They make it illegal for employers to discriminate in the following key areas:

◆ Selection procedures

◆ Terms on which employment is offered

◆ Opportunities for training and development

◆ Fringe benefits

◆ Choice of who will be made redundant

Unlawful discrimination means giving less favourable treatment to someone because of their sex or because they are married or single.

Under the Acts, discrimination can be either **direct** or **indirect.** Direct sex discrimination means treating someone less favourably than a person of the opposite sex would be treated in the same circumstances. For example, if only men are made managers, and sex is the criterion for appointment, this counts as direct discrimination.

Direct **marriage discrimination** means treating a married person less favourably than an unmarried person of the same sex.

For example, a policy not to recruit married people for a job that involved being away from home would be classed as discrimination.

Indirect sex discrimination is less easy to pinpoint. It means making a requirement which on the face of it applies equally to both men and women, but which in practice can be met by a much smaller proportion of one sex than the other – for example, when an organisation restricts certain grades of work to males.

The Sex Discrimination Act, 1986 also covers **victimisation.** Victimisation means treating someone less favourably than others because – 'in good faith' – they have made allegations about discrimination or unfair treatment.

'Can discrimination at work ever be legal?'

The Race Relations Act,1976

In the same way as the Sex Discrimination Act sets out to ensure that both sexes are treated equally in the workplace, the **Race Relations Act** sets out to protect members of ethnic minorities from discrimination and unfair treatment.

The Equal Pay Act, 1970

This states that employers must pay equal amounts to men and women if they are doing the same work, or work which rates as being equivalent, or if they are doing work of equal value.

Under the Act, anyone making a claim for equal pay must be able to compare themselves with a person of the opposite sex doing the same work.

CASE STUDY

The pay gap

The figures below show the difference in the average hourly, weekly and annual pay in 1999 of men and women.

	Hourly	Weekly	Annual
Women	£8.70	£326.50	£16,481
Men	£10.75	£442.40	£23,412
Pay gap (female as % of male)	80.9%	73.8%	70.4%

Source: National Earnings Survey

TASK

What forms of discrimination or victimisation are being employed in the following examples of job advertisements and working practices? Choose from:

a) Victimisation

b) Direct sex discrimination

c) Indirect sex discrimination

d) Direct marriage discrimination

e) Indirect marriage discrimination

f) Direct race discrimination

g) Indirect race discrimination

'NO WOMEN'

'Applicants must be over 2 metres tall'

'Bar staff must wear short skirts.'

'No hair coverings can be worn.'

'Applicants must be below the age of 30.'

'Male applicants only'

'Applicants must be single.'

Line workers are not allowed to stop work at any time during scheduled working hours.

A line worker is sacked because she claims that the supervisor is continually harassing her.

A man is refused a job as a sales assistant in a women's clothing shop because it was argued that he would be unable to go into the fitting room.

'All employees to be clean-shaven'

Disabled workers

It is against the law for employers to discriminate against employees or prospective employees on account of disability. Small companies with fewer than 15 employees are not included.

Employers may also have to make a 'reasonable adjustment' if their premises or working arrangements place a disabled person at a substantial disadvantage compared to a person without a disability.

The aim of the Act is to ensure that a disabled person is treated fairly. A person who feels that they have been the subject of disability discrimination can complain to an employment tribunal. There is no ceiling to the compensation that can be awarded by the tribunal.

TASK

1   What does the table opposite tell us about the equality of male and female earnings in this country?

2   Why do you think women's annual earnings make up a smaller percentage of men's annual earnings, than women's hourly earnings do of men's?

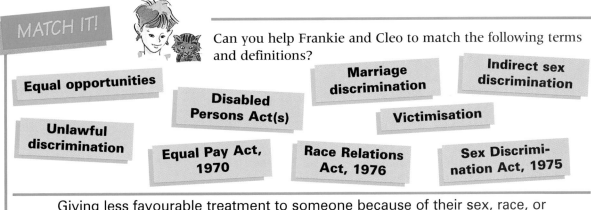

MATCH IT!

Can you help Frankie and Cleo to match the following terms and definitions?

Equal opportunities

Marriage discrimination

Indirect sex discrimination

Disabled Persons Act(s)

Victimisation

Unlawful discrimination

Equal Pay Act, 1970

Race Relations Act, 1976

Sex Discrimination Act, 1975

Giving less favourable treatment to someone because of their sex, race, or because they are married or single

Making a requirement that appears to be fair to men and women, but which in practice favours one group

Treating a married person less favourably than an unmarried person of the same sex

Treating someone less favourably after they have honestly complained of discrimination

Law requiring employers to reward employees equally for doing the same work

Law setting out that it is unlawful to discriminate on grounds including 'colour, race, nationality or ethnic or national origins'

Giving individuals identical rights, regardless of gender, racial group, age, physical characteristics, etc.

Act seeking to ensure that a disability should not bar a person from employment or promotion unless it would really prevent them from doing the job and there is nothing the employer can do to reasonably overcome the difficulties

Law outlawing any form of discrimination in the treatment of men or women in the workplace

74 Job Satisfaction

Why is job satisfaction important?

Work is a very important part of life. Ask someone what they 'do' and typically they will say 'I'm a plumber/nurse/teacher/web page designer', rather than 'I enjoy gardening', or 'I play the piano' – which may be what they enjoy doing in their leisure time. Most people have strong feelings and attitudes about their work. That is why job satisfaction is so important.

'Does job satisfaction depend on the individual concerned?'

Requirements of a satisfying job

People look for many different ingredients in a job. These include:

- A good rate of pay
- Possibilities of promotion
- Long holidays
- Job security
- Friendship with workmates
- A degree of independence
- Responsibility
- Fringe benefits
- Convenient working hours
- Status

The order in which these ingredients are arranged will be different for every individual. Pay is a major consideration, but it is not necessarily the main factor.

TASK

*R*ead the Case Study below then answer the following questions:

1 Why do you think that job satisfaction might be low in a production-line job?

2 What sort of compensation might an employer have to offer in order to make up for low job satisfaction?

3 How might it be possible to increase job satisfaction for production-line workers?

CASE STUDY

Job satisfaction (1)

The following is an extract from an interview with a worker on the production line in a canning factory:

'I find work here really boring. The pay is good but it has to be because the work is tedious. I just try to think about what I'm going to do at the weekend or how I'm going to spend my money. I feel that I'm stuck with this job because there's nothing else going and all the time I'm counting up the money against the hours. The problem is that we have to repeat the same task time after time and we don't get the chance to put something of our own personality into the work. I'd like to be a footballer, but I'd never make the grade.'

Influences on job satisfaction

There are a number of influences on job satisfaction including:

◆ The individual concerned

◆ The job

◆ The employing organisation

◆ The rewards

◆ The working environment

The individual

Everyone takes to work different attitudes and desires. Some people are mainly interested in money, so they may not care what sort of work they do providing the pay is high. Other employees may hate being bored, so they will choose a job which they see as being interesting – for example, one that gives them personal freedom, challenges, and opportunities for promotion.

The job

The work itself has a big influence on job satisfaction. For example, boring and repetitive work may suit someone who 'doesn't want to think', but would be soul-destroying for a creative person. Jobs that involve greater freedom and responsibility will motivate people who enjoy challenge and variety.

CASE **S**TUDY

Job satisfaction (2)

Below is an extract from a book about women who have lost their jobs. The example deals with the case of a textile factory:

[The firm] *rarely had to recruit labour on the open market. Once employed, their people tended to draw in members of their own family. When people said that the factory was like "family", there was some measure of truth in that, as well as indicating their attachment to the factory.*

"I enjoyed every minute, because all my friends were on that section. We used to have a right laugh and joke and I miss them all now. We could chat when we were working, that's what I liked."

Female worker

From *Redundant Women* by Angela Coyle,
The Women's Press, 1984

TASK

1   What elements of job satisfaction are expressed in the extract in the Case Study?

2   Why did the firm find it easy to recruit labour?

3   Would you expect wages to be high or low in the firm? Why?

TASK

Make a list of six jobs that you would only be prepared to do if you were paid a lot of money. Then make a list of what you consider to be the main five ingredients of a good job. Compare your list with those of another student. Note the differences.

'The only factor you need to consider in job satisfaction is the reward. Give them a rate of pay equal to your nearest rival, and a small bonus at Christmas and just before the summer break and you'll have a contented workforce. Nothing else matters!'

Do you agree with Ron?

The employing organisation

Some businesses try to involve their employees in decision-making, for example by encouraging them to work together as a team. The **Quality Circle** is a Japanese idea in which teams of workers meet regularly to discuss ideas for improving the work situation.

Other employing organisations treat employees more like pieces of machinery. Again, this can be very frustrating for creative people.

The rewards

Because money and benefits are **prime motivators** at work, employers need to think about how they can create an attractive package of rewards. **Incentives** for work may include:

◆ Bonuses and commissions

◆ Company pensions

◆ Help with school fees

◆ Company cars

◆ Mobile phones and help with phone bills

◆ Profit-sharing schemes

◆ Luncheon vouchers

◆ Discounts on company goods and services

The working environment

The environment in which an employee works is very important. There is a big difference between working in a brightly lit, well furnished office, with curtains, telephone and your own personal computer, and sharing a cramped, sparsely furnished attic office with no facilities. Working conditions are very important in helping to make people feel good about their work.

COURSEWORK ACTIVITIES

Compare the jobs of two people working in similar positions in different organisations, e.g. checkout operators in two rival supermarkets. Compare the work they do in terms of:

• The individual

• The job

• The employing organisation

• The rewards

• The working environment

How satisfied are the two people? What are the most important factors leading to different levels of satisfaction?

MATCH IT!

Can you help Frankie and Cleo to match the following terms and definitions?

Job satisfaction   **Quality Circle**   **Incentives**   **Prime motivators**

A group of employees working together as a team to improve quality and solve work problems	
Pleasure, satisfaction and sense of achievement derived from working	
Money and other key benefits offered to employees in return for work	
Benefits additional to wages or salary which can increase employee motivation	

75 Trade Unions

What is a trade union?

A trade union is an association of employees formed to protect and promote the interests of its members, and to achieve other jointly agreed aims.

'I wonder if I should join a trade union?'

What do trade unions do?

The diagram below shows some of the aims of trade unions. You can see that a union's main aim is to secure the best possible conditions of work for its members. Unions know that the decisions a firm makes will affect the livelihood of workers and their families.

'Then you couldn't work for me!'

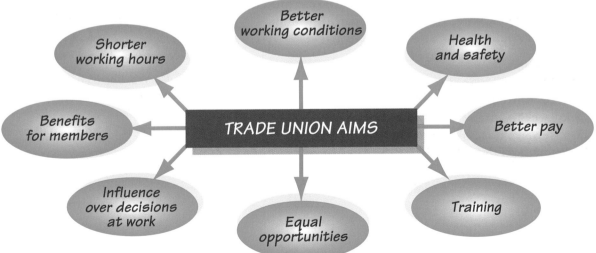

The aims of trade unions

They therefore try to influence some of the decisions made by owners and managers of businesses.

Trade unions are formed, financed and run by their members in their own interests. Several have existed for over 100 years.

In British law, a union must be 'independent' – that is, it must not rely on an employer for funds, facilities or organisation. It must show that it can provide adequate services to its members and (if necessary) sustain itself during a dispute.

The main actors in employee relations

The term **employee relations** refers to the communications that take place between employers and trade unions. Let us look at the main actors on both sides:

Employee relations: the union side

The union president
The **president** or **general secretary** of a union is elected nationally to represent the whole membership in dealing with employers, government and other unions.

The full-time official
Union officials are appointed and paid by the union. They will cover a number of firms in a particular area, and keep in close contact with union headquarters.

The shop steward
Often factories are split up into areas called **shops**, e.g. the cutting shop, the sewing shop, etc. In the past, each shop would elect at least one **shop steward** to represent them in the workplace. The work was part-time and hardly ever paid.

The convenor
Originally the **convenor** was the shop steward who called or 'convened' union meetings in a large workplace. Today the term simply means the senior shop steward. It is an important post and most convenors hold the job for long periods of time.

LATEST NEWS

Since 1979 the numbers of employees who are members of trade unions fell steadily, from over 55% in 1979 to less than 40% in 1995. Trade union membership dropped by 20% between 1990 and 1997. However, figures published in 2000 indicate that this fall in union membership may have bottomed out and that there might be a small increase in union membership to just under 7 million people.

Bill Morris, General Secretary of the Transport and General Workers Union

CASE STUDY

A day in the life of a shop steward

Sylvia Holt is a machine operator on production lines making metal packaging at Huntley, Boorne and Stevens. She has been with the company for 20 years. She is also a shop steward for the GMB (General Municipal Boilermakers and Allied Trade Union).

7.15 am   Clock in for work.

7.30 am   Start work on line.

8.55 am   A worker complains that her bonus has been underpaid. She explains to me what job she was doing and how many trays she has done. I explain the situation to the supervisor who then takes it further.

9.05 am   I return to my job.

9.20 am   Supervisor returns, informing me that the worker is owed £1.05.

9.45 am   Tea break – I inform the worker of the amount she is owed.

10.00 am   Tea break over – start back on line.

11.05 am   Another worker comes to me. He has caught his trousers on a broken wooden box. I take him down to the personnel department to report the accident. He is given the option of buying a new pair, with the firm paying a percentage, or getting them repaired at the firm's expense. I then go back to the shop floor and investigate whether the broken box can be repaired or needs to be thrown away.

12.20 pm   Lunch break.

12.50 pm   Lunch break over – start back on line.

14.00 pm   A worker tells me he has been working alongside two other men for over a week and that they have been offered one hour's overtime a night, but he has not been offered any. I tell the worker to go back to his job and that I will go and see the supervisor. I explain the situation to the supervisor and I am told that the worker is only helping out in the department. I then state that if he is good enough to work on the line in the daytime with them, helping out, it is only fair that he should be offered overtime as well. The supervisor agrees and the one hour overtime is given. I then inform the worker of his overtime.

14.20 pm   I return to my work.

16.30 pm   Clock out – day is over.

TASK

1   What type of employees does the GMB represent?

2   Does Sylvia work full-time for the union?

3   What is the leading shop steward in a large workplace called?

4   How many hours did Sylvia work? How much of this time was spent in her work as a shop steward?

5   Does the company pay Sylvia for her union work? How does the company benefit from Sylvia's union work? How important is it to the company to have shop stewards?

6   Who does Sylvia represent? How does this group benefit from her work?

7   Who does Sylvia negotiate with?

8   Do you think that Sylvia is powerful in the workplace? Explain your answer.

Employee relations: the management side

The board of directors

This is a committee chosen by the shareholders to represent their interests.

The managing director

This is the senior director with responsibility for the day-to-day running of the business.

The personnel/human resources manager

This is the manager responsible for creating the systems for the recruitment, training, welfare and safety of employees. This specialist manager will give advice and support to other managers in the organisation in carrying out human resource management work.

The charge hand

This is a working supervisor responsible for a particular group of employees in an organisation.

Union organisation

The way a union is structured varies considerably, but a typical form is shown below.

Groups of members form a **branch.** They choose branch officials to represent them. The branches also choose representatives to represent them at a regional committee. Regional groups then choose representatives to go to an **annual conference.** The annual conference makes decisions relating to the industry and chooses a full-time body of officials known as the **national executive.** The top official in the union is the **president** or **general secretary.**

A typical union structure

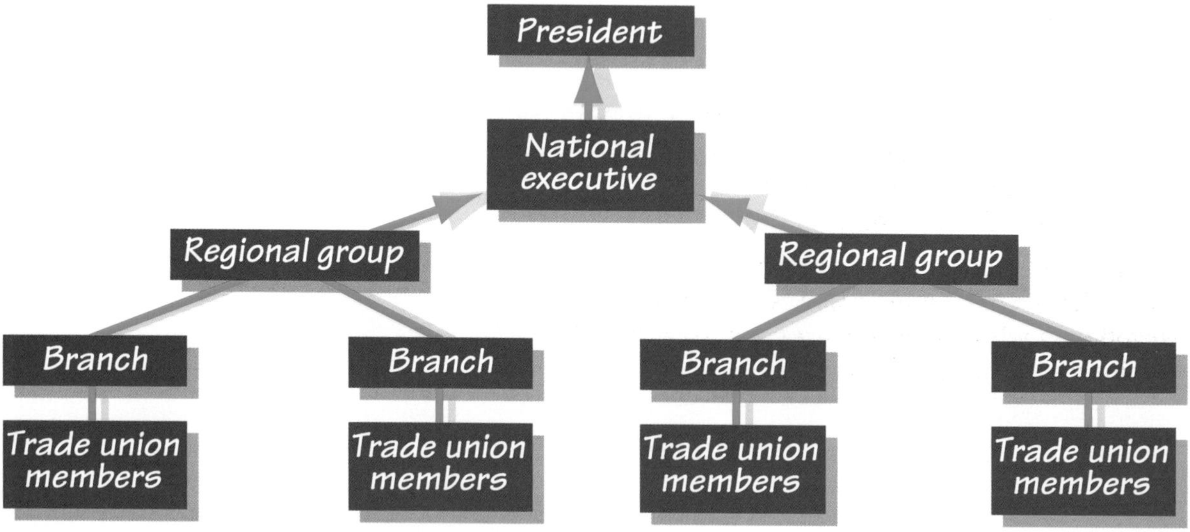

Official and unofficial action

Official action is action which has been approved by the union's headquarters. **Unofficial** action takes place when members carry out actions not approved by the union. An example of this might be when local stewards call out workers in a lightning strike.

The Employment Act of 1982 made it possible for employers to prosecute trade unions for carrying out unlawful industrial action. The 1984 Trades Union Act set out that a union would be liable if it authorised industrial action without a secret ballot and could be sued by the employer.

Types of trade union

There are four main types of trade union:

1 Craft unions

2 Industrial unions

3 General unions

4 White-collar unions

However, many unions do not fit easily into these groups. Often they have characteristics common to more than one group.

Craft unions

The earliest type of union in this country was the **craft union**. Craft unions were made up of highly skilled craft workers in a particular trade. Often these groups were mutual benefit societies before the welfare state came into being. Subscriptions could be quite high, and in return the union would provide sick pay, unemployment pay, a pension and other benefits.

These unions are less important in the UK today and their membership is relatively small.

Industrial unions

Industrial unionism is common in many European countries, notably Germany. The economy is divided up into industrial sectors and workers in each sector belong to the industrial union for that sector.

The advantage of an industrial union is that it caters for all employees in an industry, whatever their job. Negotiating with employers is greatly simplified, and all employees are united in their efforts.

Craft unions
Musicians Union
Equity (actors' union)
National Union of Journalists

Industrial unions
Fire Brigades Union
Communication Workers Union

General unions
The General Municipal Boilermakers and Allied Trade Union
Transport and General Workers Union

White-collar unions
National Union of Teachers
Banking, Insurance and Finance Union

Examples of the four main groups of union

General unions

These are some of the largest unions in the UK today. They recruit workers from several industries. They include semi-skilled and unskilled workers. A particular advantage of this form of union is that it gives strength to workers who would have little power on their own. These unions can be well funded and organised.

White-collar unions

White-collar workers are non-manual workers such as civil servants, bank workers and teachers, as opposed to **blue-collar** workers who do manual work. White-collar unions have been the most rapidly expanding groups in the 1980s and 1990s. This has coincided with the growth of the tertiary sector of the economy.

MATCH IT!

Can you help Frankie and Cleo to match the following terms and definitions?

Trade union	Craft union	General union	Shop steward
Convenor	Official action	Industrial union	Charge hand
White-collar union	White-collar worker	Blue-collar worker	Unofficial action

A manual worker in an organisation

The leading shop steward in a plant

A union made up of all employees working in the same industrial sector

The union representative of an area of workers in an organisation

Trade union activity which is approved by the union head office

A working supervisor responsible for a given section of employees

An association of highly skilled craft workers

An association of employees formed to improve working conditions and rewards

A union of office and administrative or professional employees

Union activities that are spontaneous and do not have the backing of the union head office

A union made up of people from a broad cross-section of jobs in several industries

An employee engaged mainly in non-manual work

76 Employers' Associations

Protecting common interests

Just as employees have formed trade unions in order to protect their common interests, so employers have formed and joined their own groups.

Examples are the **Confederation of British Industry (CBI)** and the **National Farmers Union (NFU)**. These and other associations have two main functions:

1 To represent employers in dealings with trade unions

2 To give help and advice to employers on a wide range of issues, such as training, calculating tax, etc.

In some industries an employers' association will bargain with a trade union to set a minimum wage for a given period of time. Individual employers will then negotiate additional payments with shop stewards at company, plant or workplace level.

Most employers' associations carry out the greater part of their work at local rather than national level – for example, through regional conferences, joint training sessions, etc.

The Confederation of British Industry (CBI)

The CBI was set up to provide a national organisation to represent the views and interests of employers. It acts as a mouthpiece for employers to present their opinions to trade unions, government, the media and other interested parties.

The CBI collects and publishes information on many things. Its *Industrial Trends* survey, published quarterly, gives up-to-date information on the state of business. It also produces a magazine, *CBI News*, giving employers up-to-the-minute information on a wide range of business issues.

The CBI has a permanent staff who collect statistics, process information, publish articles, and deal with queries from industrialists and the media. It is led by a **director general**, whose views are listened to with respect by government and many other groups.

Professional associations

A **professional association** is a special organisation to look after the interests of people who work in a particular professional field such as law, medicine or accountancy. There are many types of professional associations, reflecting the wide number of professions.

'I don't belong to any employers' association. There's nothing I can learn from other people in my industry. Anyway, we're competitors and I'm not going to share any of my secrets with them.'

Do you think that Ron is right?

TASK

Why might an employer want to join the CBI?

Many were established under the Companies Acts or by the granting of a Royal Charter. Their functions include:

- Acting as examiners and upholders of standards and providing study facilities and guides (for example, people wanting to be bankers have to sit exams organised by The Chartered Institute of Bankers).

- Controlling entry into the professions.

- Keeping up high standards of **professional conduct** in order to protect the public. (For example, the British Medical Association sets professional standards of conduct for doctors.)

- Providing members with up-to-date information about their profession and reporting on new developments in their field, e.g. conferences on medical breakthroughs.

As more people have joined the professions in recent years, the importance of these bodies has grown.

COURSEWORK ACTIVITIES

Find out who the current director general of the CBI is. Then look for reports about him/her in a national newspaper for a two-week period. Find out the sort of work that he or she is doing.

Alternatively, use the director general's name as a keyword for an Internet search.

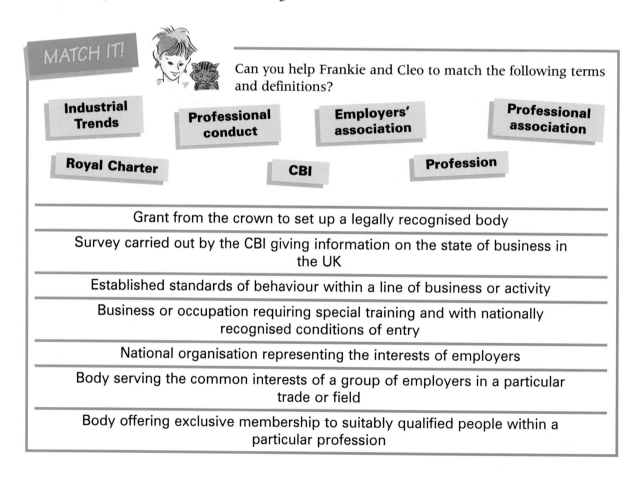

MATCH IT!

Can you help Frankie and Cleo to match the following terms and definitions?

Industrial Trends

Professional conduct

Employers' association

Professional association

Royal Charter

CBI

Profession

Grant from the crown to set up a legally recognised body

Survey carried out by the CBI giving information on the state of business in the UK

Established standards of behaviour within a line of business or activity

Business or occupation requiring special training and with nationally recognised conditions of entry

National organisation representing the interests of employers

Body serving the common interests of a group of employers in a particular trade or field

Body offering exclusive membership to suitably qualified people within a particular profession

77 Collective Bargaining

What is collective bargaining?

Collective bargaining means negotiation between a trade union and an employer, or an employers' association, over the income and working conditions of employees.

To **negotiate** means to talk with others in order to reach an agreement.

Employee relations

Employee relations refers to the communication that takes place between representatives of employees and employers.

Much of employee relations involves employees and employers working together. Indeed, part of the aim of the European Union's social policy today is to create a system of shared responsibility of employers and employees for working practices, conditions and other areas of working life. This policy of shared responsibility is called **co-determination**.

However, employers and employees do not always agree and this can lead to arguments and disputes.

Day-to-day industrial relations

On a day-to-day basis, the main process of employee relations bargaining takes place between managers, supervisors and employee representatives. Normally representatives of the groups meet regularly – say, once a week.

At this meeting will be staff, shop stewards, personnel managers and other interested managers. Discussions will be about such things as:

◆ Pay

◆ Bonuses

◆ The work environment

◆ Disputes

◆ Work schedules

◆ Grievances

◆ Health and safety

◆ Hours of work

◆ Production targets

EMPLOYEE RELATIONS

Employers

Disagreements
Agreements

Employees

Communication between employers and workforce

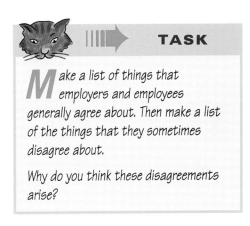

TASK

Make a list of things that employers and employees generally agree about. Then make a list of the things that they sometimes disagree about.

Why do you think these disagreements arise?

CASE STUDY

The story of an industrial dispute

Frankie's Aunty Amber is a shop steward at a local food-processing plant. Recently the workers there were upset to discover that people in other factories were getting bigger pay increases than them.

Amber and the other shop stewards called a meeting of employees in the factory. The feeling of the meeting was that they should put in for a 20% pay rise.

However, when they put this request to their employers at their weekly meeting, the personnel manager said that because the company had only been making a small profit, they could only offer 5%.

When the shop stewards told the employees about the management offer, they were furious and said that they ought to go on strike straight away, and that they wouldn't accept anything less than 15%.

Eventually the managers offered a compromise. They suggested 8%, explaining that they faced various difficulties and might have to reduce the workforce.

Eventually the two sides agreed on 9.5%, on the understanding that no employee would be made redundant for the next twelve months.

TASK

1   What factors do you think are most likely to determine the size of a pay demand made by employees?

2   What factors do you think are most likely to determine the management offer?

3   What factors do you think will determine whether the settlement is nearer to employees' demands or management's offer?

Major employee relations issues

As well as local bargaining about smaller-scale industrial relations issues, larger issues may be discussed on an industry-wide scale. Wages for government employees, for example, are normally established via an annual pay award. The parties involved are normally the central executive of the relevant union, and employers' representatives.

Union industrial action

In the event of an industrial dispute, unions can put pressure on employers in a number of ways.

1 Picketing

Primary picketing is lawful. This involves members of a union who are on strike standing outside a firm's entrance and trying to persuade other workers not to cross the picket line.

Secondary picketing is not lawful and occurs when workers from one firm try to persuade workers at a firm not involved with the strike not to go to work. Secondary picketing takes place when union members try to spread the impact of their action.

Protesting Ford workers at Halewood, Merseyside

2 Withdrawal of goodwill

This is when workers become obstructive over issues on which they normally co-operate, such as overtime *(see below)*.

3 Go-slow

During a go-slow, workers deliberately reduce their work-rate.

4 Work-to-rule

During a work-to-rule, workers reduce their productivity by strictly applying the rules governing their particular job. For instance, railway workers may check that every carriage door is firmly closed at each station before allowing the train to depart.

5 Ban on overtime

During an overtime ban, workers refuse to work more than the hours laid down in their contract of employment.

6 Official strike

Workers cease work (with the authority of the union).

7 Unofficial strike

Workers cease work (without the approval of the union).

8 Sit-in

The workers occupy their workplace. If a factory has been threatened with closure, the workers may operate a work-in, i.e. refuse to stop working.

9 Blacking

This occurs when members of a firm refuse to handle particular materials or pieces of machinery.

10 The closed shop

In the past, unions could put pressure on management to operate a closed-shop policy whereby all workers in a plant or factory had to belong to the same union.

11 Demarcation disputes

Sometimes unions have disputes with each other about 'who does what' at work. Unions are sometimes very protective about the work their members do.

Changes in union law

The **Employment Act of 1990** made it unlawful for an employer to refuse to employ a non-union member, putting an end to the closed shop. All forms of secondary picketing were made illegal. Trade unions became liable for nearly all types of industrial action by members, and employers can now dismiss employees involved in unofficial action.

The **Trade Union Reform and Employment Rights Act, 1993** set out that trade unions have to give employers seven days' notice of official action.

Forms of employer action

Although unions have certain powers, employers can also put pressure on employees in various ways.

The most obvious is to threaten to stop privileges such as the payment of bonuses. They can also threaten to close down plants or parts of the business which make a loss. They may say that a pay rise would make the firm uncompetitive. If there are no other jobs in the area, the union will be in a weak bargaining position.

Other weapons that employers can use are:

- **The sack.** The employers cease to employ certain workers.

- **Suspension.** Workers can be laid off without pay. This could be done to encourage fresh thinking about the dispute, or as a form of punishment.

- **Lockouts.** Sometimes employers will physically prevent workers from entering their premises.

SPIX

'In many developing countries trade union activities are outlawed, and people have to work in harsh conditions.' Ethical trading involves companies refusing to buy from suppliers who are involved in exploiting their employees.'

Cue the words 'fair trade' into an Internet search to find examples of exploitation. Should you buy from companies not engaging in fair trade?

Can you help Frankie and Cleo to match the following terms and definitions?

Negotiation	Picketing	Work-to-rule	Employee relations
Blacking	Closed shop	Official strike	Sack
Collective bargaining	Demarcation dispute	Lockout	Suspension

A strike that is approved by the head office of a trade union

Refusing to handle certain products, materials, equipment, etc., as part of an industrial dispute

Slowing the rate of work by sticking meticulously to the rules set down for the job

Situation in which employees are physically prevented from entering a firm's premises

Laying workers off without pay

A disagreement over 'who does what'

Communications between the representatives of employers and employees

Employees are given their cards and their work contracts are ended

Negotiations over pay and conditions between a trade union and relevant employers

Situation in which employment in a particular firm or workplace is restricted to trade union members

Talking to others with the common aim of reaching an agreement

Attempt by union members to dissuade others from working during an industrial dispute

78 Conciliation and Arbitration

Resolving disputes and grievances

The word 'conciliation' means helping the sides in a dispute to reach an agreement. The term is also used in industrial relations in situations where a third party helps employers and trade unions to settle their differences.

Arbitration means the hearing and resolving of a dispute, especially an industrial one, by an impartial referee selected or agreed upon by both sides.

The Advisory Conciliation and Arbitration Service (ACAS)

The Advisory, Conciliation and Arbitration Service (ACAS) was set up in the 1970s to act as a 'third party' in industrial disputes. It can do this in a number of ways:

ACAS – resolving industrial disputes

◆ **Conciliation** is the process by which an independent outsider, such as an ACAS official, acts as a channel of communication between an employer and a union. The conciliator will usually meet the parties separately before trying to bring them together at the negotiating table.

◆ **Mediation** is a stronger process whereby an independent outsider proposes the basis for a settlement. However, the parties involved do not have to accept it.

◆ **Arbitration** involves both parties agreeing in advance to accept the recommendations of an independent body like ACAS.

Below: The role of ACAS

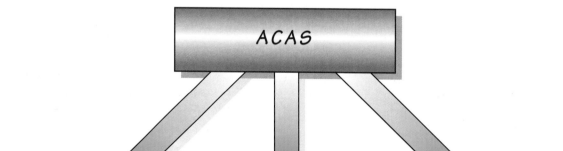

The work of ACAS

The greater part of the work of ACAS involves individual grievances. Every year ACAS has to deal with over 50,000 cases of individual arbitration. Individual disputes involve a variety of grievances, including unfair dismissal and sex discrimination cases.

If the dispute cannot be settled by any of the means described on page 306, then the case is heard before an **employment tribunal**. This is a panel made up of experts who will seek to resolve the dispute.

As part of its work, ACAS sets out **codes of practice** that provide guidelines for employers and employees. For example, it has published a code of practice on dismissal. Parties to a dispute can simply refer to these codes of practice, rather than going through the lengthy process of ACAS arbitration.

ACAS has a legal obligation to try to resolve individual grievances before they reach employment tribunals. Most individual cases will be resolved either through conciliation or because the complaint is dropped. Nine out of ten disputes involving ACAS are settled before industrial action is taken.

The rest of ACAS's resources are used for advisory work involving both unions and employers, including surveys, projects, training activities and advisory visits.

LATEST NEWS

In 2000 ACAS received 750,000 enquiries from the public about issues involving their working lives. Many of these were about the minimum wage.

CASE STUDY

Working on Christmas day

Dave Jenkins runs a large plumbing firm, employing a number of plumbers on a contract basis. In 2000 he insisted that these plumbers made themselves available on a rota to handle emergencies over the Christmas period. However, the contractors were not prepared to do this. Dave therefore threatened to replace them with others who were prepared to work over this period, and to reduce bonuses owing to them.

After a time, both sides realised that the dispute was getting out of hand. They agreed to bring in a mediator from ACAS. The mediator listened to both sides of the argument and came up with some suggestions. She then arranged for both parties to sit down together, and they quickly agreed to the following terms:

*   The existing group of plumbers were to keep their contracts.

*   They were also to keep the bonuses that they had already earned.

*   Contractors were not to be forced to work over Christmas. However, those contractors who wished to work (and enough did) would earn an extra Christmas bonus. Those that did not work over Christmas were to cover for the others in the period immediately after Christmas.

Towards co-operation

As we move into the new millennium, there are signs of increased co-operation between employers and employees in many (though not all) workplaces. The new style of management based on human relations increasingly stresses the importance of including employees in decision-making processes. In return, employees are expected to take on wider responsibility for their own actions. For example, multi-skilling involves employees being prepared to do many different jobs, rather than concentrating on a single job skill.

At the same time, many employers have introduced single-union deals. This means that rather than bargaining with many individual trade unions in the same workplace, they recognise and bargain with a single union representing all the workforce.

'You wouldn't catch me adopting a "new style of management." Allowing your employees to make decisions and to act responsibly is going soft! You have to tell people what to do or they'll take advantage of you!'

Do you agree with Ron?

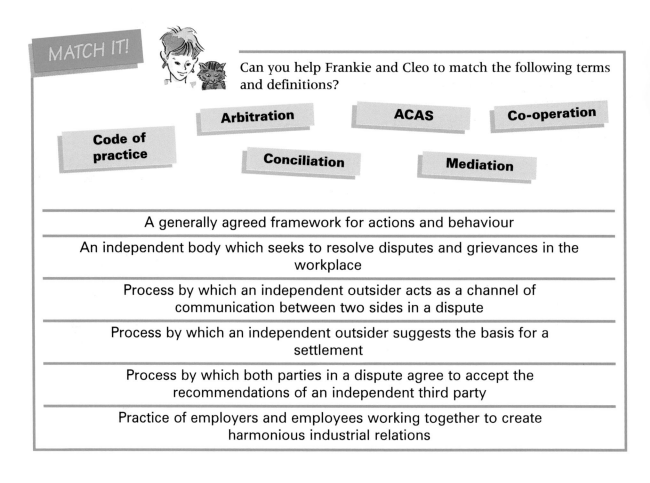

MATCH IT!

Can you help Frankie and Cleo to match the following terms and definitions?

Arbitration   **ACAS**   **Co-operation**

Code of practice

Conciliation   **Mediation**

A generally agreed framework for actions and behaviour
An independent body which seeks to resolve disputes and grievances in the workplace
Process by which an independent outsider acts as a channel of communication between two sides in a dispute
Process by which an independent outsider suggests the basis for a settlement
Process by which both parties in a dispute agree to accept the recommendations of an independent third party
Practice of employers and employees working together to create harmonious industrial relations

9 79 Limits on Business Activity

What are the factors that limit business activity?

Businesses today are not free agents. There are many different factors that limit their activity.

Internal constraints

Within a business there are likely to be a number of **internal constraints**. These include:

1 Objectives of internal stakeholders
   Businesses must take account of the wishes of internal stakeholders such as shareholders, managers, and employees.

2 The availability of resources
   The availability of resources is a key constraint on business activity. Without adequate finance, for example, a business will not be able to invest in developing e-commerce, including an effective website.

3 The management and organisation of the business
   There is no point in having the best resources in the world if you cannot manage them effectively. Successful management involves combining resources in an effective way.

The 'three Cs'

The success of a business depends on the 'three Cs' – costs, competition and customers.

◆ **Costs** can be kept down by efficient management. However, costs of materials, fuel and components will often be outside the firm's control.

◆ The **competition** must always be considered. A firm's competitors will always be trying to get one step ahead in the marketplace.

◆ Finally, **customers' needs and wants** are the biggest constraint on business activity. No organisation can succeed unless it is able to meet the needs of its customers.

SPIX

'Businesses operate in a global environment. Actions taken in one part of the world frequently affect people on the other side of the world. Nowhere is this more true than in the creation of air pollution.'

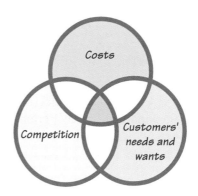

The external environment

The **external environment** in which businesses operate is constantly changing. This process of change has a great impact on what businesses can and cannot do.

The diagram on the opposite page shows how some of these changes can have an impact on business organisations.

Business in a changing environment

Social changes are concerned with changes in society and patterns of behaviour – e.g. changes in lifestyles such as people spending more time on leisure, increasing numbers of women at work, changes in fashion and tastes, etc.

Economic changes are concerned with changes in the national economy, such as periods of economic growth or slowdown, as well as changes in interest rates and exchange rates.

Legal changes are concerned with the ways in which government changes laws and the impact that this has on business – for example, new laws about health and safety or about the hours people are allowed to work.

Political changes are the changes that occur with changes in government. For example, a Labour government might impose higher taxes on business than a Conservative government would.

Environmental changes are changes that result from businesses having to change the way that they treat the environment. In recent years we have seen increasing pressures on business to respect the environment.

'How can we possibly be aware of all the chaotic changes in the modern business environment?'

CASE STUDY

Sunday trading

Sunday trading
at a busy
supermarket

As time goes on, social attitudes change. A hundred years ago, many people would have been horrified at the thought of Sunday trading. Today things are different, and Sunday trading is an accepted part of modern life.

In the early 1990s, it was against the law to trade openly on a Sunday. Some local councils tried to prosecute traders who broke the law. However, many of these prosecutions failed to hold up when taken to higher courts.

Many people felt that traders were able to escape prosecution partly because the government lacked the will to enforce the law more strictly.

Today many people find that their only chance to get to the shops is on a Sunday. Perhaps they are busy on other days of the week. At the same time there are many people who are prepared to work on a Sunday. Supermarket chains are naturally keen to increase their sales and profits by opening seven days a week.

Not everybody has welcomed Sunday trading, however. There has been some opposition from residents living near busy shopping areas – particularly supermarkets. They argue that supermarkets are noisy and cause congestion and pollution. Some have formed pressure groups to try to restrict the activities of supermarkets as a result of Sunday opening.

     TASK

1   Try to identify the social, legal, political, economic and environmental issues raised in the Case Study.

2   What effects do you think that Sunday opening has had on a supermarket's costs, customers and competition?

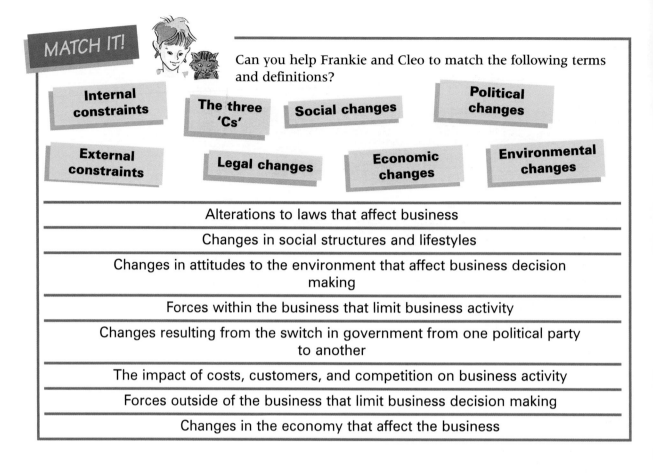

MATCH IT!

Can you help Frankie and Cleo to match the following terms and definitions?

Internal constraints

The three 'Cs'

Social changes

Political changes

External constraints

Legal changes

Economic changes

Environmental changes

Alterations to laws that affect business
Changes in social structures and lifestyles
Changes in attitudes to the environment that affect business decision making
Forces within the business that limit business activity
Changes resulting from the switch in government from one political party to another
The impact of costs, customers, and competition on business activity
Forces outside of the business that limit business decision making
Changes in the economy that affect the business

80 Changes in the Wider Economy

Unfortunately, the economy does not grow in a steady pattern. Instead we experience what is known as a trade cycle – periods in which the economy grows for a few years, followed by period in which growth starts to fall (a recession).

In a period of recession there is a marked reduction in the level of output and a considerable waste of resources.

The illustration opposite shows what the trade cycle looks like.

Note that the total value of goods produced in the economy is measured by GDP – gross domestic product.

'Is it possible for the economy to be in a continual boom period? Wouldn't that be good for business?'

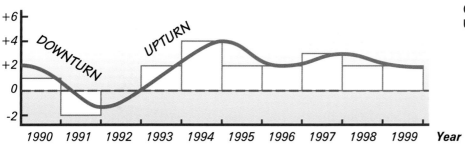

Change in GDP in the
UK, 1990–1999

The trade cycle

The twentieth century has seen regular cycles of **booms** and **slumps** in economic activity.

In a **boom**:

◆ Output rises

◆ Firms take on more employees

◆ Wages and prices rise

◆ Prosperity rises

◆ Businesses boom

In a **slump**:

◆ Output falls

◆ Firms lay off workers

◆ Wages and prices fall

◆ Prosperity falls

◆ Businesses do badly (some cease trading)

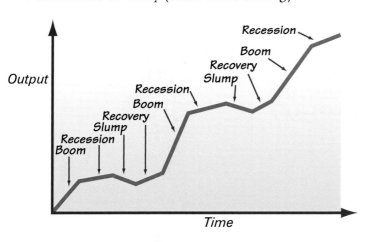

The 'boom-bust' cycle

Business and the trade cycle

Business favours a boom period in the trade cycle. This is the time when order books are most likely to be full and in which it is easiest to sell goods.

However, as the boom reaches its peak costs are likely to rise. At the top of the boom it will be more difficult to recruit labour, and wages and other costs will rise.

Business will be far more cautious in the downturn in the cycle and will tend to make cutbacks such as reducing the size of the labour force and postponing the purchase of new machinery.

Changes in interest rates

The interest rate is the cost of borrowing money. For example, if I borrow £100 today at a 10% rate of interest for one year, then I will have to repay £110 at the end of the year.

Most businesses borrow money. The interest rate is therefore very important to business.

If interest rates rise it becomes more expensive to borrow money, and the repayments that have to be made are higher.

If interest rates fall it is cheaper to borrow money, and the repayments that have to be made are lower.

The most important factor determining interest rates in this country is the interest rate set by the Bank of England's Monetary Policy Committee (MPC). If the MPC raises its interest rates other lenders will follow suit.

The MPC changes interest rates to help the government achieve its economic targets for the economy. If spending in the economy is growing too fast then the MPC will raise interest rates to discourage borrowing and hence spending. If spending in the economy is too low (leading to unemployment) then the MPC will try to encourage people to spend more by lowering the interest rate.

Changes in exchange rates

The exchange rate is the rate at which one currency (e.g. the Pound) will exchange against other currencies (e.g. the Euro).

If the Pound rises in value against the Euro then British goods will become more expensive in the European Union. If it falls against the Euro then British goods will become cheaper in the European Union.

Many businesses will be unhappy if the Pound rises too much because it will make it difficult to sell their goods, which have to compete against cheaper foreign goods.

Businesses might also be unhappy if the Pound falls too much because the goods they sell abroad will receive less revenue than before.

The Pound can thus be too high or too low when exchanged against other currencies.

'Does it make sense to borrow money when interest rates are low, and lend money when interest rates are high?'

① Art Books Ltd, based in London, sells specialist art books to Germany and France

② The books are sold in pounds

③ During 2000 the pound rose in value against the Euro

④ This meant that the books sold by Art Books Ltd became more expensive and few were sold

⑤ However in early 2001 the pound fell against the Euro

⑥ Sales have increased again

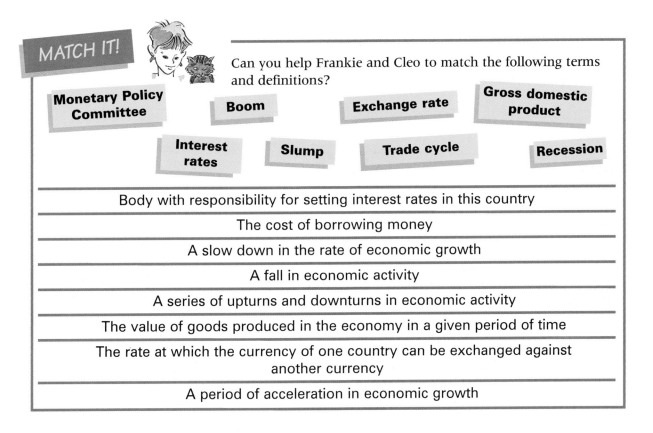

MATCH IT!

Can you help Frankie and Cleo to match the following terms and definitions?

Monetary Policy Committee • Boom • Exchange rate • Gross domestic product • Interest rates • Slump • Trade cycle • Recession

Body with responsibility for setting interest rates in this country

The cost of borrowing money

A slow down in the rate of economic growth

A fall in economic activity

A series of upturns and downturns in economic activity

The value of goods produced in the economy in a given period of time

The rate at which the currency of one country can be exchanged against another currency

A period of acceleration in economic growth

81 The Impact of Government

The government plays a major role in creating changes which affect business:

◆ **Government is responsible for creating new laws and regulations**

◆ **Government is responsible for taxing businesses and individuals**

◆ **Government is responsible for providing a range of services which businesses benefit from**

Government as law maker

New laws and changes to existing laws and regulations are voted on in parliament, as well as being created at European Union level. Once a law or regulation has been set out then it is up to business to comply with the law. Failure to comply with the law can lead to a court prosecution. We have already examined some of these laws and regulations in the sections on consumer protection and health and safety.

A good example of government law-making that affects business is that in relation to the prevention of **monopoly** and **anti-competitive practice**.

'Does the government seek to help or to hinder business?'

A monopoly exists when a firm dominates a market, enabling it to push up prices. Anti-competitive practices exist where firms prevent others from competing freely with each other – for example, a supplier of products who fixes the prices at which retailers can sell their products is being anti-competitive.

The Competition Act of 1998 created a body called the **Competition Commission**, which sets out to create fair competition.

The **Director General of Fair Trading** is appointed by a government minister to try to ensure fair competition in this country. The Competition Commission investigates cases where it is felt that organisations are trying to prevent fair competition.

In addition, where companies seek to merge (join together) they may be subject to investigation. The European Commission can ask for an investigation of mergers that are likely to restrict competition in the European Union. These involve mergers of major European companies.

The government has also set up **Public Utility Regulators**, whose job it is to ensure that there is competition in industries that were formerly government owned (e.g. water, gas and electricity) as well as to ensure that consumers are protected. Examples of regulatory bodies are OFWAT (water services) and OFTEL (telecommunications).

'How can monopolists charge higher prices than in competitive markets?'

CASE STUDY

Blow to Interbrew

On 3 January 2001 Europe's biggest brewer, Interbrew of Belgium, suffered a blow when the Government ordered it to dispose of the UK breweries it bought from Bass for £2.3 billion in the summer of 2000.

The ruling followed a report from the Competition Commission, which concluded that the take-over of Bass Brewers would lead to higher prices and less choice for beer drinkers, and was therefore against the public interest.

The table below shows a breakdown of the British beer market after the Interbrew take-over of Bass in 2000.

	Percentage of market share
Scottish Courage	26.0
Interbrew	38.0
Carlsberg Tetley	11.8
Guinness	5.6
Anheuser-Busch	3.2
Wolverhampton & Dudley	3.1
Greene King	0.9
Others	11.5

Government taxation

Government taxes increase costs for business people. From a business point of view the most important types of tax are:

◆ **Corporation tax** – a tax levied as a percentage of company profits.

◆ **National Insurance contributions** – employers have to make a contribution to the national insurance contributions of their employees. This is levied as a set percentage.

◆ **VAT** – Value Added Tax is levied on the value added to products at each stage of the production process.

◆ **Excise duties** – these are duties on items like alcohol and petrol. Excise duties should not be confused with **customs duties**, which are levied on imports.

Direct and indirect taxes

A distinction is usually made between direct and indirect taxes. **Direct taxes** such as income tax, national insurance and corporation tax are paid directly to the tax authorities by the payer. **Indirect taxes** like VAT or customs and excise duties are taxes on expenditure. For example, when I buy a DVD in a shop I am not handing over the VAT tax element directly to the government – instead it will be paid by an intermediary (e.g. the shop) on my behalf.

For business government taxation can seem a burden, particularly at times of economic recession and when a business is facing a fall in profits. Of course, at these times the business will have to pay less corporation tax, but other taxes may seem an unnecessary burden.

TASK

1 Why do you think that the Competition Commission reported against Interbrew?

2 How might the size of Interbrew have been against the public interest?

3 Why is it important to have competition in an industry like brewing?

'Government taxes cripple the business person. Scrap business taxes and you would have a much wealthier country!'
Do you agree with Ron?

Queuing for petrol, September 2000

CASE STUDY

Petrol protests in 2000

In 2000 many business people were not happy about the high price of fuel. Petrol taxes were higher in the UK than anywhere else in Europe. Businesses found that this added to their production costs and made it difficult for them to compete at a time when the price of the Pound was at a high level against the Euro and other currencies.

A protest was organised by road hauliers and others, leading to petrol shortages which almost brought the country to its knees. The government argued that the high price of fuel was necessary because (among other things) over-use of petroleum is leading to global warming. At the end of the day the government made some concessions to the road hauliers in agreeing to limit future increases in excise duties on fuel.

Government as a provider of services

The government provides a range of services that are very important to business. Improvements in these services benefit business. For example, the government plays a major part in creating an effective road transport system, as well as providing services such as health and education. Better-educated and healthier employees increase the productivity of labour. In recent years the government has been involved in a number of initiatives to ensure that the education system provides intelligent young people who are well equipped to participate in a modern technologically based economy.

TASK

1 How might the high excise duties on fuel have penalised UK businesses?

2 Why does the government levy taxes on items like fuel?

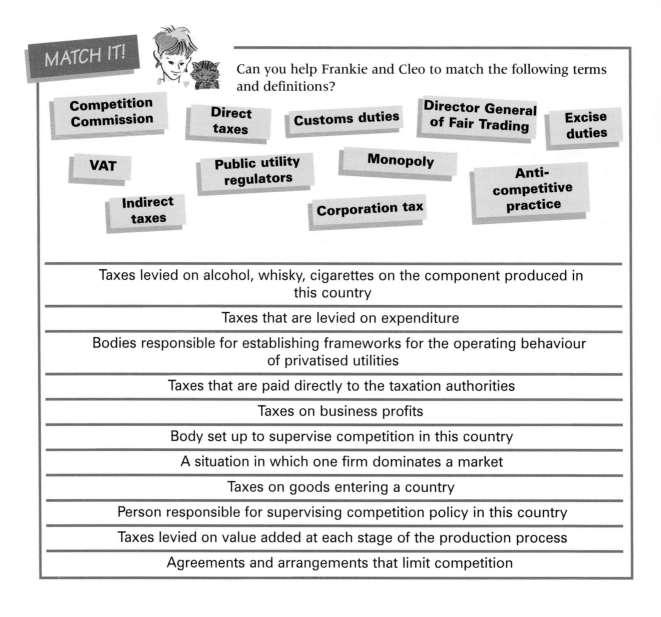

MATCH IT!

Can you help Frankie and Cleo to match the following terms and definitions?

Competition Commission

Direct taxes

Customs duties

Director General of Fair Trading

Excise duties

VAT

Public utility regulators

Monopoly

Anti-competitive practice

Indirect taxes

Corporation tax

Taxes levied on alcohol, whisky, cigarettes on the component produced in this country

Taxes that are levied on expenditure

Bodies responsible for establishing frameworks for the operating behaviour of privatised utilities

Taxes that are paid directly to the taxation authorities

Taxes on business profits

Body set up to supervise competition in this country

A situation in which one firm dominates a market

Taxes on goods entering a country

Person responsible for supervising competition policy in this country

Taxes levied on value added at each stage of the production process

Agreements and arrangements that limit competition

82 The Changing International Environment

Understanding world trade

Business activity in the UK takes place against a wider background of world trade. Many UK businesses are owned by foreign companies. Similarly, many UK businesses have operations overseas.

Increasingly, UK firms are buying and selling their products internationally. They are also facing greater competition than ever before from foreign firms.

Imports and exports

For centuries, the UK has gained enormously from international trade. We buy goods and services from other countries, and in return we sell them goods and services produced here.

◆ An **import** involves the purchase of products or services from overseas by a UK citizen or business.

◆ An **export** is a sale by a UK citizen or business to a member of another country.

'Can large UK businesses ignore overseas markets?'

Visibles and invisibles

All the tangible goods (things that we can touch and see) that we trade are called **visible** items. Services that cannot be seen or touched are called **invisibles.**

Countries trade in order to benefit from each other's resources and skills. For example, in the UK we are very good at producing whisky (mainly because of our climate), Land Rovers (because of our engineering skill) and insurance (because of our years of experience). We are not so good at producing rice (because of our climate), motorbikes (other countries can do it better) and snow tyres (because of our lack of experience).

'Are invisibles things that you can't see?'

International trade allows countries to gain from specialisation. The UK, for example, is able to concentrate on producing its most saleable goods and services, such as banking, insurance, whisky and bio-technology. By trading these items on world markets, we are able to buy things which we would find it less easy to produce, such as pineapples, washing machines, and motorbikes.

Other reasons why we trade include the following:

1 Some items, such as scarce minerals, are impossible to obtain naturally in the UK

2 To foster good relations with other countries

3 To earn foreign currency

4 Because we cannot fully supply our own market in many items

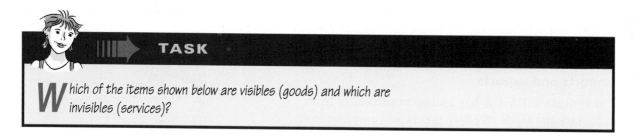

TASK

Which of the items shown below are visibles (goods) and which are invisibles (services)?

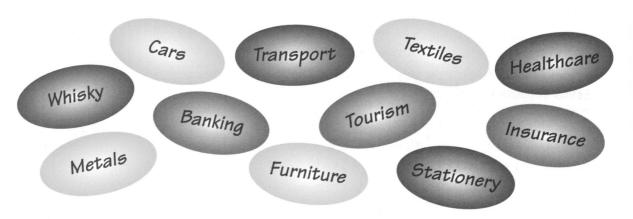

The balance of payments

Exports bring money into the UK, whereas imports lead to an outflow of money.

The UK has always done well on her invisible trading account. This is because we have developed a worldwide reputation for commercial services.

Some of our major invisible earnings come from the following:

1 Selling insurance policies

2 Offering banking services to foreign nationals

3 Carrying goods for foreign companies by sea and air

4 Attracting tourists and providing hotel and leisure facilities for them

5 Earning money on investments overseas in the form of interest and dividends

CASE STUDY

Why do countries trade?

To answer this question, let us consider the following case.

Once there were two islands separated by a sea that was too dangerous to cross.

On the first island, which was very flat, wheat could be grown in plenty, but the waters around the island contained few fish.

The second island was very hilly and only a little wheat could be grown. However, around this second island fish were plentiful.

One day an explorer found a sea passage to the south of the two islands that was not too dangerous to cross.

Let us suppose that before the trade route was discovered, half of the people in each island spent their time farming, and the other half spent their time fishing.

In a year, the amount of wheat and fish that could be produced was:

	Wheat	Fish
Hilly island	20 baskets	100 baskets
Flat island	100 baskets	20 baskets

  TASK

*R*ead the Case Study above, then answer the following questions:

1   How do you think the people of these two islands could benefit from the opening up of the sea passage?

2   Can you think of any problems that could be caused by the opening up of trade between the two islands?

3   Supposing that all the people on the flat island just grew wheat, and the people of the hilly island just fished. Can you show how the people on the two islands could be better off than before?

4   Why might this not always be true?

On the news every month we hear that the UK has made a **surplus** on invisible trade, showing that we have sold more invisible services than we have bought. The figures for a particular month might be, for example:

Invisible exports	£100 billion
Invisible imports	£80 billion
Invisible surplus	£20 billion

At the same time, the UK frequently makes a loss on her visible trade. In the early twenty-first century the UK is making a deficit on visible trading and we import more manufactured goods than we sell.

◆ The **visible trade balance** is the money from the sale of visible goods minus the money paid for the purchase of visible goods.

◆ The current trading account of the balance of payments is made up of the **visible and invisible balances**, as shown in the table below:

SPIX

'While world trade has been increasing at a very fast rate there are many people who are worried about this trend. More trade means a quicker use of scarce resources and an increase in pollution.'

Visibles		Invisibles		Totals	
Visible exports	500	Invisible exports	400	Total exports	900
Visible imports	650	Invisible imports	200	Total imports	850
Visible balance	−150	Invisible balance	+200	Current balance	+50

Balance of payments problems

While it is normal today for the UK's visible balance to run at a loss, this is greatly helped by the surplus on our invisible account. There are no easy ways of solving our balance of payments problem. Because we are a member of an international community, any actions we take at home will affect other countries and their actions will likewise affect us. The following are ways of improving the balance of payments:

Improving competitiveness

If we produce more up-to-date products than other countries, produce goods more cheaply, offer better after-sales service and meet our deadlines, then we will sell more of our products.

Raising import tariffs

If we tax foreign imports, they will be more expensive to home buyers, who will switch to buying more home-produced goods. However, the danger is that other countries will retaliate, and tariff barriers will go up around the world. This will reduce world trade and in the end everyone will lose out.

Imposing import quotas

Sometimes the UK will limit the quantities of foreign goods entering the country, such as suits from Eastern Europe. This can be done by a voluntary agreement between trading countries, or by law. Once again, this can lead to retaliation. It can also be avoided by foreign companies setting up factories in this country.

Government subsidies

The government can give financial help to UK companies to make it easier for them to sell their products at lower prices. However, again this often leads to retaliation and the breakdown of trading.

Exchange controls

In most countries the government-controlled central bank manages a central pool of foreign currency. If the government wants to cut imports, it will instruct the bank to limit the supply of foreign currency.

Usually this will mean that the central bank will only supply currency to important users. For example, importers of important raw materials will find it easy to get hold of foreign currency, whereas people wanting to holiday abroad may find that they can only take a limited amount of foreign money out of the country.

Promoting home-produced goods

The government might run a campaign encouraging citizens to buy their own, home-produced products. This has been done in the UK from time to time, and is sometimes done by other countries too, as is illustrated by the photograph from Pakistan *(right)*.

Business and international trade

International trading is very important to UK business and will continue in importance in the twenty-first century. Many firms import at least some of their inputs from overseas, and sell significant parts of their finished products overseas. Increasingly companies are having to think of their home market as an international rather than a national one.

LATEST NEWS

The last 10 years has seen large-scale reductions in many tariffs and quotas in the world.

The World Trade Organisation (WTO) is the body that has helped to arrange these reductions.

Promoting home-produced goods in Pakistan

Other forms of trade restrictions

International trade exposes UK businesses to foreign competition. This can be a major problem if UK businesses are competing with subsidised imports or with dumped products.

Dumping occurs when a firm sells goods at lower prices overseas than in its home market. It is an illegal practice.

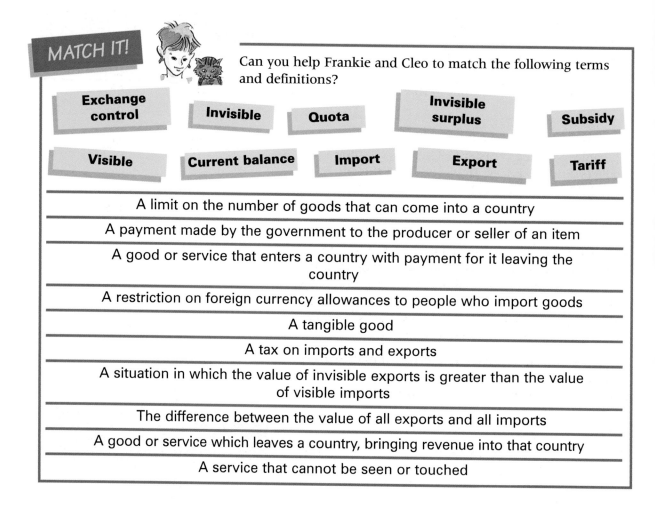

MATCH IT!

Can you help Frankie and Cleo to match the following terms and definitions?

Exchange control   Invisible   Quota   Invisible surplus   Subsidy

Visible   Current balance   Import   Export   Tariff

A limit on the number of goods that can come into a country

A payment made by the government to the producer or seller of an item

A good or service that enters a country with payment for it leaving the country

A restriction on foreign currency allowances to people who import goods

A tangible good

A tax on imports and exports

A situation in which the value of invisible exports is greater than the value of visible imports

The difference between the value of all exports and all imports

A good or service which leaves a country, bringing revenue into that country

A service that cannot be seen or touched

83 The Importance of the European Union

Today there can be no doubt that UK trade is closely linked to its partners in the European Union. In fact, over 60% of our exports go to EU countries.

'Have we always traded such a high percentage of goods and services in the European Union?'

The table below shows the importance of the EU to our visible trade.

		Percentage of total	
		1955	2000
European Union (nations that currently make up the EU)	Exports	26.8	57.6
	Imports	25.9	53.5
Other Western Europe	Exports	3.8	4.8
	Imports	2.4	5.5
North America	Exports	11.3	15.2
	Imports	19.8	15.2
Other developed countries	Exports	15.3	5.5
	Imports	12.4	8.3
Rest of the world	Exports	42.7	16.9
	Imports	39.5	17.6

When UK firms sell their goods in the UK, they are selling to a market which contains at most 60 million people. But when the same firms extend their horizons to the Single European Market, the opportunities are far greater, with 80 million people in Germany, 56 million in France, etc., all able to buy their products.

The European Union therefore presents a huge market. If a company can produce goods for a mass market, there are many economies of scale to be gained.

The Single European Market

In 1992 the **Single European Market** came into being. This means that today goods can move freely between countries without being taxed each time they cross international borders.

People, too, can move freely from one country to another and work where they like. Professionals such as doctors can also work to commonly agreed professional standards.

The Single European Market means that technical standards are gradually becoming the same in all member countries. It allows money to flow freely from one country to another for investment purposes. Common standards have also been set up in areas such as consumer and environmental protection.

The advantages of the Single European Market

Creation of the Euro

Another major development that is having a profound effect on business is the development of the single currency – the **Euro**.

European monetary union refers to the creation of monetary union between EU members. Individual currencies (such as the Pound, the Franc, the Mark and the Lira) have in effect ceased to exist and have been replaced by the Euro.

On 1 January 1999, 11 nations handed over control of their currencies to a committee of bankers. Currency (notes and coins) will appear in 2002. Up to 2002, Francs, Lire and other currencies will remain in circulation.

All decisions affecting the Euro (e.g. the setting of interest rates) are taken by the European Central Bank in Frankfurt. Unfortunately, 2000 was a bad year for the Euro. It fell against the strong dollar. However, the Euro is now expected to pick up in value.

Business and the Euro

There is a very strong business case for Britain adopting the Euro. The problem is that at the moment business has to incur transaction costs in converting Pounds into Euros in the same way that when you buy foreign currency to go abroad the bank will charge you a commission. Another major problem is that businesses which buy and sell goods on credit may find that when they come to pay for goods or receive payment after a period of credit (often 3 months) then the exchange rate might have moved unfavourably against them.

Many big businesses are in favour of adopting the Euro because of the stability that it will give to business transactions.

CASE STUDY

The Euro in 2000

2000 was not a good year for the Euro. The currency started 2000 at close to parity against the US dollar (one Euro = 1 Dollar), down from $1.17 at its launch a year earlier – and by mid-summer had fallen to a record low, below 85 cents.

However, at the end of 2000 and in early 2001 the Euro began to pick up in value and by January 2001 it was back up to 93 cents.

TASK

1   How might British exporters have suffered from the fall in the value of the Euro in 2000?

2   How might things change with an increase in the value of the Euro against the Pound?

3   Why would British business not have to worry about these fluctuations if we were part of the Eurozone?

MATCH IT!

Can you help Frankie and Cleo to match the following terms and definitions?

Single European Market	Euro	European monetary union

The common currency within the Eurozone

The development of common monetary links within the EU

A common free trade area made up of EU nations

84 The Cost of Business Activity

The price of progress

When a new supermarket opens up in your area, are you better off as a result?

On the positive side, you may be able to get a part-time job there. You may also find you have a wider range of goods to choose from than before. But what if the supermarket is right next door to your house? Suppose you have to put up with all the extra noise of cars parking and trolleys being stacked?

Counting the cost of business decisions

All communities are made up of individuals and groups who have different views about whether a particular decision is 'good' or 'bad'. This is because the decision affects each of them in a different way.

To get a clearer picture of net benefits, we therefore need to look at the **social benefits** and the **social costs** of business activity.

'So what is the difference between private costs and benefits, and social costs and benefits?'

◆ Private benefits

These are all the benefits to an individual or group resulting from a particular activity, e.g. the dividends that shareholders get from the profitable growth of their firm.

◆ Private costs

These are all the costs to an individual or group resulting from a particular activity, e.g. the cost to an individual of buying a new toothbrush, and the cost to a firm of the raw materials, labour and other inputs needed to make the toothbrush.

◆ Social benefits

These are the private benefits, plus all the good effects for other members of the community, resulting from a particular activity.

For example, if I set up as a florist I will (hopefully) receive money from my sales. This is a private benefit to me, but because I am a member of society, the money is also a social benefit.

Other social benefits will include the pleasure that customers receive from buying my flowers, the enjoyment of passersby whose day is brightened up, the wage that my assistant receives, the tax that the local council receives, the rent that my landlord earns, and so on.

Social benefit, private gain – or both?

◆ Social costs

Social costs are the private costs, plus all the bad effects for other members of the community, e.g. the extra traffic congestion caused by vehicles pulling up outside my shop, the clearing up of confetti that I sell as a sideline, and so on.

The benefits of business activity

Industry brings together resources to produce wealth. In doing so it produces the following major benefits:

1 **It provides employment.** Millions of people are employed in industry and commerce.

2 **It creates wealth.** Shareholders receive profits, landlords receive rent, lenders receive interest, workers receive wages, etc.

3 **It creates products.** Value is added at each stage of production to create a more valuable end-product.

4 **It raises living standards.** By creating wealth, industry makes it possible for people to enjoy better living standards and more leisure time.

TASK

*R*ead the Case Study below, then make a list of **five** groups of people involved in the situation. Show which are the costs and which are the benefits to each group resulting from the activities described.

CASE STUDY

The Centreville Rock Festival

Every year there is a rock festival just outside Centreville. Typically, 6,000 young rock fans converge on the park to spend three days in the sun listening to loud music and meeting up with friends. The event is organised by a millionaire 'rock entrepreneur' Justine Villeneuve. Justine runs several rock enterprises and has her own record company. The Centreville festival is always a sell-out and the rewards to Justine are considerable.

However, not everyone is happy with the festival. Local farmers say that crops are trampled and broken bottles are a danger to livestock. Cattle-owners have even reported that their cows give a reduced milk yield. Other local residents have mixed feelings. Many young people and their parents support the festival as a valuable source of entertainment. Others are strongly opposed to it, describing it as 'three days of filth, noise and declining values'. All police leave is cancelled during the festival and the bill for policing the festival is shared equally between the town of Centreville and Justine Villeneuve.

The costs of business activity

Much of this book has been about the benefits of business activity. But business also brings with it costs. When a firm produces something, it has to bear in mind a number of internal costs, e.g.:

1 Production costs

2 Marketing costs

3 Financial costs

4 Administration costs

5 Distribution costs

However, in addition to these are the external (social) costs, which go beyond the trading account of the firm. These costs are sometimes known as **externalities** or **spillover costs.**

  External costs = Social costs – Private costs

Industrial pollution

The most obvious social cost of business activity is **pollution.** This can take a number of forms:

Water pollution

It has been standard practice for a long time for industry to locate by canals, rivers and seas. Industries such as paper mills, chemical plants and breweries not only use water in their manufacturing process, but also pour out their waste into rivers and the sea.

TASK

Imagine that the eyesores shown below exist in a town near you.

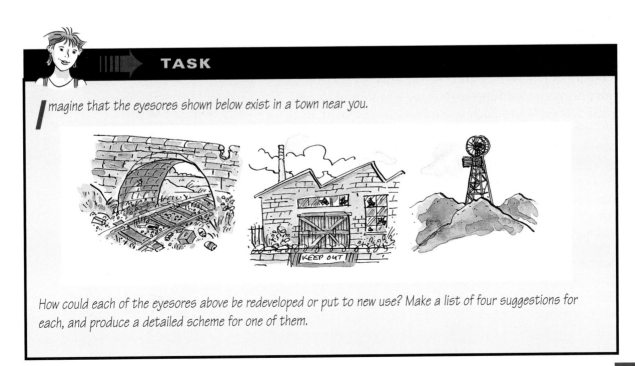

How could each of the eyesores above be redeveloped or put to new use? Make a list of four suggestions for each, and produce a detailed scheme for one of them.

Perhaps the most notorious example of this type of activity is the disposal of waste products from the nuclear fuels industry. Water itself can be treated in purification and filtration plants, but it is difficult to break down the effects of industrial chemicals, which can cause widespread and lasting damage to pond and animal life.

Air pollution

The dangers of air pollution were dramatically illustrated by several events in the 1980s. First, there was the leak of poisonous gas from the Union Carbide plant at Bhopal in India. More than 2,000 people died and at least 10 times as many suffered from breathing and eye complaints.

Disaster at Chernobyl – the deserted city of Pripyat with the nuclear reactor on the horizon

Perhaps even more dramatic was the nuclear disaster at Chernobyl in 1986. Wide tracts of land were declared unfit for farming for years afterwards, threatening the future of whole economies. The livestock of Welsh hill farmers were banned from sale because of the heavy contamination. In 2001 the impact of the Chernobyl disaster is still being felt in malformations in human and animal births in the Ukraine where the disaster occurred.

Thirdly, emissions from UK factory chimneys and power stations have been recognised as major sources of 'acid rain'. This has been shown to result in the pollution of forests and lakes in Scandinavia and Germany.

Dereliction

If we consider the decision to build a new mine, or to drill for oil or natural gas, we can see that this might destroy areas of natural beauty for ever. But often when a business pulls out of an area, the effects can be worse: not only do jobs disappear, but the community is left with derelict land which is unpleasant to look at and contains dangerous chemicals and other hazards. Today, because of the shortage of greenfield areas for housing development, the current Labour government is encouraging property developers to build on 'brownfield sites' (areas of dereliction). There are considerable dangers associated with this policy because of leftover industrial pollutants beneath the surface.

Traffic congestion

The speed of industrial development and the growing numbers of lorries and cars has put a great pressure on road networks. In the early twenty-first century we have come to question whether road building actually eases congestion. The feeling today is that improving or

SPIX

'It is possible to argue that the motor car has ruined our natural environment – look at the millions of acres put down to roads, lorry depots and car parks.'
Do you agree with Spix?

widening a road simply adds to the volume of traffic
using it.

Long-term waste

British Nuclear Fuels PLC reprocesses nuclear waste at
its plant at Sellafield.

Highly radioactive spent nuclear fuel is transported by
road or rail in nuclear-waste 'flasks'. The waste is then
either dumped in the sea or buried in stores
underground. Although defenders of the nuclear
industry claim the process is safe, critics argue that it
simply stores up problems for the future.

Noise

Noise from road and rail traffic can also be a nuisance to
householders.

In the UK, noise nuisance is controlled through by-laws
enforced by local authorities. People can be prosecuted
for continually making a noise.

The activities of businesses and construction firms are
controlled, and certain areas may be designated by the
local authority as Noise Abatement Zones.

Food additives

Today consumers often demand interesting presentation
of products and value for money. Artificial colouring and
flavourings and synthetic ingredients are used to make
food and drinks more attractive and cheaper to produce.
However, medical experts have pointed out that
additives can have dangerous spillover effects, notably
hyperactivity in children.

Food additives: an acceptable price to pay
for cheap, attractive products?

Insufficient testing of products

In the rush to become market leaders, firms may be
tempted to put their new products on the market before
they have been thoroughly tested.

A well known example of this was the production by the
Distillers Company of a drug used by women to reduce
the effects of morning sickness in pregnancy. The
spillover cost was the terrible side-effect of Thalidomide,
which caused babies to be born with limbs missing.

Cost–benefit analysis

Society benefits if resources are used well. Businesses
and governments should weigh up the costs and
benefits of any development, both in terms of private
and social effects. This is called **cost–benefit analysis**.

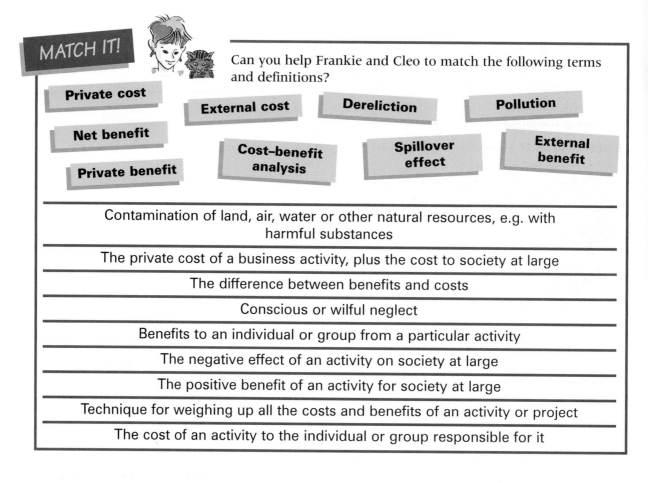

MATCH IT!

Can you help Frankie and Cleo to match the following terms and definitions?

Private cost

External cost

Dereliction

Pollution

Net benefit

Cost–benefit analysis

Spillover effect

External benefit

Private benefit

Contamination of land, air, water or other natural resources, e.g. with harmful substances

The private cost of a business activity, plus the cost to society at large

The difference between benefits and costs

Conscious or wilful neglect

Benefits to an individual or group from a particular activity

The negative effect of an activity on society at large

The positive benefit of an activity for society at large

Technique for weighing up all the costs and benefits of an activity or project

The cost of an activity to the individual or group responsible for it

85 Pressure Groups

What is a pressure group?

A pressure group is a group of people who try to influence those who make laws, form public opinion, or take important decisions.

It may be just a few people, such as a group of parents demanding a public enquiry into a local hospital. Or it may be a large organisation like the environmental pressure group, Greenpeace.

'What sorts of people form pressure groups?'

Business and pressure groups

Businesses have many stakeholders, all of whom exert different pressures on the organisation.

Internally, the business needs to make a profit for shareholders, and shareholders need to be satisfied with the way the business is being run. Externally, the business will have even more pressures to contend with.

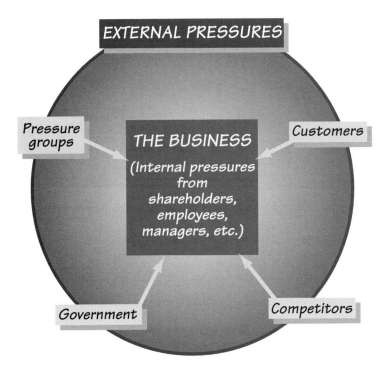

Left: Pressures on a business

1 Perhaps the biggest pressure is to sell its products. Consumers will not buy products they do not want.

2 The business must also face pressure from its competitors. Competition often acts as a spur to an organisation to perform better.

3 The government also exerts pressure on business to meet standards and comply with legislation.

4 In addition, there is the influence placed on businesses by organised pressure groups.

Types of pressure group

The two main types of pressure groups are:

◆ **Protection groups.** These are groups which are set up to fight on a specific issue, such as a dangerous road or a controversial tree-felling scheme.

◆ **Promotional groups.** These are more formal groups which fight campaigns on a wide range of issues. Some are large-scale and highly organised. Examples are Greenpeace and Friends of the Earth.

Below: Protection and promotion-type pressure groups

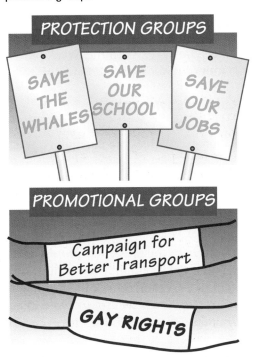

Such groups have clearly defined long-term objectives. Their sustained pressure on various authorities helps to create new ways of thinking. Groups like Friends of the Earth and Greenpeace have had a tremendous impact in changing the ways in which organisations operate.

For example, many supermarkets have moved towards 'green' and organic lines in recent times. Once a fringe concern, green issues are now an everyday part of mainstream political and business activity.

Pressure groups use a range of measures, which vary from attention-grabbing stunts (e.g. climbing up Nelson's Column with a banner) to high-profile media advertising campaigns.

Consumer pressure groups

A well known and powerful consumer pressure group is the **Consumers' Association.** This is funded by subscriptions from members who buy the consumer magazine *Which?* The Consumers' Association uses its funds to test and report on a wide variety of products. It also produces books on consumer-related matters.

Many industries, including those that have been privatised, have consumers councils representing the interest of consumers – e.g. the Rail Users' Council.

Consumer boycotts

Sometimes pressure groups will run campaigns in order to stop consumers from buying certain products. These are known as **consumer boycotts.**

Throughout the 1970s and 1980s anti-apartheid campaigners put pressure on customers to stop using Barclays Bank. This sort of pressure finally influenced Barclays in 1986 to sell off its South African branches. Today, however, with the development of 'the rainbow nation' in South Africa, Barclays have moved back.

Local lobbying

Often local residents will form pressure groups in order to force a business to change its practices. Reasons may include:

1 Traffic danger

2 Emission of fumes and pollution

3 Safety hazards such as tips, pits, etc.

If letters to the press and protest meetings fail to get results, the group may try to put pressure on local and central government to influence the activities of the firm. Wise firms will try to avoid alienating local residents in case it brings them bad publicity.

Greenpeace protesters approaching the Shell oil rig, Brent Spar

COURSEWORK ACTIVITIES

Take a look at the activities of a particular pressure group in your area.

Find out what their objectives are, when the group was set up, how it is funded, how you become a member, what members do, how the group operates, etc.

Methods of persuasion

Some groups seek to influence opinion-formers through a form of personal contact known as **lobbying.**

Others use powerful advertising and promotion to get their message across. Trade unions use this method of persuasion quite often. Groups like teachers, miners and printworkers have all used national advertising to try to win support from the public and political parties. Picketing and industrial action are another way for a union to put pressure on an employer.

The employers' organisation, the CBI, and the unions' organisation, the TUC, also exert influence at national level through statements to the press and media. Other promotional pressure groups, such as the campaign for lead-free petrol and the anti-smoking lobby, use similar techniques.

Sometimes groups use less peaceful methods to impress their views on the public. Demonstrations, protest marches and sit-ins often lead to publicity on television or in the press.

TASK

*R*ead the Case Study below then answer the following questions:

1   What does the Case Study tell you about the potential influence of pressure groups?

2   Do you think that McDonalds handled the case in a sensible way? How else might they have handled it?

3   How do you think the campaign will affect the way McDonalds operates?

4   What do you see as being the main value of pressure groups?

CASE STUDY

The McLibel case

In December 1995, the McDonalds libel trial became the longest civil case in British history.

McDonalds sued two environmentalists from North London to stop a stream of allegations against the international burger chain. Helen Steel and David Morris had claimed the company sold food that was linked to heart diseases and cancer, cut down rainforests, abused its workforce and corrupted children with its advertising. The allegations were contained in a leaflet called *What's wrong with McDonalds*.

Millions of leaflets have been handed out since the start of the trial, and reports of the story in the media have given the two campaigners worldwide coverage.

McDonalds claimed they were forced into taking legal action in order to answer the allegations being made against them. During the trial a number of high-ranking McDonalds executives were forced to testify, and resources worldwide were used to counter media stories.

The legal bill for McDonalds ran into millions of pounds. The defendants were financed by dole cheques and donations from well-wishers. A support campaign for the two produced regular trial summaries on the Internet which have been read by computer-users all over the world.

Today there is an Internet site (www.Mclibel), which contains criticisms not only of McDonalds but also of many other major corporations.

Business response to pressure groups

There are a number of ways businesses can respond to pressure groups.

1 Ignore them. Businesses may argue that consumers can choose whether to buy the product or not. In the meantime they can make sure that their products meet all the necessary legal requirements.

2 Run a counter campaign to win public support. This is the policy adopted by British Nuclear Fuels PLC. 'Come to Sellafield. Look around the place. See for yourself how safe it is' – loosely paraphrased, this is the message of a multi-million pound advertising campaign which British Nuclear Fuels has used for several years *(right)*.

3 Take advice from consumers and compromise in order to win back public support.

> BRITISH NUCLEAR FUELS PLC
>
> *request the pleasure of your company to view their Sellafield Exhibition Centre.*
>
> *Open from 10am-4pm every day of the week from Easter to the end of October, or from 10am – 4pm Monday to Friday, November to March*
>
> ---
>
> *Exhibition Centre, British Nuclear Fuels PLC, Sellafield, Cumbria.*
>
> *(Off the A595 at Calderbridge between Millom and Whitehaven)*

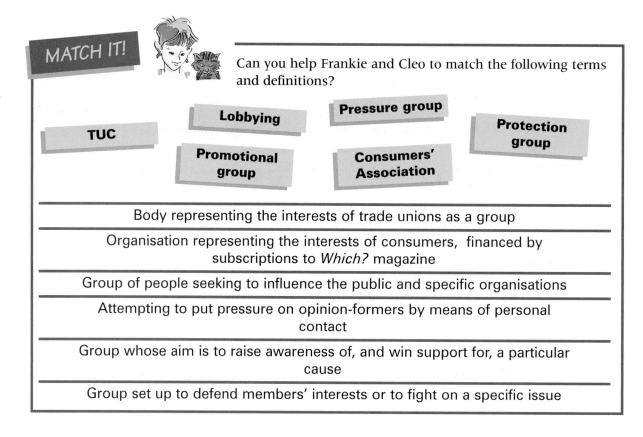

MATCH IT!

Can you help Frankie and Cleo to match the following terms and definitions?

TUC **Lobbying** **Pressure group** **Protection group** **Promotional group** **Consumers' Association**

Body representing the interests of trade unions as a group
Organisation representing the interests of consumers, financed by subscriptions to *Which?* magazine
Group of people seeking to influence the public and specific organisations
Attempting to put pressure on opinion-formers by means of personal contact
Group whose aim is to raise awareness of, and win support for, a particular cause
Group set up to defend members' interests or to fight on a specific issue

86 The Future of Business

What will businesses be like in the future?

In the future, businesses will need to be able to respond quickly to change.

Twenty-five years ago, most large business organisations had a pyramid structure. People at the top made the big decisions. These flowed down to middle managers, who then passed their instructions down to operatives.

These 'command and control' organisations are no longer desirable. They are slow and clumsy.

Today we have new **dynamic organisations** in which there are far more decision-making points. If we look at how big corporations are working, we can see that each operating company is broken down into a loose network of business units. The parts of these organisations only link up when they need to exchange information and work together on shared projects. The name of the game is flexibility.

The importance of interdependence

Today more than ever, interdependence lies at the heart of business relationships. Business has been transformed by new technology. The development of information technology means that the lowest-level operative in an organisation can now have access to almost as much information as a top-level manager. Information technology makes it possible to process vast quantities of work at great speed.

Information is one of the greatest assets of an organisation. By sharing information efficiently, it can build a strong competitive advantage over its rivals.

But it is not just interdependence within a business that is important. Companies need to build excellent links with customers. The successful business of today and the future is the one that is able to identify, anticipate and meet customer needs.

Excellent links with suppliers are vital too. Businesses need to have quality raw materials and semi-finished products delivered 'just in time' to be made into final products.

The challenge of new markets

Today many companies are moving into new markets. Large companies need to see the world as their marketplace. By doing so, they are able to spread their

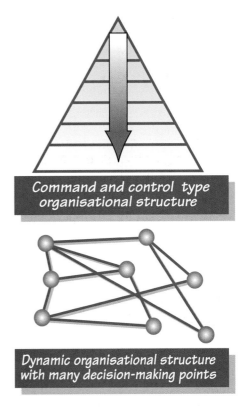

Command and control type organisational structure

Dynamic organisational structure with many decision-making points

Changing business structures

'That must mean that any student completing a Business Studies course will benefit enormously from having good IT skills!'

CASE STUDY

Power brands

With the growing globalisation of markets companies like the US-based Heinz Corporation and Anglo–Dutch-owned Unilever are increasingly concentrating on what they see as being their power brands. Power brands are those brands in which you have market leadership and are well ahead of the competition.

Unilever's power brands include Magnum ice cream and Heinz's' include Heinz Baby Food and Heinz tomato ketchup.

Heinz and Unilever are able to concentrate their resources into these products to win global leadership.

---

costs over a larger output. The costs of international communications and transport have been greatly reduced. Also, rather than transporting goods to other countries, companies are preferring to set up their own manufacturing plant there, either by building from scratch or setting up a joint venture.

The importance of new technologies

New technology has transformed our lives and will continue to do so in the future. Long-established technologies offer considerable scope for improvement. For example, the use of unleaded petrol has made the internal combustion engine much more environment-friendly, removing 90% of harmful emissions such as carbon monoxide.

In spite of its phenomenal developments in recent years, information technology still has immense potential. We quickly become frustrated with current technology, yet five years ago we would have been astounded at the speed of today's computers. Information technology will continue to astound us and to transform our lives. The year 2000 was the year of the dot.com bubble, in which newspapers puffed up every project dreamt up by two 20-something year olds. No longer will investors pile money into mere ideas – they will want to see that there is a business too.

While late 2000 and early 2001 saw the collapse of a number of e-businesses such as the European side of the US retailer eToys and LetsBuy-It.com the e-commerce sector continues to grow. The number of people buying goods and services over the Internet keeps increasing. Amazon, the best-known e-retailer, had a very good Christmas in 2000. The airlines are progressively shifting more and more of their sales online. A shakeout of unsuccessful businesses is normal.

TASK

1   Why is it important for large companies to focus on their power brands?

2   What power brands can you name apart from those listed in the case study?

The fourth and fifth division e-retailers may be under water, but with any new technology there will naturally be many failures. In the early 1900s there were 3,000 companies in the US making cars.

Whatever happens to individual dot.com companies, we can never go back to the pre-dot.com days. Today the world of business is radically different from the one that existed before the communication revolution burst upon us. The revolution rolls on and there will be very few successful businesses (if any) that do not embrace modern technologies.

Investing for the future

Business success involves a continual process of preparing for tomorrow. Businesses cannot rest on their past successes. They need to build for the future.

Many companies famous for producing typewriters failed to respond to the word-processing revolution of the 1980s – and disappeared. Others were eager to exploit the word-processing revolution, but failed to realise that the future lay with personal computers with a WP package. They too disappeared. New companies realised the importance of developing an Internet presence by developing a website. Some of these companies built websites that supported their core business interests, while others ploughed money into website presences with no clear focus.

The emphasis needs to be on making effective plans for the future and taking intelligent risks. P&O, for example, realised that aircraft could deliver passengers to their destinations faster than their own cruise liners. Instead, they turned their attention to the ferry business, where journey times were longer, but passengers could take their own car and enjoy the fun of a sea voyage.

The importance of the environment

Concern for the environment has become one of the most important business issues today. No company can survive and prosper if it neglects the developing needs of the customer and the increasingly insistent needs of the environment.

In practice, the two sets of needs go together. Customers will not want to buy products and services from companies with a bad environmental record. In addition, government regulation and taxation will put greater financial burdens on companies who do not meet agreed environmental standards. The net result is that business policies will *have* to become environmentally efficient to survive.

'In the Railway Age of the nineteenth century many railway companies went bust. But those that survived were very successful up to the Second World War. I am sure that the same will be true of the new Internet economy. Many companies will perish, while some will become tomorrow's giants.'

P&O realised that the future lay in ferries

Smaller businesses

Today there is more scope for small business than in the past. Because large organisations are 'downsizing' and streamlining, they need to buy in many of their 'non-core' requirements from outside. This is called **outsourcing**.

For example, in the past a large multinational company may have had its own photography department, perhaps employing a number of photographers with their own office.

Today these companies will buy in professional photography services from outside the organisation.

In the same way a big company will outsource design work, advertising work, training work, cleaning of offices and many other jobs, leaving it free to concentrate on its **core activities**.

At the same time, people have more leisure, and as incomes increase, they want to buy in a wide range of personal services. There are therefore plenty of opportunities for people to set up small businesses providing hairdressing, massage, gardening, cleaning, etc.

'I am now convinced that there are opportunities to set up in business – providing I do a lot of planning and take on board the business lessons set out in this book.'

SPIX

'Yes, there are lot of opportunities – but remember that business activity should always be ethical and take into account the needs of the environment and the wider community.'

MATCH IT! Can you help Frankie and Cleo to match the following terms and definitions?

Environmental policy	Non-core activities	Outsourcing	Dynamic organisations	Pyramid structure

Activities that do not lie at the heart of a particular business

A traditional 'command and control' top-down organisation

Mobile, flexible and versatile business structures that use information technology to aid swift communications

Buying in goods, services and materials from sources external to the organisation

Targets and plans directed towards helping an organisation achieve its environmental objectives

Glossary

Acceptance – when in law you are deemed to have accepted goods that you have purchased – i.e. the point at which you lose your right to a refund on the goods.

Accounting system – set of methods and procedures for organising, interpreting and using accounting information.

Acid test ratio – Current assets less stock: Current liabilities. An important measure of the liquidity of a business in terms of whether it has the ability to pay back short term liabilities.

Adding value – increasing the value of the product to the final consumer, not just through manufacturing processes but by any process that makes the product more desirable e.g. advertising, promotion etc.

Advertising Standards Authority – body responsible for controlling non-broadcasted advertising – e.g. covering press advertising, magazines, billboards, etc.

Ageing population – an increase in the average age of the population. In particular the growth in the number of elderly people sometimes referred to as the 'greying' of the population.

Agenda – written outline of issues to be discussed at a meeting.

Anti-competitive practices – actions taken to restrict competition between businesses.

Appraisal – formal evaluation of the performance of an employee over a particular period.

Arbitration – the settlement of a dispute by an arbitrator who is given responsibility for deciding on a judgement.

Articles of Association – a document setting out the details of the internal relationships that exist within the company e.g. when company meetings will be held, how directors will be chosen, and so on.

Asset utilisation – measure of how many sales assets are generating. Measured by sales/fixed assets.

Assets – what a business owns or is owed at a particular moment in time.

Authorised capital – the maximum number of shared that a company is authorised to sell by its Memorandum of Association.

Autocratic manager – a manager who makes decisions on their own and tries to force their will on others.

Automation – automatic operations involving machinery rather than people.

B2B – business to business dealing through the Internet.

B2C – direct links between businesses and consumers through the Internet.

Bad debts – sums of money owed to a business which are not paid. For accounting periods these are treated as expenses and written off in the profit and loss account.

Balance of trade – account showing the difference between the export and the import of goods and services.

Balance sheet – a snapshot of a firm's assets, liabilities and sources of capital at a moment in time.

Batch production – producing items in sets or batches for a particular length of time, before switching the production line to producing another type of batch.

Benefits – advantages, tangible or intangible, gained by customers from the product or service they buy.

Board of Directors – a body consisting of representatives of shareholders in a company with the responsibility for looking after the interests of shareholders.

Boom – period of high economic and business activity.

Branch – a local group of members of the same trade union.

Brand – a product with a unique, consistent and well-recognised character. The uniqueness can come either from a factual product detail or from its image – usually created by its manufacturer through advertising and packaging.

Break-even analysis – compares a firm's revenue with its fixed and variable costs to identify the minimum sales level needed to make a profit. This can be shown on a graph known as a break-even chart.

Break-even point – the level of output at which total revenue equals total costs.

Budget – a plan usually set out in table form setting out how financial targets will be arrived at.

Bulk-increasing industry – industries in which the product gets larger/and or more weighty during the process of manufacture e.g. producing wardrobes, producing refrigerators, etc.

Bulk-reducing industry – industries in which the product gets smaller/and or lighter during the process of manufacture e.g. reducing iron ore into steel products.

Business ethics – views on the 'right way' in terms of morality of conducting business e.g. not causing pollution, giving a fair price to suppliers, etc.

Business plan – a document designed to provide sufficient information about a new or existing business to convince financial backers to invest in the business.

CAD – computer aided design, using a computer to help design new products and processes.

CAM – computer aided manufacturing, using computers in the control and management of machinery and processes.

Capital – money or resources invested by the owner(s) of the organisation. It is a source of finance used by the business to acquire assets.Can be either 'fixed' or 'working'. Fixed capital includes land, machinery and building. Working capital includes stocks of raw material, semi-finished goods, components and money (to cover the purchase of raw material and other necessities when money from customers is not forthcoming).

Capital expenditure – expenditure on large items of fixed capital such as a computer, a machine, lorry, etc.

Cash flow – the flow of money into and out of a business.

Cash flow forecast – a future forecast of money likely to come into and out of the business over a period of time.

CBI – Confederation of British Industry, the national body representing the interests of employers, for example in talks with government and trade unions.

CD-ROM – Compact disc read-only-memory.

Central government – the body responsible for government decisions which are made at a national level e.g. by making new laws in Parliament.

Central planning – a system of running an economy where most of the major decisions are made by the government and central planning bodies.

Centralisation – where most important decisions are typically made from the centre (e.g. the Head Office) of an organisation.

Certificate of Incorporation – the document that certifies that a company has a company status – i.e. that it is recognised in law as being a body that can sue and be sued.

Certificate of Trading – the document that states that a company can start to trade.

Channels of distribution – the route through which a good or service is moved to the market.

Charismatic leader – a leader who uses their personality power to get things done.

Closed question – in a market research questionnaire, a closed question is one that gives the interviewee a choice of prepared answers.

Closed shop – only allowing people to work at an industrial site who are members of a particular trade union.

Code of advertising practice – a voluntary agreement between firms in the advertising industry to control adverts so that they are honest, legal, decent and truthful.

Collateral – assets providing security on a loan.

Commercial economies – reductions in cost that result from buying and selling in larger rather than smaller quantities.

Commission – the per centage paid to an agent e.g. a sales person for the business they conduct.

Communication – the process by which information is exchanged between one group or individual and another.

Company – a business which is registered as a company being owned by a group of shareholders and managed in their common interest.

Comparative advantage – concentrating on your best lines relative to others.

Competition – any kind of counter-attraction to the product or service you want to sell.

Competition Commission – body with overall responsibility for seeking to create competitive conditions in UK markets.

Conciliation – to calm a situation by helping sides in a dispute to arrive at an agreement.

Conglomerate integration – involves taking over a firm that produces a product different from your own.

Consultative manager – someone who listens to others views.

Consumer boycott – an alliance of consumers to stop buying particular products for example because they are produced in countries were exploitation or repression is taking place.

Consumers' Association – an organisation which sets out to further the interests of the consumers who are its members by publishing information comparing products and offers made by rival firms. Publishes the consumer magazine Which?

Contract of Employment – legal document setting out terms and conditions of employment.

Contribution – total revenue less variable costs of producing a particular line or product. When businesses produce several products this can be used to find out how much each one is contributing to covering the fixed costs.

Convenor – a leading employee representative in a place of work.

Co-operative – an organisation owned by co-operators who work together with a shared aim.

Core workers – full time employees of an organisation with better terms and conditions than others.

Corporation tax – taxes paid on company profits.ß

COSHH – Control of Substances Hazardous to Health Regulations, provides rules about how employers should manage the use of dangerous substances in the workplace.

Cost benefit analysis – a technique for appraising the net benefit of an activity. This involves adding up all the benefits and then deducting all the costs to see if there is a net benefit.

Cost of sales – the cost of making the products and services sold to customers. Calculated by: Opening stock plus Purchases minus Closing Stock.

Cost-plus pricing – working out how much each unit of product costs to produce and then adding a fixed per centage for profit.

Costs – are the expenses incurred by a firm in producing and selling its products. These include expenditure upon wages and raw materials.

Creditors – individuals or other businesses that are owed money by the business.

Current assets – shorter term assets such as stocks, debtors, money in the bank and cash-in-hand.

Current liabilities – debts which a business needs to pay in the short period (usually less than one year).

Customer attitudes – what customers think, feel and believe about a company and/or its products. Attitudes are shaped by experience of the product, the opinions of friends, direct dealings with the company, and advertising.

Customer service – the overall activity of identifying and satisfying customer needs.

Customs duty – a tax on goods imported into a country.

Data – known facts or things used as a basis for inference or reckoning. Also used to mean quantities or characters operated on by a computer.

Data protection – legal control over access to data stored in organisational records.

Database – store of information created by manipulation of a computer program.

Debenture – a loan to a company giving a fixed rate of return whether the company is making a profit or not.

Debtor days – debtors/credit sales x 52 (weeks in the year)

Debtors – individuals or companies who owe money to the business.

Deed of partnership – an agreement between a group of partners setting out the legal relationship under which the partnership is set up, how profits and work will be shared out, etc.

Delegation – passing power and authority down the hierarchy in an organisation enabling decision making to take place at lower levels.

Delivery lead times – the time between placing an order and receiving the goods.

Delivery note – note sent with goods giving their details and often their prices, may be an invoice.

Demand – consumers' wishes to purchase products backed up by their willingness to spend money on those products.

Democratic manager – a manager who shares out responsibility and encourages the opinions of others.

Demographics – the statistical study of people, their age, gender, family status, income, job type, geographical distribution, etc.

Depreciation – loss in the value of assets over time because of wear-and-tear, and obsolescence.

Deregulation – the process through which government controls of an industry are reduced.

Desktop publishing – the production of printed matter with a desktop computer and printer.

Destroyer pricing – charging a price which is lower than that of rivals in an attempt to deliberately force them to leave the industry.

Development – improving an individual in line with the requirements of that individual.

Direct competition – competition between suppliers of products which are similar to each other.

Direct taxes – a tax paid directly to the tax authority by the payer e.g. income tax.

Directives – legislation created by the European Union.

Diseconomies of scale – when a firm gets too large then inefficiencies set in leading to rising costs.

Dismissal – to discharge a person from their employment.

Dividends – shareholders share of profits earned by an organisation.

Division of labour – breaking down work so that it is carried out by specialists or using specialist equipment.

Double entry system – accounting convention of matching every credit entry in an account with a debit entry.

Downsizing – the reduction in the size of a business often by stripping out layers of employees.

Downward communication – communication from higher to lower levels within the organisation.

Drawings – money or assets taken out of the business by owners from profits.

e-business – a business organisation carrying out much of its' business through the medium of the Internet.

e-commerce – buying and selling using the Internet.

Economies of scale – the advantages that a larger firm has over a smaller one enabling it to produce larger outputs at lower costs per individual unit.

Electronic Data Interchange (EDI) – computers linked by a permanently open telephone line which enables them to swop data.

Employers' association – an organisation made up of groups of employers which represents their interests.

Employment procession – the various stages in employment starting from recruitment, selection, and induction and finishing with retirement.

Empowerment – giving decision making responsibilities to those lower down in an organisation.

Entrepreneur – risk taker in a business e.g. the shareholders, one person owner or a partner in a business.

Environmental audit – an independent check of the environmental practices of a business in terms of its meeting stakeholder requirements including meeting legal requirements.

Equal Pay Act – establishes equal pay to everyone carrying out the same work or work of the same value.

Equity – a company's equity is its total capital value less all outside liabilities including those to holders of debentures and preferential shares but excepting those to ordinary shareholders. Ordinary shareholders are the owners of the company and hence its equity – which is why their shares are also known as 'equities'.

Esteem needs – the need to be respected and to feel valued and important.

Ethical business – one that carries out its business in a moral way.

Ethical trading – trading in such a way as to avoid exploitation e.g. by paying a bit extra to ensure a decent living to your suppliers.

Ethics – sets of moral principals guiding behaviour.

Euro – a single currency for the Eurozone group of countries.

European Monetary Union – the creation of a single currency the Euro in the Eurozone countries.

European Union – an economic, social and political union between major countries in Europe such as the UK, France and Germany.

Exchange controls – limits on the quantities of foreign currencies that citizens and businesses of a country can obtain from financial institutions such as banks.

Exchange rate – the rate of exchange between one countries currency and that of another e.g. the Euro against the Dollar.

Excise duty – a duty charged on goods produced which is taxed in the country of origin.

Export – sell goods and services to another country.

External economies – advantages to a business that arise from the growth of the industry that it is in, e.g. the growth of specialist firms that supply it (and its competitors).

External recruitment – recruiting people to fill jobs from those outside the organisation.

Externality – the spillover effect resulting from a particular activity, e.g. production may cause pollution as an externality. Externalities can be both positive and negative.

Factoring – selling off your debts at a discount for another company to collect.

Factors of production – things that are used to make goods and services including labour, land, capital and enterprise.

Fair dismissal – when someone is sacked for reasons which are acceptable in law.

FIFO – first in first out. Turning over stock so that the oldest stock is the first to be sold.

Final accounts – accounts produced at the end of a period e.g. a profit and loss and trading account.

Financed by – section of a balance sheet outlining ways in which the capital of the company has been financed.

Financial accounting – ways of recording transactions and using information from these records.

Financial ratios – ratios comparing one sum as a ratio of another.

Fixed assets – assets which are kept within the business for a longer period of time – usually having a lifespan of more than one year e.g. fixtures and fittings, vehicles, etc.

Fixed costs – any costs which do not vary with the level of output, for example rent and rates.

Flat organisation – an organisation with few levels.

Flexitime – a system of working a set number of hours with the starting and finishing times chosen within agreed limits by the employee.

Forecast – an estimate of what is likely to happen in the future.

Formal communication – communication that takes place within the channels officially set up in the organisation.

Franchise – permission to use a franchise name and to sell using that franchise in a particular locality.

Franchisee – a person who has been given a franchise to trade under a franchise name.

Franchisor – person granting a franchise to someone else.

Gap in the market – a business opportunity that has as yet not been taken up by competitors.

Globalisation – a situation in which the world is shrinking because it is easier for goods, services and communications to be transferred from one side of the globe to another.

Gross pay – total pay before taking away deductions such as income tax and national insurance.

Gross profit – the profit that a firm earns from trading or from selling goods before the overheads and expenses have been deducted. It is calculated by Sales – Cost of sales = Gross profit.

Gross profit percentage - gross profit/sales revenue x 100%.

Hierarchy – an organisation with lots of layers of command.

Hire purchase – a borrowing arrangement whereby the person taking out HP – does not become the owner of an item they are buying on credit until they have paid the final instalment.

Horizontal integration – buying up another firm at the same stage of production.

Human Resource Management (HRM) – treating people as the most important resource of the organisation.

Hygiene factors – elements of working life that have the potential to cause dissatisfaction, such as salary, working conditions, status and oversupervision.

Image – what people think and feel consciously and subconsciously about a company or product.

Import – bring in foreign goods to a country or use foreign services.

Impulse purchase – one that is made on the spur of the moment, eg to pick up chewing gum at a supermarket checkout.

Incentives – a motive or incitement to action, a reward to will encourage someone to do something.

Incorporation – establishing a business as a separate legal entity from its owners, and therefore allowing it to have limited liability.

Indirect competition – competition between suppliers who are competing with other suppliers for consumers to spend their money with them. These products may be quite different.

Indirect taxes – taxes on expenditure which are paid by an intermediary to the tax authorities before being passed on to the end consumer.

Individual Development Plans – plans drawn up between an individual and their training supervisor to identify appropriate areas for personal development while at work.

Induction – introducing individuals to work and the work environment in an organisation.

Industrial union – union made up of people who work in the same industry e.g. mining, the post office, etc.

Inflation – a general rise in prices across a wide range of goods and services.

Information Technology – techniques for transmitting, storing, manipulating and retrieving all kinds of data, including speech, text, movie, graphics and reports of events.

Informative advertising – advertising which just gives the bare facts without attempting to persuade.

Innovation – using a new idea in the marketplace or in the workplace.

Integration – the joining together of firms.

Interest rate – the price charged for borrowing money.

Internal communications – communications that take place within an organisation e.g. through internal memos, team briefings, etc.

Internal customer – someone within a company that you are providing a good or service for, e.g. workers producing individual parts may 'sell' them on to the assembly unit.

Internal economies – the internal advantages that a large firm has over a smaller one e.g. being able to raise finance more cheaply, being able to offer bulk discounts, etc.

International trade – the process of buying and selling goods on international markets.

Invention – the creation of a new product or process.

Inverted organisations – organisations in which people who deal daily with customers are given lots of responsibility for decision making and are supported by others in the organisation. The organisation is turned on its head compared with the old-fashioned hierarchy.

Investment – the purchase or creation of an asset with the object of making gains in the future.

Invisible – a service which is traded on international markets.

Invisible balance – the difference between the value of services exported and services imported.

Invoice – document setting out the details of a transaction.

Issued capital – the number or value of shares that a company has issued at a particular moment in time. It may have not issued shares to the full value of its authorised capital.

Job analysis – an examination to find out what is involved in carrying out a particular job in order to be able to create an effective job specification.

Job description – a written document describing what is involved in a particular job e.g. job title, hours of work, tasks to be performed, etc.

Job production – a one off piece of work produced for a particular customer.

Job satisfaction – pleasure obtained from work irrespective of financial reward.

Job specification – a description of the mental and physical requirements that a job holder will need to have to carry out a job effectively.

Just-in-case – stocking up more than is required just-in-case they are needed.

Just-in-time production – producing goods for just when they are needed rather than building up stockpiles.

Kaizen – a Japanese word meaning seeking continuous improvement in products and processes.

Kanban system – a signal to show that a customer is ready for more parts/products, etc.

Lateral integration – involves taking over a firm producing products related to your own e.g. because they are sold through the same distribution outlets.

Leadership – the process of driving through change by getting others to do what you want.

Lean production – a philosophy that aims to produce more using less, by eliminating all forms of waste (where waste is defined as those activities that do not add value to production).

Leasing – hiring an item such as a photocopier, or a vehicle.

Legislation – laws set out by Acts of Parliament and previous court judgements. Many laws affect what businesses can and can not do.

Liabilities – what an organisation owes at a particular moment in time.

Lifestyles – patterns of behaviour associated with particular groups of people.

Limited company – one whose shareholders have a liability only to the extent of their investment.

Limited liability – the limitation on what the owners of a company can be sued for – the top limit being the sum that they have invested in the business.

Line production – producing goods in a set of sequenced steps along a production line.

Liquidity – the ease with which an asset can be converted into cash. Money is therefore the most liquid of all assets.

Location of business – where a business is set up and continues to exist.

Long-term liabilities – debts which have to be paid usually after one year e.g. a loan or mortgage.

Management – getting things done through other people.

Management accountant – someone that produces information for managers to enable them to make better decisions e.g. information about costs, the creation of budgets, etc.

Management accounting – using accounting information to support managers to make decisions.

Management style – the typical way that a manager behaves over a period of time – e.g. someone may have a management style of being open and warm.

Marginal cost – the cost of producing the additional unit.

Marginal revenue – the revenue from selling an additional unit.

Market price – the price at which the wishes of consumers in the market match those of suppliers supplying decisions.

Market research – systematically gathering, recording and analysing data about the market for a good or service.

Market segmentation – breaking down the total market into a number of more relevant sub-sections or segments. Marketing activities can then be specifically targeted at these segments, e.g. 15-18 year old females.

Marketing – identifying and anticipating what the customer requires and then providing what they want.

Marketing co-operative – a co-operative of people who sell their products through a joint co-operative which handles marketing activities on behalf of its' members.

Marketing mix – a particular programme including elements of each of the four P's of product, price, promotion and place.

Market-led – a business that identifies what customers want and need and then seeks to provide the appropriate goods and services to meet their needs.

Mass marketing – devising goods and services with mass appeal and promoting them to all types of customers.

Mass production – producing a standard product in very large quantities.

Matrix – an organisational structure based on 'teams' across specialist boundaries, with upward reporting reduced to a minimum.

Mediation – acting as a medium to help solve a dispute.

Memo/Memorandum – Short message passing on information.

Memorandum of Association – document setting out the relationship between an organisation and the outside world – for example, the name of the company, where its address is, etc.

Merchandising – the presentation and promotion of products at the point-of-sale.

Merging – the joining together of two previously separate businesses.

Mintel – a market research organisation that publishes a lot of useful marketing information.

Minutes – written record of what has been covered and discussed in a meeting.

Mission – the purpose of an organisation.

Monetary Policy Committee – a group of experts at the Bank of England who meet to set interest rates.

Monopoly – a single seller in the market.

Mortgage – loan which is made and secured on property. Mortgages are usually for long period of time and the capital and interest are paid back over time.

Motivation – the desire of an individual to work and to get involved in activities.

Multi-channel communication – communications in a range of directions across the organisation.

Multinational – a company with its head office in one country but which operates in many different countries.

Multiskilling – developing a range of work based skills rather than just specialising in narrow areas.

Mutual – a society which is run for the mutual benefit of the people who contribute to that society.

National Insurance – compulsory payments paid by those in work which contribute to items such as sick pay, pensions, etc.

Nationalisation – the taking over of a business by the government.

Net pay – pay after deductions such as national insurance and tax have been taken away from gross pay.

Net profit – the true profit of a firm. Net profit = Gross profit + Income from other sources – Expenses.

Net profit percentage – net profit/sales x 100%.

New economy – the sector of the economy that is based primarily on Information Technology and the Internet, e.g. dotcom companies, web page designers.

Noise – anything which can interfere with the clear reception of a message.

Objectives – the ends to which an organisation works towards – e.g. it may have an objective setting out how much profit it wants to make.

Obsolescence – going out of use or out of date.

Off-the-job training – training not specifically related to carrying out a work based task.

On-line – something that appear on the Internet, e.g. an online newspaper.

On-the-job training – instructing employees at their place of work while they are carrying out their normal work based activities.

Open question – in a market research questionnaire, an open question is one that allows interviewees to answer in their own words.

Operating division (or company) – a company or division directly in charge of a productive business activity, and reporting to a 'central office' or 'head office'.

Operations – the processes involved in producing goods and services.

Opportunity cost – the next best alternative that is sacrificed in making a decision.

Organisation chart – a diagram setting out the relationships between people in an organisation.

Output device – means of taking information from a computer system e.g. a printer.

Overdraft – short term finance provided by a financial institution such as a bank enabling the person taking out the overdraft to run an overdraft up to a set limit.

Overheads – costs incurred in the daily running of a business which do not vary with the quantity of production. Examples include rent, rates, heating, lighting, insurance.

Owner's capital – finance provided to the business by the owners.

Partnership – a business owned by between two and twenty partners, often carrying out professional work such as a doctors or vets.

Patent – government licence to an inventor to produce that item for a set period of time without threat of copying.

Penetration pricing – charging a low initial price to win market share in a competitive market.

Personnel – a body of employees.

Personnel department – the part of the organisation that is concerned with people management, eg recruitment, selection, employee welfare, etc.

Persuasive advertising – advertising that goes beyond providing facts about a good or service using a range of techniques to appeal to potential customers such as fear, a desire to keep up with the neighbours, sex appeal, etc.

Piece rate – payment according to the number of units or pieces produced.

Pollution – contamination of water, soil or atmosphere with poisonous or otherwise harmful substances.

Positional map – a diagram setting out the key differences and similarities in the competitive positions of different organisations.

Power brands – the key brands of large corporation, through which they hope to win domination of particular markets.

Preference shares – shares that offer shareholders preferential claims to dividends, usually at a fixed rate.

Premium price – a price which is higher than the market average. The premium helps to secure the firm a higher profit on each unit sold.

Pressure group – a group or association formed to promote a particular interest or cause by influencing businesses and public policy.

Price – the sum paid by the customer for a good or service.

Price system – a system in which decisions about which resources to use and what products to make is decided by demand and supply.

Primary industry – the first stage in a production process concerned with taking out gifts of nature such as using land for farming, cutting down trees in forests and fishing.

Primary research – research which uses first hand sources, e.g. asking people questions directly.

Private benefits – the benefits to an individual from carrying out a particular activity.

Private Company (Ltd) – a company whose shares are not up for sale on the Stock Exchange, buying and selling of shares in a private company can only be done with the permission of the Board of Directors.

Private costs – the costs to an individual of carrying out a particular activity.

Private sector – that part of the economy that is owned by private individuals and organisations rather than the government.

Privatisation – the switching of businesses from government ownership to private ownership.

Product led – a company that makes a product which it feels the customer should have with little real research into customer requirements.

Product life-cycle – the key stages in the life of a product, and how long the cycle lasts. The main stages are pre-launch preparation, launch, introduction, growth, maturity, saturation and decline.

Product mix – the range of products produced by a business.

Product portfolio – the range of products manufactured and/or sold by a company.

Production function – that part of the organisation which is concerned with production i.e. the processes that convert inputs into outputs.

Productivity – a measure of the output of a firm in relation to inputs.

Profit and loss account – an accounting statement showing a firm's sales revenue over a trading period and all the relevant costs generated to earn that revenue.

Profit centre – a division of a company responsible for creating a profit acceptable to top management and also able to control its costs and maximise the prices it charges.

Profit margin – operating profit/sales x 100%.

Profits – in broad terms, profit can be defined as the difference which arises when a firm's sales revenue exceeds its total costs.

Project production – a project involving groups of people and resources in order to produce a final end product.

Promotion – in marketing terms, money and effort dedicated to increasing sales of a product.

Promotion into the pipeline - promotions aimed at selling more goods into the distribution system i.e. they are targeted at wholesalers and retailers involved in distribution.

Promotion out of the pipeline – promotion aimed at selling more goods to the final customer.

Protection group – a pressure group set up to protect a particular interest – e.g. to protect a piece of natural environment.

Psychographic segmentation – segmenting a market because there are distinctive differences in the lifestyles of groups of consumers in different segments.

Psychographics – the categorisation of people by their behaviour and attitudes rather than by objective factors such as age and income.

Public Limited Company (PLC) – a company that is allowed to sell shares through the Stock Exchange.

Public relations – the professional maintenance of a favourable public image by a company.

Public Sector – that part of the economy which the government runs and manages.

Quality – fitness for purpose, when a good, service or process exactly does what the customer expects.

Quality assurance – checking at the end of the line that the product meets the required quality standard.

Quality circle – small groups of people who meet regularly to discuss work problems usually with a circle leader.

Quorum – the minimum number of people required for a meeting to take place.

Quota – limitation on the numbers of items that can be exchanged between countries. Used as a way of limiting imports.

Quotation – figures and details sent by a supplier to a potential buyer quoting prices and terms under which they are prepared to trade.

R & D – research and development into new products, processes and other ideas.

Ratio – the relationship between one business variable and another, e.g. sales revenue per employee.

Recruitment – the processes involved in finding new recruits for a place of work e.g. advertising a new post.

Registrar of Companies – the Registrar is responsible for keeping a register of companies.

Regulation – supervision of the way in which a business or organisation can run – setting limits to what it can do.

Remuneration – the package of rewards given to an employee including pay and other benefits.

Rent – the reward to an owner of land or other natural resource for the use of their land.

Report – detailed account produced to a set format outlining findings, and recommendations in relation to a particular issue or topic that has been researched.

Reserves – retained profits that a company decides to keep.

Resources – means that are available to achieve an end e.g. physical resources such as land and minerals.

Restrictive practices – actions carried out by businesses which limit the free working of the market place.

Retail – the final link in the chain of distribution from manufacturer to end-user. A retailer holds stocks at a location convenient to the customer and provides a choice of products, guidance on their qualities, plus after-sales service and credit facilities if appropriate.

Retailing co-operative – a group that buys products and then sell them to its members who are the joint owners of the co-operative.

Retraining – developing new skills and competences in order to be able to do a new job or area of work.

Return on capital employed (ROCE) – profit before interest, expressed as a percentage of capital employed. Simply indicates the net profit relative to the capital employed in the business.

Returns – goods which are sent back. If a firm buys faulty goods and sends them back to the supplier these are returns outwards; if a firm has sent out faulty goods and these are returned they are returns inwards.

Revenue – the value of total sales made by a business within a period, usually one year.

Revenue expenditure – day-to-day running expenses of a business, e.g. electricity and telephone bills.

Risk assessment – an investigation of likely risks in the workplace carried out by an organisation in order to take the necessary precautions against accidents occurring.

Risk bearing economies – the benefits that arise from spreading risks over several items or products rather than just one or a few.

Robot – a machine capable of carrying out a complex set of activities automatically.

Safety policy – all organisations must produce a written safety policy detailing measures that will be taken to comply with Health and Safety requirements.

Scientific management – the view that there is a science of work and that work can be organised in a scientific way to achieve maximum results. Idea put forward at the start of the last century by people like F.W. Taylor who engaged in work study, and carried out by industrialists such as Henry Ford.

Secondary industry – the stage in the production of goods which is concerned with making or building things using raw materials from primary industries.

Secondary research – using existing information sources to find out something for your own research.

Security needs – the need to be kept safe and secure from harm.

Selection – choosing someone to fill a job role.

Self assessment – a method of calculating your own tax liability, for example if you are self employed.

Self fulfilment needs – the need to use our creative and other talents to fulfil ourselves.

Selling – seeking to persuade the potential customer that you have the appropriate solutions to meet their needs.

Selling costs – the costs of packaging, advertising and promotion, the salaries and expenses of the salesforce, distribution costs and the margin paid to retailers.

Services – Intangible products – such as legal, medical or financial advice. The dealer who sells you a car also provides after-sales service. The local greengrocer delivers your purchases to your home as part of its service.

Sex Discrimination Act – law providing protection for individuals against being treated less favourably than others on account of their sex.

Shareholders – part-owners of a company with shares in the company.

Shop steward – workplace trade union representative who represents a section of workers.

Single European Market – a free market for the trade of goods in mainly Western Europe.

Skimming – charging an initial high price and then lowering it to cream off successive layers of the market, starting with those with the greatest demand for the product.

Slump – a downturn in economic and business activity.

Social benefit – the advantages to members of a society from a particular activity.

Social cost – the cost to members of a society resulting from a particular activity.

Social Trends – an official government publication which collects data in order to find out about changing social patterns in the country.

Software – the programs and other operating information used by a computer.

Sole trader – a business owned by one person.

Spare capacity – the extent to which production capability exceeds the current level of orders.

Specialisation – concentration on a narrow range of activities, tasks, processes, or products.

Spreadsheet – a computer program allowing manipulation and flexible retrieval of tabulated numerical data.

Stakeholders – people who have an interest in how an organisation or group is run.

Stock control – making sure that an organisation has the right amount of stocks, neither too many nor too few.

Stock rotation – turning over stock in order to keep existing stock fresh and up-to-date.

Stock turnover – cost of sales/stock.

Storage device – means of storing information and data – e.g. a database.

Straight line method – way of depreciating an asset in regular fixed amounts over a period of time.

Strategic decisions – decisions that involve the long-term commitment of large sums of money.

Strategies – major long-term decisions of an organisation involving the use of major resources. The means by which the firm will attain its objectives, e.g. to standardise products to become the lowest-cost producer.

Subsidy – money granted by the state to keep down the price of commodities and to support UK producers.

Supply – the quantities of goods and services that producers are willing to sell at different prices.

Tactics – day-to-day decisions within an organisation in pursuit of its longer term strategies.

Take-over – buying up at least 51% of the shares in a competing business.

Tall organisation – an organisation with lots of layers of hierarchy.

Tangible – physical items.

Tax allowances – income which is not taxed. There are a number of allowances, e.g. for looking after a dependent relative in the home.

Team – people working together to meet shared objectives and with a common sense of shared purpose.

Team briefings – meetings at which managers, supervisors or team leaders inform their teams of important developments, initiatives and targets.

Teamwork – individuals working in groups rather than being given highly specialised, individual jobs.

Technical economies – the advantages that a larger firm gains from improving its methods and processes of production e.g. by using a large sophisticated machine rather than a number of inefficient small ones.

Terms of reference – a statement of why a report is being carried out and the purpose of the report.

Tertiary industry – service industries which are concerned with providing value for people, e.g. postal carriage of letters, providing insurance and banking services, etc.

Test marketing – trying out a good or service in a small (test) market to find out how it is viewed before launching it on a much bigger scale.

Top-down decision making – where decisions are made by senior managers and passed downwards to others in the organisation.

Total Quality Management (TQM) – building quality into production at every stage in the production process rather than checking for it just at the end of the line.

Trade – the process of buying and selling goods.

Trade credit – finance provided by one firm to another to cover the period between the purchase of the goods and payment for them.

Trade cycle – series of booms and slumps in the economy.

Trade discount – a deduction made from the normal selling price when supplying trade (business) customers.

Trade union – body recognised in law consisting of employees with common work interests who seek to further their collective interests through bargaining with employers.

Trades Union Congress (TUC) – the representative body of trade unions in this country, meeting annually to determine trade union policy.

Trading account – account setting out the purchases and sales of a company in a period of time.

Training – enabling employees to develop the knowledge, skills and attitudes required to carry out the work that is needed to meet an organisation's objectives.

Training Needs Analysis – a study to find out what an individual needs to do to better help the organisation to meet its objectives by becoming a more knowledgeable and skilled worker.

Training plan – action plan setting out training activities that will need to be carried out to enable an individual to meet the requirements of their Training Needs Analysis.

Unemployment – a situation in which people who are available for work cannot find jobs.

Unfair dismissal – when someone loses their job for reasons which are not acceptable in law.

Upgrading skills – improving an employees skills to keep them up to date with the field in which they are operating.

Utilities – useful services such as the provision of water, gas, and electricity.

Value added – the increase in the value of the product at each stage in production.

Value added tax – tax levied on value created at each stage of production.

Value chain – the key processes involved in adding value to products in a linked way.

Variable costs – costs which vary with the level of output e.g. fuel costs, raw materials costs, etc.

Venture capital – money provided by existing venture capital companies usually to start-up businesses. The best known example of a venture capital company is 3i.

Video conferencing – electronic communications link enabling face to face conversations between people who may be on the other side of the globe.

Visible – a good which is traded on international markets.

Visible balance – the difference between the value of exports of goods and the value of imports of goods.

Wages – the reward to employees for carrying out their work. Fixed regular payment by an employer to employees.

Website – Internet location providing information, advertising and details of an individual/organisation/topic, etc.

White collar union – trade union made up of professional workers such as teachers.

Working capital – the financial resources that enable a firm to operate on a day-to-day basis, e.g. having stock to sell, the ability to give customers credit and having cash to pay bills as they fall due. The figure for working capital is calculated as current assets – current liabilities.

World Trade Organisation (WTO) – an international body involving most countries which seeks to reduce barriers to trade between countries.

Zero defects – a situation in which quality initiatives in an organisation is of such a high standard that there is no waste in the production process.

Index